IMPERIAL STUDIES NO. XXVI
General Editor: GERALD S. GRAHAM
Rhodes Professor of Imperial History in the University of London

Social Policy and Missionary Organizations
in Ceylon 1840–1855

IMPERIAL STUDIES SERIES

Social Policy and
Missionary Organizations
in Ceylon
1840-1855

K. M. DE SILVA

1724

PUBLISHED FOR
THE ROYAL COMMONWEALTH SOCIETY
BY
LONGMANS
1965

LONGMANS, GREEN AND CO LTD
48 Grosvenor Street, London W.1
*Associated companies, branches and representatives
throughout the world*

© *K. M. De Silva 1965*
First published 1965

*Printed in Great Britain by
The Bowering Press, Plymouth*

CONTENTS

APPENDICES

Preface

RELIGION is a very live issue in the politics of present day Ceylon, arousing as much passion and causing as many divisions as race and class. In the face of a resurgent Buddhism the Christian groups are on the defensive, rather dispirited and disturbed. This book deals with the missionary organizations and their influence on the colonial government's social policy in the mid-nineteenth century, at a time when Buddhism was on the defensive. The most fastidious author can hardly avoid causing some offence, but I have endeavoured to be dispassionate and objective, and to resist the temptation to interpret these issues from the standpoint of our own times and its own special concerns.

This book has emerged from a London doctoral thesis prepared under the stimulating supervision of Dr Kenneth Ballhatchet. I have benefited greatly from his incisive comments and constructive criticism. I am especially indebted to Mr W. J. F. LaBrooy, of the Department of History at the University of Ceylon, who assisted me with his unrivalled knowledge of nineteenth-century Ceylon and gave up many hours to reading and criticizing several drafts of the manuscript. In preparing this work for publication in the Imperial Studies Series, I have had the benefit of Professor Gerald Graham's friendly advice and encouragement. My sincere thanks are also due to a good many colleagues and friends for their most generous and valuable help in the preparation of this work, and they will understand my reluctance to make exceptions to the anonymity of my gratitude. I am very grateful to my wife who has patiently read all the chapters and helped especially, throughout the ordeal of the proofs. I need hardly add that no one but the author is responsible for the views expressed in this work.

I am deeply appreciative of the assistance given to me during my researches by the archivists, librarians and the staff of several institutions – the Library of the University of Ceylon, the Goldsmith's Library of the University of London, the Public Record Office, London; the Ceylon Government Archives, the Royal Commonwealth Society Library, the Department of Palaeography and Diplomatic, The Prior's Kitchen, The College,

Durham; the British Museum Reading Room and the Archives
and Libraries of the Baptist Missionary Society, the Church
Missionary Society, the Methodist Missionary Society and the
Society for the Propagation of the Gospel in Foreign Parts. Their
unfailing courtesy and generous assistance puts me heavily in their
debt. The Baptist Missionary Society, the Church Missionary
Society, the Methodist Missionary Society and the Society for the
Propagation of the Gospel in Foreign Parts have given me permission to quote unpublished material in their possession.

The Royal Commonwealth Society has honoured me by spon-
soring and financing the publication of this book. My grateful
thanks are due to the Board of Studies in History of the University
of London and the trustees of the Isobel Thornley Bequest for
generous financial aid towards the publication of this work.

K. M. DE SILVA

University of Ceylon,
Peradeniya, Ceylon.

Abbreviations used in footnotes:

A/R Annual Report.

C.A.S. Ceylon Agricultural Society.

C.H.J. *Ceylon Historical Journal.*

C.J.H.S.S. *Ceylon Journal of Historical and Social Studies.*

C.L.R. *Ceylon Literary Register.*

J.M.H. *Journal of Modern History.*

J.R.A.S. (C.B.) *Journal of Royal Asiatic Society (Ceylon Branch).*

Kandy F.I.N.S. The Kandy Friend in Need Society.

Miss.Her. *The Missionary Herald.*

Miss.Not. *Missionary Notices.*

Rep.Fin.Com. *Reports on the Finance and Commerce of the Island of Ceylon* (H.M.S.O., 1848).

Rep.Fxd.Est. *Report of the Committee of the Executive Council on the Fixed Establishments of Ceylon* (H.M.S.O., 1852).

U.C.R. *University of Ceylon Review.*

Wes.Mss.Cey., I Wesleyan Manuscripts, Ceylon, 1837–45.

Wes.Mss.Cey., II Wesleyan Manuscripts, Ceylon, 1846–57.

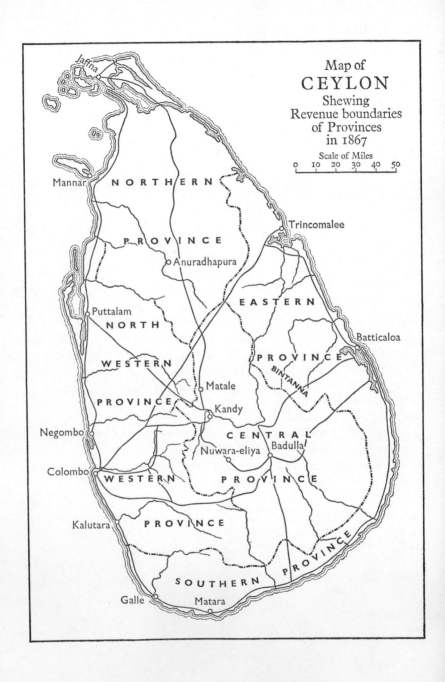

Map of
CEYLON
Shewing
Revenue boundaries
of Provinces
in 1867

Scale of Miles
0   10   20   30   40   50

Jafina

Mannar

NORTHERN

PROVINCE

Anuradhapura

Trincomalee

EASTERN

Puttalam

NORTH

Batticaloa

WESTERN

PROVINCE

BINTANNA

PROVINCE

Matale

Kandy

Negombo

CENTRAL

Nuwara-eliya

Badulla

Colombo

WESTERN

PROVINCE

Kalutara

PROVINCE

PROVINCE

SOUTHERN

Galle

Matara

Introduction

THE British occupation of the Dutch possessions in the maritime provinces of Ceylon in 1796 was an episode in the Franco-British struggle for mastery in India.[1] Ceylon's main attraction was its supremely important strategic position and in particular the harbour of Trincomalee on the eastern coast which commanded the Bay of Bengal. Indeed, the British might have contemplated the possibility of returning the island to the Dutch had they been assured that the French would not come back and exploit the strategic advantages which Trincomalee afforded. In the eyes of the British Government, Ceylon at the end of the eighteenth century, was a military station pure and simple.

The uncertain political future of the British possessions in Ceylon was reflected in the administrative arrangements devised in 1796. The administration was placed under the Madras Government of the East India Company who proceeded to adopt a variety of expedients to recoup from these territories the costs of the conquest and military occupation. The system of government adopted had not been well considered or planned – the key-note was improvization. Though the Madras officials had little experience of the region which they were suddenly called upon to administer, they preferred to rule without the assistance of the local aristocracy. They discounted tradition and convention. Not surprisingly there was, very soon, a proliferation of abuses and malpractices. The discontent that ensued was, however, not owing to any exceptional rapacity; it was merely that the forms of oppression were novel. A 'rebellion' in 1797 prompted a Commission of enquiry and the East India Company was compelled as a result to share the administration with the Crown. It was guaranteed a monopoly of trade, the most coveted portion of which was the cinnamon trade of Ceylon, once a flourishing venture but now yielding a moderate profit. This system of 'Dual Control' lasted from 1798 to 1802 when at last, following the cession to the British by the Peace

[1] For the early years of British rule in Ceylon, see de Silva, C. R., *Ceylon under the British Occupation 1796–1832*, 2 vols. (Colombo, 1942); Mills, L. A., *Ceylon under British Rule, 1795–1932* (Oxford, 1933); Turner, L. J. B., *Collected Papers on the History of the Maritime Provinces of Ceylon* (Colombo, 1923).

of Amiens in 1801, the British possessions in Ceylon were made a Crown Colony. From this brief but unfortunate association with Madras and the East India Company, Ceylon gained one inestimable benefit. In future, whenever it was suggested that for the sake of economy or administrative convenience the island of Ceylon should be treated as an integral part of the Indian Empire, the memory of these unhappy years served as a reminder of the perils involved.

The settlements so obtained consisted of a coastal belt extending around the entire Island, but in depth seldom stretching more than twenty miles into the interior. Consequently from 1802 to 1815 the most formidable problem facing the Crown Colony of Ceylon was the question of its relations with the Kingdom of Kandy in the interior, the last independent Sinhalese kingdom, whose existence was considered a threat to the security of British rule.[1] From the very beginning the British aimed at subjugating Kandy in order to round off total control over Ceylon. The first British expedition against Kandy set out in 1803; it met with disaster as had so many Portuguese and Dutch expeditions in the past. But in 1815, largely because of divisions within the Kandyan kingdom itself the British were able to overthrow the Nayakkar dynasty[2] from South India who had ruled that kingdom since 1739. For the first time for several centuries Ceylon was under the rule of a single power. The Kandyan kingdom was not conquered but ceded to the British by the aristocracy and the *bhikkus*,[3] and because the British owed so much to the assistance rendered by these two groups, the Kandyan Convention[4] which embodied the terms of the cession upheld many of their privileges and above all else promised support and maintenance to the Buddhist religion.

Dissatisfaction with the manner in which these undertakings were interpreted led in 1817–18 to a widespread rebellion of the Kandyan aristocracy against British rule. This, 'the Great Rebel-

---

[1] Pieris, P. E., *Tri-Sinhala – the Last Phase 1796–1815* 3rd ed. (Colombo, 1945), is a stimulating survey of British relations with Kandy, written with a great deal of sympathy for the Kandyan viewpoint.

[2] The Nayakkars were Telegu-speaking Hindus from South India who ascended the Kandyan throne by virtue of their marriage alliances with Kandyan royalty.

[3] *Bhikku* is generally translated 'priest' or 'monk'. A *bhikku* is a member of the Buddhist order.   [4] See Appendix II.

lion', was much the most formidable insurrection during the whole period of the British occupation of Ceylon.[1] It was crushed after a long and ruthless campaign and when the resistance of the aristocracy was broken at last, the British were effective rulers of Ceylon. Even so they did not set up a unified administration for the whole island but maintained instead two separate administrative systems, one for the Maritime provinces which had been subjected to the influence of western rule since the sixteenth century and another for the Kandyan provinces which preserved the social and cultural patterns of the traditional Sinhalese society. This separation was eminently justified, so marked and so fundamental were the differences between the two regions; indeed they were as marked as the differences between the coastal region and the interior of British West Africa.

The cession of Kandy and the suppression of the Great Rebellion made little difference to the basic pattern of British rule in Ceylon – the island was still fundamentally a military station valued for the protection it afforded the expanding British possessions in India. And for well over a decade thereafter there was still no change in this regard. This conception of the Island as a strategic entity served to inhibit reform and innovation in the administration, the economy, and the social structure.

Its extent, however, and the variety of its resources would appear to have tempted early governors to indulge in piece-meal reforms. Indeed, in the Maritime Provinces the first two decades of British rule were characterized by an urge to break away from some of the rigours of Dutch rule. There was one impulsive and unsuccessful attempt at reforming the traditional system of land tenure; there were desultory – and more successful – attempts at reducing the powers of the native aristocracy. And the judicial system as it evolved, while hardly a positive improvement on the Dutch system, at least embodied some of the more benevolent aspects of the British legal system. The Dutch educational system was maintained if not improved upon. But the sum total of these changes did not amount to a fundamental change in the system of administration which the British inherited, nor was there any system, plan, or pattern in the innovations attempted. To a large extent the chronic near-bankruptcy of the economy effectively prevented

[1] Pieris, P. E., *Sinhale and the Patriots* (Colombo, 1950), is the best study of this episode.

the adoption of measures of reform entailing substantial expenditure. The Colonial Office was opposed to financing even the most
beneficent projects so long as the Colonial revenues could not
meet the basic needs of the administration and the armed forces;
this opposition was so much the stronger because Ceylon, like
Cape Colony, was viewed at Whitehall mainly in terms of its
strategic value in relation to India and little thought was given to
the possibilities of developing or improving its natural resources.

In the 1820s one notes a steady consolidation of British rule.
Governor Barnes's road systen, built with the help of compulsory
labour under the traditional *rajakariya* system, placed the military
control of the Kandyan provinces firmly in British hands; indeed
this road system sealed the fate of this region as effectively as roads
sealed the fate of the Highlands of Scotland after the Jacobite
threat of the '45. The secret of Kandy's long and successful survival in the face of over two centuries of Western attempts at conquest lay in the fact that the bulk of the country was a wilderness
suited to guerrilla warfare of which the Kandyans were masters.
Now no longer could guerrilla tactics cut communications between
garrisons or hold up the movement of troops.

One other feature of Barnes's administration merits comment.
He was associated with attempts at experimenting in a variety of
commercial crops, coffee being the most important of them, aimed
at inducing a measure of buoyancy into a stagnant economy
tragically dependent on a visibly declining cinnamon trade.
Though these experiments bore fruit only a decade later the fact
that they were attempted is positive proof of a reformist turn of
mind. Curiously though, these experiments were in a sense a
continuation of Dutch policy. It is an indication at once of the
strength of the Dutch pattern of colonialism, and the futility of
attempts to break away from it as long as the basic assumptions of
the successor regime were so much like those of the Dutch – for
example, in their faith in 'indirect' rule through a native aristocracy under the supervision of an autocratic governor, in their
faith in mercantilist restrictions and monopolies, and their continued use of the traditional land tenure system, and obnoxious
native devices such as *rajakariya*.

Indeed, in the first three decades of British rule in Ceylon the
one consistent agent of change was the missionary. Much more
than the soldier and the administrator, he was committed to the

advocacy of change, the more because he had seldom to bear the consequences of impulsive attempts at evangelization and was therefore much less concerned about the administrator's and the soldier's preoccupation with the maintenance of political stability. The British missionary groups could look forward to no systematic support from the state, though individual governors came forward with intermittent assistance. They were thus dependent largely on their own financial resources. The reluctance of the state to afford consistent support may be explained largely by their fear that missionary activity might provoke opposition and lead to embarrassing incidents; they were always conscious of the political consequences of a disturbance of the traditional religious observances of the people. Hence it was that the missionaries were discouraged from penetrating into the Kandyan region where the traditional culture and the Buddhist religion were at their strongest. In the Maritime provinces which had been exposed to the influence of Christianity since the sixteenth century there were fewer restrictions on missionary activity.

In the meantime economic stagnation continued to affect the country until the 1830s when the gradual success of coffee culture revolutionized the economy. By the 1830s the British, as undisputed masters of the Indian seas, were in the process of consolidating their possessions in India, and had more time to ponder the possibilities of profitably developing the economy of the Island and settling its major internal political problems. The appointment of the Colebrooke–Cameron Commission was a clear indication that the Colonial Office had decided that a new phase in the colony's development should commence.

Hence began a period of experimentation in plantation crops, a period in which it seemed as though sugar cultivation might be quite as successful as coffee. But coffee soon overtook sugar and with the gradual but certain ruin of the cinnamon trade, which had been for so long the mainstay of export trade, the Island, during the next half-century, was to enjoy the doubtful benefits of monoculture.

Largely as a result of changes abroad – the rapid decline of plantation agriculture in the West Indies following the abolition of slavery; the equalization of duties on Ceylon and West India coffee;[1] and the protection given in the home market for Empire

[1] These duties were equalized in 1835.

coffee as against the foreign product[1] – the coffee industry in
Ceylon expanded with amazing rapidity.[2] So rapid was this progress – and ultimately so completely uncontrolled – that the years
preceding (and including) 1845 were justly called the years of the
'coffee mania'.

A contemporary observer remarked that

> The mania for planting in Ceylon was as great and as disastrous in
> its small way as the Railway furore in England. . . . The Governor[3]
> and his Civil Servants[4] dabbled in the speculation and scalded their
> fingers. High Civil and Military officers both of Her Majesty and
> the East India Company entered into the enterprises, many of them
> far beyond their means. Merchants, trades people and private
> individuals all took their tickets in the lottery, drew blanks and then
> too late regretted it. . . .[5]

The coffee industry of the early 1840s had an unhealthy air
about it. The planters were in the main inexperienced amateurs;[6]
the process of cultivation was crude and unscientific (many plantations were opened up where soil and location were unsuited to the
crop); there was a great deal of wasteful expenditure; and the
financing of coffee production was chaotic and extravagant.[7] The
expansion of the coffee industry was far too dependent on the
protection afforded to Empire coffee in the home market, and this
at a time when the principle of protection itself was being success-
fully challenged in England.

For a few years the booming prosperity of the coffee industry

---

[1] In 1835 the duties were: Colonial Coffee (Ceylon) 6d. a lb; East India
coffee 9d. a lb; and Foreign 1s. 3d. a lb. In 1842 the duties were: Ceylon and
East India 4d. a lb; Foreign 8d. a lb. In 1844 the duty on foreign coffee was
reduced to 6d. a lb.

[2] In the six years, 1838–43, no fewer than 130 coffee estates were opened in
the Central Province.

[3] The Rt. Hon. J. S. Mackenzie, Governor of Ceylon, 1837–41.

[4] For a full list of the Government officials who became active coffee planters,
see Appendix.

[5] Rigg, C. R., 'Coffee Planting in Ceylon', *The Ceylon Examiner*, 16 June 1852.

[6] Lewis, R. E., *Coffee Planting in Ceylon*, p.14. This slim pamphlet deserves to
be mentioned as one of the most stimulating studies of the early history of
coffee planting in Ceylon. Lewis was a pioneer coffee planter before he became
an active journalist.

[7] Rigg, C. R., *op. cit.*
Lewis, R. E., *Coffee Planting in Ceylon*, pp.19–24.

concealed its inherent weaknesses,[1] but in 1846–7 the depression in England and the reduction of duties on foreign coffee in the English market set in motion a train of events which culminated in the near collapse of the industry.[2] A contemporary missionary noted despondently that:

> The great coffee bubble has burst at length. The colony is little better than bankrupt. Estates are being abandoned fast, and all who can are leaving the Island for places more promising. Failures are daily taking place, young men are wandering without employment, and the prospect is melancholy indeed. . . .[3]

But the coffee industry proved to be more resilient than was expected. It recovered, but as an industry transformed almost beyond recognition from what it had been at the time of the coffee mania. 'The era of cultivation had dawned upon the Central Province.'[4] First, the old estates were rehabilitated, then new plantations were opened after confidence had been gained from rehabilitation of the old. The planters themselves were for the most part new men who had not suffered from the example of the time of the mania.[5] Thereafter

> . . . observation . . . discerned the true tests of soil and aspect; former delusions as to high altitudes have been exploded;[6] unprofitable districts avoided,[7] . . . and in lieu of the belief that a coffee bush once

[1] The acreage under coffee in Ceylon, doubled between 1845 and 1847. See *The Economist*, 12 May 1849.

Acreage prior to 31.12.44	25,198½
Planted between 1.1.45 and 31.12.47	24,872½
Total on 31.12.47	50,071 acres

See also Grey MSS. enclosure in Torrington's letter of 9 June 1848, where Torrington gives much the same set of figures.

[2] *The Economist*, 12 May 1849. Tennent, *Ceylon*, II, pp.231–235; Ferguson, *Ceylon in 1847–60*, p.2; Lewis, *op. cit.* pp.24 ff.

[3] *Miss. Her.*, Sept. 1848. Rev. J. Allen, 8 June 1846.

[4] Lewis, *op. cit.* p.25.   [5] *Ibid.* pp.26 ff.

[6] There was a general belief that coffee would not thrive above the 1,700 foot contour. But with the spectacular success of coffee in the Black Forest region of Pussellawa (well above that elevation) a new phase in coffee cultivation in Ceylon began. This development occured in the period of the coffee mania and it is not quite accurate to attribute it to the period after 1848.

[7] The reference is probably to the Ambagamuwa district where the civil servants had invested heavily. It was generally expected that Ambagamuwa would develop into a thriving coffee region but it did not fulfil that hope.

B

rooted, would continue ever after to bear crops without manure, and to flourish in defiance of weeds and neglect, every estate is tended like a garden, and the soil enriched scientifically in proportion to the produce it bears. Expenditure has been reduced within the bounds of discretion; an acre of forest land can be brought under crop in 1857 for one-tenth that it cost in 1844.[1]

The success of this new policy may be gauged from the fact that although in 1851 Empire coffee lost its protection in the home market completely, this did not in any way check the recovery of Ceylon's coffee industry.

In the modernization of Ceylon the expansion of plantation agriculture was the key factor; it brought into existence practically every salient feature of modern Ceylon. In the mid-nineteenth century, however, the plantations were a new and profoundly disturbing factor in the life of the Kandyan provinces. They broke the isolation of that region, but they also helped in the disintegration of the old society. Indeed the absorption of the Kandyan provinces, which would have been a formidable problem at the best of times, was rendered all the more painful by the fact that the vast bulk of the coffee plantations were situated in the heart of the Kandyan region where the traditional subsistence economy of the Sinhalese had been least disturbed. The capitalist economy of the plantations and the traditional subsistence economy of the Kandyans were not complementary (as they might have been if the Kandyan peasantry had been willing to work on the plantations), but conflicting. Land and disputes relating to land use became a perennial source of conflict between peasant and planter. The plantations had a disturbing effect upon the traditional economy. And for the first time in its history the Kandyan provinces were being transformed into a 'plural society' with all its attendant strains and stresses. Since the Kandyans would not work on the estates, the planters were compelled to rely on immigrant Indian labourers who entered the country in increasing numbers with the expansion of coffee cultivation.

The plantations did have another and more constructive role, for they provided the economic basis for the unification of Ceylon. The Colebrooke–Cameron reforms aimed at uniting Ceylon on the basis of administration and law, while the plantations with

---

[1] Tennent, *Ceylon*, II, 231 ff.

their radiating network of roads helped to consolidate this unification.

The Colebrooke–Cameron reforms, an integrated and in many
ways radical set of reforms proposals, had as their basic aim the
imposition on Ceylon of the superstructure of the *laissez-faire* state.[1]
They had much in common with Bentinck's reforms in India;
indeed they were more far-reaching in their impact, and more
consistent in the application of current liberalism. The Ceylon
reforms were a subtle blend of *laissez-faire* economics, Benthamite
legal reforms, humanitarianism and evangelicalism. As humani-
tarians Colebrooke and Cameron were both opposed to *rajakariya*
which savoured of feudalism and feudal oppression, as adherents of
laissez-faire and Free Trade they were opposed to mercantilism,
state monopolies, discriminatory administrative regulations, and
in general to any interference of the state in the economy. Their
faith in Evangelical Christianity was best expressed in their
recommendations on education reform, and their faith in Benthamism in their far-reaching legal reforms. Some of their reforms
had been anticipated by early governors and other colonial officials
but theirs was the first well integrated system of reforms. Indeed
their proposals mark the first systematic and successful attempt to
break away from the Dutch pattern of colonial administration,
and to reject its basic assumptions in favour of a more enlightened
form of government.

Perhaps their most valuable contribution to the Island's future
political development was to give it a more liberal form of government than that which prevailed before 1833; as a measure of
constitutional reform it was far ahead of anything that had been
conferred on India.[2] From 1833 onwards Ceylon was always 'the
senior colony of the new empire', and the 'constitutional pioneer'
among the 'non-European dependencies'.[3]

For all their earthiness and practicality these reforms possessed
more than a tinge of genuine idealism, and had they been implemented in the spirit of Colebrooke and Cameron, Ceylon
would have benefited a great deal more than she ultimately did.
But the civil servants who actually implemented them, to say

[1] These reforms and their significance are discussed in detail in ed. Mendis
G. C., *The Colebrooke-Cameron Papers*, 2 vols. (Oxford, 1956).
[2] Stokes, E., *English Utilitarians and India* (Oxford, 1957), p.321.
[3] Wight, M., *The Development of the Legislative Council* (London, 1950), p.74.

nothing of the Colonial Office, made these reforms a much more pedestrian product of sharp and short-sighted business than would have been the case had the basic recommendations of these reformers been accepted in their entirety.[1]

Colebrooke's approach to the Kandyan problem resembled in some ways that of Durham to the comparable problem of French Canada. In 1833, on his recommendation, it was decided to amalgamate the Kandyan provinces and the Maritime provinces. The separate existence of the old Kandyan Kingdom tolerated since its cession in 1815, was at an end. There was to be one administrative system for the whole island. The process of amalgamation was simple but crude – the low-lying provinces of the Kandyan Kingdom were broken up and attached to the Maritime Provinces with little consideration for or understanding of the traditional differences between the two regions. The basic aim was to dismember the Kandyan provinces, and to expose them to the glare of what passed as modern at that time.

This policy was carried out with whole-hearted enthusiasm by the colonial administration in Ceylon. In 1848, P. E. Wodehouse a senior civil servant made the comment that

> There should be no such thing as Kandian [*sic*]; every effort should be made to amalgamate the people of the upper and the lower country. . . . If the country is to be governed with any degree of uniformity, all distinctions between the Singhalese [*sic*] themselves must be avoided as much as possible in the Singhalese portion of the island.[2]

It was only after the peace of the Kandyan provinces was disturbed again, in 1848, that the shortsightedness of this policy was admitted.

> . . . the theory of attempting to break up the so-called nationality of the Kandians, by annexing different portions of the Kandian country to the adjacent districts of the Maritime Provinces has in

---

[1] In general, these civil servants were far too busy on their plantations to be concerned with anything else. And they were there on the plantations because Colebrooke, with an amazing lack of foresight, reduced their salaries, curtailed their privileges and eliminated many avenues of normal promotion. Meanwhile, he held out to them the prospect of making up in plantation agriculture what they lost in the disastrous civil service reforms of 1833 – if not the possibility of accumulating an enormous fortune.   [2] *Rep.Fxd.Est.*, p.175.

reality proved a failure and as such it is much better to meet and provide for the remnant of Kandian nationality, if such it can be called,
than to be voluntarily blind to the fact of its existence. By nationality
I mean the feelings, the habits, associations and customs which still
obtain among a people who only 34 years ago, were for the first
time subjected to our authority and whose amalgamation with the
Maritime population, possessing associations and feelings and customs to a great extent different, never appears to have made much
progress.[1]

But such protests were made in vain.

The riots of 1848 broke the stillness that had settled on Ceylon
since the great rebellion of 1817–8. In many ways, the last major
disturbance in Kandyan history, they were also the first occasion
on which ideas of European Radicalism showed themselves in
Ceylon. There were, in 1848, two centres of disturbance, one in
Colombo and the other in the Kandyan provinces at Matale and
Kurunegala. All they had in common was a spirited opposition
to the new taxes imposed in 1848[2] – the shop tax, the gun tax, the
dog tax and the Road Ordinance.[3]

In 1847–8 a comprehensive review of the tax system of Ceylon
was attempted and a radical transformation of the tax structure
was envisaged with the emphasis shifting decisively in favour of
direct taxation from a dependence on export and import duties.[4]
The foundation of the new system was to be a general land tax.[5]
It is 'our duty', explained the Third Earl Grey, Secretary of
State for the Colonies (1846–52):

> to maintain the policy of free trade, and to extend its application to
> the produce of the Colonies . . . the greatest service that I believed
> we were called upon as a government to render to the country was
> that of completing the work, which had been happily begun, of

[1] *Ibid.*, p.102.

[2] For a brief discussion of the nature and significance of these taxes see the
Third Earl Grey, *The Colonial Policy of Lord John Russell's Administration*, II,
161–96; and *Rep.Fin.Com.* (H.M.S.O., 1848).

[3] The Road Ordinance was designed to provide labour, particularly for
roads in the plantation districts. It was also intended as the basis of a system of
local government, though in actual practice this aspect of the Ordinance was
forgotten. See particularly, Grey, *op. cit.* II, 172–3.

[4] Grey, *op. cit.* I, 81 ff. explains why he attached so much importance to
direct taxation in a tropical colony.

[5] *Rep.Fin.Com.* (H.M.S.O., 1848). See particularly Tennent's *Report on the
Finance and Commerce of Ceylon*, 22 October 1846.

removing restrictions from industry, and securely establishing a
system of free trade throughout the empire. . . .[1]

A drastic reduction of import and export duties, and an equalization of duties on British and foreign products in 1847 were to
be the prelude to the introduction of the land tax. Unfortunately,
the depression that hit Ceylon in that year was so severe in its
impact that the administration found it impossible to levy the
general land tax. They proceeded instead to impose a series of
taxes which bore heavily on the local population, chiefly the
peasants. The new taxes imposed in 1848 were very unpopular
and there was widespread agitation against them.

In Colombo the opposition to these taxes was led by Dr Christopher Elliott, the Editor of *The Colombo Observer* and some Burgher[2]
lawyers, for whom this provided an unexpected opportunity to
make a series of demands on the Government, not all of which
had to do with the taxes. It was the year of Revolution in Europe;
and on the arrival of the news from France of the Revolution
of 1848, Elliott sought to stamp the ideas of European Radicalism on the agitation in Ceylon against the taxes. His newspaper
conducted a sustained propaganda campaign against the Government's taxation policy. On 3 July 1848 *The Colombo Observer*
published a letter by 'An Englishman' in which the people of
Ceylon were called upon to follow the example of the French, to
refuse to pay the taxes, and to agitate for the establishment of a
radical democratic society based on racial equality and universal
suffrage. Great emphasis was given to all this by saying that these
blessings were being conferred on the French colony of Pondi-
cherry and asking pointedly why Ceylon should be considered
worse or more backward.

On 26 July there was a meeting at Borella near Colombo to
protest against the taxes.[3] The crowd soon became an inflamed
mob intent on storming the fort of Colombo, and they might even
have embarked on this foolish enterprise had Elliott not persuaded
them to adopt the novel idea (perhaps borrowed from the Chart-
ists) of a petition to the Governor, urging the modification or the
repeal of the new taxes. The petition concluded with a threat of a

[1] Grey, *op. cit.* I, 12.
[2] The Burghers are townsfolk of Dutch and Portuguese extraction.
[3] Henderson, R., *A History of the Rebellion in Ceylon during Lord Torrington's
Government*, p.12; Ferguson, A. M., *Ceylon 1847–60*, pp.12 ff.

refusal to pay the taxes if the Government persisted in implementing them. In spite of Elliott's efforts there was a clash with the military, but there were no casualties.

In the Kandyan areas, there was widespread opposition to the taxes among the peasants, and Elliott who sought to influence this agitation too, had the letter of 3 July translated into Sinhalese, printed in pamphlet form and distributed in the Kandyan provinces. The Government was later to make much of this pamphlet,[1] although it is difficult to estimate its influence on the disturbances, since the vast mass of the people were illiterate. Elliott himself had little personal influence on this Kandyan movement, which took a form of which he could not have approved.

The fact that the disturbances occurred in that region of the Kandyan provinces where planting activity was at its height, prompted many contemporary observers to suggest a causal connection between plantation activity and the disturbances.[2] The expansion of plantation agriculture had created social and economic problems of the utmost complexity. The Kandyans resented the opening up of coffee and sugar plantations in their country,[3] and they were adversely affected by the land policy of the Government which tended to favour the planting interests against the peasants. But it is curious that so few plantations were attacked by the Kandyans during the riots though they were vulnerable enough.

The rapidly developing Kandyan region proved to be a great attraction to the more venturesome low-country Sinhalese. Lawlessness followed in their wake, and the coffee region soon attracted fugitives from justice, gamblers and thieves.[4] Partly at least the Government was to blame for this situation in that it was its excise policy that was attracting the less desirable of the Low Country men. The Government's excise policy encouraged the opening-up of taverns in the Kandyan area, a region not noted

[1] See particularly Tennent's evidence before the Parliamentary Committee on Ceylon; *The Third Report on Ceylon*, p.177.

[2] See the evidence of G. Ackland, merchant and non-official member of the Legislative Council; *The Second Report on Ceylon*, pp.12 ff.

[3] Grey MSS., Torrington to Grey, 11 August 1848. Torrington commented that 'our coffee estates are a source of deadly hatred to the Kandians [sic] . . .'. Skinner T., *Fifty years in Ceylon*, pp.222 ff. *The Third Report on Ceylon*, the evidence of J. E. Tennent, pp.171 ff.

[4] Skinner, T., *Fifty Years in Ceylon*, p.214.

for any large-scale consumption of liquor or the encouragement of its production.[1] Between 1815 and 1848, 133 arrack taverns were opened up in the Kandyan provinces alone. In the same period of time only four schools were established by Government in the same region. The Matale and Kurunegala districts in particular earned a reputation for lawlessness.[2]

The Kandyans despised these Low-countrymen, as well as the immigrant Indian labourers,[3] and not least the planters.[4] Torrington was to comment that 'the mass of the coffee planters many of them the very *worst* class of Englishmen has very much tended to lower and degrade our *caste* and character in the eyes of the natives ... and [among] the Kandians a coffee planter is a term of reproach. . . .'[5]

The situation in the Kandyan provinces may not have been so unfortunate if the administration had realized the gravity of some of these problems, but the truth is that the Government was not even aware of their existence. This was largely the result of the deterioration of the civil service that followed Colebrooke's disastrous civil service reforms. The Ceylon civil service had never been a particularly efficient body of men at the best of times but Colebrooke's reforms made them even more incompetent and inefficient than they were. Encouraged by the Government particularly during the administration of Governor Stewart Mackenzie (1837–41), the bulk of the civil servants took to plantation agriculture to the obvious neglect of their official duties; since most of the senior civil servants were so deeply involved in the coffee industry it was almost inevitable that they came to identify their interests with those of the planters, and in the conflict of interests between the planters and the peasants, particularly over the question of land purchases, it was not unnatural that they came down firmly on the side of the former. The Stanley–Campbell civil service reforms laid definite checks on land purchase and planting activity, but there was little immediate improvement in

---

[1] *Ibid.*

[2] *Ibid.*

Forbes, J., *Recent Disturbances and Military Executions in Ceylon* (London, 1850), p.16.

[3] *Third Report on Ceylon*, evidence of J. E. Tennent, p.171.

[4] Skinner, *op. cit.* p.223.

Forbes, *op. cit.* p.16.

[5] Grey MSS., Torrington to Grey, 11 August 1848.

the efficiency of the civil service. The civil servants had neglected their study of the indigenous languages, and they were still reluctant to go on circuit to the remoter areas of their districts; indeed some of those remoter regions had not seen a European official for decades. Thus a wide gap separated the administration from the people. The Government did little for the peasants; peasant agriculture was on the decline, and the bulk of the irrigation works of the Kandyan areas (and of the Southern province too) were in a sad state of neglect and disrepair. It was natural therefore for the peasants to conclude that they were faced with a most unsympathetic administration and one totally unconcerned about their welfare.

In these circumstances much depended upon the chiefs whom Tennent described as 'the only medium of communication between the civil officers of the Government and the people'.[1] The British Government was deeply suspicious of the Kandyan chiefs and ever since the Great Rebellion of 1817 had sought to reduce their powers. They had succeeded in this to a great extent, but the loss of their former powers and privileges had not resulted in any appreciable decline in the influence of the aristocracy over the people.[2] The aristocracy had little reason to be loyal to a government which had so little trust in them.

And when in the 1840s there developed in Ceylon an agitation to dissociate the state from Buddhism,[3] the local administration, aware of the unpopularity of any such move, and fearing that this religious agitation would result in civil strife, refused to be stampeded into indiscreet action. The missionaries, however, succeeded in imposing their views on the Colonial Office where James Stephen, the Permanent Under-Secretary, became an ardent advocate of their aims and under his influence successive Secretaries of State urged a reluctant Ceylon Government to attempt this dissociation. The outcome was to alienate the Kandyan aristocracy and the *bhikkus* who, as the natural leaders of Kandyan opinion, looked upon these proceedings as a gross betrayal of a solemn undertaking given at the Kandyan Convention. Thus the Buddhist policy of the Colonial Office alienated the two most influential groups in Kandyan society; and by 1848 the aristocracy and the *bhikkus* had developed a deep sense of grievance.

[1] *Third Report on Ceylon*, evidence of J. E. Tennent, p.177.
[2] Skinner, *op. cit.* p.223.   [3] See below, Chapters II and III.

The immediate cause of the disturbances at Matale and Kurune-gala was undoubtedly the decision to impose the taxes of 1848. And it was from the period immediately preceding the imposition of the taxes to the actual outbreak of violence (i.e. from about 1 July to 29–31 July 1848) that the shortcomings of the British administration in the Kandyan region were revealed in all their immensity. The gap that divided the administration from the people was never wider than it was then. Here was an administration intent on imposing a variety of taxes – many of which were novel – affecting every stratum of society; it was a prime obligation of the administration to take the people into their confidence and to explain to them the nature of the taxes. But no such attempt was made. And since there was a variety of taxes it is not surprising that there should have been rumours of more taxes to come. These rumours followed in the wake of the Government's attempt to collect detailed information for the annual Blue Book of statistical information regarding the colony. It was in this atmosphere of rumour, suspicion and doubt that the hostility to the taxes developed. And it is a measure of the extent of the Government's separation from the people that all its leading members were unaware of the depth of this hostility to the taxes.

On 6 July a crowd of several thousands gathered at Kandy to protest against the taxes. The crowd got out of hand, the police lost control of the situation, and the military was called in to restore order. It was at this stage that the administration realized that the taxes were unpopular. On 8 July, Tennent called a meeting of the chiefs and the people at which he endeavoured to explain to them the nature of and need for taxes. Back in Colombo he convinced himself that the people were satisfied with his explanation, but he had misjudged the situation.

Between 8 July and 29 July – the day of the riots at Matale – the mass movement against the taxes was taken over by a small group of men who sought to channel this discontent into an attempt to drive the British out of Kandy. The leaders of the new movement were men of peasant stock, some of them hailing from the Low Country. Their aim was a return to the old Kandyan system with its traditional values, which – somewhat naïvely perhaps – they aspired to cherish by making one of their number king.

Theirs was a blind protest against the changes and uncertainties brought by British rule, and they yearned for the old society, the only one they knew and understood. They had the support of a substantial section of the population, and some at least of the *bhikkus*, though the aristocracy stood aloof from their movement. In spite of the reforms introduced by the British Government the people were dissatisfied. The pretender and his associates provided them with an opportunity to return to the rule of their own 'kings', to the traditional society, to a world where there were no planters, no Indians, and no new and revolutionary taxes. They could understand monarchy, and the paternalism of an authoritarian regime, but they could make little sense out of the cold and impersonal British administration.

The riots at Matale and Kurunegala were easily stamped out. They broke out on 29 July; two days later, order had been restored. It is not difficult to see why they failed so signally in all their objectives. A contemporary planter described the rebels as being

> ... merely a mass, a mob, with not the slightest pretension to military discipline, display or armament; the men were armed with old flint guns, crude spears, knives. . . . The only source of danger was in their numbers but even that, without a trained military leader, was of little use. . . .[1]

The leaders of the 'rebellion' were men with little knowledge of the world of their day; they were naïve and unsophisticated men, far too simple in their outlook to lead a revolt against a major imperial power. Had the Kandyan aristocracy backed the rebels as the Government alleged they did, it would have been rather more difficult to have put them down.

The character of the victims of the riots provides an index to the general aims of the movement. Though there were scores of isolated plantations very vulnerable to attack from the Kandyans, very few estates were actually attacked, and at both Kurunegala and Matale 'the rebels' concentrated their assaults on Government buildings in the town – the Kachcheri, the jails, the Government Rest-House and the houses of officials. In the process they did attack other buildings in the vicinity of Government buildings but in these instances it is very likely that it was only proximity

[1] Millie, P. D., *Thirty Years Ago, or the Reminiscences of the Early Days of Coffee Planting in Ceylon* (Colombo, 1878), Chap. XIII. See also the evidence of Capt. Lillie – the man who led the expedition against the Kandyan 'rebels' – in the *Third Report on Ceylon* (1850–1).

to Government buildings that prompted the attack.[1] As far as the peasants were concerned they participated in these attacks to show their disapproval of the taxation policy of the Government; but as regards the leadership the riots were a quixotic attempt to expel the British from Kandy.

In spite of the ease with which the 'rebels' had been defeated, the Government panicked;[2] they had visions of the great rebellion of 1817–18 all over again. The rebellion of 1817 had been led by the chiefs and the *bhikkus* and it was these two groups that Torrington and Tennent suspected once again of organizing a rebellion, though they could not provide any proof that they had really done so.[3] The Government were fighting the battles of 1817–18 all over again, and it became Torrington's aim to avoid all the mistakes that Governor Brownrigg had made then. Brownrigg had been criticized in 1817 because he had delayed to impose martial law and had thereby unnecessarily prolonged the rebellion, and so Torrington immediately declared martial law and ruthlessly suppressed the 'rebellion'. Martial law was not lifted till 10 October, though there was no clash with the army after the incidents of 29 and 31 July. The British had only one soldier wounded in this whole campaign; at least two hundred Kandyans were killed.[4]

The policy of ruthless repression may be attributed to Torrington's lack of administrative experience. It is also significant that he and his closest advisers were moved to take these harsh steps for fear that the coffee crop of 1848 would be completely lost. The man on whose advice martial law was imposed was Colonel 'Tiger' Fraser, who had earned his sobriquet for his ferocity during the rebellion of 1817–18.[5] He was a coffee planter with an estate thirty miles from Matale the scene of the disturbances.[6] The

---

[1] Among the buildings attacked at Matale was the Baptist chapel in the town. See *Miss.Her.* 1848, Rev. J. Allen's letters of 12 August and 13 September 1848.

[2] At Kurunegala, a subaltern and 30 men routed a mob of about 4,000. See evidence of T. Y. McChristie in *The Second Report on Ceylon*, p.329., and evidence of H. L. Layard, *ibid.* p.233.

[3] C.O. 54/250, Torrington to Grey, no.165 of 15 September 1848. Tennent's evidence in the *Third Report on Ceylon*, pp.183 ff.

[4] The *Third Report on Ceylon*, Capt. Lillie's evidence.

[5] Tennent in his evidence in the *Third Report on Ceylon*, p.190, stated that Fraser was the first person consulted by Torrington.

[6] Tennent, *op. cit.* p.192.

Government's closest adviser at Kandy was Lieut.-General Herbert Maddock, a retired East India Company official who was a coffee planter at Matale.[1] His coffee store in Matale bazaar had been burnt down by the rebels.[2] It was on Maddock that both Tennent and Torrington relied for advice during the disturbances,[3] and he was the evil genius behind the whole policy of repression. During the disturbances Maddock persuaded Tennent to attempt the establishment of colonies of Indians – to work on the coffee plantations – on the lands to be confiscated from the 'rebels'. Tennent later admitted that the plan was not implemented only because the confiscations had fallen far short of expectations.[4]

During the early stages of the disturbances Elliott had decided to support the Government in its policy of dealing firmly with the 'rebels'. Apparently he had wanted a peaceful agitation against the taxes, and had been as surprised and alarmed as the Government at the violence of the 'rebels', but when the Government's policy became needlessly repressive, Elliott began to campaign against it, and was more than once in danger of arrest.[5] He succeeded in interesting Joseph Hume, the Radical M.P., in the situation in Ceylon, and through his efforts succeeded in getting a Parliamentary Committee to investigate it, but though this Committee issued three reports it could reach no satisfactory conclusion on the affairs of Ceylon.

In Ceylon itself, the disturbances led ultimately to the recall of Torrington and Tennent; they led to the repeal of the taxes of 1848 (all save the Road Ordinance); and they made the Government more wary in dealing with the Kandyans. But their greatest influence was on Buddhist policy. Both Torrington[6] and Earl Grey[7] were convinced that it was the *bhikkus* and chiefs who had organized the disturbances, and that it was the Government's

[1] The *Second Report on Ceylon*, pp.49 ff., the evidence of Sir Herbert Maddock.
[2] *Ibid.* p.74.
[3] Grey MSS. Earl Grey's correspondence with Torrington during the disturbances indicates that he too had a very high regard for Maddock and encouraged the Ceylon officials to rely on Maddock's advice.
[4] The *Third Report on Ceylon* (1850–51) p.253, the evidence of Tennent. Grey MSS. Torrington to Grey, 11 August 1848.
[5] Grey's letters to Torrington in the Grey MSS. suggest that it was he who dissuaded Torrington from arresting Elliott.
[6] Grey MSS., Torrington to Grey, 11 August 1848.
[7] Grey, *op. cit.* II, pp.182–3.

Buddhist policy that had driven them to this opposition. There-after the policy of the Government became noticeably more liberal and less 'Evangelical'. But the disturbances had little im-pact on other aspects of policy. The plantations continued to expand, and even if the Kandyans objected, it was impossible to stop that expansion, or to prevent the entry of the Indians into the Kandyan provinces in search of employment on the planta-tions. All in all, the process of amalgamating the Kandyan with the Maritime provinces did not receive anything more than a temporary setback.

When the reports of Colebrooke and Cameron reached Ceylon in 1833, it seemed as though Benthamism would have the same impact on Ceylon as it had on India. But it was not to be, for Ceylon lacked what was most essential for this purpose – a hard core of civil servants imbued with these ideas. Few civil servants in Ceylon had any Benthamite leanings.[1] At a time when there was a remarkable store of intelligence, talent and administrative ability in the civil service of the East India Company in India there was a dearth of first-class men in the administration in Ceylon, where in the 1840s the bulk of the civil servants were incompetent and inefficient men; a great many of them were coffee planters as well as civil servants. New ideas had few attrac-tions for them. Thus Benthamism petered out in Ceylon in the 1840s.[2] Cameron's[3] Benthamite legal reforms, and Colebrooke's undisguised liberalism were much too radical for the civil servants of the day, whose task it was to implement them.

Moreover, not one of the governors of Ceylon showed any Benthamite leanings, and none of them were men of outstanding

[1] Arthur Buller, Queen's Advocate (till 1848), showed glimpses of Ben-thamite leanings. He was the brother of Charles Buller, the radical imperialist; he moved out of Ceylon in 1848 to take up a judicial appointment in India.

[2] Perhaps the most lasting contribution of the Benthamites was the judicial system, established in 1833 on Cameron's recommendations. The Charter of Justice of 1833 marks the beginning of the modern judicial system in Ceylon. In his minute of 20 January 1842, in C.O. 54/191, James Stephen commented that 'this Ceylon Charter was a pure innovation . . . based on speculation (chiefly those of Bentham)'.

[3] C. H. Cameron was a member of the first and second Indian Law Com-missions. Leslie Stephen (in the *D.N.B.* III, 741) referred to him as 'a disciple and, ultimately, perhaps the last surviving disciple of Jeremy Bentham.'

Ceylon[1] is the most sensitive and perceptive study of the subject in existence. Two of his despatches and reports would rank among the best half dozen ever written by a Ceylon civil servant – his brilliant Report on the Finance and Commerce of Ceylon, written in 1846, is a mine of information on the subject,[2] while his despatch on Indian immigration to Ceylon, written in 1847, was at once a Blue Book and a passionate demand for humanitarian reform.[3]

He failed as an administrator, partly because of the hostility of Ceylon civil servants who resented his appointment to the key post of Colonial Secretary which had hitherto been filled by one of themselves; partly because he was unfortunate enough to hold office during a time of acute economic depression and violent political storms; but also because of his own shortcomings – tactlessness, insincerity and an indecision that bordered on timidity.

Viscount Torrington, a descendant of the ill-fated Admiral Byng, was Governor of Ceylon from 1847 to 1850. The Third Earl Grey, Secretary of State for the Colonies had picked this impecunious courtier (Torrington was a Lord of the Bedchamber in Queen Victoria's Court) only after two very able men had refused the appointment.[4] Queen Victoria hastened to inform Grey that Torrington was little qualified by education or experience for the post, and events were to prove the sagacity and accuracy of her assessment of his abilities.[5] He was unfortunate in having to face a severe economic depression and disturbed political conditions within a year of his appointment; but it is doubtful if a man of Torrington's limited ability could have fared better even if circumstances had been more favourable.

His successor, Sir George Anderson (1850–55), was a far abler man with considerable experience of administration in the service of the East India Company in western India, and in that of the

[1] Tennent, *Christianity in Ceylon* (London, 1850).
[2] *Report on the Finance and Commerce of Ceylon, 22.10.1846, Rep. Fin. Com.* pp. 46ff.
[3] C.O. 54/235, Tennent to Grey, no.6 of 21 April 1847.
[4] Doig, R. P., 'Lord Torrington's Government of Ceylon: 1847–50', *Durham University Journal* (March 1962), p. 50.
   The two men who refused the appointment were C. H. Cameron and John (later Sir John) Shaw-Lefevre; the latter had distinguished himself in the service of the Colonial Office, and in 1847, when the appointment to Ceylon was offered, he was Vice-Chancellor of the University of London.
[5] *Ibid.*
c

Colonial Office as Governor of Mauritius (1849–51).[1] The tasks that faced him in Ceylon were, in a sense, even more formidable than those that faced his predecessor. The colony needed a period of peace and stability after the disturbances of 1848; the colonial economy and the coffee industry were in need of a few years of quiet consolidation after the depression and coffee crisis of 1846–7; the morale of the civil service had to be restored after the sordid intrigues that followed the appointment of the Parliamentary Committee on Ceylon in 1849, and above all it was necessary to solve the complicated Buddhist problem. To the solution of these problems Anderson brought a sturdy commonsense, a practical turn of mind, and a spirit of compromise. But if these qualities enabled him to rise to the tasks that faced him, by their very nature they prevented him from rising above them to the sphere of long-term plans and bold and imaginative solutions. For a man who had served under Elphinstone in Bombay, and had helped in the framing and preparation of the first systematic code of laws attempted in British India, the Bombay Code of 1827,[2] he brought with him to Ceylon very little of that subtle Benthamism that inspired Elphinstone.

Benthamism had no great hold on the Colonial Office. In the affairs of the colonial empire, any continuing trend of policy derived its strength and consistency from the forces of *laisser-faire* economics and Evangelical Christianity. In the tropical colonies the Evangelical impulse gave to colonial administration a continuity and a sense of purpose even more marked than that provided by the secular creed of *laisser-faire*.

To a large extent the strength of Evangelicalism at the Colonial Office may be attributed to the personal influence of James Stephen,[3] the formidable Permanent Under-Secretary (Mr 'Over-

[1] *D.N.B.*, I, 377–8. He was employed principally in judicial duties until December 1831, when he was placed in charge of the Southern Maratha districts under the designation of Principal Collector and political agent. In 1835 he was selected as the Bombay member of the Indian Law Commission, an office he held till his appointment to the Council of Bombay in 1838. From 1841 to 1842 he was Governor of Bombay. He retired from the service of the East India Company in 1844.   [2] *D.N.B.*, I, p.377.

[3] For an assessment of Stephen's career see Beaglehole, J. C., 'The Colonial Office, 1782–1854', *H.S.A.N.Z.* 1; Knaplund, P., *James Stephen and the Colonial Office 1813–1846*; Pugh, R. B., 'The Colonial Office', *Cambridge History of the British Empire*, III; Williams T., 'The Colonial Office in the Thirties', *H.S.A.N.Z.* (1943) 11.

Secretary' Stephen as he appeared to the Radical Imperialists), a distinguished member of the Chapham Sect who has been justly described as 'one of the most remarkable men of his generation.'[1] For nearly two decades '. . . during short tenures of strong Secretaries of State, and entire tenures, whether short or long, of some who were not strong, he more than any other man virtually governed the Colonial Empire'.[2] He commanded the respect of his political superiors by his remarkable ability, indefatigable industry and great devotion to the affairs of the Colonial Empire. But his influence was derived from other circumstances as well, and chiefly from the fact that successive Secretaries of State treated the Colonial Office as a mere stepping stone to political advancement and left the affairs of the colonies in the hands of the permanent officials, the most prominent of whom was Stephen.[3]

Of the Secretaries of State only the Third Earl Grey had any wide experience of colonial affairs, and he was the only one with a definite colonial policy of his own.[4] He has been described as 'a man of strong and independent mind, capable of taking a long view and quick to grasp a principle, hard-working and public spirited'.[5] Stephen and he had much in common – their temperaments were so much alike – and they got on well together. Grey was somewhat of a doctrinaire on Free Trade, systematic colonization, and self-government in the 'white' colonies, while Stephen

[1] Taylor, H., *Autobiography* II, 302.

[2] *Ibid.*

Stephen's relations with successive Secretaries of State varied with the personalities concerned. Glenelg and Normanby were under his close supervision; indeed during Glenelg's tenure of office Stephen virtually ruled the Colonial Office. Russell won Stephen's respect but was only slightly less dependent on him than Normanby and Glenelg. Stanley's attitude was much less cordial, and he kept much colonial business away from him, while Grey, who got on well with Stephen and respected his opinions, consulted him on every imaginable issue, and on many occasions was deeply influenced by him.

[3] The Colonial Office was politically impotent, and the Secretary of State sat in the Cabinet only because the portfolio of Colonial Affairs was combined, from 1801 to 1854, with the War Ministry, though the two departments were run separately. Ambitious politicians seldom stayed long at the Colonial Office; Earl Grey's long spell (1846–52) was an exception to the general rule.

[4] Morrell, W. P., *British Colonial Policy in the Age of Peel and Russell*, pp.201–8, 472–527, and Bell and Morrell, *Select Documents on British Colonial Policy 1830–60*, Introduction. See also Grey's own work, *The Colonial Policy of Lord John Russell's Administrations*, 2 vols. 2nd ed. (London, 1853).

[5] Morrell, W. P., *op. cit.* p.201.

was much more of a doctrinaire on proselytization, and native policy in New Zealand and South Africa. But Grey was far from being unsympathetic to the Evangelical impulse as his strong support of Stephen on Buddhist policy in Ceylon would indicate.

One of the most noteworthy features of the social policy of mid-nineteenth century Ceylon was the importance of religious issues. This was partly owing to the influence of Evangelicals like Glenelg and Stephen at the Colonial Office, and of men like Governor Stewart Mackenzie (1837–41) and a host of subordinate officials in Ceylon who believed in the urgency of converting the 'heathen' to Christianity; and partly to the agitation of missionary organizations for a redefinition of the relationship between Buddhism and the Ceylon Government. Glenelg laid it down that the spread of Christianity should be made a vital aspect of state policy in Ceylon,[1] and his successors, to a greater or lesser extent, shared this belief: of the governors of Ceylon in this period only Anderson showed little interest in it.

Since the spread of Christianity was so important an aspect of state policy, it was inevitable that missionary organizations should seek to influence government policy. The influence of these missionary bodies on the formation of social and religious policy is the theme of this book. Six missions – the Church Missionary Society, the Society for the Propagation of the Gospel, the Wesleyans, the Baptists, the Roman Catholics, and the American Board of Missions – worked in Ceylon during the period covered by this book. The Roman Catholics had been in Ceylon since the time of the Portuguese in the sixteenth century; the other missions had begun their activities after the establishment of British rule in Ceylon, and were all, with the exception of the S.P.G., whose mission work in Ceylon really started with the Establishment of the Bishopric of Colombo in 1845, now in the second phase of their activity. The preliminary period of laying the foundations was over; the age of expansion had begun.

Of these missions, the Americans confined themselves to the Jaffna peninsula and its environs in the north of the island. The Baptists were unique among the missions in having no station in the Tamil regions of the north and east. They concentrated their efforts on the south-west coastal region and on the Kandyan

[1] C.O. 55/79, Glenelg to Mackenzie, no.18 of 2 October 1837.

region, and they were the best represented mission in the latter area. The other missions spread themselves over all parts of the island, with the exception of the Wesleyans who had no mission station in the Kandyan region. The Wesleyans and the C.M.S., the two most powerful missions in Ceylon at this time, observed an administrative division between North Ceylon (Tamil) and South Ceylon (Sinhalese).

Generally, missionary activity was concentrated on the maritime regions of the north, the south-west, and the east, the regions that had been under Western influence since the sixteenth century, while the Kandyan region, where the resistance of Buddhism and the traditional Sinhalese culture was at its strongest, were not so effectively penetrated.

In countries like Ceylon with well-established cultures and civilizations the propagation of Christianity was a more formidable undertaking than the missionaries anticipated. And a great many of their disappointments sprang from their over-confidence, and their under-estimation of the strength of indigenous religions. It was impossible to spread Christianity without reducing the influence of, if not altogether destroying, these indigenous religions. This was particularly true of the Kandyan region where Buddhism had so strong a hold on the people, and where, moreover, the British Government, at the cession of Kandy in 1815, had given a solemn undertaking to support and protect Buddhism. Under the impression that the severing of this connection between the State and Buddhism would accelerate the decline of Buddhism, the missionary organizations in Ceylon made it one of their major aims to force the Government to dissociate itself from its connection with Buddhism. Inevitably, therefore, Buddhist policy became the major religious issue of this period. As it happened, however, the religious problem of mid-nineteenth century Ceylon was introduced with an attempt to reform the Anglican establishment.

Part I

CHAPTER I

The State, the Church and the Missions

WHEN the Rt. Hon. J. S. Mackenzie was appointed Governor of Ceylon Lord Glenelg, the Secretary of State for the Colonies, wrote him a long despatch, setting out in detail the tasks that awaited him there, and explaining the line of policy to be followed. Glenelg, an Evangelical greatly interested in the conversion of the 'heathen', made it clear to Mackenzie that the 'moral and religious education of the people of Ceylon' was 'the most important subject' to which his attention could be directed.[1] This despatch marked a definite and deeply significant change in the attitude of the Government to missionary activity. Ever since the conquest of the Kandyan Provinces there had been some diffidence in encouraging missionary activity in that region (there was no reluctance to encourage it in the Maritime Provinces) since religion was the one factor capable of rousing the people to active opposition to the Government, but now for the first time the Governor was instructed not only to encourage actively missionary enterprise but to treat it as the most important subject to which his attention could be directed. The despatch in fact marked the beginning of a closer State interest in Christianity, and for the rest of our period active evangelization was never far from the minds of most of the administrators.

This despatch was equally significant for the criticism made in it of the Anglican Establishment[2] that, taking into consideration the

[1] C.O. 55/79, Glenelg to Mackenzie, no. 18 of 2 October 1837.

[2] In this chapter the term 'Anglican Establishment' will refer to the Archdeacon of Colombo, the Colonial Chaplains and their subordinates, paid by the Government of Ceylon: it will not include the missionaries of the C.M.S. and the S.P.G. who, though they were members of the Church of England, were not part of the Establishment. It must be added that they did not qualify in any way for the criticisms made of the Anglican clergymen of the Establishment.

money spent on it,[1] the results of its labours were decidedly meagre. Glenelg suggested that the government chaplains should take a greater interest in the conversion of the people, that, in brief, they should look upon themselves less as chaplains than as missionaries.

There was a great deal of justification for Glenelg's criticisms of the Anglican Establishment. It was found that of the 74,787 Christians then attending public worship in Ceylon, 72,870 were Roman Catholics; that of the remaining 1,917, 1,600 were considered to belong to the Anglican Church, and that only 900 of these attended the services conducted by the Chaplains. The salaries of the Archdeacon and the five Colonial Chaplains amounted annually to £5,400 of which the Archdeacon of Colombo was paid £2,000.[2] This was apart from the £1,234 paid to the Sinhalese, Portuguese and Tamil Colonial Chaplains, who between them had congregations amounting to 317 persons. Besides, while the clergy of the Establishment and the Archdeacon of Colombo had always been actively associated in the educational activities of the Government and had since the establishment in 1833 of the School Commission played an active though hardly constructive role in it,[3] they had seldom been actively interested in evangelization. Indeed, as was pointed out later, the Letters Patent of the Archdeacon did not require him to take such an interest.[4]

Glenelg's instructions, in spite of the clarity of the language in which they were couched, might have been treated as merely the expression of an Evangelical's personal interest in the expansion of Christianity, not to be treated as a matter of great urgency, and they may have been watered down to suit the convenience of the

[1] Glenelg made it clear that, while the Government of Ceylon should actively assist the spread of Christianity among the people, there should be a strict check on the expenditure involved, and Mackenzie was asked to make economies wherever possible.

[2] C.O. 55/79, Glenelg to Mackenzie, no. 18 of 2 October 1837.

Ceylon had been part of the Bishopric of Calcutta till 1837. Since 1837 it formed part of the See of Madras. The Archdeacon of Colombo was its local head.

[3] This problem will be discussed in greater detail in the chapter on education policy.

[4] C.O. 54/203, Campbell to Stanley, no. 60 of 16 March 1843. The confidential report of the Bishop of Madras enclosed in this despatch.

Ceylon Government, as would very likely have been their fate had Mackenzie's immediate predecessor, Horton, or his immediate successor, Campbell, dealt with them, but as it was, these instructions tallied with Mackenzie's own notion of his duties as a Governor. An ardent supporter of missionary enterprise and an advocate of social reform (he was deeply interested in the education of the people), he treated these instructions, as Glenelg wanted them to be treated, as a matter of the first importance.

Mackenzie realized quite early in his administration that the great obstacles to all his projects of social reform were the Archdeacon and the High Church group in the Anglican Establishment who, unconcerned with these problems, were content to concentrate on their duties as Chaplains – such as they were. Almost in despair he turned for a lead in these problems to the Wesleyans and the Baptists, but this tended to complicate matters, because the Anglican Establishment were as bigoted and intolerant as they were lethargic and inefficient and looked on the Governor's cordial relationship with these 'Dissenters', 'Schismatics' and 'Anabaptists' with suspicion and concern.

Mackenzie's response to Glenelg's despatch was to draft a questionnaire on the duties and functions of the Anglican Establishment, which he sent to the Archdeacon and the Colonial Chaplains.[1] Coinciding as this did with his efforts to curb the activities of the Archdeacon and his associates in the School Commission it convinced the Anglican Establishment that Mackenzie's policies were fundamentally dangerous to their interests, and this conviction strengthened an urge, never very weak, to fight rather than accept them. Indeed they were in no position to fight, for as their replies to Mackenzie's questionnaire indicated they had taken an extremely narrow view of their duties and had neglected even those which they acknowledged as being theirs, but they were aided by the fact that Mackenzie, enlightened and far sighted as he was, was at the same time a weak and ineffective administrator. Moreover, although he criticized the Arch-

---

[1] C.O. 54/163, Mackenzie's private letter to Glenelg, 1 June 1838.

Ibid., Mackenzie to Glenelg, no. 117 of 18 July 1838. It is significant that Stephen had doubts about this questionnaire. His minute dated 4 December 1838 reads as follows: 'I doubt whether the Bishop will not think that this is an usurpation of his province, and I am inclined to the opinion that he will be well founded in that objection.' But Glenelg over-ruled him and supported Mackenzie. C.O. 54/163, Glenelg to Mackenzie, no.161 of 21 December 1838.

deacon for his worldliness and his concentration on his activities as a coffee planter, he could hardly make too much of it, because he himself had the reputation of being a speculator in land. Besides he was a Liberal in politics, and, though an Anglican, was a friend of Wesleyans and Baptists in a Colony where the great majority of the senior civil servants were Tories and High Church Anglicans.[1] Some of them, notably the able and experienced George Turnour, Government Agent of the Central Province, made no secret of the fact that their sympathies were not with Mackenzie in his conflicts with the Archdeacon.[2]

The Archdeacon of the Anglican Church, the Ven. J. Glennie was a resourceful, if choleric and unscrupulous man. A typical Anglican clergyman of his day he would have fitted in comfortably in some affluent parish in the English countryside. A Tory in politics and High Church in his religious attitude, he had little interest in spiritual matters and no time for theology, his time being divided between the defence of the secular interests – and privileges – of the Anglican Establishment, and the cultivation of coffee.[3] Indeed he deserves to be remembered more as a pioneer coffee planter than as an Archdeacon of the Anglican Church. He was not without influence in England for he was known to be a friend of the then Bishop of London. Two of his daughters were married to West Indian planters while he had two sons in the Church, one in England and the other, Owen Glennie, in Ceylon.

Owen Glennie, who had inherited his father's resourcefulness and temper, proved to be an even more formidable defender of Anglican privilege, by virtue of a wider education[4] and his skill as a journalist. He ran *The Ceylon Herald* with great zest and vigour and in his hands that journal became an outspoken defender of Toryism and High Church Anglicanism, and a most vehement and unprincipled critic of Liberalism and all those who stood opposed to the perpetuation of Anglican privilege. But like the

---

[1] C.O. 54/177, Mackenzie to Russell, separate private despatch of 5 February 1840.

[2] C.O. 54/179, Mackenzie to Russell, no.69 of 24 April 1840, C.O. 54/180. Mackenzie to Russell, separate miscellaneous despatch of 7 July 1840.

[3] He had 1,976 acres of the best coffee land at Pussellawa in the Central Province.

[4] Apart from his training in England, he had also been educated in Germany where he had acquired a thorough grounding in theology.

man the journal lacked both a sense of humour and a sense of proportion, though it compensated for this by the courage with which it championed its twin causes. Owen Glennie defied Governor Wilmot-Horton – as he was to defy Governor Mackenzie in the future – when he believed the latter's actions or policies jeopardised the interests of the Anglican Establishment. Together the two Glennies set on foot a skilful campaign of personal vilification and sustained opposition to the liberalizing policy of Stewart Mackenzie.

This conflict, however, led to consequences which neither of the two parties could have anticipated, the most important of which was the thorough reform of the Anglican Establishment and the establishment of the Bishopric of Colombo. The more virulent the opposition of the Glennies, the more radical became Mackenzie's recommendations on Church reform. His early despatches would indicate that he was willing to co-operate with the Archdeacon in any scheme of Church reform the latter may have had in mind but the Archdeacon, who had been irrevocably antagonized by Mackenzie's determination to reconstruct the School Commission and to deprive the Anglicans of their near monopoly of the power and patronage of that body, had little trust in Mackenzie and little desire for any reform at all.

Mackenzie's great difficulty was that he had two irons in the fire: he became interested in the reform of the Anglican Establishment while he was actively engaged in a radical reconstruction of the educational system. He was able to devote more time to – indeed it would appear that he gave priority to – educational reform, and his achievement here was more substantial than that in his schemes of Church reform. Perhaps this pre-occupation with educational reform left him less time for the latter task. It is significant that while he had a coherent programme of educational reform, on the issue of Church reform he had merely a conviction that reform was necessary if the Established Church was to serve any useful purpose. Besides, the Glennies cleverly outmanoeuvred him on this latter issue by compelling him to dissipate his energies on trivialities like the Heber Scholarship,[1] and the matter of an

[1] The Heber Scholarship was an annual award at the Bishop's College, Calcutta, for two Ceylonese students. The Archdeacon claimed the right to nominate to this Scholarship, while Mackenzie claimed it as the right of the Governor.

increase of salary for Owen Glennie, on which he wasted the better part of two years, leaving little time for the broad principles at stake. The Glennies egged him on with attacks – bitterly personal – in the columns of *The Ceylon Herald*[1] and from public platforms. The vehemence of these attacks compelled Mackenzie, in the first quarter of 1840, to appeal to the Secretary of State against the Archdeacon, who, he complained, was lowering the Governor's prestige. He deplored most of all the virulent attacks on the Governor by *The Ceylon Herald*. One result of these attacks was to convince Mackenzie that in any scheme of reforming the Anglican Establishment the removal of Archdeacon Glennie must take high priority. He suggested the abolition of the post of Archdeacon,[2] but he found the Colonial Office in a most uncooperative mood.

It was Glenelg's despatch that had prompted Mackenzie to attempt a reform of the Anglican Establishment, but now Glenelg had left the Colonial Office, to be succeeded by the Marquis of Normanby, who after a tenure of a few months was himself replaced by Lord John Russell. James Stephen continued in his post but he proved to be no friend of Mackenzie's. The Colonial Office did not give Mackenzie the support that he was led to expect by the tone of Glenelg's despatch. Between 1836 and 1840 Mackenzie's prestige at the Colonial Office had declined considerably.[3]

---

[1] In 1839–40 the Government unsuccessfully prosecuted the Editor of *The Ceylon Herald* for criminal libel, with reference to a statement made in that paper about Mackenzie.

    The Ceylon Herald's fire was directed at Mackenzie, the Baptists, the Weseyans and Liberalism in that order. See Mackenzie MSS. File 18.

[2] C.O. 54/177, Mackenzie to Russell, no.15 of 29 January 1840 and separate private despatch of 5 February 1840.

[3] From the very beginning of his administration, Mackenzie came in for a great deal of criticism at the Colonial Office. James Stephen and his assistant, G. Barrow, took great exception to Mackenzie's habit of writing long private letters to Glenelg, in which he touched upon all the problems of his administration in a most haphazard manner. He was instructed to write carefully drafted despatches instead. In spite of this admonition, he persisted in this practice, though these letters became less frequent thereafter.

    Stephen's annoyance probably sprang from a suspicion that this unorthodox correspondence was designed to reach Glenelg direct, without the intervention of the permanent officials of the Colonial Office; or it may have been that he felt it somehow reflected Mackenzie's inefficiency. Whatever the explanation, there was no doubt that it antagonized Stephen who, throughout Mackenzie's

The Colonial Office was aware of his activities as a land speculator, and he was being blamed – unfairly in this instance – for the deterioration of the civil service. His appeals for help against the Glennies had not improved matters for him for it left behind an impression of ineptitude and incompetence. He was left to fend for himself.

Lord John Russell would not consider the abolition of the post of Archdeacon, except in the event of the resignation or the death of Glennie. His despatch studiously avoided any reference to the activities of the Glennies against Mackenzie. The latter could however, derive some comfort from Russell's observation (in agreement with his own view) that

> . . . the salaries of the clergy of the Established Church in Ceylon appear . . . to be unnecessarily high; and it will be proper to consider when vacancies occur on the Ecclesiastical Establishment whether some reduction may not with propriety be made in the emoluments of its members.[1]

But it was cold comfort at a time when the Glennies had won the support of the Bishop of Madras, who proceeded to inflate the petty problem of an increase of salary for Owen Glennie into an affair of considerable importance. The Bishop took the offensive in a series of letters he wrote to the Colonial Office,[2] stoutly defending the Glennies and powerfully arguing the case for the *status quo* in education and Church affairs in Ceylon.[3] If it was any consolation to Mackenzie his quarrel with the Established Church was at last being fought on the level of principles rather than of detail.

The Colonial Office was greatly embarrassed by this correspondence.[4] For one thing, the Bishop was guilty of a breach of con-

---

administration, adopted a most unsympathetic and hostile attitude towards him.

See particularly: C.O. 54/160 Mackenzie's private letter to Glenelg, 12 February 1838, and Stephen's minute of 8 May 1838; C.O. 54/163, Mackenzie's private letter to Glenelg, 1 June 1838, and Stephen's minute on it.

[1] C.O. 54/177, Russell to Mackenzie, no.44 of 19 March 1840.

[2] C.O. 54/185; see under Ecclesiastical, and Bishop of Madras. This volume is the miscellaneous volume for 1840.

[3] The Bishop rather overplayed his hand when he went on to defend the Archdeacon against the charge of being more a coffee planter than an ecclesiastical dignitary, and to defend the Church in Ceylon from charges of inefficiency and neglect of duty.

[4] C.O. 54/185, Stephen's minute of 10 January 1840.

stitutional etiquette in writing direct to the Colonial Office on a matter relating to Ceylon, instead of through the Governor. Besides the Colonial Office grudgingly recognized that the Governor's criticisms of the Archdeacon and the Anglican Establishment were justified. They resolved therefore to refrain from corresponding with the Bishop on this matter. But very soon the Governor and the Bishop were involved in another dispute.

Mackenzie, in the interest of the prestige of the Civil Government, threatened to remove Owen Glennie from Colombo to a less congenial station. This was reported to the Bishop, whose immediate reaction was to suspect this threatened removal as a calculated attempt to intervene in the internal affairs of the Church. He asked for instructions from the Colonial Office on the urgent question of 'the removal by a Governor of a British Chaplain from a station to which he has been licensed by me, to one to which I might be unwilling to license him'.[1] But it was not this detail that mattered to the Bishop, but the vital principle behind it all, the constitutional position of the Governor in relation to the Colonial Church. He demanded to know 'whether the Governor is the Head of the Protestant Church of England and Ireland in Ceylon and if this assumption is recognized by Her Majesty's Government, to instruct me as to the character and extent of the obedience due from the Bishop of the Diocese to His Excellency in that capacity'.[2]

This new controversy caused a great deal of anxious thought at the Colonial Office, for questions of this nature relating to the Church in the Colonies were not often raised. The exact relationship between the Governor of a Colony and the Colonial Church had never been clearly defined, and even when it was necessary to do so there was an understandable reluctance to be too explicit. Vernon Smith, the Under-Secretary, looked upon the governor as the 'Head of the Church of England and Ireland' in the Colony, but he thought it best not to lay it down so clearly.[3] It was an opinion shared by his superior, Lord John Russell, who saw some of the difficulties that stood in the way of a clear definition. He declared that 'the Queen is the Head of the Protestant Church in England and Ireland and in Scotland by law –

---

[1] C.O. 54/185, see under Ecclesiastical, and Bishop of Madras.
[2] C.O. 54/185, ibid.
[3] C.O. 54/185, Vernon Smith's minute of 27 February 1840.

but how far the Governor of a Colony is so, it is difficult to say. I presume a Roman Catholic might be made Governor of Ceylon, though a Roman Catholic Prince of Wales could not succeed to the Crown . . .'.[1]

Even at this stage the Colonial Office was clearly anxious not to get itself involved in this dispute. For one thing it was difficult to decide firmly for one side or the other, and for another a Whig Government would have to be careful about annoying the Church in England. It was better therefore to stand studiously aloof than to intervene decisively, and even if a decision had to be made it was safer to embarrass the Governor than to annoy the Bishop. Thus while the Colonial Office refused to be drawn into this conflict between the Governor and the Bishop, or to defend the Governor against the unscrupulous attacks of the Glennies, they decided – at James Stephen's prompting – to lay before the Bishop of Madras a complaint against Owen Glennie by the Governor. It would be difficult to defend this decision.[2] Stephen was not unaware of the gravity of this move for he wrote that 'the effect of such a proceeding must be to place the Head of the Civil Government in the condition of a Prosecutor before the Local Ecclesiastical Government and what are the consequences in every part of the world of sub-ordinating the secular to the spiritual authority it is needless to state.'[3] But the reasons he gave for placing this dispute before the Bishop hardly justify a decision of such gravity.[4] For, by taking this step the Colonial Office gave the appearance of supporting the Glennies against the Governor at a time when they had openly challenged the authority of the Governor and had publicly humiliated him. It was for the Colonial Office to intervene in support of the Governor against the attempts to undermine his authority.

Stephen's political superiors gave in to his suggestions though Vernon Smith did so only because 'too much had been submitted

[1] C.O. 54/185, Russell's minute of 27 February 1840.

[2] The decision was taken against the advice of Philip Anstruther, who was consulted on the matter. C.O. 54/185, Philip Anstruther's memorandum A of 24 February 1840.

[3] C.O. 54/185, Stephen's minute of 26 February 1840.

[4] *Ibid.* The reasons given were: that the Bishop as the Head of the Church in Ceylon had the right to be consulted; that he had already been consulted in other matters concerning the Church; and that Mackenzie, himself, had laid a complaint against Owen Glennie before the Bishop.

to the Bishop to decline his authority now.'[1] Since neither Stephen[2] nor Vernon Smith[3] had any illusions about Owen Glennie, it strengthens the suspicion that Stephen was moved by some deep personal animosity towards Mackenzie.

But the very persistence with which Mackenzie advocated a reform of the Anglican Establishment began to have some belated effect. Mackenzie seized the opportunity provided by Russell's remark that the salaries of some of the clergymen of the Establishment were too high[4] to suggest that these salaries should be on a graduated scale according to the duties performed.[5] He pointed out that '. . . one and all of the Colonial Chaplains have officially declared that the conversion of the Heathen . . . is not part of *their* duty and they most faithfully live up to that declaration.'[6] He suggested that the salary of the Archdeacon '. . . who neither makes nor has made during 14 years any visitation through his Archdeaconry nor has the cure of souls within it . . .', should be made available on the abolition of that post – a step which he again strongly recommended – for the construction of churches and the maintenance of additional Chaplains.[7]

On this occasion James Stephen was moved into making a sharp criticism of the Established Church in Ceylon.

Why an Archdeacon who had no cure of souls and who never performs a visitation of his Archdeaconry should receive £2,000 per annum, why largely paid clergymen with scarcely any congregation should hold themselves absolved from all obligation to attempt the instruction of the heathen population in the midst of which they are living are questions which it would not I think . . . be easy to answer satisfactorily. . . .[8]

---

[1] V. Smith's minute of 27 February 1840.

[2] *Ibid.* Stephen in his minute above, referred to Owen Glennie thus: '[He] is a person utterly unbecoming of any spiritual charge whatever, and fitted rather to conduct some scurrilous newspaper or the broils of a Civic Corporation than to act as a Minister of the Gospel. . . .'

[3] *Ibid.* V. Smith said of Glennie that '[he] is a bold bad man and lucky enough to meet with just such Governors that he could deal with. . . .'

[4] C.O. 54/177, Russell to Mackenzie, no.44 of 19 March 1840.

[5] C.O. 54/180, Mackenzie to Russell, no.111 of 8 July 1840.

[6] *Ibid.*   [7] *Ibid.*

[8] C.O. 54/180, Stephen's minute of 7 October 1840 in Mackenzie to Russell, no.111 of 8 July 1840.

In spite of this criticism, however, Stephen could suggest no remedy. He merely added that

> the difficulties of Ecclesiastical reformation are, however, not pecu-
> liar to Ceylon or to the present time, and I should fear that the evils
> which the Governor laments must be considered as irremediable
> unless there should appear amongst us Bishops and Archbishops
> ready to sacrifice the temporal interest of the clerical order to the
> spiritual interests of the Church, a moral martyrdom which few men
> have ever had energy enough to undergo.[1]

But Russell did not adopt this defeatist attitude. He was convinced that Mackenzie was right, and on his own initiative decided that the question of the position of the Archdeacon of Colombo should be referred to the Archbishop of Canterbury and the Bishop of London. He had made up his mind that the Archdeacon should be offered retirement on favourable terms.[2]

Mackenzie did not stay long enough in Ceylon to proceed with the task of reforming the Anglican Establishment, but his successor, Sir Colin Campbell, was in a much stronger position to do so. Russell gave him clear instructions that Glenelg's important des-patch to Mackenzie, when the latter assumed the Government of Ceylon in 1837,[3] should be treated as a definitive statement of Government policy on the question of conversion. He added that he had seen with regret 'the little advance which is made at so great an expense in teaching the doctrines of Christianity and I beg to call your attention to this important subject.'[4] Then, remembering the opposition that had rendered the final stages of Mackenzie's administration so ineffective, he gave instructions that

> in any difficulties which may arise . . . any purely Ecclesiastical
> functions must be left to the guidance of the spiritual authorities of
> the particular church affected, but in that case where undue civil
> or political interference is proved on the part of the Ecclesiastical
> Authorities, the offender must be dealt with in the most summary
> and decisive manner.[5]

In spite of the advantages deriving from these instructions, Campbell bided his time. It was not until 1843 that he began

---

[1] *Ibid.*
[2] C.O. 54/180, Russell's minute (no date) in the same despatch.
[3] C.O. 55/79, Glenelg to Mackenzie, no.18 of 2 October 1837.
[4] C.O. 54/195, Russell to Campbell, no.12 of 13 February 1841.
[5] *Ibid.*

D

the process of reform and even then he left it to the Bishops of Madras and Calcutta (who visited Ceylon early in 1843 to report on the ecclesiastical situation there) to initiate it.

The Bishops were shocked by the inefficiency and lethargy they found in the Anglican Establishment in Ceylon.[1] They reported that the Archdeacon performed no spiritual duties, except the preaching of an occasional sermon; had no 'cure of souls', made 'no regular Visitation', and had 'maintained . . . none of the dignity or hospitality of his highly remunerated functions'. He had neglected his spiritual duties to devote his attention to the more remunerative business of coffee planting.

Nor were the rest of the clergy a credit to the Church. At least one was, like the Archdeacon, a coffee planter. All were accused of worldliness and secularity. Two of the chaplains were so short-tempered and quarrelsome that 'but for the attendance on duty of the military, there was reason to fear that the churches of both chaplains would be almost deserted'.[2] Only one station, Trincomalee, appeared to be in good shape.[3]

There was a remarkable degree of agreement in the two Bishops' assessments of the defects of the Church in Ceylon, but they differed – equally remarkably – in the remedies they suggested. The report of the Bishop of Madras was the less radical of the two. Although he was critical of the Archdeacon, his recommendations, couched in the most colourless language, amounted to a mere tinkering with the existing structure – a few additional appointments in the existing stations, a new station at Jaffna, and a few transfers between stations.

At first glance the report of the Bishop of Calcutta would appear to be as innocuous as that of his colleagues. He insisted on an increase in the number of churches and chaplaincies (he sought an increase of 12 chaplains) as the most effective remedy for the situation. And he pleaded that the Anglican Church in Ceylon should be maintained in a position of primacy over other missions and sects.

---

[1] C.O. 54/203, Campbell to Stanley, no.60 of 16 March 1843. Letters of the Bishop of Madras of 7 and 17 February 1843, and his confidential report of 23 February 1843. C.O. 54/204, Campbell to Stanley, no.154 of 18 August 1843. The confidential report of the Bishop of Calcutta of 21 January 1843.

[2] The reference is to the Chaplains of Kandy and Galle.

[3] Surprisingly enough, it was Owen Glennie's station.

hardly be right to provide them with substitutes and pensions to encourage their continuance in their faults.[1]

Stephen probably hoped that Stanley's reaction to this report would be to recommend measures of drastic reform, but all that Stanley did was to send these papers to the Archbishop of Canterbury for the latter's comments. The Archbishop's suggestions were decidedly mild, very much like those of the Bishop of Madras, and Stanley had already decided to sanction them when the situation changed with the arrival of the report of the Bishop of Calcatta. It provided Stephen with the backing he needed to persuade Stanley that it was only by getting rid of the Archdeacon that there could be any progress in the Church of Ceylon.[2] And Stanley was sufficiently impressed by this report to change his attitude completely. To the Archbishop of Canterbury[3] and the Bishop of Madras went letters to the effect that the situation in Ceylon called for radical rather than piecemeal reform; that the compulsory retirement of the Archdeacon was an absolute necessity; and that it would be necessary to create a separate Bishopric of Colombo. These two dignitaries agreed with Stanley, and it was only necessary to convey this information to Campbell. The Archdeacon was to be pensioned off (he was to be given the alternative of retirement or dismissal) because of 'his want of temper . . . his worldly mindedness and neglect of his sacred duties', and this was to be the prelude to the creation of a Bishopric of Colombo. Other matters concerning the Anglican Establishment in Ceylon were to be left for the decision of the future Bishop.[4]

The establishment of the Bishopric of Colombo was the culmination of a series of events that followed upon Glenelg's despatch of 1837.[5] Glenelg himself did not recommend it. (It was only in 1837 that the Archdeaconry of Colombo had been transferred from the jurisdiction of the Bishop of Calcutta to that of the Bishop of Madras.) In 1840 Lord John Russell had ignored a suggestion of the S.P.G. that a separate Bishopric of Colombo be

---

[1] *Ibid.*

[2] C.O. 54/204, Stephen's minute of 19 Oct. 1843, in Campbell to Stanley, no.154 of 16 Aug. 1843.

[3] C.O. 54/204, Stanley's letter to the Archbishop of Canterbury of 14 November 1843.

[4] C.O. 54/204, Stanley's confidential despatch to Campbell, 1 February 1844.

[5] C.O. 55/79, Glenelg to Mackenzie, no.18 of 2 October 1837.

established.[1] The Bishopric was established in 1845 because the Church in Ceylon was so badly in need of reform that only a radical change in its organization could have sufficed. But in a sense that decision stemmed from Glenelg's despatch, for the creation of the Bishopric was meant to render the Anglican Establishment a more effective weapon of evangelization, and it was Glenelg's despatch that first laid down that evangelization should be one of the main concerns of the Government.

The decision of the Home Government to make evangelization a legitimate sphere of Government activity had far-reaching effects, the establishment of the Bishopric of Colombo being one of the remoter of these. Of much greater importance were the questions it raised about the relationship between the State, the Established Church, and the Missions. Was the Anglican Church in Ceylon to enjoy the privileges its parent organization had at home? Or were the various missions to be placed on a footing of equality?

The answer to these questions was given unequivocally. The Christian Missions in Ceylon were, in the eyes of the Government, equal; and the Anglican Establishment did not possess any special privileges. The finest exposition of official policy on this matter was the speech made by Arthur Buller, then Queen's Advocate of Ceylon, in defending the Church Ordinance of 1844.[2] (That speech provides at the same time an example of the absolute conviction with which a great many colonial administrators of this era believed in the value of Christianity as a civilizing force. There was a touch of arrogance about it, but this was redeemed by its deep sincerity.) Buller declared that

> ... Christianity is the best known means of producing good and useful citizens ... [It] is the best known means of inducing men to practice virtue and morality, and the best known means of deterring them from ... vice. I shall not give myself the trouble of proving this. I assume it and I also assume that it follows as a corollary thereto, that it is the duty of a Christian Government, by every mild and inoffensive means within its reach to promote the conversion of its

---

[1] Pascoe, C. F., *Two Hundred Years of the S.P.G., 1707–1900* (London, 1901), pp.660 ff.

Thompson, H. P., *The History of the Society for the Propagation of the Gospel in Foreign Parts, 1801–1950* (London, 1951), p.193.

[2] Ordinance 9 of 1844.

heathen subjects. Accordingly, it is the duty of such a Government to give encouragement and support to *all* who labour towards that end, and the fitting measure of their encouragement must be the zeal and the success of the labourer. The conversion of the heathen is the great object, and it matters little whether it is effected through the agency of the Catholic, the Dissenter or the Churchman; and as long as the heathen becomes a Christian, I care not whether he is qui vult, or qui non vult episcopari.[1]

At no stage did the Colonial Office make any firm declaration of its views on the precise position of the Anglican Establishment in Ceylon; but it is noteworthy that Buller should have laid so much stress on decisions made on the position of the Anglican Church in Australia. In support of the Ceylon Government's policy Buller quoted the declaration made in 1835 by Sir Richard Bourke, then Governor of New South Wales, that

in a new country to which persons of all religious persuasions are invited to resort, it will be impossible to establish a dominant and endowed church, without much hostility and great improbability of its becoming permanent. The inclination of these colonists which keeps pace with the spirit of the age is decidedly adverse to such an institution; and I fear the interests of religion would be prejudiced by its establishment. . . .

From Buller's point of view Glenelg's firm support of Bourke on this issue was even more important and he quoted with relish Glenelg's statement that

In Colonies formed and rapidly multiplying under most peculiar circumstances it is evident that the attempt to select any one church as the exclusive object of public endowment, even if it were advisable in other respects would not long be tolerated. . . .

Without actually making an explicit statement of policy the Colonial Office left it to be understood that they would not defend Anglican privileges in Ceylon and that the position of the Anglican Establishment there was in no way analogous to that of its parent body in England.

[1] Speech of Arthur Buller, in the Ceylon Legislative Council during the debate on the Church Ordinance of 1844 on 1 July 1844 printed in *The Colombo Observer*, 8 July 1844. The official minutes of the Ceylon Legislative Council provide only a brief record of business transacted, the voting at the various readings of a bill, amendments proposed and the voting on these amendments. But for just two or three years (c. 1842, 1843, 1844) an official stenographer kept a record of all speeches and these were made available to the newspapers.

The policy of equalization was bound to be extremely unpopular with the Anglican Establishment in Ceylon who had a privileged position in education, church construction and the registration of births, marriages and deaths; equalization was nothing more than the elimination of Anglican privilege in these matters. Sectarian jealousies existed before the policy of equalization began but the process of equalization transformed latent jealousies into blazing enmities and rendered sectarian strife into one of the dominant features of the missionary activities of this period. The Wesleyans and Baptists who kept a discreet silence on the issue of the reform of the Anglican Establishment egged the Government on in the policy of equalization.

Mackenzie – on the instructions from Lord John Russell – had changed the conditions on which the State contributed to the construction of churches. Where, hitherto, the Government had borne the whole cost of building churches for the Established Church, Mackenzie had introduced the principle that in districts where colonists were sufficiently numerous and wealthy the community should contribute a fourth of the cost.[1]

The Anglican Establishment – theirs were the only churches built at Government expense – opposed the adoption of these new rules. The opposition to the new policy was led by G. Turnour, then Acting Colonial Secretary, who sought to introduce in the Legislative Council a Bill to provide a State-sponsored loan for the construction of churches for the Anglicans.[2] He believed that the rules laid down by Lord John Russell were based on a misunderstanding of the situation in Ceylon, and that these rules could be applied whenever a second church was to be built at stations where there was already a church.[3] Mackenzie refused him permission to introduce a statement on this matter into the proceedings of the Legislative Council, or to sanction his originating a debate upon his scheme for church construction.

Instead he insisted that they should await the decision of the

---

[1] C.O. 54/177, Mackenzie to Russell, separate private despatch of 5 February 1840.

C.O. 54/180, Mackenzie to Russell, separate miscellaneous despatch of 7 July 1840.

[2] C.O. 54/179, Mackenzie to Russell, no. 69 of 26 April 1840.

[3] *Ibid.*

Home Government on the question of the reform of the Anglican Establishment before making any further investment for church construction. He had good reason to believe that Turnour had raised this issue to embarrass him just when he was being subjected to the taunts and ridicule of the Archdeacon and the High Church group for his desire to reform the Anglican Establishment. Besides, it was his fear that once the principle of incurring debts by loans, even for so unimportant a matter as church construction, was introduced there would be a precedent created for raising money by loans for other and more important matters. Mackenzie was a great believer in balanced budgets. But he had a more fundamental objection yet. He was opposed to the principle of taxing 'a heathenish and idolatrous population for the erection of churches into which they do not enter'. He taunted Turnour with the remark that

> . . . it is not by building large churches for the military and a few respectable Christians to worship within their walls, that converts will be made . . . [it] is the working missionaries, if any, who will reckon the converts among the congregations. I know how loathsome the very utterance of the word is to the feeling of High Churchmen.[1]

The Secretary of State did not support either Turnour's project of a loan, or his desire to introduce legislation on this matter in the Legislative Council against the Governor's wishes.

Mackenzie's term of office was over before he could proceed any further with these changes in the financing of church construction. Once again it was left to Campbell to continue with reforms that Mackenzie had originated. In 1843 Lord Stanley stated anew the principles which should govern the financing of church construction. Campbell was instructed to prepare an Ordinance based on Australian legislation on this subject.[2] He proceeded to prepare this Ordinance but, acutely conscious of the feelings that it was likely to arouse, he took the precaution of first circulating its main principles among the various Churches and Missions.[3]

[1] C.O. 54/179, Mackenzie to Russell, no. 69 of 26 April 1840.

[2] C.O. 54/212, Stanley to Campbell, no. 52 of 10 June 1843.

[3] C.O. 54/212, Campbell to Stanley, no.131 of 8 August 1844. Enclosing Ordinance 9 of 1844. 'To promote the building of places of Christian worship and to provide for the maintenance of Ministers of the Christian Religion'. See also, C.O. 54/212, Campbell to Stanley, despatches no.133 and no.134 of 10 August 1844.

The Anglican Establishment resolutely opposed this Ordinance; their opposition could not have come as a surprise, for this Ordinance was based on a principle which they would not tolerate, much less accept. Arthur Buller, in the course of the debate on this Ordinance, explained that the real issue was 'whether the principle of a dominant church, or the principle of religious equality [was] henceforth to prevail in Ceylon. . .'.[1] He declared that the main principle on which the Ordinance was based was 'that it is competent to a Colonial Legislative to give support to all Christians alike within its rule, and that it is not only competent to them but their duty to do so'.[2]

Once the Government had chosen to accept the principle of religious equality a defence of Anglican privilege was difficult in the extreme, but this did not prevent the High Church minority from making a spirited defence of their position, and in the Legislative Council P. E. Wodehouse, the Government Agent of the Western Province, and C. E. Norris, the Surveyor-General, the most outspoken representatives of High Church Anglicanism, led the attack on the new Ordinance.[3] The Archdeacon and some of the Anglican clergymen petitioned the Colonial Office against it,[4] while *The Ceylon Herald* conducted a sustained campaign against it which was at once pugnacious and irresponsible.[5] The main argument of the High Church group was that this new Ordinance would be contrary to the spirit of the British Constitution which had recognised the privileged position of the Anglican Establishment. Further, it was contended that though an Ordinance of this nature would perhaps suit Australia with its white population it would hardly suit Ceylon with its mainly 'heathen' population. But these arguments could not conceal the basic fact of a blind opposition to all reform, and the selfish insistence on the perpetuation of privileges neither sanctified by tradition nor

[1] A. Buller's speech of 1 July 1844. Report in *The Colombo Observer*, 8 July 1844.   [2] *Ibid.*

[3] *The Colombo Observer*, 8 July 1844, in which the speeches of Wodehouse and Norris in the Legislative Council are printed.

[4] C.O. 54/212, Campbell to Stanley, no.131 of 8 August 1844, letter of the Archdeacon and his associates enclosed.

[5] One argument used by the Anglicans – though a comparatively minor one – was that the Ordinance would benefit the Catholics. *The Ceylon Herald*, in its issue of 16 July 1844, contained an attack on the Ordinance particularly noteworthy for its undisguised anti-Catholicism.

earned by hard work. The spokesman for the Government was the Queen's Advocate, Arthur Buller, who proceeded to demolish the arguments of the High Church minority with his usual professional competence.

He ridiculed the habit of drawing fanciful comparisons between England and Ceylon and pointed out that though the Anglican Establishment in England enjoyed a privileged position by tradition, convention and law, in the Colonies the Church of England did not enjoy any special privileges. He quoted in his support the authoritative opinions of Glenelg on the Church of England in the Australian Colonies.[1] The argument that the Ordinance, based as it was on Australian experience, was not suited to Ceylon was even easier to demolish. Buller cleverly stood it on its head, declaring that, 'the circumstances of our being surrounded by a heathen population, so far from operating as an argument against our Ordinance, on the contrary is an argument in its favour, which could not be urged in the Australian Colonies'.[2]

The Colonial Office ignored the objections of the High Church minority and ratified the Ordinance. They objected, however, to the seventh clause, which they felt might lead to sectarian disputes. Campbell was instructed to reintroduce this Ordinance in the Legislative Council with this clause excluded.[3] When the Ordinance was reintroduced in 1845 there was little opposition to it in the Legislative Council and it was passed without discussion.[4]

This Ordinance, in spite of Buller's declaration that it was meant to apply to all sects, was originally not intended to apply to missionary bodies 'on the ground that they were voluntary associations . . . and therefore had no legal status'. It would appear that the first draft of the amended Ordinance of 1845 specified aid only to the Churches of England, Scotland and Rome. When objections were raised the terms were changed to 'places of Christian worship', and 'to ministers of the Christian religion duly appointed to officiate', but it was done on the private understanding that the provisions of the Ordinance could only apply to recognized churches.[5]

---

[1] Arthur Buller's speech of 1 July 1844. *The Colombo Observer*, 8 July 1844.
[2] *Ibid.*   [3] C.O. 54/212, Stanley to Campbell, no.331 of 3 May 1845.
[4] On this occasion the Ordinance was introduced by the deputy Queen's Advocate, H. C. Selby.
[5] Wes.Mss.Cey. I, Gogerly, D. J., 24 September 1844.

It was a situation which the dissenting sects, particularly the Wesleyans, could not accept, and they soon set about looking for ways and means of qualifying for aid. They succeeded in this, largely because of the tactical skill of the Rev. D. J. Gogerly, the chairman of the South Ceylon Wesleyan Mission, and the high respect in which he was held by Campbell and Anstruther. Gogerly's main aim was to show the Government that the Wesleyans were a legally recognized church. When the Legislative Council was debating the Ordinance, he wrote a long explanatory letter to Anstruther in which he made the point that the Wesleyans in Ceylon should be treated not merely as a Mission, but also as a Church.[1] In his discussions with the Government on other subjects he lost no opportunity to explain that the Wesleyans were more a Church than a Mission. Drawing a distinction between the Wesleyan Missionary Society and the Wesleyan Conference, he insisted that it was the latter that controlled and financed the Missions of the Wesleyans. According to Gogerly the funds raised by the Wesleyans were placed at the sole control of the Conference to be administered by a mixed Committee of Ministers and laymen appointed by the Conference; the sole ecclesiastical jurisdiction was in the Conference, and this jurisdiction was 'subordinately exercised' by the District Committee. All this, he suggested, proved that the Wesleyan Mission in Ceylon was an integral part of the Wesleyan Church.[2] This line of argument – whether it was valid or not[3] – apparently satisfied the Ceylon Government.

Gogerly's main aim was to obtain endowments for native ministers, who were to remain in all ecclesiastical matters as fully under the Conference as they originally were, except that they could not be appointed or removed without the sanction of the Government.

---

[1] Wes.Mss.Cey. I, Gogerly, D. J., 15 September 1845. The letter was intended for the Governor but Anstruther instructed Gogerly to withhold it till the Ordinance had received the royal sanction, after which the Governor could meet Gogerly's wishes. He withheld the letter but did not wait till after the Ordinance had been ratified to put forward the Wesleyan point of view.

[2] Wes.Mss.Cey. I, Gogerly D. J., 15 September 1845.

[3] There is nothing in the records to show that the Wesleyan Missionary Society itself ever accepted this argument. In any event, the constitutional position was not clear and Gogerly made the most of it, drawing a sharp distinction between the Society and the Conference which does not, in fact, appear to have existed.

To obtain this concession two guarantees were necessary – one, that the Wesleyans would appoint a fresh native minister to be supported by their own funds for every one endowed by the Government; the other, that they would continue to maintain from their own funds as many native ministers as they had on their lists at the time the Ordinance was passed.[1]

For the Anglican Establishment the Church Ordinance was a humiliating reverse. It was also a decisive reverse; for the debate on the Ordinance had concentrated on the vital issue of privilege against equality, and it was the principle of equality that had prevailed. It became more difficult in future to defend the other monopolies of the Anglican Establishment.

Of these other monopolies, the most important was their monopoly of the registration of births, marriages and deaths. It was a profitable monopoly – chiefly to the native assistants, who were paid a small sum of money for each entry in the registers – but its real importance lay in the fact that it gave the Anglican Establishment a greater hold over the Christian converts than the Dissenters had.

The Law of Marriages in early Victorian Ceylon was particularly confused, as confused as the regulations on the Registration of Births and Deaths. The existing law – Administrative Regulation 9 of 1822 – applied only to the native inhabitants of the Maritime Provinces. (In the Kandyan provinces the ancient native tradition remained almost undisturbed.) The system as it developed gave a monopoly in the registration of births, marriages and deaths to the Anglicans, a monopoly which the other sects found most irksome and none more so than the Baptists. It was one aspect of the monopoly of the Established Church which affected the Baptists very badly and they attacked the Anglicans on this with a vigour that they did not display on the matter o church construction.[2]

[1] Wes.Mss.Cey. I, Gogerly, D. J. 15 Sept 1845. In this same letter Gogerly appealed to the Wesleyan Missionary Society to make these guarantees without delay. But it was well over a year before they were given, and not before Gogerly had explained that without them it would be impossible to qualify for aid, and that without this Government aid expansion of missionary activity would be seriously retarded.

[2] It was among the first issues the Baptists raised in the early 1840s. Frequent topics of discussion in two Baptist journals, *The Investigator* (in English) and

Since Regulation 9 of 1822 related to the native inhabitants alone, it in effect excluded from the registry it provided the children of Europeans and Burghers; and as Baptists did not christen their children Baptists of these two communities could not enter their children's names in the books of Presbyterian and Episcopalian Churches (where registration followed on christening). But the seventeenth clause of the same Ordinance excluded even native Baptists from its benefits by requiring that 'if such children of Christian parents, the dates of the Baptism and the name of the Minister who administered the rite shall be added to the Registry'. Thus, for the registration of the births of the children of all Baptists – European and Native – there was no legal provision whatever. There was no Civil Registration in Ceylon till 1868.

On the question of marriages too the Baptists had a genuine grievance for although their Ministers when licensed could perform a marriage ceremony for native Baptists, yet the Baptists of European and Burgher extraction were obliged to resort to clergymen of other denominations for legal marriage. Besides, the only registry of deaths was that kept by the Colonial Chaplains, so that no recognized entry of the deaths of Baptists was made unless the burial service was performed over the remains by an Episcopalian or Presbyterian clergyman.[1]

The Anglicans were not disposed to part with their monopoly lightly. For the power of registration gave them an advantage over other Christian groups in the matter of converting people to Christianity, and, more important, keeping them converted. For, as a Wesleyan Missionary explained, 'the people had a partiality

---

The Uragaha or The Touchstone (in English and Sinhalese), were the existing marriage and registration laws in Ceylon, and the manner in which they favoured the Established Church.

The Investigator: vol. 1, nos.1 and 2.

See also, Baptist Mission Society Mss. 'Letters from various Fields collected by Dr. E. B. Underhill, 1842–55'.

[1] The position of the Wesleyans was only slightly better – if at all – than that of the Baptists.

See Wes.Mss.Cey. II, Gogerly D. J. 10 February 1847.

C.O. 54/226, Campbell to Grey, no.47 of 15 October 1846. See enclosed petition of Dr C. Elliott and others on behalf of the Baptists of Ceylon.

C.O. 54/261, Torrington to Grey, no.189 of 14 December 1849. See enclosed petition of Baptists and Wesleyans.

The Investigator, I, nos.1 and 2. B.M.S. MSS. Letters of Dr E. B. Underhill, 1842–55.

. . . for Christian marriage, which rite admitting of some ceremony and being connected with a registry has become very acceptable to them'.[1] *Bhikkus* were themselves well aware of this and in some areas they had resolved to petition the Government to grant them a Buddhist register to be deposited in the *Viharas* and to be kept by them.[2] The Sinhalese as a people have always been noted for their love of litigation;[3] they were anxious to have their marriages registered and their children baptized,[4] because this registration was invaluable in deciding questions of inheritance. Since there was no civil registration in Ceylon at this time, it was necessary to resort to the registers of the Anglican Church.

The Anglicans were well aware of the strength of their position, and very often their native assistants took advantage of the existing registration procedure to persuade people to attend Anglican churches, by showing them that they could not get the benefit of registration by attending the churches or chapels of other denominations.[5]

Both the Baptists and the Wesleyans had a grievance against the existing system. The Wesleyans could solemnize marriages, but they could neither publish the banns of marriage, nor register marriages or baptisms.[6] The registration was performed by men called Government Schoolmasters or thombo-holders, serving under the Archdeacon who, as Registrar-General, appointed them to their posts.[7] After the passage of the Marriage Act in England in 1836 the Wesleyans petitioned the Government year after year protesting against their inferior status in these matters

[1] Wes.Mss.Cey. II, Kessen, the Rev. A., 2 June 1847. See also Gogerly, D. J., 14 September 1847 and Spence-Hardy, R., 9 June 1847.

[2] Wes.Mss.Cey. II. Kessen, A., 2 June 1847.

[3] The Roman-Dutch Law of Inheritance, a legacy of Dutch rule in the Maritime Provinces, contributed greatly to this; it did not recognize the principle of primogeniture, but, on the contrary, distributed parental property among the children in equal shares. This led to successive divisions of property and to a fragmentation of land holdings. Along with this, there were interminable disputes and litigations over these lands.

[4] Large numbers of people became 'Christians' merely to get their names on the registers, and the great bulk of these 'converts' were Buddhists in all but name. See Tennent, *Christianity in Ceylon*, p.82; Buchanan, C., *Christian Researches in Asia* (London, 1849).

[5] Wes.Mss.Cey. II, Spence-Hardy, R., 9 June 1847.

[6] Wes.Mss.Cey. II, Gogerly, D. J., 14 September 1847.

[7] See C.O. 54/204, Campbell to Stanley, no.154 of 18 Aug.1843.

in Ceylon, and calling for the application of the principles of this act there. But the Anglicans 'threw hindrances in every direction'.[1] and it was not until 1843 that the Government, aware of the grievances of the Wesleyans and the Baptists, and of the defects of the marriage and registration regulations, seriously considered new legislation on these matters. In the preparation of this legislation the Rev. D. J. Gogerly had great influence.

The Government and Gogerly did not always see eye to eye on the aims of this legislation – all they had in common was a desire to end the monopoly of the Anglicans. The Government was more inclined to make registration a responsibility of the State, with lay registrars instead of clergymen, while Gogerly's aim was to let the dissenting sects share the privileges enjoyed by the Anglicans.

The first draft of the new Ordinance envisaged the appointment of lay registrars to solemnize marriages and to register births and deaths. To Gogerly this was a remedy worse than the disease. He protested to the Colonial Secretary, Philip Anstruther, against this development. After much delay and discussion the Queen's Advocate, Arthur Buller, summoned Gogerly and went over all the clauses of the Ordinance with him. The Ordinance was amended to give the missionaries the power to publish banns, and to solemnize and register marriages.[2] But pressure of business prevented the passage of the Ordinance in the Legislative Sessions of 1843 and when it was taken up again in 1844 the Ordinance was amended once more and 'neither missionaries nor clergymen [were] allowed to solemnize marriages, but the whole was made a Civil obligation after the mode of the French Code in the time of Napoleon'.[3] Once again Gogerly intervened. He interviewed the Chief Justice and the Queen's Advocate on the subject, and his letter of protest was circulated among the members of the Executive Council. His lobbying proved successful; he wrote home that

> Mr Buller (Queen's Advocate) and I again went over the whole and the arrangement is to me and the brethren perfectly satisfactory, as we have the power to put out the banns and solemnize and register the marriages of all classes of Christians, Europeans, Burghers and Natives. We regard all this as of very high importance in our connection with the natives, as removing the opposition we have ex-

---

[1] Wes.Mss.Cey. II, Gogerly, D. J., 24 September 1844.
[2] *Ibid.*
[3] *Ibid.*

perienced from the underlings connected with the Church. Our
Assistant Missionaries regard this Ordinance as the most important
one the Government could pass.[1]

The Ordinance, however, was disallowed by the Secretary of
State on some technical, legal grounds respecting the evidence
necessary to prove a valid marriage. Campbell then shelved the
Ordinance and made no further attempt to proceed with it during
the last year of his administration in spite of requests from the
Baptists for changes in the law.

The situation changed with the arrival of Tennent (as Colonial
Secretary) and Torrington (as Governor). The Wesleyans had a
good friend in Tennent,[2] and their influence with the administration increased rather than decreased with the retirement of
Campbell and Anstruther. Gogerly applied to Torrington to have
a separate register given to the Wesleyans so that they might
publish banns, solemnize marriages and register them as was done
in the episcopal churches.[3] The permission was granted. But the
Anglicans reacted sharply, particularly the thombo-holders or
native registrars, who received a sum of money for each entry in
their registers, and now found themselves faced with the prospect
of a sharp drop in their income.

The opposition of the thombo-holders was strongest at Kurana
in the Negombo district. The Wesleyan Minister there, the Rev.
R. Spence-Hardy, complained that the alarmed thombo-holders
did all they could to intimidate the Wesleyan converts by telling
them that the Wesleyan registers were not valid, and that they
would be denied the use of public burial grounds.[4] 'As the mass of
the people seek the name of Christian for no other purpose than to
receive the benefit of these registers,'[5] the power of the thombo-
holders over them was very great, and their propaganda against
the Wesleyans proved to be disastrously effective. There was a
steep drop in attendance at the Wesleyan chapels in the district –
only twenty adults attended the church in the circuit and they all
belonged to families paid by the Mission.[6]

[1] *Ibid.*
[2] Wes.Mss.Cey. II, Gogerly, D. J., 11 July 1846. At every stage of his stay
in Ceylon, Tennent, actively supported the Wesleyans.
[3] Wes. Mss.Cey. II, Gogerly, D. J., 14 September 1847.
[4] Wes.Mss.Cey. II, Spence-Hardy, R., 9 June 1847.   [5] *Ibid.*
[6] Wes.Mss.Cey. II, Gogerly, D. J., 14 September 1847.
    E

This clash between the Wesleyans and the Anglicans led to great ill-feeling and bitter division among the Christian converts in the villages of this district. But the incident – particularly the success of the Anglicans in winning over so many of the Wesleyan converts – revealed the essential superficiality of most acts of conversion at this time; it also showed the value of possessing the power of registration, as a means of attracting converts. Not surprisingly the Anglicans were unwilling to part with their monopoly.

The Anglican Establishment attached great importance to this conflict at Negombo. The Bishop of Colombo accompanied by the Archdeacon visited those villages in the Negombo District where the thombo-holders had organized opposition to the Wesleyans, and, it was alleged with good reason, encouraged them in the stand they had taken.[1] The situation deteriorated with the Bishop's intervention. Gogerly was compelled to protest to the Bishop against the activities of the thombo-holders of Kurana. To this the Bishop sent a pacific but non-comittal reply, but made no attempt to check them. This time Gogerly complained to Tennent about the thombo-holders, the Archdeacon and the Bishop.[2] Gogerly's influence with the administration was such that within two days the Governor had written to the Bishop, upholding the right of the Wesleyans to register births, marriages and deaths on their own. But his letter was more important for its outspoken defence of the principle of religious equality. He emphasized that in the eyes of the Government all Christian groups in Ceylon were equal, and no one – not even the Anglican Establishment – was entitled to any exclusive privileges.[3]

One consequence of this controversy was the preparation of 'an Ordinance to amend in certain respects the Law of Marriages and to provide for the better registration of marriages, births and

[1] Wes.Mss.Cey. II, Gogerly, D. J., 14 September 1847; Spence-Hardy, R., 9 June 1847; Kessen, A., 10 September 1847.

[2] Wes.Mss.Cey. II, Gogerly to Tennent, 1 July 1847.

[3] *Ibid.* Tennent to Gogerly, 3 July 1847, enclosing a copy of Torrington's letter to the Bishop of the same date. Torrington suspended the two thombo-holders from office and, after an investigation conducted by the Government Agent of the Western Province and Gogerly and Spence-Hardy (these two were in the position of being both complainants and judges on the same issue!), one of them was dismissed from office while the other, who had been less active, was recommended for mercy.

deaths' – Ordinance 7 of 1847.[1] The preparation of the Ordinance was a difficult task; it had to satisfy the Colonial Office; it had to avoid antagonizing the Anglicans too much; and it had to satisfy the Dissenters. In its preparation Torrington and the Executive Council were careful to remove several of the objections of the Law Officers at home to the previous Ordinance – Ordinance 22 of 1844. But the scruples of the Colonial Office were less of a problem than sectarian antagonisms in Ceylon. And it is a measure of Torrington's achievement that the Ordinance satisfied the Dissenters without moving the Anglicans to any widespread opposition.

The following extract from a letter of a Baptist missionary is indicative of the spirit of compromise which characterized the drafting of this Ordinance:

> The new Marriage Ordinance which has cost us so much trouble and anxiety has just passed the Council. It is upon the whole satisfactory and will be of great advantage to us. We failed to carry it on the ground of perfect religious equality; yet practically it will amount to this. The majority of the Council conceded all that we asked but: (1) that all places of worship be alike, either licensed or not licensed; but it was carried that all consecrated[2] places be exempted from licence. (2) That licences, however, will be granted by the Civil power exclusively or by one minister appointed in each denomination; but it was carried that the Bishop retain this power, and that the District Judge should have the same power to grant licences to those who do not apply to the Bishop. In all other respects there is perfect liberty.[3]

The Colonial Office confirmed the Ordinance but its publication in Ceylon was delayed till the end of 1849, 'owing to certain doubts having been cast as to the best method of carrying it into operation'.[4]

In consequence of the delay this occasioned, petitions were sent to the Government in September 1849 by Gogerly on behalf of the Wesleyans,[5] and by three principal missionaries among the

[1] C.O. 54/240, Torrington to Grey, no.148 of 5 November 1847.
[2] It would appear that under the Ordinance, chapels of the Baptists and Wesleyans were not regarded as being consecrated places.
[3] *Miss.Her.* January 1848, pp.5, 6; Davies, the Rev. J., 21 October 1847.
[4] C.O. 54/261, Torrington to Grey, no.189 of 14 December 1849.
[5] C.O. 54/261, Torrington to Grey, no.189 of 14 December 1849. Gogerly's memorandum of 21 September 1849, enclosure in above.

Baptists,[1] representing the great inconvenience it caused and so the matter was again brought before the Executive Council (on 5 October 1849) when it was finally decided that the Ordinance should be promulgated at once.[2]

With this the second of the monopolies of the Anglican Establishment in Ceylon was broken,[3] and a great measure of equality established between the Christian groups. The one privilege the Anglicans continued to possess in spite of occasional but increasingly more vociferous protest was their connection with the state.

This question had been raised as early as 1840 when the High Church group, then at loggerheads with Governor Mackenzie over the latter's policy of Church reform, had insisted that the Anglican Church was the Established Church in Ceylon ('The National Church of Ceylon') and therefore justly entitled to the privileges it enjoyed.[4] Their arguments did not impress Mackenzie who doubted whether there was any Established Church in Ceylon at all and – here he was on much weaker ground – whether there was one National Church in Britain. The Colonial Office itself gave no lead on this issue; it was one of those dangerously combustible issues which it preferred not to handle. But the fact is that without actually defining the status of the Anglican Church, the Colonial Office treated the Anglican Church in Ceylon as the Established Church.

When Mackenzie and the High Church group were involved in this dispute, the Baptists intervened with an altogether more formidable criticism of the whole principle of an Established

---

[1] *Ibid.* Memorandum of the Baptists, 17 September 1894, enclosure in above.

[2] C.O. 54/261, Torrington to Grey, no.189 of 14 December 1849.

[3] Even at this stage the Anglicans did not give up without a struggle. In the early part of 1852 there was a disturbance at Moratuwa, arising from the refusal of the Bishop of Colombo and his chaplain to let the Wesleyan missionaries of Moratuwa read the burial service in the churchyard. The Anglicans even resorted to physical force to prevent the Wesleyans from doing so; the parties involved were charged before a magistrate for rioting and were fined £2 each. H. C. Selby, the Queen's Advocate who reported on the case to the Governor, strongly criticized the intolerance of the Anglicans, and Governor Anderson decided in favour of the Wesleyans when the matter came before him. *The Colombo Observer,* 10 January 1853.

[4] *A Letter to the Editor of the Ceylon Herald, occasioned by the question of Rt. Hon. J. A. S. Mackenzie as to the National Church of the United Kingdom and Ceylon,* Colombo, 17 March 1840.

Church.[1] They saw no need for any Church establishment at all and condemned 'the injustice and enormous evils of Religious Establishments'. Churches should be voluntary organizations. They held the view that Christianity was at its noblest when it upheld the principle of spiritual liberty and had no connection with the State. Christianity's connection with the State was involuntary and had meant an end 'to her beauty, her innocence, her power and her divinity'. On a more mundane level they took strong objection to the expenditure of public funds for an Established Church, particularly because these funds were obtained by the taxation of the whole population of the British Empire.

This was essentially a Baptist point of view, though it coincided with Mackenzie's own. It was heard with increasing regularity in this period and it had the support not only of Mackenzie but also of other influential persons who were not members of the Baptist Church.

After the passage of the Church Ordinance in 1845 it should logically have become more difficult to maintain an Established Church. Once the equal treatment of all Christian missions and churches was officially accepted as Government policy, the position of the Anglican Church as the Established Church became dangerously insecure. The Colonial Office – and for that matter the Ceylon Government – did not however see that the next step should have been the disestablishment of the Anglican Church, though it was the logical consequence of their own policy.

There were powerful voices urging this next step. H. C. Selby, Arthur Buller's successor as Queen's Advocate, in the course of reintroducing the Church Ordinance in 1845 insisted that there was no need at all for maintaining an exclusive Church Establishment.[2] The Government was not with him on this issue. Strangely enough, in the Legislative Council there was no criticism of Selby's radical views. But outside it, *The Ceylon Examiner* took serious objection to both the Church Ordinance and H. C. Selby's arguments. An anonymous correspondent published a series of

---

[1] *The Non-Existence of a National Church and the Injustice of Established Religion*, Civis the Second. The Colombo Observer Press (May 1840).

[2] Selby's arguments on this occasion were a repetition of those used by Civis the Second in his pamphlet, *The Non-Existence of a National Church and the Injustice of Established Religion* (1840).

letters attacking both.[1] The Church Ordinance itself was condemned as 'a most reprehensible departure from the strict line of
duty to the church by offering indiscriminate aid to all denominations of Christians . . .'.[2] This was 'sinful in itself' for, the argument
continued: 'If a state should extend its protection and support to
religion at all, its choice is necessarily limited to true religion . . .
and where is true religion to be found but in the church, the
guardian of the truth.'[3] But even more reprehensible was Selby's
argument that the 'exclusive compact subsisting between the
Church and State', should be abolished. This, Selby's critic insisted, was an 'atheistical' argument involving the most serious
consequences for both Church and State; and it 'mystified . . . the
end for which all Governments are ordained and [broke] up the
foundations on which all Governments are built'.[4]

This issue was not raised again till the early 1850s. In 1852,
when the Buddhist problem was a matter of acute controversy,
the Baptists queered the pitch by urging that the State should
sever its connection with all religions and not merely with Buddhism alone.[5] That suggestion was ignored by both the Ceylon and
the Imperial Governments, but the campaign revived with the
publication in 1852 of the Report of the Committee of the Executive Council on the Fixed Establishments of Ceylon which recommended that the Government's financial contribution to the
Anglican Establishment should be drastically reduced.[6] The Committee could see 'no reason why the provision for a Bishop should
ever have been imposed on the revenues of this island any more
than on that of the Cape of Good Hope, Hong Kong and other
Colonies . . .'[7]. Anstruther, whose evidence the Committee treated
with great respect, was even more outspoken in his demands for
retrenchment in the Anglican Establishment. (He even suggested
that Ceylon would do well to revert to the old system of having
an Archdeacon at the head of the Anglican Church in Ceylon,

---

[1] These letters were later reprinted as a pamphlet, *Three letters on the necessity
of a Church Establishment in Ceylon*, The Examiner Press Colombo (n.d., c. 1846).
[2] *Ibid.*   [3] *Ibid.*   [4] *Ibid.*
[5] C.O. 54/293, Anderson to Grey, no.17 of 13 January 1852, enclosing petition of Baptists, 2 January 1852.
[6] This committee was appointed in 1848 during the depression. It completed
its work by 1849, but it was only in 1852 that its report was published. The
members of the Committee were: J. E. Tennent, C. J. MacCarthy and F. J.
Templar.   [7] *Rep.Fxd.Est.*, pp.307–15.

under the Bishop of Madras.)[1] Torrington too was in general agreement with the recommendations of the Committee.[2] But by the time the report was published (in 1852) the situation had changed and the Government was unwilling to make any changes. In 1853 however the annual budgetary allocation for the Church was made a local responsibility, to be debated annually by the Legislative Council, while previously it had been part of the Fixed Establishments beyond the control of the local government, not subject to debate in the Legislative Council.[3]

In the meantime, when the Executive Council reviewed the recommendations of the Committee on the Fixed Establishments of Ceylon, H. C. Selby once again challenged the need for an expensive Church Establishment.[4] Selby's comments on the Church-State relationship have a very modern ring. He was a nineteenth-century Liberal urging the separation of Church and State. He contended that since Ceylon was not a Christian country such reasons as might exist for an Established Church in England were wholly inapplicable to Ceylon; in England there may have been 'political' reasons for a Church Establishment, but there were no such reasons for a Church Establishment in Ceylon. Nor, in his opinion, was the argument that it was the duty of the Government to make provision for the spiritual needs of the people any sounder.

He considered it the exclusive duty of each Christian Church to maintain its ministers, and he believed that Christianity in Ceylon would flourish only if the Churches were independent and self-supporting. He was severe in his criticism of the Anglican Church in Ceylon, whose position he considered to be anomalous in that, in spite of its wealth, it continued to ask for State support. He obviously agreed with the opinion of the Committee, though he did not say it in so many words, that 'considering the very small number of persons professing to belong to the communion of the Church of England in Ceylon . . . it [was] not advisable to continue the charge of this Establishment on the Colonial Revenues.'[5]

[1] *Rep.Fxd.Est.*, p.173.

[2] C.O. 54/265, Torrington to Grey, no.192 of 14 December 1849.

[3] *The Colombo Observer*, 8 January 1854.

[4] C.O. 57/19, Selby's minute of 30 September 1853; minutes of Executive Council Meetings of 29 September 1853 and 1 October 1853.

[5] *Rep.Fxd.Est.*, pp.307–15.

And he believed it to be absurd for the Church of England in Ceylon to argue that without State support they could not maintain their churches or clergymen, for the Catholics, by far the largest Christian group in Ceylon, did so without the support of the State. Selby declared that as long as the Government made an annual allocation of money the Anglicans would make no attempt to raise the money on their own. If they could not raise this money, it was only further proof that the State was preserving merely a shell of a church.

In spite of Selby's protests the Executive Council agreed to maintain the Ecclesiastical Establishment. He had no one to support him. Even C. J. MacCarthy, who had been a member of the Committee that recommended retrenchment, would not go as far as Selby.[1]

Selby's views were in no way original even for Ceylon. Dr Christopher Elliott had popularized these views for more than a decade in his newspaper, *The Colombo Observer*. He continued to advocate the 'disestablishment' of the Anglican Church even when he realised that the chances of winning the administration over to this policy were remote. Thus, along with two other Baptists, J. Allen, a pastor, and P. Schumaker, a fellow deacon, he petitioned the Legislative Council against State interference in religious affairs not only with Buddhism but with the Anglican Establishment.[2] But the Council gave him little support. The truth was that the idea of 'disestablishment' was too advanced for this age.

The period ends, however, with a reverse for the Anglican Establishment. The Bishop had asked the Government to appoint a native Chaplain to Batticaloa. The local government declined to make this appointment, and the whole question was referred to the Duke of Newcastle, the Secretary of State for the Colonies, who distinctly affirmed that the British Government could recognize only an Ecclesiastical Establishment to meet the spiritual wants of its European Civil and Military Servants, and could not provide for the wants of the native inhabitants. Gogerly was

---

[1] C.O. 57/19, meeting of the Executive Council, 29 September 1853. It was after this Council had decided to maintain the Ecclesiastical Establishment that Selby wrote his minute protesting against the decision.

[2] *The Colombo Observer*, 18 December 1854; Baptist petition dated 5 December 1854.

quick to realize the possible consequence of this decision. He explained that 'this strikes at the root of all the native chaplaincies, and if carried out would produce a powerful effect on the natives, who adhere to the Church because they believe it to be the Government religion'.[1] But on a different level there is a touch of irony in this. At the beginning of this period, as has been noticed, Glenelg was criticizing the Anglican Establishment because it had confined its ministrations to the Europeans alone. At the end, Newcastle was recommending the opposite course – that the Anglican Establishment should restrict its activities to the European population.

[1] Wes.Mss.Cey. II, Gogerly, D. J., 10 November 1854.

CHAPTER II

James Stephen and the Missionary Agitation against the State's connection with Buddhism, 1840–47

ON 2 March 1815, the Kandyan Kingdom was ceded to the British by its chiefs and *bhikkus*; the Kandyan Convention of the same date, signed on behalf of the British by the Governor, Sir Robert Brownrigg, and on behalf of the Kandyans by the chiefs, preserved intact the powers of the chiefs, the laws, customs and institutions of the country, and – what in the eyes of the Kandyans was more important than all else – the Buddhist religion. The fifth clause of that Convention, employing language described by Brownrigg as being 'more emphatical than would have been my choice',[1] declared that 'the Religion of Buddhoo, professed by the chiefs and inhabitants of these provinces is declared inviolable; and its rites, ministers and places of worship are to be maintained and protected.'[2]

When he sent a copy of the Convention to the Colonial Office, Brownrigg explained that because it was vitally important to quiet the apprehensions of the Kandyans about their religion, he had been obliged to consent to 'an article of guarantee couched in the most unqualified terms'.[3] He added that it was only by making

---

[1] C.O. 54/55, Brownrigg to Bathurst, 15 March 1815.

[2] It must be pointed out that Buddhism, as it exists today and as it existed in 1815, was an amalgam of the original Theravada Buddhism and elements of Mahayana Buddhism and Hinduism. The fifth clause of the Kandyan Convention undertook to protect and maintain all this and not merely Theravada Buddhism, pure and simple. A Sinhalese version of the Convention, printed in Pieris, P. E., *Sinhale and the Patriots*, pp. 591–3, makes this clear. There specific reference is made to the religion of the Buddha and the *Agama* [Religion] of the *Devas* [Hinduism] and protection is promised to the *Viharas* [Buddhist temples] and *Devalayas* [Hindu temples]. It is important to stress the threefold nature of popular Buddhism because one of the arguments used by those who sought to sever the connection between the British Government and Buddhism was that the Kandyan Convention protected only the 'pure' Therevada Buddhism.

[3] C.O. 54/55, Brownrigg to Bathurst, 15 March 1815.

it clear that the fifth clause of the convention would be scrupulously observed that the British could gain the adherence of the *bhikkus* and chiefs.[1] The Convention was approved by the home Government though they were at first inclined to favour one in which the guarantees on religion were less emphatic. There were other critics of the Convention, the Evangelical, William Wilberforce, being the most prominent. He strongly objected to the fifth clause, as being likely to exclude any future attempts at conversion, and was frankly apprehensive of the use of the word 'inviolable' to describe the position of the Buddhist religion.[2]

Bathurst had his own misgivings, but Brownrigg expressly disclaimed any idea of interpreting the fifth clause in the manner objected to, and explained that the Sinhalese words translated as 'inviolable' really meant 'cannot be broken down'. At the same time he made no move to change the wording of the Convention in any way.[3] But two years later he did utilize the opportunity provided by the Kandyan Rebellion of 1817–18 to modify the declaration a little. The Proclamation of 21 November 1818[4] greatly reduced the privileges of the chiefs and slightly changed the guarantees on religion. The sixteenth clause of the Proclamation minimized the categorical promises made in the Convention of 1815; while reserving to Buddhism the respect promised in 1815, it extended protection to all other religions as well.

The Kandyans believed that the relationship between Buddhism and the British Government defined in 1815 was to be permanent. Their insistence on the continued connection of their religion with the British Government puzzled officials and missionaries alike. Tennent came nearest to providing a reasonable explanation, when he suggested that

> it is not *protection* which they look to us for. . . . It is not our *management* they want. . . . But what they really want under the semblance of interference and appearance of control is really our identification with their religion and the prestige of the Government name as associated with their appointments and patronage.[5]

[1] C.O. 54/55, Brownrigg to Bathurst, no.100 of 1 April 1815, and no.104 of 20 July 1815.   [2] Pieris, P. E., *Sinhale and the Patriots*, pp.596 ff.
[3] C.O. 54/57, Brownrigg to Bathurst, no.143 of 1 June 1816, and private despatch of 21 June 1816.   [4] See Appendix III.
[5] C.O. 54/296, Tennent, *Memorandum on Buddhism and the means of severing the connection between the British Government and the Buddhist rites and temples in Ceylon*, paragraphs 138 and 139.

Like most of his contemporaries, he believed that the connection of the State with Buddhism 'confers dignity on their religion, which would otherwise sink into insignificance'. What he did not understand was that the Kandyans sought to maintain the connection of the State with Buddhism because it was hallowed by tradition. That connection no doubt brought 'dignity' and 'prestige' to Buddhism, but in their eyes it was a connection worth maintaining as an end in itself. The connection between the State and Buddhism had very seldom been broken, and the Kandyans in 1815 hoped that their new alien rulers would accept this responsibility as the Nayakkar dynasty (1739–1815) had done.[1]

The Kandyans for their part erred in thinking that the relationship established in 1815 would be maintained unchanged. There was a strong belief among them that the Kandyan Convention of 1815 and in particular its fifth clause could never be abrogated and the promises embodied in it could never be broken.[2] They did not see that the peculiar form of the Kandyan Convention depended on political factors operating in 1815, factors which were subject to rapid change. The concessions made to Kandyan interests in 1815 were made because of the comparative weakness of the British position then, but with every year that passed the position of the British had improved and that of the Kandyans had weakened. The years 1815 to 1840 were years of rapid, even revolutionary, change in the Kandyan provinces. The failure of the rebellion of 1817–18 had broken the power of the Kandyan aristocracy and helped to consolidate the British position. With the Colebrooke–Cameron reforms of 1833 the Kandyan Kingdom lost its separate identity. The whole trend of legislation thereafter was directed at breaking down the old conservative, aristocratic, status-ridden and caste-oriented society, and at replacing it with a new commercial and more egalitarian society.

[1] See, Rahula, W., *A History of Buddhism in Ceylon* (Colombo), pp.62 ff.
[2] For an excellent account of the opinions of the Kandyans on these matters see the Kandyan Petition (with 1,941 signatures) to the Queen, enclosed in Campbell's despatch to Stanley, no.37 of 2 February 1846, in C.O. 54/223. The main arguments used by the Kandyans were (1) that, since 1815, the policy of maintaining Buddhism had been continued unchanged, and the Government had acted in strict conformity to its promises at the Convention of 1815. (2) That the Convention of 1815 did not mention any time or period after which the patronage would cease. It had, in fact, declared that that patronage should continue forever, and would not be withdrawn in time.

If Wilberforce had had his way, the Kandyan Convention would have taken a different form, but Evangelicalism lacked strength in 1815. In the course of the next two decades, however, it had developed into a powerful influence on colonial policy. The new generation, more inclined to put their faith in militant Christianity, poured scorn on alien cultures, religions and traditions and, acting under the impulse of Evangelicalism, challenged the relationship established in 1815 between Buddhism and the British Government in Ceylon. The Evangelical impulse was strengthened by the influence of that strand in Liberal political thought which emphasized the separation of Church and State, though the latter was not as pronounced in the mid-nineteenth century as it was to be a generation later.

Between 1815 and 1840 there were no substantial modifications in the relationship between the Government and Buddhism. The British Government, though with obvious lack of enthusiasm, sought to play much the same role in relation to Buddhism that the Kandyan King had played. At moments of crisis, or when a radical social change was envisaged, the Government always made it clear that the relationship with Buddhism was unaffected. Thus in 1833, when the Colebrooke–Cameron reforms were introduced in Ceylon, the home Government, leaving the decision on matters relating to Temples and Temple lands to the Ceylon Government, merely pointed out that any direct sanction of 'heathenism' must be carefully avoided. It was emphasized, however, that the British Government would secure to the inhabitants of the country the free exercise of the religious rites guaranteed them in 1815, and that the Order-in-Council abolishing compulsory service (*rajakariya*) was not to affect temple lands.[1]

But the abolition of *rajakariya* in 1832 did indirectly affect the State's relationship with Buddhism. For the Government lands, traditionally belonging to the Kandyan King, were used in part to support Buddhist ceremonies. When they were sold, after 1832, it was necessary therefore to make some new arrangement to continue these ceremonies. Governor Wilmot-Horton arranged to make an annual monetary grant, usually £310, which remained in force until it was abolished on Lord Stanley's instructions after 1844.

[1] C.O. 55/72, Goderich to Horton, no.52 of 3 May 1832, and the Order-in-Council of 12 April 1832.
   C.O. 54/296, Tennent, memorandum on Buddhism.

In 1834 a number of Kandyan chiefs were arrested on very flimsy evidence on a charge of 'conspiracy' against British rule. They were tried, but were all acquitted. During the trial it was suggested that among the reasons for the continued hostility of the Kandyan aristocracy to British rule was their fear – particularly after the implementation of the Colebrooke–Cameron reforms – for the safety of their religion. To satisfy the Kandyans that the changes brought about by the Colebrooke–Cameron reforms were not meant to impose on them a new religious policy detrimental to the interests of Buddhism, Horton issued a Proclamation on 15 September 1834 declaring that the old religious policy was to be maintained without substantial change.

Thus in the year 1840, when the connection between the British Government and Buddhism first became a matter of great controversy, the Buddhist religion enjoyed many privileges. The lands of the *viharas* and *devales* were exempt from the operation of the ordinance that abolished *rajakariya*, and tenants of temple lands continued to perform their traditional services for the lands they held. The British Government was the custodian of the Temple of the Tooth at Kandy.[1]

> The [Tooth] relic is in the official custody of the Government Agent [of the Central Province], the keys of the Karanduwa [the case] in which the relic is immediately deposited is also in his possession. For the purpose of opening and closing the temple an aratchy [a native official] is appointed by the Agent, who receives from the Government a monthly allowance and is called the aratchy of the Maligawa.[2]

[1] The possession of the Tooth Relic and the Alms Bowl Relic was essential to a ruler of Ceylon. These two relics had always been in the possession of the chief ruler of the island – they had passed into the hands of the King of Kandy after 1591 – and they were associated with the continuity of Sinhalese kingship. Rahula, W., *A History of Buddhism in Ceylon*, pp.62–74.

[2] Spence-Hardy, R., *The British Government and the Idolatry of Ceylon*, p.23. See also Tennent, memorandum on Buddhism, in C.O. 54/296.

The Ceylon Government undertook the custody of the Tooth Relic only after the rebellion of 1817–18. It had been in the possession of the *bhikkus* between 1815 and 1817. The relic was stolen during the rebellion; it was recaptured in 1818. Governor Brownrigg attributed the suppression of the rebellion in great measure to the superstitious awe of the people, on the relic again – accidentally – falling into the hands of the British, for it was a common belief that no conquest of the Kandyan Kingdom could be complete without the possession of the Tooth Relic. Hence the care with which it was guarded after 1818. See de Silva, C. R., *Ceylon under the British Occupation*, I, pp.196 ff.

A soldier stood guard at the entrance to the Temple.

The principal *bhikkus*[1] were appointed by the Governor[2] as were the *basnayake nilames*,[3] or the lay chiefs of the principal *devales*, and some of the *kapuralas*, or priests of the *devales*.[4] The Government granted a trifling monthly allowance for the support of the *bhikkus*.[5] It made a more substantial grant for the performance of various traditional religious ceremonies, the chief of which was the Kandy *Perahera*.[6]

The campaign against the connection of the British Government in Ceylon with Buddhism in the Kandyan provinces coincided with, and was deeply influenced by, the campaign against the

---

[1] A list of the *bhikkus* and *basnayaka nilames* so appointed is provided in Appendix IV.

[2] The process of appointment was as follows: The body of *bhikkus* in each district nominated the chief *bhikkus*; the Government Agent of the area forwarded the nomination to the Governor, and – on approval by the Governor – an Act of diploma was issued, recognizing this nomination. Thus the Governor merely accepted the nominee of the *bhikkus*: he did not select any *bhikku* on his own.

[3] A list of the *bhikkus* and *basnayaka nilames* so appointed is provided in Appendix IV.

[4] The *basnayake nilame* was the organ of communication between the Government and the *devale*: he appointed people to the various duties to be performed, took charge of the money presented at the shrine and kept the buildings in repair. The warrant of appointment to this office was given by the Government Agent, and not, as in the case of the chief *bhikkus*, by the Governor. The *kapuralas* were intermediaries between the deity of the *devale* and the devotee. They were not members of an organized religious order; they were not distinguished by any particular dress, nor had they to subscribe to any vow of celibacy. They had only to be of good family, i.e. generally of the *goigama* or farmer caste. When a *kapurala* was appointed to office his name was merely mentioned to the Government Agent whose approbation was necessary to confirm him in the post. The Government Agent did not normally interfere in the appointment, but in cases of contumacy he displaced the offender upon the petition of the people.

[5] Forty-two *bhikkus* were paid by the Government. The heads of the two Chapters – Malvatta and Asgiriya – each received a monthly allowance of 7s. 6d. The *bhikkus* who officiated at the Temple of the Tooth received 3s. each and 4 parrahs of paddy. The others received an allowance of $7\frac{1}{2}$ to $3\frac{3}{4}$ parrahs of paddy and a monthly allowance for salt and oil. These payments and the grants to the out-station temples cost the Government about £150 annually. Spence-Hardy, *The British Government and the Idolatry of Ceylon*, pp.26–8.

[6] See Appendix V.

Pilgrim Tax in India.[1] It began with the publication in 1839 of a pamphlet[2] by the Rev. R. Spence-Hardy, a Wesleyan missionary, calling on the Government to sever its connection with Buddhism.[3] For a missionary pamphlet of this nature and this age it was singularly free from appeals to emotion; it had in fact a thoroughness and a solemnity normally associated with the Blue Books of that period. Its importance lies in the fact that in the long controversies on this problem no one introduced an argument against the State's connection with Buddhism that Spence-Hardy had not included in this pamphlet.

Spence-Hardy's task in Ceylon was curiously much more difficult than that of his contemporaries in India. In India the missionary agitation against the Pilgrim Tax concentrated on two things. Firstly, they condemned the fact that the East India Company was associated with the organization of Hindu religious ceremonies and – what was more – derived a considerable income from the Pilgrim Tax. (The missionaries held that it was immoral to obtain a revenue from this 'tainted' source.) Secondly, they drew attention to such ritual ceremonies as those associated with the temple of Jaganath, where scores of frenzied devotees threw themselves under the wheels of the temple chariot to be crushed to death. This was all so much grist to the missionaries' mill. They organized a superbly sustained campaign, noteworthy for its heady emotionalism, its high moral tone, and its intelligent and realistic appreciation of what was necessary to impress public opinion in England. But the campaign in Ceylon had to be organized on different lines for the State derived no revenue from its association with Buddhism and there were no ritual ceremonies

---

[1] On the missionary agitation against the Pilgrim Tax, see Ingham, K., 'The English Evangelicals and the Pilgrim Tax in India, 1800–1862', *The Journal of Ecclesiastical History*, vol. 3 (1952), pp.191–200.

[2] Spence-Hardy, R., *The British Government and the Idolatry of Ceylon.*

[3] Spence-Hardy collected the material for his pamphlet during his brief stay at the Wesleyan mission station at Kandy. (The Wesleyans abandoned their mission station at Kandy in 1839.) This pamphlet was greatly influenced by the campaign in India against the connection of the East India Company with Hinduism. Spence-Hardy quoted, with approval, the policy declaration made under strong Evangelical pressure in 1838 that the East India Company should, as soon as possible, sever its connections with Hinduism in those parts of India under its control. The aim of Spence-Hardy's pamphlet was to persuade the Ceylon Government to adopt a similar policy in the Kandyan provinces.

such as those of the temple of Jaganath. The connection between Buddhism and the State could only be contested on the grounds of principle – that the association with Buddhism, however tenuous it might be, was still inherently harmful.

The chief argument used by Spence-Hardy – and it was to be the main argument used by all those who opposed the association of the State with Buddhism – was that the connection between the British Government and Buddhism was a connection between a Christian Government and an idolatrous religious system.[1] Nineteenth-century missionaries, and laymen interested in religious problems, held nothing in greater contempt than 'idolatry' – and to them most oriental religions were 'idolatrous'. It was therefore a connection that must be severed no matter what the circumstances in which it originated or the consequences of the step suggested.

Apart from this main argument, Spence-Hardy used two others. He complained that Government 'interference' in the religious practices of the country would be interpreted by the people as official approbation of their religion. And Spence-Hardy believed, as did most missionaries of his day, that it was only Government 'support' that kept Buddhism alive. If that were removed (by dissociating the State from Buddhism) the religion would lose its hold on the people.[2]

Not content with a lucid and skilful presentation of the case for dissociation, he went on to suggest the arguments likely to be used by the defenders of the established policy and proceeded to demolish them. Anticipating that one line of defence would be that the interference of the Government was too slight to be productive of harm, Spence-Hardy asserted that all Government interference, however slight, must cease because it was a matter of vital principle to dissociate the State from Buddhism.[3] While admitting that no financial advantages were involved, he still claimed that the British Government used its connection with Buddhism 'to consolidate the British power in Ceylon'. This, he insisted, was quite as sinful as deriving a revenue from its association with that religion.[4]

Spence-Hardy was too intelligent not to realize that those who defended the existing arrangements would hardly rely entirely on

[1] Spence-Hardy, *op. cit.* pp.12–13.
[2] Spence-Hardy, *op. cit.* p.44. [3] *Ibid.* [4] *Ibid.*
F

arguments such as this. Their defence lay on altogether more secure grounds, viz. that the connection with Buddhism had been solemnly guaranteed at the convention of 1815. No one realized the strength of this argument more than Spence-Hardy. He suggested two arguments against it neither of which was wholly satisfactory from his point of view. The first was that even if the convention of 1815 was not contrary to the Law of Nations it was contrary to the Laws of God. It was a weak argument in a secular age and realizing its weakness he proceeded to a second line of attack by suggesting that even if the Treaty was valid in law there were certain aspects of the existing connection with Buddhism that could not have been guaranteed by it. Here he was referring to the Hindu practices in popular Buddhism.[1] But this argument was as weak as the first because the convention guaranteed protection to Buddhism as it existed and not to Theravada Buddhism in its pristine purity.[2]

Spence-Hardy's pamphlet aimed at attracting the attention of those missionary organizations in England who were campaigning against the Pilgrim Tax in India. It was equally important to win the support of Governor Mackenzie in Ceylon. This latter task Spence-Hardy left in the capable hands of Rev. D. J. Gogerly, the Chairman of the Wesleyan Mission Society in South Ceylon, who had a great influence with Mackenzie.[3] But Mackenzie was not as enthusiastic in his support of this cause, at this stage, as he was to be later. Realizing that what these missionaries wanted was a complete reversal of the policy that had been accepted since 1815, he confessed his inability to effect this change, much as he sympathized with their aims. He pointed out that in these matters the most sensible thing to do was to attract attention in England to the Ceylon situation, to get the support of the missionary organizations there, and to persuade them to use their influence at the Colonial Office to have the policy changed.

Since the pamphlet had already been published, Mackenzie could not ignore it. His speech to the Legislative Council of December 1839, moving the first reading of a Bill to provide for the contingent expenditure of 1840, contained a cautious defence of the existing policy and a broad hint that this policy was being

[1] *Ibid.*, pp.43–9.   [2] See above, n.2, p.64.
[3] Wes.Mss.Cey., I, Spence-Hardy, 8 July 1840. See also Spence-Hardy's letters of 14 December 1839 and 7 May 1840.

challenged.[1] Mackenzie, aware of the difficulties of his position, and conscious of his inability to make any substantial modifications in that policy on his own initiative, refused to be precipitated into indiscreet action. He warned that the 'all important object' of converting the 'heathen'

> . . . will not be advanced by violent assaults upon the Religious Establishments of a nation or upon those who administer the heathen ceremonies so long cherished amongst them.[2]

Spence-Hardy had in the meantime sent several copies of his pamphlet to missionary organizations at home. He sent urgent appeals to the Wesleyan Missionary Society to review it in their journals, to publish extracts from it and, most important of all, to use their influence at the Colonial Office to persuade the home government to reverse the established policy.[3] The Wesleyans did review his pamphlet and published extracts from it, but it is doubtful if they ever petitioned the Colonial Office on this matter. (In the files of the Colonial Office there are no letters from the Wesleyans on Spence-Hardy's behalf.) But Spence-Hardy had found an eager and influential convert in Dandeson Coates, the Secretary of the Church Missionary Society and a close friend and associate of the evangelical James Stephen. Coates sent copies of this pamphlet to three missionaries of the C.M.S. who had served in Ceylon asking for their views on the subject. Their replies confirmed the main conclusions of Spence-Hardy's pamphlet and all of them agreed on the need to dissociate the British Government from all connection with Buddhism. Armed with these letters, Coates took upon himself the task of championing Spence-Hardy.[4] In a letter to James Stephen he called for an urgent reappraisal of the existing policy on Buddhism.[5] The theme of his letter was simple – State support of idolatry, i.e. Buddhism, was an obstacle in the way of missionary activity, and the countenance thus given

---

[1] *Governors' Addresses, Ceylon 1833–60.* Mackenzie's speech of 16 December 1830, pp.88 ff.   [2] *Ibid.*

[3] His pamphlet was reviewed in the Wesleyan journal, *The Watchman*, on 18 March 1840.

[4] For a discussion of the close relationship between Coates and James Stephen, see Bell and Morrell, *British Colonial Policy*, Select documents, introduction, pp.xxii. Williams, T., 'The Colonial Office in the thirties', *H.S.A.N.Z.*, II, pp.158 ff.

[5] C.O. 54/193, Coates to Stephen, letter of 23.3.41. The replies of the three C.M.S. missionaries were enclosed in this letter.

to this idolatry created the impression in the minds of 'heathen' people that the British Government approved of 'practices which throughout the whole of Divine Revelation are condemned with the utmost severity as most affronting to the Majesty of the True God'. Therefore the State must sever its connection with Buddhism.[1]

James Stephen needed little coaxing on this matter. From the moment that Coates's letter arrived, till the day of his retirement in 1847, Stephen fought ceaselessly for a reversal of the established policy on Buddhism in Ceylon. On this subject his mind was more than half made up before he began, and he took an increasingly hostile attitude, coaxing, cajoling and pushing his political superiors into accepting a stronger line than they were likely to have taken on their own. His prestige and his reputation were so high and his capacity for hard work so well known that he was very often not a mere technical adviser but a policy maker on his own. This was particularly so when Glenelg was Secretary of State and Russell was only slightly less dependent on him. On the theme of the State's relations with Buddhism Stephen became the real policy maker.

When a subject like the reform of the Ceylon Civil Service caught Stephen's eye, or when a serious social evil like slavery attracted his attention, his usual method was to make an exhaustive study of the subject, to write lengthy and carefully detailed memoranda, and to carry out persistent lobbying of his political superiors. Stephen had very little knowledge of the Buddhist question, however, and showed no desire to acquaint himself with the facts. His memoranda, lengthy and detailed though they were, contained more emotion than fact; only his lobbying possessed its usual qualities. Stephen's attitude to this subject is a study of the darker side of Evangelicalism – its confident assumption of moral superiority, its intolerance and its bigotry.

The day after Coates's letter arrived at the Colonial Office, Stephen wrote a stiff minute recommending immediate action on this matter and suggesting that the Governor should be called upon to send home a report, and that an injunction should be given that he take immediate steps to redress 'these evils' if Spence-Hardy's report was substantially correct. He declared that:

[1] *Ibid.*

I cannot but agree with the writer of these letters [Coates] that no Christian Government should countenance or actively participate in idolatry which we are all agreed in regarding as not merely absurd but positively criminal. I should hold it wise to hazard any consequence however formidable of acting on this principle, but I totally disbelieve that there is anything to be dreaded, unless it be perhaps the sacrifice of some revenue.[1]

This minute was aimed at gaining the support of Vernon Smith, the Under-Secretary at the Colonial Office who, however, frankly admitted that he would have preferred a policy of 'quieta non movebit'.[2] He pointed out that the missionaries who now denounced the connection of the State with Buddhism were silent when they were in Ceylon but, taking a politician's approach to the subject, he agreed that since the matter was being agitated in England 'it may be as well to ask the government for a report'.[3] He commented that:

it has hitherto been our policy to govern the natives of India and Ceylon by non-interference with their religion which has been extended in instances to support. After the changes in India, we must follow the example in Ceylon, and perhaps the time has come when we may very safely, and as good Christians, violate our engagements.[4]

It was a practical, if rather cynical, approach.

Stephen was disappointed with Smith's attitude, for it lacked the warmth and enthusiasm that this subject provoked in him. A week later he produced a longer and more substantial minute, more critical of Mackenzie and more vehement in his support of Spence-Hardy, and this was directed at winning the support of Lord John Russell, who was then the Secretary of State. The burden of this minute was that since Mackenzie's speech of 16 December 1839 did not meet Spence-Hardy's arguments, it would be necessary to call for a full report without any further delay.[5]

Stephen organized in impressive array the arguments for dissociation. There was first the familiar one that the connection of the British Government with Buddhism was a connection with idolatry, which was in principle so utterly wrong that it had to be

[1] C.O. 54/193, Stephen's minute of 24 March 1841.
[2] C.O. 54/193, Vernon Smith's minute of 25 March 1841.
[3] *Ibid.*   [4] *Ibid.*
[5] C.O. 54/193, Stephen's minute of 30 March 1841.

severed notwithstanding any possible risks. But he paid much
greater attention to the construction of an Evangelical interpretation of the Kandyan Convention of 1815. He took the view that
the convention of 1815 should not be supposed to infer that:

> the British Sovereign succeeded to the obligations of the Kandyan
> Sovereign and must maintain and protect their idolatry in the same
> way in which it was maintained and protected by their former
> princes. . . . It could never have been meant by the contracting
> parties that the conquering state should locally adopt a system of
> religious observances condemned in the strongest possible terms by
> its own religion. . . .

He insisted that the Convention was a mere

> contract for absolute toleration . . . which bound the British Govern-
> ment to prevent . . . every interference with . . . the Kandyan reli-
> gion . . . or every encroachment upon the property dedicated to the
> maintenance of it. But it could not mean that King George the Third
> bound himself and his successors in the persons of his and their
> officers to tread in the footsteps of the Kandyan Princes by lending
> to the idolatry of the country the same active support and direct
> countenance.
>   Or if such was the meaning of the Treaty it was a compact which
> in my judgement no British Sovereign had a right to make or having
> made, is at liberty to fulfil.[1]

James Stephen never changed these views. For the rest of his stay
at the Colonial Office he continued to give his superiors the same
advice: but the nearer he came to the end of his duties, the more
violent became the language in which he expressed them. If his
understanding of the subject did not increase, his bigotry and
intolerance did.

Spence-Hardy himself could hardly have put the missionary
viewpoint in stronger or more effective language. Stephen was
doing a better job for the missionaries than they could have done
for themselves.

Once again Vernon Smith was less than enthusiastic,[2] but
Stephen had made a complete conquest of Russell, who not only
recommended a despatch asking for a report, but also suggested
the inclusion in it of a statement of policy embodying Stephen's
main arguments in a modified form.[3]

---

[1] *Ibid.*   [2] C.O. 54/193, Vernon Smith's minute of 30 March 1841.
[3] C.O. 54/193, Lord John Russell's minute of 31 March 1841.

It was a significant triumph for James Stephen but unfortunately for him the despatch was never written because the Whig Ministry was defeated soon afterwards, and Lord John Russell was succeeded at the Colonial Office by Lord Stanley whose relations with James Stephen were by no means as cordial as those of his predecessor Russell, and much less so than those of Glenelg. He would not have policies dictated to him or even initiated for him by James Stephen. Stephen had therefore to bide his time and wait for an opportunity to arise when he could convert Stanley as he had converted Russell to his line of thinking.

In Ceylon, in the meantime, Mackenzie on the eve of his return home had become an enthusiastic supporter of the missionary point of view on the question of the Government's relations with Buddhism. Realizing that he could not attack the problem in detail, he decided to concentrate on one aspect of it – temple appointments. He called for reports on this problem from each member of his Executive Council, and in concert with the Chief Justice he prepared the draft of an Ordinance on temple appointments to be introduced in the Legislative Council during the session of 1841.[1]

But time was against him and he was recalled before he could bring this measure before the Council. All that he had the time to do was to lay down a written protest against himself or any other Governor being called upon to interfere in any future appointments to the *vihares* or *devales*.[2]

Mackenzie's successor, Sir Colin Campbell, was a Presbyterian by conviction, much less enthusiastic than he on the question of separating the State from Buddhism, and, when faced with this problem, showed a greater awareness of the legal and administrative difficulties involved.

But in the early months of his administration he followed Mackenzie's line of policy. Thus in 1841 when the Government Agent of the Central Province asked to be informed of the Gover-

---

[1] C.O. 54/210, Campbell to Stanley, no.14 of 24 January 1844. See memorandum of T. W. C. Murdoch on this despatch. It is difficult to account for this radical change in Mackenzie's attitude on the question of Buddhism. Perhaps it was due to Gogerley's influence, but one cannot be certain of this.

[2] He laid down this protest at the Executive Council meeting of 24 March 1841.

nor's views on the regular appointment of persons to the posts of *Basnayaka Nimales* of the Pattini and Alwatugoda Devales, where two persons had been acting without regular appointments, Campbell acting in accordance with his predecessor's resolution declined to make an appointment, and informed the Government Agent that 'it is highly desirable to abstain as far as possible from all interference in regard to the management of heathen temples'.[1]

Campbell's attitude changed considerably with the passage of time. Some of the consequences of this new policy on temple appointments gave cause for concern. One of the direct results of this policy was that some of the temple tenants refused to render the services due from them in return for their lands, and the *bhikkus* found it impossible to assert their rights at law. In 1843 the *bhikkus* petitioned the Government, and urged that a new law be enacted to give them redress; but the Governor and his Executive Council, while they admitted that the new policy had created difficulties for the *viharas* and *devales*, confessed their inability to apply the remedy the *bhikkus* desired. A Minute of the Executive Council of 11 August 1843 recorded that

> The Governor and Council are of opinion that there is much ground for complaint. The Temples were formerly supported by the Government who compelled the attendance of those who held lands under them. Now all such interference is withdrawn, and the Temples are referred to the Courts of Law to establish their rights. It must be understood that they cannot so enforce them, and they have thus been material sufferers, by this change in the policy of the Government.

In 1843 there was the far more serious problem of a scare of rebellion, and though the rumours of plots and secret gatherings were clearly exaggerated the Government, remembering the rebellion of 1817–18, took no chances. Campbell believed that the Government's changed attitude to Buddhism had much to do with the existing discontent in the Kandyan areas. He noted that

> some degree of dissatisfaction exists attributable to an impression that has gone abroad of the Government being hostile to the Native Institutions and Religion and the refusal of the Government to fill up appointments which are absolutely required to protect the tem-

---

[1] C.O. 54/210, Campbell to Stanley, no. 14 of 24 January 1844. See enclosed letters of J. A. Mooyart, G.A. Central Province to P. Anstruther, Colonial Secretary, of 16 November 1841, and the latter's reply of 3 December 1841.

poral interests of the religious establishments is regarded as evidence of this hostility.

He called a meeting of the Executive Council to discuss this problem, both because of the excited feelings among the Kandyans, and also in 'justice to the Native Religious Establishments'.[1] The Executive Councillors were unanimous in recommending that the vacant temple appointments or at least the more important of them should be filled at once.[2] The Pattini *Devale* at Kandy immediately benefited from this change of heart. Legal measures were necessary to recover certain dues of this *devale* but the acting *basnayake nilame* was unable to produce a warrant of appointment and could not therefore be recognized by the Courts of Law. When Campbell was informed of this he instructed the Government Agent of the Central Province to issue an Act of Appointment to the acting *basnayake nilame*, with the clear understanding, however, that it was a purely provisional arrangement designed solely to protect the temporal interests of the *devale*.[3]

The Pattini *Devale* was an important religious institution and the arrangements made with regard to that *devale* were not intended to be applied to smaller and less important institutions. It was perhaps with regard to these that the Executive Council suggested that Campbell should call a levee at Kandy of the principal headmen and *bhikkus* to explain to them that though the Government would not interfere in the appointment of officers to *viharas* and *devales* it was by no means intended that such vacancies as existed should not be filled. Campbell was to suggest that election to these vacancies should be left to a Committee of Kandyan chiefs. Presumably the Government would then recognize their nominee.[4] There was no evidence to suggest that such a levee was held in 1844, and even if one had been held it would not have led to any important results, because the Kandyans were strongly opposed to any change in the existing connection between the Government and their religion.

In 1843 there occured an event that was to be of great significance for the future, not because of any intrinsic importance of its own but because of unexpected developments that sprang up from it. A deputation of Siamese Buddhist monks from the King

---

[1] C.O. 54/210, Campbell to Stanley, no. 14 of 24 January 1844.
[2] *Ibid.*   [3] *Ibid.*   [4] *Ibid.*

of Siam arrived in Kandy to see the Tooth Relic, and the Kandyan *bhikkus* applied to the Government for permission to hold a special exposition of the Tooth Relic for the occasion. Permission was granted, and on 27 March 1843 there was a picturesque ceremony at which the Governor and Lady Campbell, C. R. Buller, the Acting Government Agent of the Central Province, and several other civil servants and their wives were present. The presence of these officials attracted the critical comments of missionaries. In June 1843 the Indian Baptist Journal, *The Friend of India*, published an account of this ceremony severely critical of Campbell and C. R. Buller.

Spence-Hardy joined in this criticism.[1] But the article in the *Friend of India* attracted the attention of a far more formidable individual, the Baptist missionary the Rev. James Peggs, who more than any other person had been responsible for the success of the missionary campaigns against the connection of the East India Company with Hinduism in India, and against the Pilgrim Tax there.[2] Peggs was in England at this time, and he wrote to the Colonial Office on the question of the State's connection with Buddhism in Ceylon.[3] Unlike Spence-Hardy he had no first-hand knowledge of Buddhism in Ceylon, but he was a master in the techniques of propaganda and in the devious arts of pressure group agitation. His reputation as a missionary was so high and his influence at Exeter Hall so considerable that Lord Stanley felt obliged to send a copy of his letter to Ceylon with instructions to Campbell to report on the recent exposition of the Tooth Relic there.

Stanley's despatch to Campbell drew attention to several subsidiary issues arising from the State's connection with Buddhism. Among these, the one in which Stanley showed most interest was the question of whether C. R. Buller's presence at the recent ceremony was in his capacity of Government Agent of the Central Province. Campbell was asked to provide information on two other issues – whether Government officials, civil or military, had in recent times assisted 'at heathen rites and ceremonies', and if so under what authority that assistance had been afforded, and

---

[1] Wes.Mss.Cey. I. Spence-Hardy, 8 July 1843.

[2] Ingham, K., *Reformers in India*, pp.39 ff.

[3] C.O. 54/209, Peggs' letter to Stanley, 28 August 1843; Peggs' letter was entitled *The British Connection with Idolatry in the Island of Ceylon*.

what considerations of policy were involved in the matter; and whether the Ceylon Government was associated in any way in making appointments to *viharas* and *devales*.[1]

In the meantime Peggs proceeded to bombard Stanley with pamphlets (his original letter of two pages had grown into a pamphlet of forty pages)[2] urging him to sever the connection with Buddhism without any further delay. As Campbell took his time in sending the report he had asked for, Stanley was unable to reply to Peggs' original letter as early as he would normally have done. In a letter of 20 December 1843, Peggs, who suspected that Stanley was deliberately delaying, hinted that this might compel him to adopt different tactics.

> I have not sent copies of this letter to the Public papers because I wish your Lordship to have the opportunity of removing those evils in Ceylon without their being much known to the Public. . . .[3]

Campbell's reply was sent in January 1844.[4] His despatch was a cautious defence of Government policy. He admitted his presence as well as that of C. R. Buller and other officials at the ceremony but denied that this could be interpreted as official support of Buddhism. The *bhikkus*, he continued, had a perfect legal right to display the Tooth Relic, and that, because of a strong belief in the country that those who possessed the Tooth Relic were the real masters of the country, it was Buller's responsibility to see that strict precautions were taken for the security of the relic. This explained the presence of Government officials at the ceremony. He emphasized that no official took any part in the religious ceremony.

He informed Stanley that the Government no longer interfered in the appointments to *viharas* and *devales*; it merely recognized those who were elected by their colleagues. The Legislative Council made an annual grant of £310 to the Temple of the Tooth, the *viharas* and *devales*, but though it was legally possible to stop this grant, there were doubts whether the Government could do it in good faith; since it levied the greater part of its

---

[1] C.O. 54/209, Stanley to Campbell, no.76 of 15 September 1843.

[2] The new pamphlet was entitled *The Present State of the British Connection with Idolatry in Ceylon*.

[3] C.O. 54/210, Peggs' letter to Stanley, 20 October 1843.

[4] C.O. 54/210, Campbell to Stanley, no.14 of 24 January 1844. This was in reply to Stanley's despatch, no.76 of 15 September 1843.

revenue from Buddhists, it would be difficult to justify a refusal to continue this trifling grant.

Campbell's main aim was to show Stanley that, while the official connection of the State with Buddhism did exist, it was so slight as to be harmless. He sought to show also that the outstanding difficulty in the way of a complete dissociation from Buddhism was in regard to the management of the large landed property belonging to the *viharas* and *devales*; if the Government did not appoint the *basnayake nimales* of the *devales*, it was possible that there would be large-scale peculation and fraud. Moreover it was impossible 'to find any body in whom this species of patronage may be vested'.[1]

Campbell admitted, however, that these appointments were not made without advantages. 'The appointments are valuable and constitute nearly the most valuable patronage that remains in the hands of the Government, and it is used to reward deserving public servants.'[2]

In a later despatch he warned Stanley against taking Peggs too seriously, pointing out that he had never been in Ceylon, and that his knowledge of Buddhism and its position in Ceylon was decidedly meagre. As an example of this ignorance Campbell referred Stanley to the frontispiece of Pegg's pamphlet, where there was a picture of what was supposed to be a Buddhist *bhikku*, but the picture was really one of a Kandyan chieftain in his traditional clothes with his attendants, while the *bhikku* was the robed figure in the background.[3]

James Stephen seized the opportunity provided by Peggs' pamphlet and Campbell's despatch to continue from where he had been compelled to stop in 1842. He rushed to Peggs' defence and, picking with unerring accuracy the weak links of Campbell's arguments, he wrote another of his more impulsive minutes in which the civil servant's caution gave way to the Evangelical's

[1] C.O. 54/210, Campbell to Stanley, no.14 of 24 January 1844.
[2] *Ibid.*
[3] C.O. 54/210, Campbell to Stanley, no.53 of 16 March 1844. See also P. E. Wodehouse's evidence before the Parliamentary Committee of Ceylon, *Second Report on Ceylon*, p.269, where he stated that 'Mr Peggs sent in to the Colonial Office a pamphlet with a frontispiece giving a picture of a Buddhist priest in Ceylon; it was in reality extracted from an old History of Ceylon; it contained a picture of a chief in Ceylon, with a priest walking by his side, but he suppressed the word 'chief' and he left the readers of the pamphlet to infer that the dignified person was a Buddhist priest. . . .'

fire.[1] In all his minutes on this problem Stephen was less the civil servant recommending carefully considered alternatives than the religious zealot egging on his superiors to an uncompromising stand.

He began with a subtle hint that the Tooth Relic might perhaps be destroyed. ('The obvious course is to destroy it, which however might provoke an Insurrection.')[2] But he checked himself and suggested that the 'Middle course w^d appear to be that of keeping it but refusing to make an exhibition of it. Possibly it might be safe to send it off the isl^d.' He was very critical of the presence of Government officials at the ceremony, and the voting of the public money for the support of Buddhism, both of which appeared to him to be 'gratuitous homage' to that religion.

With Stephen and Peggs both urging immediate action, Stanley could no longer postpone a decision on this matter, even if he was so inclined. After a careful study of the papers on the subject (chiefly a memorandum on the history and the nature of the connection of the British Government with Buddhism prepared by Murdoch) he issued instructions to Campbell to sever the connection between the State and Buddhism. Stanley's despatch of 27 March 1844 was a clear and well formulated declaration of policy, reversing the British policy on Buddhism which had prevailed since 1815.[3] The strength of this despatch lay in the fact that it recognized that there were two different aspects in the existing relationship between Buddhism and the Government.

First, what relates to the support of the Religious Rites including the custody of the Relic – the appointment of the Priesthood and the maintenance of idolatrous ceremonies, and second, the management of the landed property belonging to the Temples.[4]

The weakness of the despatch was that it did not recognize that this second aspect was as important as the first, and that if the connection between the Government and the Buddhist religion were to be severed, it was necessary to issue clear and detailed instructions on the question of temple lands.

[1] C.O. 54/210, Stephen's minute of 13 March 1844 on Campbell's despatch to Stanley, no.14 of 24 January 1844.
[2] Ibid.
[3] C.O. 54/210, Stanley to Campbell, no.210 of 24 July 1844. This despatch was based, to a very great extent, on Stephen's minute of 13 March 1844.
[4] Ibid.

Concentrating on the first aspect, Stanley declared that the time had come 'when the British Government may, without risk to the tranquillity of the Colony, relieve itself from all connection with idolatry'. It was one of those matters of principle on which there could be no compromise. Campbell was instructed to refrain from making any appointments to *viharas* and *devales*.

Since these recent discussions had arisen out of an exhibition of the Tooth Relic, the despatch paid great attention to that aspect of the problem. Echoing Stephen's remarks, Stanley insisted that

> ... there can hardly be a doubt that the scrupulous care with which it [the Tooth Relic] has been guarded by the British Government must have tended to sanction in the minds of the natives the idolatrous veneration with which they are accustomed to regard it. This, therefore, is an arrangement in the continuance of which I cannot acquiesce . . . I see little risk and much advantage in making over the custody of it to the Priests . . . and in strictly prohibiting the Government Agent and his subordinates from taking any part in the exhibition of the relic.[1]

Largely because of Campbell's doubts on the subject, Stanley was unable to issue clear instructions on the question of the annual monetary grant, though he would have preferred to see it struck out of the public expenditure. In Stanley's opinion: 'Nothing but the clearest evidence of an obligation on the part of the Government could justify the grant of money by a Christian Legislature for such purposes.'[2] A decision was postponed till Campbell informed him whether there was such an obligation.

The despatch laid it down that Campbell was to treat the question of the dissociation of the Government from Buddhism as a matter of the greatest urgency; an Ordinance giving legal effect to this dissociation was to be introduced in the Legislative Council. The handing over of the Tooth Relic was to be the most delicate, as well as the most dramatic, manifestation of the policy of dissociation, and Campbell was urged to use his own judgement as to the precise manner and moment of this transference but to allow no 'unnecessary delay'.

These instructions were clear enough, but they should have been accompanied by equally clear instructions on the questions of temple lands. It was impossible to treat this, as Stanley's despatch

---

[1] *Ibid.*   [2] C.O. 54/210, Stanley to Campbell, no.210 of 24 July 1844.

did, as an entirely separate subject, for the severance from Buddhism could not be effected without a settlement of this problem. To do so would have been to undermine the whole legal position of the temples over their lands and tenants. Stanley postponed a decision on this problem, on the grounds that he did not have sufficient information on which to base any positive instructions, and Campbell was instructed to send home a report, providing the most ample information on the temple lands.

Stanley's despatch was of very great significance in the history of Ceylon. At first glance it would not appear to do much – it merely instructed that the Tooth Relic be handed over to the Buddhists; that the sentry at the Temple of the Tooth be removed; that Government officials should not be present at expositions of the Tooth Relic; and that the Governor was to refrain from making appointments to *viharas* and *devales*. But these instructions in effect severed the tenuous connection of the British Government with Buddhism. In the eyes of the Kandyans, however, this connection was not tenuous,[1] but symbolic of the ancient bond between their religion and the ruler of their country, and the severing of that bond was therefore an event of great significance. The connection between Buddhism and the State which had lasted with only insignificant interruptions from the very beginnings of the recorded history of Ceylon was now at an end.

Stanley's despatch could not have come as a surprise to Campbell, because even before its arrival he was considering two schemes submitted by C. R. Buller and P. E. Wodehouse for dissociating the Government of Ceylon from its connection with Buddhism. Once the despatch was received the discussion of these plans was intensified, but still it was several months before the Government had any concrete proposals to lay before the Kandyans. A meeting of the Kandyan chiefs and *bhikkus* was summoned to discuss the

[1] P. E. Wodehouse (Government Agent, Western Province, and Assistant Colonial Secretary), in his evidence before the Parliamentary Committee on Ceylon (1849–50), commented that the great mass of the people attached the greatest importance to any connection of their religion with the Government, in any shape whatever. *Second Report on Ceylon*, pp.264 ff.

G. Ackland (Merchant and non-official member of the Legislative Council) stated that the people felt that the custody of the Tooth Relic by the Government was equivalent to the religion being established in the country. *Second Report on Ceylon*, pp.13–14.

changes recommended by Stanley. At this meeting – held in
Kandy on 23 April 1845 – Campbell explained to them the sub-
stance and significance of Stanley's decision.[1]

The transference of the Temple of the Tooth to the Kandyans
was to be the most dramatic manifestation of the policy of dissociation. The Kandyans were informed that this temple would
be handed over to them as the representatives of Buddhism, and
that they were to devise the best means for its safe custody.

Needless to say, the chiefs and the *bhikkus* were unanimously
opposed to Stanley's policy. They argued and pleaded with Campbell that the existing relationship should be continued, but when
they realised that it was beyond his power to give them satisfaction, they decided to send a memorandum to Stanley protesting
against these projected changes.[2]

On Campbell's return to Colombo, the Buddhist problem was
brought before the Executive Council. The discussions centred on
the two schemes of C. R. Buller and P. E. Wodehouse. Buller's
scheme envisaged a Board of five Commissioners (to be chosen by
an electorate composed of *bhikkus*, chiefs, sons of chiefs, and all
persons who had held or were holding office), to which the powers
exercised by Government in relation to Buddhism were to be
transferred. Wodehouse criticized Buller's Board of Commissioners
on the ground that, founded as it was on the principle of centraliza-
tion, and vesting as it did the entire management of the temples
and their property in this board, it would have 'the effect of
gradually placing the whole of the revenues and influence of the
Temples in the hands of a small body of influential chiefs, principally resident at Kandy'.[3] It would appear, however, that Wodehouse's main objection was not to the power thus given to these
chiefs, for his own scheme too envisaged the transfer of powers to
a similar board; he feared that Buller's Board of Commissioners
would not give their consent to the diversion of a portion of the
revenue of the temples for purposes of education. Wodehouse
suggested that one of the great advantages of his own scheme was
that it was designed to make it easier to obtain money for educational purposes from temple revenues, since it was to be enacted

---

[1] C.O. 54/217, Campbell to Stanley, no.120 of 8 May 1845.
[2] *Ibid.*
[3] P. E. Wodehouse's minute of 30 April 1845, in Campbell to Stanley, no.
120 of 8 May 1845.

that the default by any group of electors to fill a vacant incumbency would result in the forfeiture of the revenues of such incumbency to the Crown which, Wodehouse assumed, would spend it on education. In his opinion the ultimate aim of all these schemes should be the 'moral improvement' and conversion to Christianity of the Buddhists.

The great merit of Wodehouse's scheme was that, unlike Buller's, it touched upon the important question of temple lands, and was therefore more comprehensive and valuable. He recommended that the Government should proceed with the registration of these temple lands, acknowledging generously wherever possible the claims of the temples to them. But, in return, the Government should be relieved of all concern in the management of temples, and of the annual contribution from public funds towards the expense of temple festivals[1]. He laid down a second important condition, namely that the services due from the peasants to the temples in return for the lands they held should be commuted.[2]

Although the discussion at the meeting of the Executive Council centred round these two schemes, the most noteworthy incident at that meeting was a clash between Philip Anstruther and Arthur Buller. It was not a mere clash of personalities but a clash of two sharply contrasted points of view on the question of Buddhism; one, reflecting the influence of missionary opinions, called for immediate and radical changes; the other was the traditionalist view, arguing for the *status quo*. Anstruther represented the first, Arthur Buller the second.

Anstruther did not make any frontal assault on the Kandyan Convention of 1815 (he did indeed suggest that the Convention was not a binding treaty but this was more in the nature of an afterthought than a serious argument), but concentrated instead on drawing a distinction between pure Buddhism which alone in his opinion was guaranteed protection by the Convention, and Hindu ceremonies and institutions forming part of the popular religion, which he contended were not entitled to it. Indeed he

---

[1] *Ibid.*

[2] There was, at this time, a genuine concern for the condition of these temple tenants who did not benefit from the abolition of *rajakariya* in 1833; men like Wodehouse and, later on, Tennent believed that these temple tenants were mere serfs. These officials, with genuine humanitarian motives, made regular pleas for the commutation of the tenants' services.

suggested that while the *viharas* should hold their lands free of taxes, the property of the *devales* should either be taxed or seized and their revenues used for the support of Christian education and the propagation of Christianity.[1]

This distinction between 'pure' Buddhism and popular Buddhism did not in fact exist, nor did the Kandyan Convention draw any such distinction, but it was a popular argument with those who were opposed to the connection of the state with Buddhism. Arthur Buller as a lawyer, had a clearer understanding of the implications of the Kandyan Convention, and had little difficulty in meeting this argument. He explained that it was

> perfectly true that the worship of those dieties forms no part of *pure* Buddhism, but it was not *pure* Buddhism which we undertook to maintain. It was the Buddhism of the people . . . [or] to use the words of the Convention itself, it was the 'Religion of Buddha as professed by the chiefs and the inhabitants'. It was impossible to deny that the Dewales were objects of protection to the Kandyan Kings as fully as Viharas, nor could it be any more doubted that the guarantee given at the Convention extended to both institutions alike.[2]

The question of the Temple of the Tooth figured prominently in these discussions, with Anstruther strongly in favour of handing it over to the Buddhists forthwith. He argued that the fifth clause of the Kandyan Convention gave no undertaking 'to protect Buddha's Tooth'; he pointed out that the British Government did not undertake its protection till after the great rebellion of 1817–18, and even then only for political reasons. Since these political reasons did not exist any longer there was nothing in the Convention to prevent the Temple of the Tooth and its property being transferred to the custody of the Kandyan *bhikkus* (to whom Anstruther suggested a salary should be reserved out of the revenues of the Temple), on the clear understanding, however, that if the Tooth Relic was ever 'lost' the lands of the Temples would be confiscated to the Government. Anstruther assured the Government that there was little prospect of political danger in this course of policy.[3]

Arthur Buller would have preferred to let the existing arrange-

[1] C.O. 54/217, Campbell to Stanley, no.120 of 8 May 1845. Anstruther's minute of 30 April 1845.

[2] *Ibid.*, Arthur Buller's minute of 30 April 1845.

[3] Anstruther's minute of 30 April 1845, *op. cit.*

ments remain undisturbed but he realized that the possession of the Tooth Relic had attracted a great deal of censure from missionary organizations at home. He had little objection therefore, to giving up the Tooth Relic, but he insisted that it must be done in a quiet and conciliatory manner, after judicious and friendly discussion and without any unnecessary announcement of a determination to break all connection with the religion of the Kandyans.[1]

Warrants of appointment were the third issue on which Anstruther clashed with Buller, the former urging that the Governor should not sign them in future.[2] Anstruther's argument in favour of this line of policy was based on the false assumption that the *bhikkus* were averse to the Government giving up the practice of signing their Commissions because they feared that if they did not hold the Governor's Commission few would pay them any respect. The evidence would suggest, however, that the *bhikkus* wanted these warrants of appointment because without them the Courts would not recognize their legal right to the temple lands and property.

These conflicting views arose from two diametrically opposed interpretations of the Government's obligations to the Kandyans under the fifth clause of the Kandyan Convention. To Arthur Buller's keen legal mind it was perfectly clear that as long as the Convention of 1815 and the Proclamation of 1818 were respected by the Government – and he saw no good reason why they should not be respected – it would be impossible for the State to dissociate itself from Buddhism. Besides, there was also a moral obligation quite as strong as the legal obligation for the Government had given a solemn undertaking that the national religion of the Kandyans would not be left to shift for itself, but should be maintained and protected by the whole might of the secular power.[3] Anstruther, on the other hand, urged that the Government's connection with Buddhism must be completely withdrawn; and he believed that with this withdrawal the whole structure of Buddhism could collapse.[4] He had little to say about, and little concern for, moral and legal obligations.

There was no support in the Executive Council for Arthur

---

[1] Arthur Buller's minute of 30 April 1845.
[2] Anstruther's minute of 30 April 1845.
[3] Arthur Buller's minute, *op. cit.*
[4] Anstruther's minute, *op. cit.*

Buller's rigid insistence on the maintenance of the existing relationship, but even among the staunchest advocates of the policy
of dissociation there was little doubt that Buller's interpretation
of the Convention of 1815 was fundamentally correct. It was for
this reason that Anstruther himself had refrained from making a
direct attack on the Convention itself; and it was for the same
reason that James Stephen was to concentrate his attack on Arthur
Buller's interpretation of the Convention.[1]

Buller was so strong a supporter of the existing relationship that
he would not have it disturbed even by an Ordinance such as that
suggested by Wodehouse. He criticized Wodehouse's Ordinance
on the grounds that it would be an ostentatious parade of a breach
of faith, inasmuch as it announced to the Kandyans that '[The
British Government] will have no more to do with your religion.
You may manage its affairs as best as you can. . . .' But a much
stronger objection lay in the fact that if the Government withdrew
from Buddhism the '. . . present merely nominal protection' it
would, if Wodehouse's Ordinance were adopted, 'substitute in its
place a protection that will be of great avail'.[2] In his view such an
Ordinance was an elaborate and well considered scheme for the
endurance of Buddhism.

Faced with this great divergence of opinion in his Executive
Council, Campbell merely sent along to the Colonial Office the
views of the individual Executive Councillors and the schemes of
Wodehouse and C. R. Buller, without any significant comment
of his own apart from urging caution in the implementation of the
new policy. He explained that the object aimed at could be
attained without alarming the prejudices of the people, and asked
Stanley to leave it to his discretion to determine the proper time
and method of effecting the change of policy.[3]

When these papers arrived at the Colonial Office James Stephen,
whose task it was to examine them, picked on Arthur Buller's
interpretation of the Convention of 1815 for special attack, aware
that it was the foundation on which the old policy was based.
Referring to the Convention of 1815 Stephen declared that its
object was simply to

[1] James Stephen's minute of 4 July 1845 in C.O. 54/217, Campbell to Stanley, no.120 of 8 May 1845.

[2] Arthur Buller's minute, op. cit.

[3] C.O. 54/217, Campbell to Stanley, no.120 of 8 May 1845.

reassure, on the subject of their religion, a people from whom we had taken everything else. The treaty did not and could not mean that King George III should succeed to the Religious duty and character of the King of Kandy, and the Defender of the Christian Faith should in the same sense be the defender of the Buddhist Faith. The Treaty merely meant this . . . 'If you will surrender to Great Britain all secular dominion you may keep up your Religion. If you will deliver up to us your Treasury, your Temple Lands shall be inviolate. If you will become subjects of our King he will permit no one to interrupt your Religious Offices or to depose your Priests or your Temples.

He rejected Arthur Buller's interpretations as totally unacceptable.[1]

Then turning to the schemes formulated by Wodehouse and C. R. Buller, he asserted that both would involve the Government in direct intervention in idolatry, while there was the possibility that Buller's scheme would go far towards the establishment of something like a 'Buddhist Papacy'. Thus both schemes departed from the principles laid down in Stanley's despatch.

It was Stephen's firm conviction that the Home Government alone should lay down the main principles of Buddhist policy. Since Stanley's despatch had already done that, nothing further remained to be done but to refer to those instructions and to insist on as prompt and exact a compliance with them as possible, leaving to the local authorities only the power to determine the time and the manner in which they could be most conveniently carried into effect. He added that 'I think it evident enough from these papers that the obstacles . . . have been rather personal than substantial – the want of agents willing and able to act with decision, rather than any inherent difficulty in the subject itself.'[2] Lord Stanley, accepting James Stephen's views completely, called for a strict adherence to his instructions conveyed in the despatch of 24 July 1844. He would leave in the hands of the Ceylon Government merely the details of time and method. Campbell was asked not to postpone needlessly a decision on this matter.[3]

In the Colonial Office there was a deplorable refusal to understand the difficulties that faced the Ceylon Government. It was

[1] James Stephen's minute of 4 July 1845 in C.O. 54/217, Campbell to Stanley, no.120 of 8 May 1845. [2] *Ibid.*

[3] C.O. 54/217, Stanley to Campbell, no.388 of 7 August 1845. This despatch instructed Campbell to omit from future Bills of Supply the monetary grant hitherto made for traditional religious ceremonies.

not merely the formidable problem of the temple lands, but the more important fact that in its organization Buddhism was fundamentally different from Christian Churches in possessing no central organization – the individual *viharas* had a great degree of independence in most matters. In such a situation before the Government dissociated itself it had to create or evolve a central organization to take over those functions which it performed in relation to Buddhism. The schemes of Wodehouse and C. R. Buller had precisely this aim in view, but the Colonial Office under the influence of James Stephen treated Buddhism as though it were a centrally organized religion like Christianity, and when the despatches from Ceylon recommended caution they merely suspected the local officials of lethargy, unaware that they required of the Ceylon Government nothing less than doing, at a moment's notice, what Sinhalese rulers had for centuries failed to do – to give Buddhism a central organization.

Faced with this uncompromising attitude, Campbell had no alternative but to proceed at speed with the business of dissociating the Government from Buddhism. He sent Wodehouse to Kandy to confer personally with the chiefs and *bhikkus*, and to persuade them to accept the changes recommended by the Colonial Office.[1] Adopting a very conciliatory tone, Wodehouse informed the Kandyans that the Governor would receive any proposals they wished to make, but he did make them understand that he would receive these proposals only on the distinct understanding that the announcements recently made to them were to be taken as the solemn and final decision of the Queen's Government. The only significant concession that Wodehouse had been instructed to promise was that all lands recognized and registered as temple property would be entirely exempted from taxation. The Kandyans, on their part, rigidly adhered to the view that the Convention of 1815 should be carried out as regards the maintenance of their religion in the same way as it had been by the Kings of Kandy.[2] Then, both at this conference and at a private

---

[1] This conference was held on 10 November 1845. See memorandum of the conference held by P. E. Wodehouse with the Kandyan Chiefs and Priests, dated 14 November 1845, enclosed in C.O. 54/223, Campbell to Stanley, no.37 of 7 February 1846.

[2] Petition of the Kandyans to the Queen dated 7 January 1846 enclosed in C.O. 54/223, Campbell to Stanley, no.37 of 7 February 1846.

interview with Wodehouse, they sought to appeal to the home authorities, but Wodehouse told them that the Home Government was acting under missionary influence, and that the local Government alone was likely to be conciliatory. The Kandyans had no alternative but to accept these decisions, and had to get what satisfaction they could from a brief and sharply worded petition to the Queen protesting against the new policy.

The Government then proceeded to frame an Ordinance to effect the dissociation based largely on Wodehouse's scheme with modifications to meet the criticisms heaped on it by Stephen and Stanley. This Ordinance – Ordinance No.2 of 1846, 'An Ordinance to provide for the management of Buddhist *viharas* and *devales* in the Kandyan Provinces' – was based on the principle that 'that which a Government could do, or was bound to do by itself as the Sovereign authority, it could delegate to an Authority'.[1] It provided for the appointment of a 'committee of sixteen persons (of whom, in the first instance, six were to be *bhikkus*), who were to be the guardians of the Tooth Relic and the treasures belonging to it, and to whom all the ecclesiastical authority vested in the Government by the Kandyan Convention was to be transferred. Provision was made for the appointment of a commissioner to register the temple lands and, if required, to commute the tenants' services. Lands could not in future be donated to temples without the Governor's licence; nor were the temple lands to be alienated without the consent of the Governor and the Committee to be appointed under this Act.[2]

Campbell sent this Ordinance home, along with the petition of the Kandyan chiefs and *bhikkus*, with another word of warning, stressing the need for tact and understanding in discontinuing a connection that had been so solemnly promised at the moment of cession of the Kandyan Kingdom.[3] Stanley had by this time left the Colonial Office – his successor was W. E. Gladstone – and there was thus the possibility of a fresh start in this matter.

The new Ordinance was reviewed by Frederick Rogers, the recently appointed Assistant Under-Secretary of State, in a long

[1] *Second Report on Ceylon*, evidence of Ackland, G., p.5.
[2] C.O. 54/223, Campbell to Stanley, no.37 of 7 February 1846.
[3] *Ibid.*, the Kandyan petition of 7 January 1846 (1,941 signatures).

and comprehensive minute noteworthy for the cogency of its arguments and its freedom from 'Evangelical' religious fervour and emotion. He concluded that while the Ordinance effected the dissociation so strongly recommended by Stanley, it nevertheless contained some features potentially so dangerous, that it would be best to reject it; he was referring to the committee of *bhikkus* and chiefs, which he believed would give to the Buddhist religion 'a most dangerous force and unity', and to the *Sangha* a 'dangerous organization'.[1] But while he recommended the rejection of this Ordinance, his attitude was free from the innate hostility and intolerance that characterized Stephen's.

On the wider theme of Buddhist policy Rogers emphasized three points; first, that the dissociation was an exceedingly difficult and intricate business; second, that the Kandyans had a genuine grievance against the new policy; and third, that more attention should be paid to the opinion of local civil servants, particularly to those who had a thorough understanding of the problem.[2]

For the first time since this controversy began James Stephen found himself faced with the problem of opposition to his views within the Colonial Office itself, and he lost no time in seeking to convert Gladstone to his view. Taking up the challenge offered by Rogers' opinions, he wrote a startlingly prejudiced and hostile minute.

Turning to the Kandyan Convention he declared that

> If this compact means that Sovereign in whose name it was made was to become the Guardian and Defender of all the crimes and pollutions practised in the Candian[*sic*] country in the name of Religion and as an integral part of this religion, it was a compact absolutely void ab initio. No Christian King can contract a valid obligation to do any act which Christianity unequivocally forbids. . . . This appears to me a conclusive answer in the absence of any other to all

---

[1] *Ibid.*, Rogers, T. F., minute of 25 June 1846.

Frederick Rogers, Fellow of Oriel College, Oxford, was appointed to the dual post of Assistant Under-Secretary of State at the Colonial Office and third Emigration Commissioner, by Order-in-Council of 18 May 1846. A barrister of ability, one of his duties was to report on colonial laws; he was in effect the nearest, since Stephen's original appointment in 1813, to a legal adviser at the Colonial Office. See Knox, B. A., 'The Provision of Legal Advice and Colonial Office Reorganization, 1866–7', *Bull.Inst.Hist.Res.*, XXXV, 181.

[2] *Ibid.*, Rogers' minute of 25 June 1846.

the arguments used by Mr Buller[1] and employed (by the aid of some English lawyers) by the Sinhalese Petitioners.[2]

He then proceeded to his own usual interpretation of the Convention. Campbell's Ordinance, he insisted, was contrary to his (Stephen's) interpretation and should on that account alone be rejected.

On the Committee envisaged in the Ordinance Stephen found himself in wholehearted agreement with Rogers. This Committee 'when created, w^d probably be found, if not irresistible, at least most intractable, and inconvenient'. Thus the Ordinance, far from 'actually and apparently disconnecting' the State from Buddhism, would only make that connection stronger.

But while Stephen's main target was Campbell's Ordinance, he was not a little perturbed by Rogers' recommendations on Buddhist policy, in particular the latter's suggestion that the opinions of local officials should be given greater weight than hitherto and that there should be a more sympathetic consideration of Kandyan sensibilities. It was precisely this that Stephen wanted to avoid, for if these views were accepted as Colonial Office policy it would mean a significant modification of the policy hitherto pursued which, under his direction, was based on diametrically opposite assumptions. The first of these assumptions was that the dissociation of the State from Buddhism was an urgent necessity; that there were religious and moral considerations of such vital importance that the separation must be effected notwithstanding the possibility of disturbances. (In any case he did not believe there would be any.) His second assumption was that the dissociation, far from being a complicated or intricate business, was in fact a matter of remarkable simplicity. Finally, the principles of the policy were to be laid down by the Colonial Office alone, with little regard for the opinions of Ceylon officials with their myopic concentration on local circumstances. Pervading all these considerations was a deep religious fervour which was totally absent in the case of Rogers.

As regards the Ordinance itself Stephen's recommendations were simple – the Ordinance was to be rejected and the Buddhists instructed 'to make any kind of agreement among themselves . . .

[1] He was referring to Arthur Buller (Queen's Advocate).
[2] C.O. 54/223, Campbell to Stanley, no.37 of 7 February 1846, Stephen's minute of 26 January 1846.

for the Regulation of their own religious affairs, the custody of their Relics, and the choice of their Priests'.[1] All that would be necessary would be 'a Law to recognize, or perhaps, to establish this right'.[2]

Stephen, a shrewd judge of character, probably realized that it was difficult to move the deeply religious Gladstone to adopt a line of action that would involve the abrogation of promises made or obligations assumed under the terms of a treaty.

As regards the dissociation of the State from Buddhism, Gladstone confessed that he was willing to agree with Stephen on 'abstract grounds', but one is justified in concluding that these 'abstract grounds'[3] were as much political as they were religious – it was not merely the refusal of a Christian to countenance the association of a Colonial government with another religion, but also that liberal instinct which looked with suspicion on 'established' religions and was deeply hostile to the association of Church and State. In Ceylon we see glimpses of this attitude in Charles MacCarthy and H. C. Selby. He agreed that the Ordinance should be disallowed for the reasons outlined by Rogers, but realized that a rigid adherence to evangelical principles in matters relating to Buddhism would be unjust to the Kandyans. Faced with a choice between the diametrically opposed policies advocated by Rogers and Stephen, he came down heavily on the side of Rogers and moderation.

The foundation of Gladstone's Buddhist policy was his insistence that the British Government was morally obliged to create some sort of organization to whom the functions of the State in relation to Buddhism could be transferred.[4] Thus while Campbell's Ordinance was to be disallowed, Gladstone was convinced that it was imperative to instruct the Ceylon Government on the framing of a fresh

[1] Stephen's minute of 26 June 1846.

[2] *Ibid.*

[3] C.O. 54/223, Campbell to Stanley, no.37 of 7 February 1846, Gladstone's minute of 29 June 1846.

[4] Rogers himself was deeply conscious of this moral obligation. In a minute dated 30 June 1846 (on the same despatch), he declared that '. . . we shall break our original promise that Buddhism shall be maintained . . . if we first appropriate or allow to vest in ourselves [the] power necessary to the existence of Buddhism and then abandon them without enabling anyone else to take them up. . . .'

Ordinance. At the same time he was willing to concede that much more attention should be paid to the opinions of local officials in these matters.

Rogers, to whom he turned for assistance, convinced Gladstone that the principles of the new legislation should be outlined by the Colonial Office before Campbell's Ordinance was rejected.[1]

It was left to Gladstone now to lay down the principles to be followed in the new Ordinance. His suggestions read thus:

> As to our obligation, I think we are not entitled to turn around upon our construction of the Convention or to allow our protection in such a way that Buddhism shall *suffer* from it: . . . on the other hand it has no claim to stand better.
>
> These I think are the principles on which we should write with regard to the new Ordinance. We want for the future an effective practical separation and we should give to these religionists, of course avoiding at the same time whatever endangers law and the public peace, neither more or less (or as nearly as we can hit that mean) that it may be fair to presume they would have had if we had never interfered: so that no man may be able to say with justice hereafter either that we destroyed the religion unavowedly or that when it was destroying itsclf, we went out of our way and beyond our obligations and raised it from its natural death.
>
> The application of these principles can only be regulated on the spot.[2]

The significance of this minute lies in its rejection of James Stephen's ideas, and in its attempt to adopt a less uncompromising attitude. Had Gladstone stayed longer at the Colonial Office, the question of the State's connection with Buddhism might have been tackled with less rancour and more understanding and tolerance, but his was a brief stay of a few months, too brief indeed to leave his mark on this problem.

A double change, one at the Colonial Office where the third Earl Grey replaced Gladstone, and one in Ceylon where Viscount Torrington replaced Sir Colin Campbell, postponed for a few months a final decision on Campbell's despatch. This delay was sufficient for Stephen to regain lost ground. Earl Grey was in this matter a man after Stephen's own heart, and quite early in his administration he had become an active supporter of Stephen's point of view on the question of Buddhism. In a long minute

---

[1] Rogers' minute of 30 June 1846.   [2] Gladstone's minute of 1 July 1846.

which deserves extensive quotation he declared himself in complete agreement with Stephen, asserting that he would

> altogether deny the possibility of our being bound by any stipulation in a treaty to take an active part in maintaining and encouraging the abominable superstition called the Buddhist religion, nor do I see that the words quoted from the Treaty are susceptible of any such construct[n]. I also deny that in human affairs any immutable arrangement can be made by men of one generation wh[ich] men of all future generations are bound to abide by – The Sovereign authority in no country possesses or ought to possess the power of making laws binding even upon its successors. . . .[1]

He insisted that the convention should be 'construed liberally', the liberality of construction lying, it appears, in changing it to fit the needs and opinions of a new age. He believed like Stephen that it would be best to abstain from all legislation on the subject. In Grey's opinion it would be best

> simply to abdicate all those functions connected with . . . [Buddhism] which have hitherto devolved upon the Govt, leaving those who profess that religion to make such arrangements as may seem proper to themselves upon the subject but not giving to those arrangements any legal force – If however a law is absolutely necessary the objects to which it is directed ought to be very carefully and precisely determined; as far as I can understand the subject I can see none for which it is so necessary to provide except the regulation of the right of exempt[n] from taxat[n] of the temple lands.[2]

It was not necessary for Stephen to spend much time in winning Grey over to his point of view for the latter had reached these conclusions independently.

Grey did not seek the assistance of Rogers but instead he invited Stephen to 'oblige me by considering what instruct[ns] ought to be given upon it to the Governor and suggest them to me'.[3] The longed-for opportunity had arrived; Stephen was anxious to see that Torrington arrived in Ceylon with clear instructions on the policy to be followed. On Grey's instructions he prepared a draft of a despatch which he hoped 'will at least serve as a basis on which to proceed'.[4] This draft was adopted by Grey as his own

---

[1] Grey's minute of 30 Sept 1846.   [2] *Ibid.*
[3] *Ibid.*
[4] C.O. 54/227, Grey to Torrington, no.2 of 13 April 1847, Stephen's minute of 6 April 1847.

despatch: he did not change one single word in it, or for that matter a single comma or period. It was Stephen's last despatch on Buddhism rathern than Grey's first.

A remarkably uncompromising despatch, it was the high water mark of missionary influence on Colonial Office policy on Buddhism in Ceylon. It began with a criticism of Arthur Buller's interpretation of the Kandyan Convention – the petition of the Kandyans had used much the same arguments – and Stephen reiterated for Torrington's benefit his own interpretation.

> The Convention declares that the Religion of Buddha is inviolable and that its Rites, Ministers and places of worship are to be maintained and protected. The obvious meaning of these words is that the Buddhists should be free to celebrate their religious Rites and to hold all the places and property devoted to their worship without molestation from their new Sovereign or from any one else. The stipulation was little less than a copy of the language usually employed during the last war on every capitulation to British Arms. It is a form of which the meaning is, at first sight, sufficiently obvious and which usage in a great variety of cases has exempted from all ambiguity.[1]

Stephen was quite wrong in assuming that it was little else than a copy of the language employed 'on every capitulation to British Arms'. The hesitation of Bathurst and the criticisms of Wilberforce were quite incompatible with the idea of a stereotyped formula, and Brownrigg's assertion that the Convention employed language 'more emphatical than would have been my choice'[2] is compatible only with a deliberate departure from the usual form.

It must be remembered, too, that in the first place the Kandyan provinces were not conquered; they were ceded by the chiefs and the *bhikkus* without whose aid the expulsion of the last King of Kandy from his throne would have been extremely difficult. Secondly, whatever the form of the document, Britain undertook to maintain and protect Buddhism as a condition of the cession of the Kingdom. As Brownrigg himself admitted, without an undertaking couched in the most emphatic form it would have been impossible to placate the chiefs and *bhikkus* in 1815.

Even Stephen himself seems to have had doubts on this matter.

[1] C.O. 54/227, Grey to Torrington, no.2 of 13 April 1847.
[2] C.O. 54/55, Brownrigg to Bathurst, 15 March 1815.

For his despatch informed Torrington that even if Buller's interpretation were correct it ought to be rejected on the grounds that:

> The Christian Sovereign of a Christian State had no authority to
> bind himself and his successors to a course of conduct which Christian-
> ity unequivocally forbids. . . . [It meant] the maintenance of abomina-
> tions, to which, not merely the revealed Law of God, but the general
> conscience of mankind is irreconcilably hostile.[1]

The great defect of this argument, apart from its rampant
emotionalism and bigotry, was that it failed to draw a distinction
between a Government of Christians, which the British Government was, and a Christian Government, which it clearly was not.
The Kandyan Convention, from the point of view of the British
Government, was a political document. Religion had little to do
with it. Evangelical Christianity had in Stephen's case triumphed
over the rational consideration of political realities.

He informed Torrington that Campbell's Ordinance was rejected because it was based on a principle to which the Colonial
Office took strong objection:

> . . . the principle namely that we are not only bound to secure the
> Buddhists against molestation and injury in their persons or in their
> property on account of their religious observations, but [also] to
> advance further, and to enact and execute laws having for their
> express object the more easy, convenient, and orderly celebration
> of the Buddhist rites and ceremonies. . . .

He declared that the Ordinance assumed that 'the Convention
of 1815 vested in the Governor of Ceylon the appointment and
removal of the Priests and a controul [sic] over the internal discipline of the Ministers of the Buddhist Religion.' He denied that
'such is the real effect of the Convention'.

Stephen maintained that, in instances such as this, it was for the
Imperial Government to lay down the principles to be followed.
For,

> the present is a case in which the principles brought into debate
> depend, not upon any local circumstances, but upon considerations
> which can be appreciated with equal clearness in whatever country
> they may be discussed, or which (it may be no exaggeration to say)
> can be appreciated more clearly at a distance from the scene of
> action, than in the centre of a Society agitated by the proposed
> application of them to practice.

[1] C.O. 54/227, Grey to Torrington, no.2 of 13 April 1847.

He then proceeded to lay down, in the strongest possible language, the policy to be followed.

> To separate the British Government from all active participation in practices at once idolatrous and immoral, is a plain and simple, though a most urgent duty. That they who live in Ceylon may have a far clearer and more comprehensive perception than I have of the difficulties, and even of the dangers of performing that duty there, I do not, for a moment, dispute ... I trust that on a review of the subject, they will agree with me that the difficulties, whatever they may be, must be encountered, and that the danger whatever it may be, must be incurred, in order to maintain inviolable the sacred principle in question.[1]

P. E. Wodehouse was to complain that this despatch embodied a far more religious view of this question than Lord Stanley's despatches. 'It carried out the views, as we say in Ceylon, of the missionaries rather than any system of Government.'[2] Stephen, who could be so clear and precise in rejecting the Ordinance, did not bother to suggest an alternative. He merely stated that 'as far as I can judge, at this distance from the place, it appears to me that no Law whatever is necessary.'[3] The *bhikkus* should be told that they may regulate these matters for themselves and execute their own regulations as they should see best. He was still reading English experience into a different set-up, still imagining that Buddhism had an institutional structure akin to that of a Christian Church, and that the *bhikkus* had the organization with which to regulate those affairs which the State was to hand over to them.

James Stephen emerges in this period as by far the most important influence on the formulation of British policy on Buddhism. He was at the hub of affairs in his post of permanent Under-Secretary at the Colonial Office, an industrious, much maligned, and yet respected figure, wielding enormous influence on his political superiors. In a period of ten years from 1837–47, when six different Secretaries of State – Glenelg, Normanby, Russell, Stanley, Gladstone and Grey served at the Colonial Office, he was the one constant factor. He seemed to know precisely what was wanted, and set about getting it with ruthless efficiency.

To the missionaries, his presence at the Colonial Office seemed

---

[1] C.O. 54/227, Grey to Torrington, no.2 of 13 April 1847.
[2] *Second Report on Ceylon*, Evidence of Wodehouse, P. E., pp.253 ff.
[3] C.O. 54/227, Grey to Torrington, no.2 of 13 April 1847.

to be the Lord's own work. If the campaign against Buddhism and its connection with the Government reached its goal with so much less agitation[1] than that against the connection between the East India Company and Hinduism, two factors would explain the difference. First, there was the success of the Indian campaign, waged in England and in India, which made the task of preserving the connection of the Ceylon Government and Buddhism almost impossible. Secondly there was James Stephen, who was to the missionaries 'Our man in the Colonial Office', fighting their case for them better than they could have done themselves.

[1] It is significant that in the whole of this period, 1840–7, only once was this matter raised in Parliament; and even that was in the form of a question in the House of Commons, by Sir R. Inglis. See *Hansard*, 3rd series, LXXVII, 1320–1.

CHAPTER III

The Problem of Buddhism and the Attitude of the British Government, 1847–55

THE arrival of Viscount Torrington as Governor of Ceylon in 1847 marked a new phase in this problem. Stephen had made a complete conquest of Grey; through Stephen the missionary viewpoint had been accepted as Colonial Office policy.

Grey had briefed Torrington on the subject of Buddhism before the latter had left for Ceylon.[1] Indeed, he came to Ceylon with orders to effect the separation of the State from Buddhism as early as possible, and with specific instructions disallowing Ordinance 2 of 1846.[2] Torrington did not waste much time. He convened an assembly of Kandyan chiefs and *bhikkus* at Kandy, where he conveyed to them the gist of Grey's proposals.[3] He made it clear to the Kandyans that they had been invited to discuss the details of the dissociation and not the fact of dissociation itself. On 2 October 1847 the Temple of the Tooth was handed over to a committee consisting of a chief and two *bhikkus*,[4] a decision which the Kandyans accepted only with the utmost reluctance.

There were grave misgivings in Ceylon about Grey's despatch to Torrington disallowing the proposed Ordinance. Wodehouse explained that '. . . it left everything unsettled [and] laid down what we looked upon as very extreme views as to the future legislation that was to take place on the subject.'[5] There were fears that the handing over of the Temple would result in civil commotion because the Kandyan people, who attached great importance to the connection of the Government with Buddhism in any shape

---

[1] C.O. 54/227, Grey to Torrington, no.2 of 13 April 1847, Stephen's minute of 6 April 1847 and Grey's minute of 30 September 1846.

[2] *The Second Report on Ceylon*, the evidence of Wodehouse, P. E., pp. 249 ff.
Ibid., the evidence of Ackland, G., pp. 5 ff.

[3] C.O. 54/229, Torrington to Grey, no.133 and no.134 of 14 October 1847. Despatch 133 contains the minutes of the conference.

[4] *Ibid.* The idea of a Committee was Torrington's own; the Colonial Office had given him no instructions as to who was to be given charge of the Tooth Relic.

[5] *The Second Report on Ceylon*, the evidence of Wodehouse, P. E., pp.250 ff.

H

whatever, believed that the custody of the Tooth Relic by the Civil Government was equivalent to their religion being 'established' in the country.[1] At the conference there was strong opposition to the new policy, particularly from the *bhikkus* who took up the position that 'the Queen is the head of our religion, and that we wish it to be: that is what you promised and what you are bound to do'.[2] The chiefs too – though to a lesser degree than the *bhikkus* – considered the dissociation a most impolitic step. The common people were equally disappointed with the new policy.[3]

One of the great practical difficulties stemming from Grey's refusal to ratify the Ordinance was that vacancies in *viharas* and *devales* could not be filled, and temple authorities had no legal status. Some tenants of temple properties took advantage of the situation to withhold the services due from them, and this, even more than the handing over of the Tooth Relic, alienated the *bhikkus* who felt that by this means they were being deprived of all their temporal power.[4] Tennent declared that the dissociation would not have alienated the *bhikkus* and people so much, 'if we had legislated to restore their temporalities and their property to the state of order in which we found them; but on the contrary our policy has thrown it into confusion.'[5]

It was not long before Torrington realized that the Buddhist problem was more complex than Grey had suggested. In a private letter to Grey he observed that the problem had not been understood or explained properly to the Secretary of State: 'The question at home has been considered as a religious one – Religion is the least part of the question.'[6] Instead, he emphasized the importance of the question of Buddhist Temporalities, which he felt would become the great problem of the immediate future. But he had other and more serious misgivings. He confided in Grey that 'Mr Carr, the Acting C[hief] J[ustice] says, argue it as you will on

---

[1] C.O. 54/229, Torrington to Grey, no.134 of 14 October 1847, P. E. Wodehouse's minute of 13 October 1847.

The Second Report on Ceylon, evidence of Ackland, G., pp.15 ff.

Ibid., evidence of Wodehouse, P. E., p.264.

[2] *The Second Report on Ceylon*, evidence of Wodehouse, P. E., p.253.

[3] *Ibid.*, the evidence of Ackland, G., pp.10–11.

[4] *Ibid.*

[5] *The Third Report on Ceylon*, the evidence of Tennent, p.215.

[6] Grey MSS., Torrington to Grey, 15 August 1847.

the highest moral grounds, in Law we have committed a breach of faith . . .'[1]

Torrington's Executive Councillors had equally serious doubts of their own on these matters. Wodehouse feared that the act of dissociation – particularly the ostentatious handing over of the Tooth Relic – would lead to disturbances.[2] (In fact, it passed off without incident.) His colleagues were not so pessimistic, but they all insisted on the urgent need for a legislative enactment safeguarding the property rights of the Temples. Both MacCarthy and Tennent explained that the protection of property rights was not a religious question but an indisputable civil right. MacCarthy pointed out that these property rights and interests 'are so many and various that it [would] . . . be quite out of the power of the British Government without formally abdicating its sovereignty to abstain from legislating on them in the fullest detail.'[3] He had grasped the fundamental fact that Buddhism had no central organization; that there was

> no such recognized or organized body in existence as a Bhuddist [sic] priesthood or church; and above all there [was] no sort of analogy, between the position of the British Government as regards the Temple lands and other temporalities of the Kandyan provinces, and its relations with any Christian Church or community in any part of its dominions. . . .[4]

But both Wodehouse and MacCarthy took objection to the committee to whom the Tooth Relic had been handed over – Wodehouse, because he believed that the committee was 'without law and title';[5] MacCarthy, because it would create 'a state within a state, [and] would throw a strong engine of political and social power into hands often unfaithful, always unsteady'.[6]

The Executive Councillors ended on a note of cautious optimism. MacCarthy and Tennent believed that the dissociation of the State from Buddhism would lead to the ultimate triumph of Christianity and the corresponding decline of Buddhism. Tennent was very emphatic on this point, confidently asserting that the

[1] *Ibid.*

[2] C.O. 54/229, Torrington to Grey, no.134 of 14 October 1847, Wodehouse's minute of 13 October 1847.

[3] *Ibid.* MacCarthy's minute of 7 October 1847.   [4] *Ibid.*

[5] *Ibid.* Wodehouse's minute, 13 October 1847.

[6] *Ibid.* MacCarthy's minute, *op. cit.*

severance of the State's connection with Buddhism would in reality mean 'the withdrawal of the only stay that could much longer have retarded its decay'.[1]

The extent to which Torrington's views had been influenced by the opinion of his officials is indicated by the fact that, apart from supporting them in the despatch that accompanied their minutes, he also sent a private letter to Grey in which he explained that he attached the greatest importance to the opinions expressed in those minutes.[2] And he endeavoured to make Grey understand that once the connection between Buddhism and the State had been severed, it was imperative that the energies of the Government should be concentrated on the provision of detailed legislation concerning Temple lands and Temporalities, without which much serious confusion and evil would result.[3]

But Earl Grey was too delighted with the quiet efficiency with which the dissociation had been effected to heed these pleas and warnings. He hailed Torrington's acts as '. . . open and outward manifestations of the great principles on which my instructions of the 13th April last [were] based; that of a complete and thorough dissociation of the British Government from religious practices repugnant to their essential Christianity. . . .'[4] He was willing, however, to admit that the British Government, as a temporal soverign power, still had a function to perform in its relations with Buddhism; he left the local Government to resolve the important question of what this function was to be. In fact, he stated explicitly that the initiative on the problem of Buddhism was in future to lie with the Ceylon Government. In spite of these concessions, however, Grey gave no indication that he had realized the importance of the question of temple lands in the settlement of the Buddhist problem.

Before this despatch reached Ceylon, the disturbances of 1848 broke out in the Kandyan provinces. Torrington ascribed them chiefly to the measures of the Government in regard to Buddhism from Mackenzie's time to his own. During the disturbances he was obliged to direct the Government Agent of the Central Province, C. R. Buller, to resume the custody of the Tooth Relic,

---

[1] *Ibid.* Tennent's minute, 11 October 1847.
[2] Grey MSS., Torrington to Grey, 14 October 1847.
[3] *Ibid.*
[4] C.O. 54/245, Grey to Torrington, no.257 of 19 July 1848.

which the Kandyans regarded as the 'palladium of political power'.[1]

For Torrington the disturbances were a bitter and unforgettable experience. He was convinced that the chiefs and priests had indeed engineered them; but he was equally convinced that they had been driven to this opposition mainly by the religious policy of the Government. He explained to Grey that the Government's Buddhist policy had struck '. . . a blow . . . at Buddhism which each year has been more severely felt. Temples are without Head Priests; those *who act* cannot legally enforce their rights and are cheated of their dues'.[2] He was deeply impressed by the words of a Kandyan Chief who had asked him: 'What good have we gained by British Rule if you violate our Treaties – not only cease to protect our Religion but on the contrary endeavour to destroy it?'[3] The same individual had complained that the Kandyans 'had been unfairly and unjustly used in this, *a matter to us of the utmost importance*'.[4] Torrington was moved to inform Grey that: '. . . unless we hold some moral control over the Chiefs and Priests, unless they have some advantage by supporting the Government, we shall always be liable to Treason and Rebellion. They have great power over the people who blindly obey their orders.'[5] He explained that this 'moral control' could be obtained by evolving a new Kandyan policy, in which the early settlement of the Buddhist problem, by the enactment of an Ordinance to protect Buddhist Temporalities, would have the highest priority.

Torrington's first move in the direction of a new policy was the exemption of the *bhikkus* from liability to service or payment in commutation of service under the Road Ordinance of 1848, which he did in the face of strong opposition from the Bishop of Colombo and some of the clergy.

Then in January 1849 he submitted to Grey the draft of an Ordinance which, while effecting the desired dissociation between the State and Buddhism, at the same time protected the legal rights of the *viharas* and *devales*. In sending this draft Ordinance home he did not go the length of positively recommending it, but

---

[1] C.O. 54/258, Torrington to Grey, no.54 of 14 April 1849; Grey MSS. Torrington to Grey, 11 August 1848.

[2] Grey MSS., Torrington to Grey, 11 August 1848.

[3] *Ibid.*   [4] *Ibid.*

[5] *Ibid.*

merely indicated that if Grey agreed he would introduce it in the
Legislative Council in June 1849, as a final settlement of this
vexed problem.[1] This Ordinance, a hastily drafted rehash of
Campbell's Ordinance 2 of 1846, was prepared at a time when
the country had not yet recovered from the disturbances of 1848,
and was obviously meant to pacify the Kandyans. The powers of
the Government in relation to Buddhism were to be handed over
to a committee of Chiefs and *bhikkus*; it followed Campbell's
Ordinance in this, as in most other matters, the only difference
between the two committees being that in Torrington's the chiefs
outnumbered the *bhikkus*. Whether this was a matter of deliberate
choice cannot be established, but it is significant that at the
conference on the Buddhist problem held in 1847 it was always
the *bhikkus* who were more vehement in their opposition to the
new policy.[2]

This projected Ordinance was severely criticized by P. E.
Wodehouse and, ironically, his criticisms were concentrated on
the committee to which the powers of the Government were to be
handed over. It was Wodehouse who had drafted Campbell's
Ordinance of 1846, in which these same powers were handed over
to a similar committee. Wodehouse contended that the committee
envisaged in the new Ordinance would create a powerful, close,
corporation of chiefs, likely to be injurious to the interests of the
Government and oppressive to the mass of the people. At the
same time, the authority and influence of the *bhikkus* would be too
much diminished, partly because they would always be a minority
on the committee, and partly because the power of election of
bhikkus to the committee was vested not in the whole body of *bhikkus*
but in the committee only.[3] This first criticism could just as well
have been made of the committee envisaged in his own Ordinance;
the validity of his second criticism, from the point of view of the
British administration in Ceylon, would depend very much on the
question of which of the two groups – the Kandyan Chiefs or the
bhikkus – was held to be potentially more dangerous to British rule.
Perhaps Torrington thought the *bhikkus* to be the more dangerous
group, while Wodehouse was more afraid of the chiefs. But the
issue was never as clear cut as that; there were individuals in

[1] C.O. 54/257, Torrington to Grey, no.16 of 5 January 1849.
[2] C.O. 54/229, Torrington to Grey, no.133 and no.134 of 14 October 1847.
[3] C.O. 54/257, Torrington to Grey, no.24 of 12 February 1849.

both groups who were willing to support the British, and there were others who were implacably hostile.

At the Colonial Office, too, the disturbances of 1848 had a sobering effect. Religious factors were believed to be a major cause of these disturbances, at least to the extent that the chiefs and *bhikkus* had been antagonized by the new policy on Buddhism.[1] There was some reluctance, now, to proceed further with that policy for fear of aggravating the sense of grievance that prevailed among the Kandyans. Grey himself began to have doubts about the virtues of his Buddhist policy, and he gradually abandoned the uncompromising stand he had adopted earlier. His uncompromising attitude had been strengthened by Stephen's advice, but the latter's retirement in 1847 cleared the way for a more generous and less doctrinaire attitude. His successor, Herman Merivale, in no way his inferior in ability, was also more practical and much less 'religious' in his approach to this problem. The new Colonial Office 'expert' on Buddhism was William Strachey, a man with some practical experience of Indian administration,[2] whose attitude to the Buddhist problem was remarkably free from the religious intolerance that had characterized Stephen's. In the background there was the Parliamentary Committee investigating the affairs of Ceylon, remorselessly cross-examining officials and private persons on the affairs of the colony.

It was Strachey who examined Torrington's Ordinance. In a long minute, and an equally long memorandum, he explained why the draft Ordinance ought not to be approved. His main criticism was that it resembled Campbell's rejected Ordinance too much; that it provided for much the same sort of committee to take over the functions of the Government and, in Strachey's opinion, this committee gave to Buddhism a degree of comprehensive and efficient organization such as it had never possessed before. He took objection to this, on the grounds that 'all that we are bound to do is to secure to Buddhists a fair equivalent and substitute for the Government interference now to be withdrawn

[1] Grey, *op. cit.*, II, pp.182–3.

[2] See: Sanders, C. R., *The Strachey Family 1588–1932* (Duke University Press, 1953), pp.211 ff. Strachey had served the East India Company as a writer from 1838 to 1843. He joined the Colonial Office sometime in 1848, and largely because of his Indian experience he was consulted on the more important problems relating to Ceylon and, in particular, the question of Buddhism.

– to see that Buddhism does not suffer – not to revive a declining system in unusual vigour'.[1]

His second criticism was that this Ordinance did not dissolve, but re-established the connection between the State and Buddhism. True, neither the Governor nor the Government Agent had to appoint or confirm the appointment of any persons but minor officials, native chieftains holding government appointments, were *ex-officio* members of the committee which was to possess great powers both secular and religious, holding full control over every kind of question relating to the management of Temples and the religious discipline of *bhikkus* and votaries.[2]

Strachey's objections to the inclusion of minor native officials in the committee anticipated similar objections which missionary organizations and representatives of Christian groups in Ceylon were to raise in 1853–4. But Strachey's objections sprang as much from considerations of liberal political thought – an antipathy to the association of State and Religion – as from a Christian's reluctance to allow the continued association, in any form whatever, of a colonial government with an alien religion.

Strachey concentrated his attention on the committee. Recent events in Ceylon were very much in his mind when he wrote this minute. He feared that the committee would increase the political power of the Kandyan aristocracy and the *bhikkus* – 'that very aristocracy and hierarchy which are the natural enemies of our rule and have been at the bottom of every insurrection since our rule began'. The Ordinance, he asserted, did not even possess the advantage that it would be popular with the *bhikkus* and chiefs who in 1847 had strongly opposed a similar plan. Then, referring to the divisions that had been evident among the chiefs and priests in 1847, he remarked that:

> the existing jealousies between the chiefs and priests should have been made the ground by us for making no general committee at all. The Committee once formed, designing men will find means to reconcile those jealousies and to convert the combined influence of both parties to purposes inimical to the British. The present Ordinance is at once irritating and invigorating to the native aristocracy and hierarchy.

[1] C.O. 54/257, Torrington to Grey, no.16 of 5 January 1849, Strachey's minute of 20 March 1849 and his memorandum of 21 April 1849. This memorandum reproduced his minute of 20 March 1849.   [2] *Ibid.*

Further, Strachey believed that the powers given to the committee would constitute a revolution in local customs; he was referring to the fact that under this Ordinance the *viharas* and *devales* would be under one common management, while they had hitherto been kept separate. Besides, he noted that there was no evidence to show that the mode prescribed by the Ordinance for electing *bhikkus* and other functionaries was at all consistent with existing customs.

But Strachey did not stop with a mere criticism of the Ordinance; he also suggested that Torrington ought to be censured for submitting an Ordinance so much like the one rejected in 1846–7. He recommended – and this was to be his main recommendation – that a new and thorough enquiry into the whole problem ought to be instituted by someone other than Wodehouse.[1]

One concession he was willing to allow to the Kandyans without this preliminary enquiry. He contended that Grey's despatches did not convey any specific instructions to Torrington to stop the annual grant to the Temple from public funds. Here Strachey was surely right, for a reading of Grey's despatches would suggest that no specific instructions were given, the matter being left to the Governor's discretion. Strachey recommended that this grant be renewed, if there were a positive undertaking to make it.[2]

Grey was so impressed with Strachey's minute that he had it printed, with only very slight alterations, as a memorandum for the Parliamentary Committee. (The rebuke to Torrington was omitted on Merivale's advice.) The same memorandum was sent to Ceylon as an enclosure in Grey's despatch on Torrington's Ordinance.[3] The memorandum recommended the grant of a free gift of land to the Temples, 'somewhat commensurate in value with the money grant which had been discontinued'. It suggested the appointment of some competent person to review the whole problem of the State's connection with Buddhism, and recommended that the powers hitherto possessed by the Government should be transferred to some less 'powerful' and more

[1] Strachey's suggestion was that this person should 'examine the records, visit the temples, confer with the different parties interested [and] . . . ascertain the precise functions hitherto performed by the Government in relation to Buddhism.' Strachey believed that Wodehouse was responsible for 'misleading' both Campbell and Torrington.

[2] Strachey's minute of 20 March 1849.

[3] Enclosed in C.O. 54/261, Grey to Torrington, no.384 of 13 April 1849

'general' Buddhist association. Grey's own despatch was brief; he left it to be understood that he agreed on the whole with Strachey's memorandum. Among the reasons he gave for arriving at this decision was the fact that he found Wodehouse's objections to be of so 'fundamental a character', that they materially strengthened the case against approving the Ordinance. He suggested that Torrington should reconsider the whole problem, paying particular attention to another plan recommended to Grey, according to which each of the different Buddhist establishments connected with the Government in the Kandyan provinces should receive its own independent organization in place of the politically dangerous measure adopted in Campbell's, as well as Torrington's, Ordinance. It was obvious that Grey, like Strachey, rejected this Ordinance mainly because of its political implications. That was not the only moral he drew from the disturbances of 1848; he had also learnt to be less doctrinaire on this issue. His despatch concluded with the advice, which Torrington and his civil servants hardly needed, to settle this difficult problem in a mode less open to controversy. With this in view, he stated his willingness to defer the relinquishing of Government interference in temple appointments.[1]

In the meantime, the Buddhist problem overshadowed all others in Ceylon. Torrington had now come round to the view that the policy pursued since Stanley's tenure of office should be quietly abandoned, and that there should be a reversion to the old policy.[2] He considered Stanley's policy to be altogether mistaken on religious grounds, while the disturbances had shown how dangerous it was politically. But it was Mackenzie who came in for the severest criticism; Torrington commented that 'he [Mackenzie] refused to fulfil a duty as binding and imperative on him as any other portion of the trust committed to his charge. He mistook an act purely temporal for one of a spiritual nature'.[3]

Torrington had received several petitions from *bhikkus* complain-

[1] C.O. 54/261, Grey to Torrington, no.384 of 23 April 1849.

[2] C.O. 54/258, Torrington to Grey, no.67 of 10 May 1849. (This despatch was sent before the arrival of Grey's despatch no.384 of 23 April 1849.) Torrington believed that it was best for the Government to retrace their steps and to attempt no legislation at all on the Buddhist question. He had an interesting reason for this – he believed that if there was no legislation, Buddhism would sink of itself; legislation would only perpetuate it.

[3] C.O. 54/258, Torrington to Grey, no.67 of 10 May 1849.

ing of the difficulties they had in asserting any of their traditional rights of property for the lack of warrants of appointments, which had been discontinued since 1847. The disorganization that stemmed from this also affected the tenants and cultivators of temple lands, for they were deprived of their former security of tenure. He was anxious to give the *bhikkus* satisfaction on this issue, as it would be a positive demonstration of goodwill. He asked for authority to resume the practice of granting these warrants of appointment, urging that it was a purely secular act affecting rights of property. He added that it was the duty of the Government to protect all parties in the enjoyment of their property, whatever their religion might be.

But the real emphasis of his arguments was on the fact that this was among the obligations on Buddhism undertaken at the Kandyan Convention. He explained that

> We are bound to protect [the Buddhists] in the exercise of their religion, . . . [Buddhism] is the religion of the people, and till the ministrations of [Christian missionaries] . . . shall have dispelled the darkness which still hangs over the minds of the people it is both wise and prudent to protect it.

He outlined the advantages of the line of policy he advocated:

> By Government appointing priests we have a hold and a satisfactory check on their proceedings; we can ensure the appointment of the best intentioned and most respectable of the priests; and their knowledge of the power we possess will ensure the proper fulfilment of their duties, and prevent any attempts at treasonable practices.[1]

Torrington's views were supported by most members of his Executive Council. MacCarthy also believed that it was necessary for Government to interfere in the matter of Buddhist temporalities, if only as a temporary measure, in the absence of a final settlement. But, since the difficulties of legislation were almost insurmountable, he suggested that it would be best to resume the practice, which had worked well in the past, of the Government appointing the *bhikkus* and *basnayake nilames*, without reference to their spiritual duties, but simply to protect their temporal rights. There was another argument as well; Government interference in these matters was a 'purely temporal function of sovereignty itself, and therefore an abandonment of it was tantamount to an aban-

---

[1] C.O. 54/258, Torrington to Grey, no.67 of 10 May 1849.

donment of that sovereignty'.[1] This was a rather radical contention for that age, but then MacCarthy was more secular in his outlook than the great bulk of his contemporaries.

Tennent gave his support to Torrington and MacCarthy. His
minute was noteworthy for the analogy he drew between what
was happening to temple property in Ceylon as a consequence of
the refusal to grant warrants of appointment, and what might
happen in England if the Established Church were precipitately
dis-established.[2]

The only member of the Executive Council to disagree with
these opinions was H. C. Selby, the Queen's Advocate, but even
he admitted that the Buddhist temporalities had suffered much as
a consequence of the refusal to sign warrants of appointment. He
also admitted the great difficulty of legislating in a manner satisfactory to all parties. But if Selby was unique in suggesting the
continuation of Grey's policy, he did so for reasons that had little
to do with religion. He recommended the continuation of Grey's
policy because of the great publicity that had been given to it,
maintaining that to go back on it would be a loss of face. Besides,
an attempt on the part of the Government to retrace its steps
'would have an injurious effect' on the native mind; the people
would misunderstand the reasons for the change of course (they
would perhaps attribute it to fear engendered by the riots) and
not look upon it as a simple act of justice.[3]

In the Colonial Office there was a great deal of sympathy with
much that was said by Torrington and MacCarthy. Merivale and
Benjamin Hawes, Grey's Parliamentary Under-Secretary, agreed
with the general views of Torrington, Tennent and MacCarthy;
they both regretted the course begun by Mackenzie, whom they
blamed for the existing confusion.[4]

But it was one thing to regret the past and another to take as
strong a step as Torrington recommended, '. . . viz. to retrace our
way altogether, undo all that has been done since 1840 and revert
to the old state of things.'[5] Merivale rejected this suggestion for

[1] *Ibid.*, minute of MacCarthy, C. J., enclosed.
[2] C.O. 54/258, minute of Tennent enclosed.
[3] C.O. 54/258, Torrington to Grey, no.67 of 10 May 1849, Selby's minute.
[4] *Ibid.* Merivale's minute of 30 June 1849. Hawes' minutes of 1 July 1849
and 13 August 1849.
[5] *Ibid.* Merivale's minute, *op. cit.*

much the same reasons as Selby and recommended instead a middle course; the draft Ordinance was to be rejected for the reasons given by Strachey, and at the same time the Governor was to be directed to devise some scheme involving less political danger. In the meantime he was to be authorized to revert, without delay, to the old plan of issuing warrants for the appointment of *bhikkus* and other officers connected with the Temples, until some more satisfactory method was devised.

Strachey, who believed that it was Torrington rather than Mackenzie who was to blame for the existing confusion, returned to his view that the settlement of this question depended not so much on the framing of instructions as on the selection of a man, a special Commissioner, to proceed to the Temples, make minute enquiry into this and related subjects, and submit a detailed plan.[1] Hawes, on the other hand, suggested that the old practice (as suggested by Torrington) should be reverted to, temporarily, pending a settlement of the problem. Rejecting Strachey's suggestion of a special Commissioner, Hawes recommended that the matter be left for the decision of the Parliamentary Committee.[2]

What was Grey to make of all these suggestions? To let the Parliamentary Committee settle the whole problem would be a 'most improper abandonment of the duties of the Executive Govt. to a parly. Comm.', and Strachey's suggestion of a Commissioner was 'a different way of evading the responsibility of a dec'sⁿ'. As far as his own views on a settlement were concerned, Grey realized that there was no completely satisfactory solution possible, and that the best that could be done was 'to effect such a settlement of it as may upon the whole be open to the fewest objections'.[3] While he took the view that Torrington's draft Ordinance should be rejected for the reasons that Strachey had given, he was now inclined to sympathize with the stand taken by Torrington and MacCarthy, though he would not go as far as accepting their suggestion of a return to the old system.

Nothing demonstrated the change in Grey's attitude to the Buddhist problem better than his acceptance of the need for legal measures for the protection of temple property. A sober pragmatism had replaced his old doctrinaire approach: '[Experience] having shown that the preservation of the property [of temples],

[1] Strachey's minute, 8 August 1849.   [2] Hawes' minute of 1 July 1849.
[3] Grey's minute of 18 September 1849.

which we have promised, cannot be ensured without the assistance of Government we will do what is necessary for this purpose.'[1]

Grey's new-found diffidence was to serve the Ceylon Government well. It certainly made it much easier to settle the problem on an equitable basis. But the recall of Torrington and Tennent in the course of 1850 made it inevitable that a settlement would be postponed.

Torrington's successor, Sir George Anderson, was a man with wide Indian experience (he had served the East India Company in Western India). In 1849 the Colonial Office had sent him as Governor of Mauritius, and he had hardly served two years there when Grey appointed him to Ceylon. Tennent's successor as Colonial Secretary was C. J. MacCarthy.

Anderson and MacCarthy had one thing in common – neither of them was actively interested in the propagation of Christianity, or associated with missionary activity. With Anderson, this was largely the result of his experience in India, for he knew that religion was a most combustible element in the social structure of the Indian sub-continent.[2]

He had not been long in Ceylon before he realized that the Buddhist issue was the most important problem that faced his administration. He was quick to grasp the crucial fact that Buddhism had no central organization, and that this made it difficult for the State to abandon its connection with that religion abruptly.[3] In August 1851 he informed Grey that, after a full consideration of the subject, he saw no alternative but to continue the former practice in the appointment of *bhikkus* and *basnayake nilames*.[4] He had the unanimous support of his Executive Council on this matter.

Anderson had no sooner made up his mind that the old system of warrants of appointment should be resumed, than it became publicly known that he had done so. The strong opinions of Viscount Torrington and some members of the Executive Council, in support of the same course of action, were made public at about the same time. The evidence given before the Parliamentary Committee on Ceylon was published in the local newspapers,

[1] *Ibid.*
[2] Grey MSS., Anderson to Grey, 13 December 1851 and 13 January 1852.
[3] Grey MSS., Anderson to Grey, 13 August 1851. C.O. 54/281, Anderson to Grey, no. 134 of 14 August 1851.   [4] *Ibid.*

along with Torrington's despatches and the minutes of the Executive Council on Buddhism.[1]

Some time after his arrival he sent a circular to the Government Agents and their assistants, empowering them to grant warrants of appointments to *bhikkus* and *basnayake nilames* in the Kandyan provinces. This circular alarmed the supporters of the policy of dissociation, who found in *The Ceylon Times* an eager and enthusiastic critic of Anderson's policies. This newspaper denounced the new policy as a disgrace to a Christian Government, and called upon the Bishop of Colombo to petition the Queen on this matter. It urged all Christian groups, Baptists and Catholics included,[2] to 'raise the banner of protest and preach a Crusade against the system of Christian connection with a heathen system.'[3] The appeal did not go unheeded. Though the Bishop refused to be drawn into this campaign, the rest of the Anglican clergy – led by the Archdeacon of Colombo, Dr B. Bailey, and the Principal of the Colombo Academy, Dr B. Boake (himself an Anglican clergyman) – took the initiative in this matter for the first time. Their first move was a petition signed by the Archdeacon and seventeen other Anglican clergymen, condemning the resumption of the practice of signing warrants of appointment.[4] The petition declared that this was tantamount to a support of heathenism, and claimed that it would be a fresh obstacle in the way of conversion. Anderson patiently explained that the Temples requiring these warrants of appointment were few in number, and that the warrants were to be issued only in essential cases to enable the temples to protect their rights of property in the courts of law.[5] But this explanation did not satisfy the Christian groups in Ceylon, who proceeded to bombard Anderson with petitions, while *The Ceylon Times* backed the Archdeacon and other missionary campaigners with a series of

[1] *The Ceylon Times* of 14 June 1850, contained a bitter attack on the views of Wodehouse, Tennent and MacCarthy on the Buddhist problem. The *Colombo Observer*, in its issue of 11 November 1850, singled out MacCarthy for criticism on the same score. In its opinion MacCarthy was responsible for the shift in the Government's attitude to Buddhism.

[2] At this time the Anglicans were seldom willing to associate themselves openly with either of these groups.

[3] *The Ceylon Times*, 8 August 1851; see also the issues of 5 and 19 August 1851.

[4] C.O. 54/288, Anderson to Grey, no.10 of 10 January 1852.

[5] *Ibid.* See enclosed letter of Anderson to the Bishop of Colombo, 29 December 1852. C.O. 54/282, Anderson to Grey, no.170 of 4 November 1851. Grey MSS., Anderson to Grey, 13 January 1852.

violent editorials and letters to the editor. The Archdeacon and his supporters sent in another petition protesting against any relaxation of the policy laid down by Stanley and Grey. It earned much the same reply from Anderson as the previous petition; but Anderson included in his reply an appeal for tolerance in this matter. The appeal read as follows:

> [The Government] gives [Buddhism] no other favour, no other countenance, no other protection as a religion than what the British Government gives in all countries which it has acquired, and yet where idolatry may exist and prevail, that is, a perfect toleration; but we must ever recollect that offensive and abusive attacks on a religion by an opposing but dominant party is [sic] not toleration but persecution.

It was the first time in the history of this dispute that a Governor of Ceylon had adopted so firm an attitude against the missionaries.

A petition signed on behalf of the Baptists, by Dr C. Elliott and two other deacons of the Baptist congregation at Colombo, was of a rather different sort. Though they regretted as much as any of the other Christian groups the connection between the State and Buddhism, they nevertheless deplored the tendency to ignore the obligations that the Government had undertaken at the Kandyan Convention of 1815. They commented that when

> the British Government have expended a considerable part of the Revenue in building places of Christian worship in the Kandyan country and in supporting an ecclesiastical establishment whose duties are avowedly hostile to and aggressive upon Buddhism, there can be no question that the compact has been violated.[1]

Their solution was simple, but radical; Government should sever its connections with all religions and not merely with Buddhism alone. They wanted the 'disestablishment' of the Anglican Church as well, but Anderson ignored their suggestions.

Anderson found himself faced with a well-organized missionary campaign; indeed, never had the missionary agitation on this issue reached such a pitch. At the back of his mind there was always the

---

[1] C.O. 54/288, Anderson to Grey, no.17 of 13 January 1852, the petition of the Baptists enclosed. The petition pointed out that, while Buddhist temples had been allowed to go to ruin, the Government had constructed 'a beautiful' church beside the crumbling Temple of the Tooth in Kandy; and that, while *bhikkus* were being deprived of their 'trifling' emoluments from the Government, the money spent on the Anglican Establishment had been augmented.

fear that this missionary campaign would result in religious strife. He explained to Grey that the warrants of appointments were to be issued

> only in those cases where they are absolutely necessary for the protection of the secular rights of the incumbents of Temples; and until some other arrangement can be made for securing that object without the intervention of Government, I conceive that we are bound in justice as well as by treaty to continue to afford them protection in the manner in which it has hitherto been done.[1]

He added the warning that

> under the state of excitement which has been so industriously fomented, it would at all events at present be very impolitic to make any change, for such would not be attributed to any desire on the part of the Government to be relieved of the existing difficulties, but to the influence and violence of the clergy against the religion of the country.[2]

He was forced to emphasise this theme again and again in the course of 1852. From November 1851 to January 1852 a series of six *Letters of Vetus* was published in *The Ceylon Times* condemning not only Anderson's attitude to the problem of Buddhism, but also the whole trend of Government policy on that problem since the disturbances. There was a bitter division within the Anglican Church on this issue; the Bishop supported Anderson, while the Archdeacon and Dr Boake attacked the Bishop for his stand in pamphlet, speech and sermon. The *Letters of Vetus* concentrated on government officials, paying particular attention to Torrington's despatches, and the minutes prepared by MacCarthy and Tennent. These letters did not introduce any new argument, but the violence of the language used, and the insulting references made in them to the indigenous religions, attracted Anderson's attention. On inquiry it became evident that these letters were written by the Archdeacon, who, when challenged by the Governor, boldly acknowledged himself to be the author.[3]

---

[1] C.O. 54/293, Anderson to Grey, no.11 of 10 January 1852.   [2] *Ibid.*

[3] The only original note in these letters was the reliance on Blackstone's *Commentaries on the Laws of England* to prove the nullity of the Kandyan Convention. 'But in conquered or ceded countries that have already laws of their own, the King may indeed alter and change these laws; but till he does change and alter them, the ancient laws of the country remain – UNLESS SUCH AS ARE AGAINST THE LAW OF GOD, AS IN AN INFIDEL COUNTRY.'

I

Bailey was not the man to relent, even when it was obvious that the Governor disapproved of his tactics. He turned on the Bishop and condemned him for what he considered to be his lack of courage, faith and principle in not joining in this campaign. Boake, not to be outdone, delivered a sermon condemning not only the Bishop but the Governor as well. Then followed a furious triangular correspondence between Bailey and Boake on one side and Anderson and Bishop Chapman on the other two, in the course of which the Bishop considered himself to have been insulted by Bailey and Boake. Bailey went a step further and published, under his own name, a letter in *The Ceylon Times* appealing for public sympathy against the Governor.[1]

Anderson was shocked at the insubordination of the clergy to their Bishop, and their turbulence alarmed him. He was concerned about the attacks on the Government, and annoyed by Boake's sermon. But it was the intemperate and abusive attack on Buddhism in the *Letters of Vetus*, 'in language so violent and offensive as calculated to excite and exasperate the whole Buddhist population,' that alarmed him most. A recent incident in Bombay, where the attacks of a Parsee journalist on Mohammedanism had led to a riot which was quelled only by the army, was fresh in Anderson's mind and he feared these attacks on Buddhism by the clergy might have similar results in Ceylon.[2]

In the meantime, the Kandyan chiefs and *bhikkus* presented Anderson with a petition in which they invoked the Kandyan Convention to support their claim for renewed warrants of appointment. They emphasised the fact that these certificates had nothing whatever to do with their religion, and that any criticism of the Government on this account was baseless. The petition was clearly meant to help Anderson in meeting the criticisms of the missionaries. Anderson called Grey's particular attention to its contents as, confirming Anderson's own views on the matter.[3] But he was less concerned about buttressing his policy with Kandyan support than with the need to check the activities of the Archdeacon and his associates.

At the Colonial Office, Strachey sympathized with the Archdeacon, and considered Anderson's line of policy to be misguided,

---

[1] C.O. 54/293, Anderson to Grey, no.18 of 14 January 1852.
[2] Grey MSS., Anderson to Grey, 12 December 1851 and 13 January 1852.
[3] C.O. 54/293, Anderson to Grey, no.18 of 14 January 1852.

but he had no support from either Grey or Hawes. Grey, in particular, was now anxious that the whole problem should be settled as quietly and as soon as possible. He directed that Anderson's suggestions should be accepted, but as purely provisional and temporary measures until a fresh policy should be formulated. He made the significant confession that he was

> prepared to admit that much mischief had resulted from measures adopted by my predecessors and myself upon imperfect information and which were not consistent with the spirit of our engagements to the people of Ceylon. This is indeed the justification of the course it is now proposed to adopt.[1]

Grey was in no mood to tolerate the intransigence of the Anglican clergy. After some deliberation, he called upon Bailey to resign his appointment or face dismissal. Boake was severely reprimanded and informed that he would not be considered for appointment to another Diocese. Grey commended the Bishop for his support of the Governor and declared firmly that he disapproved of the practice of clergymen, paid by the State, attacking Government policy in the newspapers or from the pulpit.[2]

The punishment meted out to Bailey and Boake did not pass unnoticed in Ceylon. *The Colombo Observer*, which normally supported Anderson, felt on this occasion that he had committed an error of judgement in taking Bailey and Boake so seriously.[3] *The Ceylon Times* treated the punishment of these two clergymen as a betrayal of Christianity itself and an ignoble surrender to 'idolatry'.[4] *The Ceylon Examiner*, which had always been an outspoken supporter of Anderson's policy on Buddhism and had more than once criticized Bailey for his intransigence, commented that the Archdeacon could hardly be called a Christian martyr. 'A martyr is one who suffers for conscience sake, which is not the case with the Archdeacon; he is simply the victim of his own unhappy temper.'[5]

But Bailey's retirement, far from being the end of the battle,

---

[1] Grey's minute of 7 January 1852 in C.O. 54/282, Anderson to Grey, no. 170 of 4 November 1851.
[2] C.O. 54/293, Grey to Anderson, no.59 of 8 July 1852.
[3] *The Colombo Observer*, 5 February 1852.
[4] *The Ceylon Times*, 21 September 1852.
[5] *The Ceylon Examiner*, 4 September 1852.

brought the issue of the State's connection with Buddhism into the limelight in a manner that his letters had been unable to do. The Anglican clergy, supported by over five hundred Christian laymen of all denominations, petitioned the Queen and the Houses of Parliament, condemning Anderson's policy and calling for its reversal.[1] This petition was sent to England in September 1852, by which time Earl Grey had left the Colonial Office.

More important in its effect was Anderson's attempt to fill the long standing vacancies in the Asgiriya Temple – one of the two important Colleges of *bhikkus* in the Kandyan province – where the posts of *Maha Nayaka* and *Anu Nayaka* were vacant. C. R. Buller, as the Government Agent of the Central Province, informed Anderson that the Kandyan *bhikkus* were anxious to have these vacancies filled. At a conference at Kandy, the *bhikkus* suggested that the Government Agent should, as had been done originally, direct the *bhikkus* and Chiefs to hold a meeting to select two *bhikkus* for these posts. Their nomination should then be submitted to the Governor for confirmation.[2] Anderson had no practical objection to this course of action, but he could not make a final decision without consulting his Executive Council. At a meeting of the Executive Council, on 15 July 1852, the issue of warrants of appointment was again debated,[3] and with one exception the Councillors were agreed that the appointments in question, and indeed all appointments, must be made, both because of the hardship caused to the Buddhists and because it was an obligation assumed at the Kandyan Convention. The exception was H. C. Selby, the Queen's Advocate, who argued that it was not necessary for the Government to sign warrants of appointment, and he recommended that they should not be signed in future. However, he saw the need for legislation of some sort. All that was necessary, he believed, would be the appointment of a Trustee for the property of the Temples, with some provision made for the election of his successors. The advantage of this plan in Selby's view was that it would satisfy the *bhikkus*, and that it would enable the Government

---

[1] C.O. 54/291, Anderson to Pakington, no.92 of 11 September 1852. Enclosed petition.

[2] C.O. 54/290, Anderson to Pakington, no.61 of 6 August 1852, C. R. Buller's letter of 20 March 1852 enclosed; also enclosed was a letter of the Maha Nayaka of Asgiriya of 5 February 1852.

[3] C.O. 54/290, Anderson to Pakington, no.61 of 6 August 1852.

to dissociate itself from Buddhism.[1] Selby's plan was likely to achieve this second objective; it could not have achieved the first. At any rate, Selby was more interested in the second, being a great supporter of the view that the State should have no connection with any religion, let alone Buddhism. He was a strong advocate of the 'dis-establishment of the Anglican Church'.[2]

More constructive was the plan submitted to Anderson as early as March 1852 by C. R. Buller, which envisaged the establishment of an Ecclesiastical Court of twenty *bhikkus* (chiefs were to be excluded) to administer all the properties of the temples, and to adjudicate on religious issues. Provision was to be made for the inclusion, at some future date, of a clause which was to declare that where two-thirds of the tenants of any temple property desired to utilize that property for some other purpose than the support of the temple, they should have the right to do so. Buller, who had great hopes for the ultimate replacement of Buddhism by Christianity, wished to accelerate the process by means of this clause.[3]

His other aim was to prevent the formation of a close corporation of chiefs and *bhikkus*. His scheme – and he pronounced it his main aim – sought to make each *vihara* a separate incumbency, wholly independent of the two main colleges,[4] with each incumbent having full power to name his successor. (The *basnayake nilames* were to be elected in the same way.) Buller hoped by this means to divide the interests of the chiefs and the *bhikkus*.

It was obvious that legislation would be necessary to create this court. Buller suggested that any such legislation should be as brief as possible – no more legislation in fact than was absolutely necessary. In his view his scheme had the advantage that it could, by effecting the dissociation quietly and without any unnecessary dis-

[1] C.O. 54/290, Anderson to Pakington, no.61 of 6 August 1852, Selby, H. C., minute of 1 July 1852.
[2] See Chapter I.
[3] C.O. 54/290, Anderson to Pakington, no.61 of 6 August 1852.
  C.O. 57/18, meeting of the Executive Council, 15 July 1852. C. R. Buller was not a member of the Executive Council but he was invited to attend this and other meetings because of his knowledge of the intricacies of the problem, gained, presumably, by virtue of his long service as Government Agent of the Central Province.
[4] It is difficult to see what Buller was aiming at here, for the individual *viharas* had always been separate incumbencies, with very little control by the two Colleges of Asgiriya and Malvatta.

play of Ordinance and proclamation, avoid increasing the strong feeling among the Kandyans against the policy of dissociation.[1] But Anderson disregarded Buller's scheme as he disregarded Selby's, and relied heavily on MacCarthy's advice.

Naturally *The Ceylon Times* and the missionaries made much of these developments, but Anderson was less amenable to missionary influence in this matter than any of his predecessors. His approach to this problem was pragmatic and his motives were practical and political, hardly every religious.

At this stage Earl Grey resigned from office, and with his resignation there was every possibility that the settlement that Grey and Anderson were slowly but deliberately working out would be upset. Grey's successor at the Colonial Office was Sir John Pakington, who did not have either Grey's wide knowledge and experience of Colonial affairs or his enormous capacity for work. But Pakington had the quality of resolution; he was determined to settle the Buddhist problem. This he left in Merivale's capable hands, thus ensuring – even if he did not intend it – that there would be a continuity in Colonial Office policy on Buddhism.

Strachey was given the task, under Merivale's supervision, of bringing the controversy on Buddhism to an end, and he produced a despatch which was to prove the basis of the settlement. Pakington had as little to do with the actual drafting of this despatch as Grey had with his first despatch on Buddhism. It was Strachey's work and, surprisingly enough, Tennent's. (It is curious that Tennent's greatest influence on Buddhist policy may have come at a time when he was no longer in the Colonial service.[2] Pakington and Merivale had the highest regard for his abilities and consulted him on many matters affecting Ceylon, but most of all on Buddhism.) Strachey's draft despatch was ready by 16 September 1852, and he wanted to send it at once to Anderson, but it was delayed because Tennent had chosen this particular moment to send Merivale a copy of a memorandum on Buddhism, originally

---

[1] C.O. 57/18, meeting of the Executive Council of 15 July 1852.

[2] C.O. 54/296, Tennent's letter to Pakington, 30 September 1852. Torrington had always treated MacCarthy's views on Buddhism with more respect than Tennent's. In a letter to Grey (Grey MSS., Torrington to Grey, 14 October 1847) he commented that Tennent's opinions on this matter were 'more showy than practical'. There is nothing to suggest that he ever changed this view.

prepared for the Parliamentary Committee on Ceylon.[1] Never reluctant to praise his own efforts, he informed Merivale that the facts in his memorandum 'have all the authenticity of an official enquiry conducted with the sanction and under the authority of the Governor [Torrington]'.[2] He suggested that Merivale should send a copy of this memorandum to Ceylon:

> as I am enabled to assure you that *much* of its contents are wholly new and unknown to the officials there: and it will facilitate their execution of your orders to have the facts and to be able to verify them.[3]

The officials in Ceylon could have done without Tennent's memorandum for it contained nothing that was not known there, but Merivale did study it carefully, and held up Strachey's despatch till he had had time to digest it. At Tennent's suggestion, Strachey's despatch was amended, though the amendments added little to the value of the document. It was, however, an indication of the extent to which Merivale – and Pakington – were willing to use Tennent's experience. It must be kept in mind that Strachey's original draft itself had been prepared with the assistance of Tennent, who had gone over every point in that despatch with great deliberation.[4]

The amended draft was adopted as Pakington's own despatch to Anderson on the solution of the Buddhist problem. This despatch, unlike Stanley's and Grey's major despatches on Buddhist policy, was a compromise between the views of the missionaries and the evangelicals on the one hand, and those of the Kandyans and the traditionalists on the other. Anderson could have recognized in it many of his own suggestions. It was also a superb piece of fence-straddling, seeking to reassure the Buddhists, while at the same time appeasing the missionaries.

The details of the settlement were – perhaps deliberately – vague. It declared that the system of warrants of appointment constituted '. . . an admission by the Government of responsibility

---

[1] C.O. 54/296, Tennent's 'Memorandum on Buddhism and the means of severing the connexion between the British Government and the Buddhist rites and Temples in Ceylon'.

[2] C.O. 54/296, Tennent to Pakington, 30 September 1852.

[3] *Ibid.* Tennent to Merivale, [n.d.]

[4] C.O. 54/290, Anderson to Pakington, no.61 of 6 August 1852, Strachey's minute [n.d.] to Pakington.

for the person appointed'; and that this gave offence to the Christians in Ceylon. Therefore, it was recommended that these warrants of appointment should be abolished.[1] Instead,

> the present system of recognizing by diploma or certificate the priests or lay chiefs elected by their own organizations should continue, but it would be best to organize a regular electoral body either by agreement among the Buddhists or by arrangement in the first instance, and no attempt should be made to get rid of any part of the present Government's functions until such a body has been organized.[2]

This seemed clear and sensible enough, but when it came to giving Anderson instructions on what he was to do on the next occasion he was faced with a specific request for a warrant of appointment, Pakington was much less precise. The despatch instructed Anderson

> . . . on the next vacancy, if possible, if not as soon as possible, to cease to issue an appointment; to dispense (if safe and injurious to no rights of property) with any certificate; if this cannot be done, to substitute either a simple certificate, or a grant of temporal rights.[3]

To have extracted any positive directions from these instructions would have taxed the energies of any but the most sagacious and experienced administrator. Anderson, fortunately, was up to the mark.

This despatch – which Anderson was asked to publish – made the firm declaration that the guarantees of 1815 and 1818 on Buddhism would be respected, but at the same time it asserted that the Government was not bound

---

[1] C.O. 54/294, Pakington to Anderson, no.123 of 4 December 1852.

[2] *Ibid.*, para 13. The distinction between 'warrants' and 'certificates or diploma' lay in the formulae used. The 'warrant' generally copied the somewhat flowery language of the letters of appointment of Kandyan days. Missionaries and those who supported them insisted that this formula itself constituted the '. . . admission by the Government of responsibility for the person appointed' as there was reference to the Governor having confidence in the 'probity' and 'piety' – to mention just two qualities – of the person appointed.

On the other hand the certificate or diploma was to state in very plain language that the Governor recognized the recipient as the person properly chosen by an electoral college or chapter.

[3] *Ibid.*, para 24. The same policy was to be followed in the case of the *basnayake nilames* of the various *devales* (para. 26).

to preserve untouched the particular forms of temple appointments, and the like, at present in use, if the substantial object, the protection of the rights themselves, is equally attainable without them.[1]

The Buddhists were assured that

no representation from other portions of the Community will induce H.M.'s Government to permit any withdrawal of the protection or any infringement of the immunities guaranteed to the Buddhist religion by the Convention of 1815.[2]

It would be in the interests of the Buddhists themselves, however, that some change should be made in the relationship between the 'Buddhist Establishments' and the 'Executive Authority'. The despatch hinted that this change had to be made to satisfy the 'Christian portion of the Community', and to prevent the continuation of 'inconvenient controversies' between Buddhists, Christians and the Government.[3]

On two aspects of policy the despatch was clear enough: the Tooth Relic was to be handed over as it was in 1847 to the representatives of the Buddhists; and the annual grant of money stopped in 1847 was to be restored as an act of justice, 'if possible to coincide with the change in the system of appointment', and thus make this latter step more palatable to the Buddhists.[4]

Pakington recognized that legislation would be necessary to give effect to these changes. If there was no elective body, legislation would be necessary to give validity and permanency to such a body when it was created. It would also be necessary to legislate for any certificate or instrument that might be devised as a substi-

---

[1] *Ibid.* para.2. The reference here is to the change from elaborate warrants to simple certificates.

[2] Para.30.   [3] *Ibid.*

[4] In para. 8, Anderson was informed that one aim of his policy should be to make Buddhists '. . . rely upon the powers of self-government which are preserved by any religious community, or may, by proper arrangements, be developed in it'. It is not clear what Pakington intended here. On the one hand, it may be that he was asking Anderson to convert the loose collection of *viharas* in Ceylon into a centrally controlled organization. This would be a revolutionary process, easy to suggest, but exceptionally difficult to achieve. Again, it may be that all Pakington intended was to revive a procedure (said to have been followed in Ceylon) which resembled the capitulary elections of western monasticism. There was to be no central organization involved but each *vihara* would chose its own head. It would have been very difficult to make either scheme uniformly accepted, as practice evidently varied a great deal.

tute for the present certificates.[1] But these matters of detail were left to Anderson's discretion with a strong recommendation 'not to legislate unless on an established case of necessity'.[2]

Anderson was informed that these new arrangements would constitute 'an entire cessation of interference in Buddhist affairs'. The despatch instructed him that

> if there is at present any interference otherwise than by appointments, such other interference is also to be made to cease, either by simply withdrawing it, or transferring the functions to be discontinued to the proper Buddhist agency.[3]

If Pakington had hoped that his policy of compromise would be hailed in Ceylon as an act of statesmanship, he was mistaken. None of the missionary organizations was satisfied and *The Ceylon Times* was as violent as ever in its condemnation of matters concerning Buddhism. But more significant was the fact that the sober and moderate *Colombo Observer* thought his despatch a disappointment. It declared that

> a document more unsatisfactory and uncertain as regards the action contemplated, more involved in sense and imperfect in style, scarcely ever proceeded from a high public officer. It is a perfect contrast to the beautiful compositions on the same subject which have proceeded from the pens of Mr MacCarthy and Sir Emerson Tennent; and whatever may be thought of some parts of the policy of Earl Grey or whatever estimate may be formed of his temper, he must be at least allowed the merit of making himself acquainted with his subject and conveying his meaning in clear and vigorous phraseology.[4]

It was on the whole a fair criticism.

Anderson, however, decided to make the most of the concessions that Pakington had made to his opinions, and the discretion allowed him by the Ordinance. His first task was to organize the new electoral colleges and to devise a method of election. In the main, he followed the principles laid down in paragraph 24 of Pakington's despatch.[5] It was originally intended that the electoral colleges should consist of temple tenants and officers of each *vihara* and *devale*, but ultimately Anderson decided to devise

---

[1] Para.26.   [2] *Ibid.*   [3] Para.27.
[4] *The Colombo Observer*, 7 February 1853.
[5] C.O. 54/298, Anderson to Pakington, no.22 of 24 March 1853.
   C.O. 57/19, Minutes of the Executive Council Meeting of 9 March 1853.

electoral colleges in which the chiefs would have the controlling vote. He felt that an electoral college in which the temple tenants had a majority would in the long run

> be fatal to the integrity of the property belonging to the different temples, as the majority of the electors would have a direct interest in the election of a temple officer who would not be faithful to his trust, i.e. the maintenance of temple rights, and the application of property to Temple purposes.[1]

Once the electoral college had chosen an individual, the question of Government recognition arose, and here Anderson considered it neither just nor safe to deprive the managers of these temporalities of such legal documents as would guarantee their undisturbed possession of these properties. For these reasons, he decided to substitute, in place of Acts of Appointment, a simple certificate of a purely declaratory form recognizing the validity of the election. He decided to hand over the Tooth Relic to the Committee who held it from October 1847 to July 1848. The question of a grant of lands as compensation for the monetary grant terminated in 1847 did not present any difficulties.

Once he had made up his mind on these various problems, he issued specific instructions to the Government Agent of the Central Province, explaining to him the composition of the electoral colleges, the mode of election, and the nature of the certificate of recognition. The Tooth Relic was to be given to the Committee with a clear warning that they would be held responsible for the property handed over to their care, and that the Government would not hesitate to resume possession of it if the Tooth Relic were used for anything other than religious purposes. He was to submit, as soon as possible, a statement of the extent of compensation to be given in lieu of the grant stopped in 1847.[2]

On the very day that these instructions were issued, Anderson (in a Minute drawn up with the assistance of MacCarthy)[3] made a policy declaration of the utmost significance. He declared that

> our sole motive should be that of support and protection to what exists [Buddhism] and . . . we have nothing to do with anything else.

[1] C.O. 54/298, Anderson to Pakington, no.22 of 24 March 1853. Anderson's minute of 18 February 1853.   [2] *Ibid.*

[3] Anderson's minute of 18 February 1853. It was on the basis of this minute that these instructions were issued to the Government Agent of the Central Province.

Nor would he accept the view that in the event of the ultimate collapse of Buddhism, Buddhist property should be used for the purpose of education. On the contrary Anderson insisted that Government was bound to help to protect these lands

> on all principles of honesty and justice, and [we] ought to repudiate every idea that it is our purpose sooner or later to possess ourselves of these lands for objects different from the original purpose of the Grants, however these objects in themselves may be virtuous, good and excellent.[1]

This was nothing less than the rejection of the whole basis of the Buddhist policy of his predecessors. Not even Torrington, chastened by the events of 1848, went as far as this. To a large extent this attitude to Buddhism explains the virulence of the missionary opposition to Anderson's policies.

This time there was no unanimity in the Executive Council. Three Executive Councillors – H. C. Selby, the Queen's Advocate; W. C. Gibson, the Auditor-General; and J. Caulfield, the Acting Treasurer – presented a joint minute which recommended a course of action rather different from Anderson's.[2] On certain matters there was indeed a measure of agreement but these were generally matters of lesser importance. The difference of opinion came on the major issue of temple appointments and temple lands. The three Executive Councillors suggested that the chief *bhikkus* and *basnayake nilames* should be elected (they were not clear as to who should elect them), and that the persons so elected should be granted a certificate of recognition. Thereafter a grant was to be made to them of all the lands belonging to the temples, and these lands were to be held on a tenure known as *sisya paramparawa*, a grant in perpetuity from priest to pupil.

At the same time they introduced the argument, for which there was no support in the facts of the situation, that the property of *viharas* should revert to the Crown on the death of the *bhikkus*.

---

[1] *Ibid.*

[2] C.O. 54/298, Anderson to Pakington, no.22 of 24 March 1853, joint minute of 9 March 1853. It must be noted that these three officials did not form any permanent opposition 'bloc' in the Executive Council. Even on this question there was the significant difference that, while Selby's opposition to Anderson's policy was based on his view that the State should have no connection with any religion at all, the other two appear to have shared some, at least, of the opinions of the missionary opposition.

They believed that such property was not vested in the Buddhist community, the *bhikkus* being merely its administrators. These arguments could hardly be reconciled with their recommendation that temple lands should be granted in perpetuity.[1] Anderson was to show that this was all based on C. R. Buller's idea that temple property belonged to the Crown, and was granted by the Crown to the appointed priest for the time being, reverting to the Crown on his death. Anderson explained that this view was certainly not held by the *bhikkus* themselves, and that the *Maha Nayake* of Malvatta, whose opinion Buller had quoted as the basis of his argument, had declared that Buller had completely misunderstood him.[2]

There were two other points on which the three Executive Councillors differed from Anderson. First, they believed that it was necessary to issue a Proclamation setting out clearly the terms of the settlement. Anderson objected to the idea of a Proclamation as being too ostentatious and likely to prove unpopular among the Kandyans. Secondly, it was Anderson's firm conviction that legislation was necessary to effect the settlement. Indeed, Pakington's despatch had recognized the need for legislation, for the twenty-sixth paragraph of the despatch outlined the circumstances in which legislation would become necessary. The Executive Councillors on the other hand contended, 'that no new law is required to enable them [the Buddhists] effectually to manage their own concerns, and to maintain their just rights before the tribunals'.

The fact is, however, that the basic differences between Anderson (and MacCarthy) and the three Executive Councillors stemmed from different views on the extent to which the separation of State and Buddhism should be effected. For Anderson, and indeed for Pakington, the compromise settlement of 1852 was to constitute 'an entire cessation of interference in Buddhist affairs'.[3] But in this settlement the Government still had certain minor functions, and there was still some very tenuous connection. The Executive

---

[1] The fact is that none of the local civil servants had any clear idea of the tenure of temple lands. From the records only one thing is clear—there was no uniform practice.

[2] C.O. 54/300, Anderson to Newcastle, no.70 of 10 June 1853.

[3] C.O. 54/294, Pakington to Anderson, no. 123 of 4 December 1852, para. 26.

Councillors wanted a total separation,[1] which in the circumstances of the day was both impossible and undesirable. Their arguments were to be taken a stage further by men like Strachey in the Colonial Office, the missionaries, and the more articulate members of the Christian community in Ceylon, who looked upon such matters as the certificate granted by the Government and the presence of native Government officials in the electoral colleges created by Anderson as positive evidence of continued Government interference.

Anderson, realizing that speed was essential if he was to thwart the missionaries and the opposition in the Executive Council, persuaded C. R. Buller to carry out his instructions with all possible speed. In June 1853 he sent the Colonial Office a copy of the instructions he had given Buller, and along with it he sent the news: that the separation between Buddhism and the State had been effected without much trouble; that the Tooth Relic had been handed over on 20 May 1853; that the first elections under the new system had already taken place; and that certificates of recognition had been granted to the new *Maha Nayaka* of Asgiriya, the new *Diyawadana Nilame* of the Temple of the Tooth, and the new *Basnayaka Nilame* of the Kataragama *devale* in Kandy.[2] In presenting the Colonial Office with an accomplished fact perhaps Anderson believed that there would be less likelihood of their overruling him altogether.[3] He realized that the Colonial Office was more diffident now on Buddhist policy than it had been earlier.

Nevertheless, it was necessary, particularly because Pakington had left the Colonial Office, to explain why he had rejected the recommendations of Selby, Caulfield and Gibson. The bulk of these proposals were concerned with temple appointments and the tenure of temple lands. Anderson explained that the three Executive Councillors had based their recommendations on certain mistaken notions of C. R. Buller's. The *Maha Nayaka* of Malwatta, whom Buller quoted as his authority for these views, informed Anderson that Buller had completely misunderstood him,[4]

---

[1] This probably explains why they were so vague about the electoral college, its composition and functions.

[2] C.O. 54/300, Anderson to Newcastle, no.70 of 6 June 1853.

[3] Pakington had left the Colonial Office at this stage, and Anderson could never be certain about the views and attitudes of Pakington's successor, the Duke of Newcastle.   [4] See above, page 131.

which considerably weakened the arguments of the three Executive Councillors.

Anderson believed that these suggestions would lead to a revolutionary change in the existing tenure of temple properties. He was certain that the property of the temples could never revert to the Crown:

> Temple property once dedicated to religious purposes [was inalienable]; and again, if the property was made to descend, as is proposed, from priest to pupil, this practice would set aside succession of election, which is certainly on all hands admitted to be the mode in which priest should succeed priest in their temples.[1]

He had grave misgivings on some of the other recommendations of the three Executive Councillors, particularly on their suggestion of a proclamation embodying the terms of the settlement. Such a proclamation would be too ostentatious, and was certain to be unpopular among the Kandyans.

Only one concession was made to the three Executive Councillors. On their suggestion, a new electoral college was devised for the purpose of electing the *basnayake nilames*, which was to consist of the *rate mahatmayas* and *basnayaka nilames*. Anderson realized that this electoral machinery was likely to increase the power and influence of the headmen among the people, 'which it has not been the policy of the English Government to augment', but it was the least objectionable method that could have been devised.[2]

At the Colonial Office only Strachey had any objections to Anderson's policies; but these were confined to the proposal to have the *rate mahatmayas* and *korales* in the electoral college, which he believed would strengthen 'the hands of the native official aristocracy'.[3] Besides, the presence of these men in the electoral college would be the substitution of an 'indirect for a direct system of Government nomination',[4] since they were, after all, Government officials. Further, though these men were all Buddhists, they or their successors might in the future be converted to Christianity, in which event they might have objections to serving on that electoral college.

But Merivale, clearly anxious to be rid of this problem, was

---

[1] C.O. 54/300, Anderson to Newcastle, no.70 of 6 June 1853.
[2] *Ibid.*
[3] C.O. 54/298, Anderson to Pakington, no.22 of 24 March 1853, Strachey's minute of 5 May 1853.   [4] Strachey's minute, *op. cit.*

satisfied that Anderson had 'very fairly carried out instructions'.[1]
He noted the difference of opinion between Anderson and Mac-
Carthy on the one hand, and Selby, Caulfield and Gibson on the
other, but he would not let it stand in the way of a settlement,
sagely remarking that the difference 'turns on a rather refined
point of Sinhalese jurisprudence, and the variety of opinion
respecting it seems to indicate how little is known after 35 years of
conquest of the fundamental usages and notions of the Kandyans'.[2] The Duke of Newcastle, who had replaced Pakington at
the Colonial Office, also approved of Anderson's policy though he
had doubts on one point – the new constituencies created for the
election of the *diyawadana nilames* and the *basnayake nilames*.[3] Like
Strachey, he felt that the presence of Government officials in the
electoral colleges would substitute an indirect for a direct connection with the Government. But he generously conceded that any
other arrangement would likewise be open to criticism, and that
'no arrangement appears to have been suggested, nor could [he]
suggest any, free from objections.[4] Newcastle approved Anderson's settlement with the comment that it was 'a good Compromise between the demands of the Buddhists and Christians'.

Newcastle and Merivale wholly misjudged the temper of the
Christian community in Ceylon. When Anderson's instructions to
Buller were published in the local newspapers, it raised a storm of
protest.[5] The Press was unanimously against it; the missionary
groups – united on this as on no other issue – added their criticisms. In the Legislative Council two non-official members, E. J.
Darley and James Swan, presented a petition declaring their
opposition to the new settlement. The main theme of their criticism was that Anderson's instructions to the Government Agent
were contrary to Pakington's despatch, and that Anderson had
not effected a complete break with Buddhism. They suggested
that since the sole use of the new certificate was to secure recognition of the election in the Courts of Justice, the same object could
be secured with greater certainty by simple registration in the
courts. That the Tooth Relic was no longer in the possession of the

---

[1] C.O. 54/298, Merivale's minute of 4 May 1853, on the same despatch.
[2] C.O. 54/298, Merivale's minute of 4 May 1853, on the same despatch.
[3] *Ibid.* Newcastle's minute of 13 July 1853.
[4] C.O. 54/300, Newcastle to Anderson, no.103 of 18 August 1853.
[5] *The Colombo Observer*, 20 April 1854. Petition of E. J. Darley, James Swan
and others, dated 20 March 1854.

Government was a matter of great satisfaction to them, but they objected to the receipt obtained by the Government for the property handed over with it. The new electoral colleges were condemned, particularly because native Government officials had the right to vote in them; the petitioners looked upon this as an indirect connection between the Government and Buddhism. Fears were expressed that this would exclude the appointment of Christians to posts of *rate mahatmaya* and *korale*; or that by appointing Christians it would give Buddhists a cause for complaint.[1]

Anderson defended his policy as best as he could, explaining that: the certificates merely gave the *bhikkus* and *basnayaka nilames* their secular rights to temple property; that the treasures of the Temple of the Tooth included jewellery valued at £60,000 or so; that the receipt had been taken in order to prevent a dispute in future as to the extent of the property handed over; and that the electoral college was a temporary device until something better could be devised. He explained that the native officials would not wield any influence for the Government at these elections and, therefore, their presence in the electoral college could not compromise the Government. And he pointed out that if Christians held these posts, it was optional for them to vote; and that, in any case, it was not supposed that they would want to. He made it clear that he would not change his plans to accommodate these criticisms.[2]

But his firmness only strengthened the opposition to these policies among the various Christian groups in Ceylon. This time they petitioned the Queen, declaring that while they concurred in the statement of policy made in Pakington's despatch of 4 December 1852, they regretted that Anderson's instructions to the Government Agent of the Central Province violated the principle, as well as the spirit, of that despatch.[3] At about the same time, the

---

[1] The petition of E. J. Darley, James Swan and others, *loc. cit.*

[2] *The Colombo Observer*, 20 April 1854. Anderson's reply of 8 April 1854.

[3] *The Colombo Observer*, 14 December 1854; C.O. 54/310, Anderson to Sir George Grey, no.74 of 25 December 1854. This petition, dated 4 December 1854, was signed by two members of the Legislative Council, E. J. Darley and James Swan, the Archdeacon and nine other clergymen of the Church of England, two Presbyterian Chaplains, seven Wesleyan and Baptist missionaries, several merchants and planters, some civil servants and army officers, and over 500 others. This new petition embodied most of the criticisms made in the earlier one.

K

Secretary of the S.P.G., E. Hawkins, submitted a petition to the Colonial Office making much the same complaint.[1]

These petitions did not impress Merivale. He realized that the petitioners wanted the elimination of all Government connection with the Buddhist religion, and that it would be impossible to concede this demand, for that would be an act of injustice towards the Kandyans.

Merivale stood loyally by Anderson and defended him against all his critics. He noted with approbation that Anderson's 'part of the correspondence [with the petitioners] seems to have been conducted with much moderation and propriety.'[2] The petition itself he dismissed with the sagacious comment that:

> . . . much is said in Sir J[ohn] P[akington]'s despatch of ulterior measures as desirable and ulterior objects to be kept in view, and these expressions are treated by the memorialists as directions, which when taken along with the context they clearly are not.[3]

Above all, there was a firm determination that there should be no disturbance of the settlement made by Pakington and Anderson:

> As to the general question, I am by no means sanguine enough to believe it set at rest for ever; but I hope nothing short of very strong grounds will be allowed to cause the re-opening of a matter which Lord Grey endeavoured for years to settle, which were reputed not the least significant among the causes of rebellion in 1847 [sic] and which Sir J. Pakington arranged at last only on the footing of a compromise.[4]

The Pakington-Anderson settlement, ungainly compromise though it was, lasted practically unchanged into the twentieth

---

[1] C.O. 54/312, Hawkins' petition December [n.d.] 1854. Hawkins actually asked for an interview on this subject but Merivale refused him this request, asking him to put his suggestions on paper.

[2] C.O. 54/310, Merivale's minute of 9 January 1855 in Anderson to Sir George Grey, no.74 of 25 December 1854.

[3] C.O. 54/310, Merivale's minute of 9 January 1855, in Anderson to Sir George Grey, no.74 of 25 December 1854.

[4] Ibid.

Mainly because of a series of changes at the Colonial Office, the Secretary of State's reply to this petition was delayed till 1856. The reply emphatically stated that Anderson was correct in his interpretation of Pakington's despatch, and that the Home Government had no intention of re-opening a question '[so] fully considered by their predecessors'. See Palmerston to Ward, no.25 of 5 February 1856, the draft of which is enclosed in C.O. 54/310.

century. Missionary interests which had been so largely responsible for the original severance of the connection between the State and Buddhism had little influence on a settlement which was dictated largely by practical considerations of politics.

Part II

The first part of this book dealt with problems that were fundamentally religious, but which were at the same time the central
social issues of the day. We turn next to some other social problems
of mid-nineteenth century Ceylon: the problem of illiteracy; the
question of the aborigines of Ceylon – the Veddahs; the issue of
slavery; and the great question of caste. In practically every problem, and particularly in education policy, religious considerations
were prominent, the influence of Evangelicalism being easily
discernible. At this time in England there developed, under the
influence of Evangelicalism, a gradual moral awareness of positive
cruelty, tyranny, injustice, and, more important, of the evil consequences of indifference and neglect. To quote Dicey:

> At the beginning of the nineteenth century, Evangelicalism was
> among religious Englishmen supreme, and Evangelicalism, no less
> than Benthamism, meant as a social creed the advocacy of every form
> of humanity.[1]

It was the influence of this force that, in the main, shaped policy
on the Veddahs, on slavery and on caste in Ceylon. It is significant
that Glenelg's despatch to Mackenzie on the latter's appointment
to the Governorship of Ceylon instructed him to take an interest in
the aboriginal Veddah.[2] A few months earlier a select committee
of the House of Commons reported on the state of the aborigines in
the Empire.[3] They declared that 'the protection of the Aborigines
should be considered as a duty peculiarly belonging and appropriate to the Executive Government, either in this country or by
the Governors of the respective Colonies'.[4] The committee was
strongly Evangelical in outlook, and in the policy they recommended to the Imperial Government 'Religious Instruction and
Education' took a prominent place.[5] From the first Governor

[1] Dicey, A. V., *Lectures on the Relation between Law and Public Opinion in
England*, (1924), p.108.
[2] C.O. 55/79, Glenelg to Mackenzie, no.18 of 2 October 1837.
[3] *Report of House of Commons Committee on Aborigines in British Settlements*,
26 June 1837, *P.P*, 1837, vii.
[4] *Ibid.*, quoted in Bell and Morrell, *Select Documents on British Colonial Policy*,
1830–1860, p.547.
[5] *Ibid.*, p.548.

Mackenzie, strongly Evangelical by temperament and conviction, was an enthusiastic supporter of a Mission to the Veddahs to be organized as a joint venture by the missionaries and the State. 'Religious Instruction and Education' formed the kernel of the policy which followed.

In Ceylon at this time the State, when it took an interest in social problems, was greatly handicapped by the lack of guiding precedents and administrative machinery sufficiently well-developed for such projects. It was here that the missionaries proved to be of great use. Since the State lacked the administrative machinery for these projects, the missionaries, possessing a rudimentary organization, were useful as auxiliaries. They had the men, the time and inclination to work; the State merely provided the finances, and its moral support. Their influence was rather on the day-to-day administration of these projects than on the formulation of basic principles of policy; but even here, there was no great divergence of opinion. The officials and the missionaries both agreed that conversion to Christianity was a worthy end, and that welfare projects were as good a means to that end as any other.

Two other points of interest must be noted. First, such State activity in social welfare as existed was the result of individual effort on the part of officials, rather than any collective effort of the administration. Thus Mackenzie, liberal politician, enlightened church reformer, farsighted educationist (and enterprising capitalist), proved to be keenly interested in the social problems of the day. He initiated work among the Veddahs,[1] the Rodiyas[2] and the Gahalayas;[3] State action followed on his individual efforts. There is no evidence that his successors had the same interest in these projects, though it would appear that Tennent at least was interested in the Veddah Mission. There was no one among the top administrators of the day to take the same paternal interest in these projects as Mackenzie took. The reasons are not hard to find.

[1] The Veddahs are the aborigines of Ceylon, inhabiting the wild forested region of the Bintenne District in the south-east of the Island. An excellent bibliography of the Veddah is provided in H. A. I. Goonetileke, 'A Bibliography of the Veddah: The Ceylon Aboriginal', in *Ceylon Journal of Historical and Social Studies*, Vol. 3, no.1, pp.96 ff.

[2] The Rodiyas are a small community, the only 'untouchables' of the traditional Sinhalese society.

[3] The Gahalayas, an even smaller group than the Rodiyas, were one of the lowest castes in the Kandyan caste heirarchy.

Since most of these projects were in the interior, away from the main centre of administration, only the most intrepid or the most enlightened would show any interest, and at this time both qualities were lacking in the Ceylon Civil Service. Besides, these projects were contrary to the prevailing conceptions of State activity. The early Victorian State was essentially negative in character, seeking rather to enlarge the sphere of individual activity than to adopt a positive role in the social and economic life of the community. This was so even in colonies such as Ceylon. It is hardly surprising, therefore, that these schemes did not bear the fruit they were expected to yield. But in the context of that age, it is significant enough that they were attempted at all.

Secondly, it is noteworthy that while the missionaries played a role of great significance in these projects, they had hardly any influence on the abolition of slavery in Ceylon. This was the achievement of the administrators alone. There is practically no mention of the problem of slavery in the letters of the missionaries, and they appear to have made no contribution to the agitation (in England) for the abolition of slavery in Ceylon.

CHAPTER IV

Missionary Organizations and the Evolution of Education Policy

IN Ceylon, as in India, State intervention in education came earlier than in England. Before 1833 State activity in education in Ceylon was both slight and sporadic, but thereafter with the implementation of Colebrooke's recommendations it assumed a regular and definite form.

Colebrooke observed that the schools maintained by the Government were 'extremely defective and inefficient',[1] and he did not hesitate to acknowledge the superiority of the schools run by the missionaries. Nor was he inclined to encourage the establishment of government schools in areas served by the missionary schools.[2]

To 'facilitate the reform of the government schools' he recommended that they be placed 'under the immediate direction' of a School Commission composed of the Archdeacon of Colombo and the clergy of the island, as well as the Government Agents of the provinces and other civil and judicial officials.[3] The School Commission was a distinct improvement on the system that it replaced;

[1] Mendis, G. C. (ed.), *The Colebrooke-Cameron Papers*, I, p.72.

Colebrooke remarked that the schoolmasters in the government schools – there were 94 schools – were largely ignorant of the English language, and were often extremely unfit for their situations. He added that 'nothing is taught in the schools but reading in the native language, and writing in the native characters; and as the control exercised is insufficient to secure the attendance either of the masters or of the scholars, many abuses prevail, and the government schools in several instances exist only in name, children being assembled occasionally for inspection, many of whom had received instruction in the schools of missionaries, of which the government schoolmasters are alleged to be jealous'.

[2] *Ibid.*, p.73.

[3] Subordinate committees were established at Kandy, Galle, Jaffna and Trincomalee; these sub-committees were composed of the Government Agent of the Province, the District Judge and the clergy resident at the station. They were expected to inspect the schools in their several divisions and to report to the Central Commission on their efficiency and management.

See Gratien, L. J., *The Story of our Schools. The First School Commission, 1832–1841* (Colombo, 1927), p.4.

previously, the government schools were superintended by one of the Colonial chaplains, who received a salary of £270 per annum as Principal of Schools.

Colebrooke's reflections on education were prosaic and disjointed, extraordinarily so for a man who is generally believed to have been a utilitarian. There was nothing of that subtle utilitarianism that distinguished the writings of C. E. Trevalyan on education in India, or the generosity of Elphinstone's outlook, which was unperturbed by the possibility that extension of educational opportunities might lead to India's ultimate political freedom.[1] For Colebrooke, education was to serve two purposes: as a preparation of candidates for public employment, and as an aid to 'natives to cultivate European attainments'.[2] The missionary organizations in Ceylon looked upon education solely as a means of propagating Christianity at the expense of the indigenous religions, and Colebrooke himself was not unsympathetic to this line of thinking.[3]

The only consistent theme in Colebrooke's recommendations on education was his insistence on English as the medium of instruction. He complained that the 'English missionaries have not very generally appreciated the importance of diffusing a knowledge of the English language through the medium of their schools'.[4] By the 1840s, however, the missionaries were deeply appreciative of its importance. As a Baptist journal of the day explained:

> . . . There is no language in the world which has richer treasures of wisdom and knowledge. . . . They who study the English language will find out by what methods that country has risen so high in civilization and commerce, as well as in religion, and will be glad to avail themselves of similar opportunities to attain the great ends for which all were created.[5]

[1] Ballhatchet, K. A., *Social Policy and Social Change in Western India, 1817–1830* (O.U.P.), pp.248 ff.

[2] Mendis, *op. cit.* I, 72.

[3] Ballhatchet points out that while C. E. Trevalyan, among others, would support English education in public with the use of utilitarian arguments, in private – particularly in his letters to the Governor General – he would present it as a means for the eventual conversion of India to Christianity.

[4] Mendis, *op. cit.* I, 73, 74. Colebrooke pointed out that the American missionaries in the north of the island '. . . were fully impressed with the importance of rendering the English language the general medium of instruction, and of the inestimable value of this acquirement in itself to the people'.

[5] *The Investigator*, I (2), pp. 26 ff.

The Wesleyan missionaries working in Jaffna suggested a narrower but, from the point of view of the missionaries, an even more important reason for the use of the English language as a medium of instruction. '. . . [Instruction] imparted through English is eminently fitted to weaken the strongholds of Hinduism.'[1] And they might have added, of Buddhism, too.

Indeed, one of the most notable features of the education provided both in missionary and government schools was the importance attached to the teaching of Christianity. It was generally believed that '. . . Schools and a preached Gospel must go together . . .'[2] The Baptists described the education imparted at one of their girls' boarding schools thus: '[The] children are carefully instructed in the great doctrines and duties of Christianity, and their conversion is sought as the first and paramount object.'[3] This was the general pattern in the schools of the other missions as well.[4] The Wesleyans explained that, '. . . the education given in [our] institutions is essentially a Christian education. Instruction is so communicated that Christianity is made to appear the end for which all other mental processes are conducted.'[5]

This emphasis on education as a means of conversion had two inevitable consequences. It led to a proliferation of sectarian disputes. Educational activity was marred by the religious conflicts which were, in the main, the extension into Ceylon of the general

---

[1] A/R North Ceylon (Wesleyan) Mission (1850), p.15.

[2] Wes.Mss.Cey. I, Gogerly, 16 September 1845.

[3] A/R Baptist Mission (1854), p.47.

[4] CMS Mss. C/CE/O.20 contains copies of the curriculum of the CMS schools in the Sinhalese areas of the island. The most striking feature of this curriculum is the emphasis given to the teaching of Christianity. In all the CMS schools in the island there was an hour and a half devoted daily to purely religious teaching, a practice that was common in all the missions working in Ceylon. Attendance at these classes was not compulsory, but it does appear that pressure was used to persuade students to attend. Bishop Chapman's Visitation Journal for 1850 (SPG MSS. 1840–55) has this significant passage.

> The parents of one Moorish boy [in a Wesleyan Tamil school at Batticaloa] objected to the teaching of scripture, and the necessary direction was given that he should submit or withdraw. Our teaching must not only be Christian but scriptural, or no real good is done. No infringement of this principle can be admitted. It is a mere fallacy, the worst self-delusion, to teach reading and writing alone in a heathen country.

[5] A/R North Ceylon (Wesleyan) Mission (1849), p.14.

conflict between Anglicans and Dissenters for the control of education in England. Secondly, it was in this sphere that missionary influence on the Ceylon Government was most sustained and at its strongest, though it might have been even stronger and more effective had the Anglicans been less selfish, and had there been fewer sectarian squabbles.

From its inception the Central School Commission was controlled by the Anglican Establishment, who relished the power and patronage it provided. Very soon the School Commission was plagued by sectarian strife and personal disputes,[1] a situation which provoked a contemporary newspaper to observe that,

> With the clergy as usual it's 'war to the knife',
> A general diffusion of malice and strife.[2]

Mackenzie, a great believer in the social benefits of education (apart from its use as an instrument of conversion), found that the greatest obstacle to the educational progress of the colony was the School Commission itself. As early as 1838 he had made up his mind to reconstruct it, principally by adding other members, chiefly laymen, to the existing organizations. He was deterred from doing so mainly by the fact that the civil servants, the only laymen qualified by education and training to serve on that body, could not afford the time.[3] But, though he could not reconstruct the Commission, he devoted his time to developing plans for far-reaching changes in education.

The most radical change he had in mind concerned the medium of instruction. From his brief experience in Ceylon, and his longer acquaintance with education in the British Isles, particularly in Scotland, Wales and Ireland, he had reached the conclusion that an exclusive reliance on the English language was an impediment to progress in education.[4] It was his belief that educa-

[1] C.O. 54/184, Mackenzie to Russell, no.135 of 12 August 1840. Mackenzie referred to '. . . the disgraceful wrangling between the Archdeacon Glennie and his son on one side, and the Rev. Mr Marsh, late at the Head of the Colombo Academy, on whose side the senior Colonial Chaplain and the Head of the Church of England Mission at Cotta [Kotte] was [sic] found ranged . . .'

[2] The Ceylon Chronicle, 23 April 1838.

[3] C.O. 54/184, Mackenzie to Russell, no.135 of 12 August 1840.

[4] C.O. 54/181, Mackenzie to Russell, no.124 of 10 August 1840.

Mackenzie laid great store by the educational experiments of the Society for the Promotion of Christian Knowledge in Scotland, Wales and Ireland. They

tion in the vernaculars would not only attract a larger number of students, but would at the same time actually increase the demand for English education. These views were influenced to a great extent by the opinions of the Rev. D. J. Gogerly, Mackenzie's adviser in matters of education reform, and the practical experience of the Wesleyan missionaries working in their South Ceylon division, who had built up an efficient system of schools in which the medium of instruction was Sinhalese.

The core of the new scheme of vernacular education was a committee whose task was to translate useful works into the indigenous languages, to print these books at the expense of the Government, and to distribute them among the schoolmasters. Without the system of translations, vernacular education would have been impossible; both Mackenzie and Gogerly grasped this fact and in all their schemes of educational reform a translation committee occupied a position of prime importance.[1] Indeed, without the prior approval of the Colonial Office, Mackenzie appointed a Translation Committee with Gogerly as Secretary.

While Mackenzie and Gogerly championed vernacular education, they always insisted that education in the indigenous languages was merely a prelude to education in the English language. In Mackenzie's own words, he believed in '. . . the necessity of teaching all children to read in their native language before they attain the benefits of instruction in our English works.'[2]

Mackenzie had also come to believe, though with less precision than on the question of language, that an attempt must be made to educate the masses and not merely a small *élite* – a view which had

---

had wasted nearly a century in trying to instruct the Gaelic population of the Highlands and Western Islands of Scotland in English. But about the middle of the eighteenth century the Gaelic School Society had been established to teach the Highlanders to read the Bible and the Psalms in their own language; that experiment had proved to be a great success and the Society had multiplied their translations and religious and moral tracts. More important a desire for the English language followed on this experiment. A similar experiment in Wales had had much the same results. Mackenzie recommended something on the same lines for the Sinhalese and Tamil populations of Ceylon.

[1] C.O. 54/184, Mackenzie to Russell, no.135 of 12 August 1840. See also Wes.Mss.Cey. I, Gogerley's letters of 9 February 1839, and 15 September 1840. Mackenzie MSS., File 31.

[2] C.O. 54/179, Mackenzie to Russell, no.42 of 11 March 1840; see enclosed letter, Mackenzie to the Bishop of Madras, 2 March 1840.

the support of Gogerly, if indeed it had not been suggested by him. Mackenzie's ideas on this aspect of education were vague, perhaps necessarily so, because the extra outlay in money would have prompted a peremptory refusal by the Colonial Office. His suggestions were feelers rather than detailed propositions, merely informing Russell that if an attempt were really made to educate the masses, a much larger sum of money than had hitherto been spent would be necessary, . . . for the poverty of the inhabitants generally is so great that only a very small amount in the shape of fees could be expected from them.[1]

He set out five indispensable rules for the reform of education in Ceylon.[2] (1) All schools, to be supported in whole or in part from the funds of the Government, should be open to children of parents of all denominations. (2) The great object of the Government being the promotion of education in general and religious education in particular, the basis of the system should be the Holy Scriptures, with such extracts as were then used by the British and Foreign School Society. (3) No catechisms or books of peculiar religious tenets were to be taught in the schools, but every child was at liberty to attend regularly the place of worship to which its parents belonged. (4) These regulations were to constitute the basis on which financial aid was to be extended to schools, whether public or private; when such assistance was given, the schools were to be under the superintendence of the School Commission. (5) No teacher was to be employed unless he provided satisfactory recommendations as to his religious and general character, and proof of his competence as a teacher.[3]

From these rules it is clear that in Mackenzie's mind the purpose and primary aim of education was religious; education was a Christian education and a means of conversion. Indeed there could be no stronger contrast in the matters of education than that

[1] *Ibid.* Mackenzie always insisted that no fees should be charged in the schools because of the poverty of the inhabitants. See C.O. 54/181, Mackenzie to Russell, no.124 of 10 August 1840.

> In Great Britain, I think no education should be quite gratuitous. Here the excessive poverty would make me question whether, if school fees of any amount were attempted to be exacted, the parents would send their children for education.

[2] Mackenzie to the Bishop of Madras, 2 March 1840.

[3] C.O. 54/179, Russell to Mackenzie, no.42 of 11 March, 1840; see enclosed letter Mackenzie to the Bishop of Madras, 2 March 1840.

between the East India Company in India and the Colonial administration in Ceylon. In Ceylon, at this stage, there was no attempt to consider the deeper political implications of the expansion of educational opportunities – that education would lead ultimately to political freedom. ('Our highroad back to Europe', as Elphinstone called it.) Nor was education viewed as a panacea for social evils. The emphasis was always on the religious aspect, always on conversion.

But Mackenzie's scheme was also notable for its emphasis on non-sectarian religious education,[1] an emphasis which was an undoubted challenge – as it was meant to be – to the privileged position of the Anglican Establishment in Ceylon, who in spite of their many shortcomings were fighting a rearguard action against his moves to rob them of their near-monopoly of the power and patronage of the School Commission. Mackenzie's emphasis on the religious nature of education would find the missions in support; but his insistence on a non-sectarian education would inevitably divide them.[2]

In the first quarter of 1840 Mackenzie's plans had matured sufficiently for him to discuss them with Bishop Middleton of Madras, the statutory head of the Anglican Establishment in Ceylon.[3] In a letter to the Bishop he explained in great detail the projected scheme of vernacular education, taking particular care to emphasise the importance of the Translation Committee as an integral part of the new policy.[4] But he was more anxious to get across to the Bishop the idea that, while the new scheme of educa-

---

[1] Mackenzie was a man singularly free from sectarian bias, and he supported the requests of groups such as the Catholics and the Baptists for Government aid for their schools. In a despatch, C.O. 54/182, Mackenzie to Russell, no.190 of 17 December 1840, he strongly supported their requests for a grant in aid for education; he recommended a grant of £100 each to these two groups and to the C.M.S. Russell approved of this grant. C.O. 54/182, Russell to Campbell, no.46 of 21 April 1841. In 1839 he had made a grant of £200 to the Wesleyans at a time when they badly needed the money. (Wes.Mss.Cey., I, Gogerly, 9 February 1839).

[2] At this time missionary groups in Ceylon were deeply divided and conflicts over education were among the major causes of disunity.

[3] Mackenzie to the Bishop of Madras, 2 March 1840.

[4] Nor did he neglect to mention the more prosaic question of training teachers for these changes – 'the basis of all future excellence and uniformity in instruction'. He suggested the establishment of two training colleges, one for Tamil teachers and one for Sinhalese teachers.

tion gave a decided prominence to the Holy Scriptures, it was at the same time designed to avoid all taint of sectarianism. In this regard, he emphasised the second of his five rules, and warned that the home Government would not provide financial assistance '. . . on any other than the broad basis of Christianity with reference to Religious creed'.[1]

Generally the Bishop's support of these educational reforms would have been less essential to Mackenzie than it was on this occasion, when it was not at all certain that the Colonial Office would accept these proposals. For one thing they would involve the expenditure of a large sum of money and the Colonial Office was notoriously averse to sanctioning additional expenditure in a colony like Ceylon which could not balance its budget. Besides, the projected reforms challenged some of the best-established theories and some of the most powerful vested interests of the day. They were a challenge to the privileged position of the Anglican Establishment in the education system of the colony. At the same time his emphasis on vernacular education, and his suggestion that educational opportunities should be provided for a much larger segment of the population than was thought desirable by contemporary opinion, challenged the then accepted theory of education in the Eastern Empire.

Thus Mackenzie had to move cautiously. His first step was a despatch to Russell (in which he enclosed a copy of his letter to the Bishop) with a few discreet comments and tentative suggestions on the need for a change of policy.[2] Just at this time the Colonial Office, independently of Mackenzie's proposals, was considering a reform of the structure of education in Ceylon. Mackenzie found that the remodelling of the School Commission, which he had been working on for some time, was now being recommended by Russell himself. But the despatch which recommended the formation of a new School Commission also disapproved of the system of translations and the use of the vernaculars[3] thus rejecting, in effect, the essence of his recommendations.

Mackenzie was too deeply interested in education reform to be discouraged by this initial rebuff. His next move was to gather as

---

[1] Mackenzie to the Bishop of Madras, 2 March 1840.

[2] C.O. 54/179, Mackenzie to Russell, no.42 of 11 March 1840.

[3] C.O. 54/181, Russell to Mackenzie, no.32 of 3 March 1840 and no.63 of 26 April 1840.

much support as possible for his schemes, and to get the more prominent missionaries to write to the Colonial Office in his support. Naturally enough Gogerly, whose eminence both as missionary and educationist was likely to impress the Colonial Office, played a key role in these schemes.

Mackenzie sent Russell a memorandum from Gogerly, strongly recommending his system of education.[1] Since Gogerly was Mackenzie's mentor and confidant in these projects (indeed it is very likely that he was their real author),[2] his support was not a surprise, but his memorandum was important both for its able defence of the new scheme, and for its critical review of the existing system of education. Gogerly pointed out that in Ceylon educational opportunities were scarce; he calculated that to put the Sinhalese on an educational equality with what he termed 'the agricultural lands of England' there should be 150,000 pupils in the schools,[3] but the number actually in school was a mere fraction of that total, and of that number only half could even read fluently. In the immediate vicinity of European settlements educational standards were moderately high, but in the interior they were deplorably low. The inadequacies and shortcomings of the existing system of education greatly disturbed him.

Gogerly observed that, while the mission schools could not, in general, afford the equipment necessary for the provision of a satisfactory system of education, there was the more disturbing circumstance that such equipment was difficult to obtain. There were, for instance, no maps with the names of places marked in Sinhalese, and this prevented the introduction of geography into the curriculum, while '. . . science, history and general literature are completely out of the reach of the people, there being no books on the subject.' The mission schools had a limited number of spelling and reading books, but the people were too poor to afford them.

He believed that the remedy for this situation was the system of translations recommended by Mackenzie. By delineating the com-

---

[1] C.O. 54/181, Mackenzie to Russell, no. 124 of 10 August 1840. See Gogerly's memorandum to Mackenzie of 5 August 1840.

[2] Wes.Mss.Cey., I, Gogerly, 15 September 1840.

[3] Gogerly's memorandum of 5 August 1840, and his letter of 15 September 1840 above. In this second letter he referred to Mackenzie's plans to teach 6,000 Sinhalese and 2,000 Tamil students in the native languages. In the Sinhalese areas there were to be 100 schools for the 6,000 students.

plex challenge posed by vernacular education and the system of translations (he envisaged nothing less than the creation of a whole new vernacular literature), Gogerly endeavoured to emphasise the need for state support.[1] 'The whole is to be here created. We have at present neither booksellers, publishers, nor a book-buying population.'[2]

Mackenzie expected this strong support from Gogerly, but he could hardly have expected the Bishop of Madras to have gone as far as he did in supporting his schemes of educational reform. The Bishop came out firmly in support of vernacular education, and he agreed that a Translations Committee would be 'very desirable'.

The 'religious' tone of Mackenzie's educational reforms was for the Bishop their most attractive feature. He agreed with Mackenzie that education was above all things a necessary prelude to the conversion of the people to Christianity, and that '. . . the translation of the Holy Scriptures into the dialects of the Island' would be the best means of spreading Christianity.

But there were aspects of the Bishop's recommendations that Mackenzie found most unpalatable. He could agree with the Bishop that education was a means of conversion, but he saw many difficulties in the Bishop's suggestion that 'theoretical Christianity' – by which Mackenzie understood the Bishop to mean Anglican doctrine – should be an integral and indispensable part of the curriculum. Besides, the Bishop hinted that it might be advantageous to compel non-Christians to study 'theoretical Christianity'. Deeply suspicious of these suggestions, Mackenzie was alive to the difficulties and dangers their implementation would involve. He explained that if the Government were, 'to force, for instance, on the Mohammedan population . . . "theoretical Christianity", to use His Lordship's words, even to the extent he suggests, I am persuaded they would not let their children attend school'.[3] Even more reprehensible, in Mackenzie's eyes, was the Bishop's demand that the schools run by the Anglicans should receive privileged treatment. He regretted, too, the Bishop's suggestion that the Archdeacon should continue to be head of the School Commission.[4]

[1] He suggested that a sum of £300 a year be set aside for printing and publishing books in the vernacular.
[2] Gogerly's memorandum of 5 August 1840.
[3] C.O. 54/181, Mackenzie to Russell, no.135 of 12 August 1840.
[4] *Ibid.*

The Bishop's suggestions would have left the Anglican Establishment in continued control of the School Commission which, above all else, Mackenzie was determined to end.

Mackenzie sent these recommendations of the Bishop (despite his misgivings on some of them) and the suggestions of Gogerly to the Colonial Office in the hope that their support would win the home Government over to a realization of the importance of his proposals, particularly that of a Translation Committee, on which he set high hopes. He added another plea for his scheme of vernacular education, explaining that, far from competing with English education, it would actually help its spread. He assured Russell that there would be no reduction in the number of schools where English was taught exclusively; and he held out the prospect of a systematic improvement in the standard of education in such schools if his proposals were accepted.[1]

At the Colonial Office these recommendations on vernacular education drew heavy fire, notably from James Stephen who shared the widespread belief in the exclusive virtues of the English language as the medium of instruction in the Eastern Empire. He scornfully dismissed the arguments used by Mackenzie and Gogerly, particularly their reference to the activities of the Society for the Promotion of Christian knowledge:

> That the Scotch, the Welsh and the Irish should cling to their native languages and refuse instruction in English may I fear be referred to causes of which England has no reason to be proud. The influence of them can hardly be supposed to extend to Ceylon.[2]

In spite of Stephen's opposition, however, Mackenzie might have persuaded Russell to agree to his scheme, for Russell was inclined to be accommodating, as his minute of 17 October 1840 would show:

> I can hardly give an opinion of my own in this matter, I followed that of Mr Anstruther. I cannot help thinking however that some good translations into Sinhalese might help reading with a large class. Thus recommended I could not object to the expense of £400 a year for this particular purpose.[3]

---

[1] C.O. 54/181, Mackenzie to Russell, no.135 of 12 August 1840.

[2] C.O. 54/181, Mackenzie to Russell, no.124 of 10 August 1840. Stephen's minute of 15 October 1840.

[3] *Ibid.* Russell's minute of 17 October 1840.

But Russell had previously decided against the use of the vernacular languages and the establishment of a Translations Committee, and the decision had been conveyed to Mackenzie in the despatch which directed the formation of a new School Commission.[1] This decision, too, had been taken on Anstruther's advice as a Colonial Office Minute of 14 October 1840 would indicate. It reads thus:

[that] opinion was adopted from one expressed by Mr Anstruther which was in effect that the labour and expense . . . might be better devoted to the instruction of the natives in the English languages. That they were rapidly acquiring that language and that it was desirable to encourage its acquisition as a means of civilization. . . .[2]

Anstruther's standing at the Colonial Office was very high; he was consulted on every problem relating to Ceylon, and his opinions were greatly respected. Mackenzie's despatch (with the Bishop's recommendations and Gogerly's suggestions) were sent to him for his comments,[3] and he re-affirmed his opinion that 'little or no advantage would result from any attempt to supply translations of English works and the analogy of Gaelic schools in the highlands of Scotland does not apply to Ceylon'.[4] The effect of this minute of Anstruther's was to make Russell less accommodating than he had shown himself willing to be. Russell's reply to Mackenzie briefly disapproved of the Translation Committee, and recommended that more emphasis should be given to English as the language of instruction.[5] Anstruther's was the decisive voice in the rejection of Mackenzie's scheme of education.

Mackenzie could take some consolation in the fact that Russell

[1] C.O. 54/181, Russell to Mackenzie, no.63 of 26 April 1840.

[2] C.O. 54/181, Mackenzie to Russell, no.124 of 10 August 1840. Gairdner's minute of 14 October 1840. It must be emphasized that Anstruther was not the only person in Ceylon at this time to be convinced of the inadequacy of the Sinhalese language as a medium of instruction, and the shortcomings of the system of translating English books into Sinhalese. The Baptist Journal *The Investigator* held these views equally strongly. See *The Investigator*, January 1841, p.22.

[3] C.O. 54/181, Mackenzie to Russell, no.135 of 12 August 1840. All the previous correspondence on education had similarly been sent to him.

Anstruther was at this time on holiday in England. He was away from Ceylon for over twelve months from the end of 1839 to the beginning of 1841.

[4] Anstruther's minute [no date] on above.

[5] C.O. 54/181, Russell to Mackenzie, no.162 of 20 December 1840.

approved of his nominees to the reorganized School Commission.[1] He had spent the last months of his stay in Ceylon in remodelling the Commission, and it was perhaps a disappointment to him that he could achieve merely a change in its composition without any substantial change in the language of instruction. But by his reorganization of the School Commission he had, at last, broken the hold of the Anglican Establishment on education in Ceylon, and this was achievement enough. Almost the last important official act of Mackenzie's administration was his Minute of 27 March 1841, which constituted 'The Central School Commission for the Instruction of the population of Ceylon'.

His successor, Sir Colin Campbell, redefined the broad aims of the education policy of the Ceylon Government. In a minute, dated 26 May 1841, Campbell informed the Commission that it was their duty

> by every means in their power, to promote the education in the English language of their fellow subjects of all religious opinions in the Colony. They will therefore be particularly careful to introduce into their schools no books or system of instruction which might have the effect of excluding scholars of any religious belief whatever. . . . [It] will be the especial care of the Central Commission to exercise such caution as to raise no religious scruples on the part of any.[2]

The Commission was informed further that,

> though the general education of the whole population is the duty of the Commission, it will also be a most important part of their duty to promote the religious education of such of the community as belong to the Christian faith, and the funds under their management will therefore be equally applicable to this purpose.[3]

---

[1] Mackenzie's remodelled Commission had seven members, with Philip Anstruther as chairman. The others were to be: the Senior Colonial Chaplain; a Presbyterian Minister; a Roman Catholic priest; the Government Agent of the Western Province; a non-official member of the Legislative Council; a Missionary of the Church of England (C.M.S. or S.P.G.) or a Wesleyan. Power was left to the Governor to add two more. He had broken the hold of the Anglican Establishment on the School Commission effectively. But he was able to make only four appointments before he left Ceylon: Rev. J. Bailey, CMS; Sir Anthony Oliphant (Chief Justice); D. J. Gogerly (Wesleyan); and J. Armitage, a non-official member of the Legislative Council.

Note that the Archdeacon was not a member of the Commission. Mackenzie insisted on a lay Chairman.

[2] C.O. 54/188, Campbell to Russell, no. 18 of 27 May 1841.   [3] *Ibid.*

The Commission was to undertake: the administration of the funds voted by the Legislative Council for the purpose of education, the appointment of all schoolmasters, the fixing of their salaries, and the purchase of school books, furniture and other equipment. (They were not permitted to incur any charge for erecting or repairing buildings without the usual sanction of the Government.) Apart from the establishment of Government schools, the Commission was at liberty to grant money in aid of any private schools which they considered to be worthy of encouragement, but always on condition that they retained the full right of inspection and examination, without interference in any way from the management. Also, there were to be sub-committees to control education in the provinces, under the supervision of the Central Commission.

The years 1841–8 may be looked upon as years of quiet achievement in education. The Anglican preponderance on the School Commission was gone, and a lay head kept sectarian jealousies under control. But the chief feature of this phase was the gradual acceptance of many aspects of Mackenzie's education policy, despite their rejection by the home Government. The man chiefly responsible for this remarkable reversal of policy, so quietly achieved that there was hardly a murmur of protest from officials in Ceylon or abroad, was D. J. Gogerly, who came to wield the same influence with Anstruther and Campbell as he had with Mackenzie. Gogerly came to dominate the School Commission as much by the strength of his personality and his erudition, as by the fact that in that organization he alone had a definite policy. It was easy for him to dominate the School Commission at this time. The Anglican Establishment, out of favour with both governments and in the throes of a painful process of reorganization, were too demoralized to offer an effective challenge. Anstruther, though he was greatly interested in education, was in no position to control the Commission himself. Busy with his coffee plantations and reform of the civil service, a task on which he was latterly to devote all his energies, he came to rely increasingly on Gogerly in the School Commission. Nor were the other officials in a position to impose their views on the Commission; perhaps they lacked both the inclination and the time. Thus the path was clear for Gogerly.

The first two years of the School Commission saw little achievement. Indeed, nothing could be done because the negligence of the previous Commission compelled the new one to devote all its attention merely to keeping the system of education going. Besides, the Anglican Archdeacon was hostile to the new Commission from its inception, in spite of the conciliatory attitude adopted by the latter.[1]

Perhaps the most constructive achievement of these first two years of the new Commission was the establishment of three central schools, where part of the education provided was designed to prepare poorer students for a career in commerce and the professions. The education provided in the ordinary schools was more academic than practical; aware of this the Commission established the central schools to teach such subjects as surveying, mensuration, navigation, draughtmanship, commercial arithmetic, bookkeeping and the new sciences of chemistry and physics.[2] The first of these schools was established at Colombo, in August 1843, under W. Knighton.[3] The second was opened at Galle, and the third at Kandy.[4] The establishment of these three central schools was the one redeeming feature of the first two years of activity of the second School Commission.

The constructive phase in the history of this new School Commission began in 1843, with a significant new development in the financing of education; it also marked the beginning of Gogerly's assertion of authority in the Commission. A scheme which originated with Gogerly in the School Commission was adopted, by which some 'Ministers' Schools' were supported by the Govern-

---

[1] A/R Sch.Com. 1841–2.

[2] C.O. 54/196, Campbell to Russell, no.47 of 5 April 1842.

[3] Knighton gained some distinction as the author of two works on Ceylon; one, a history entitled *A History of Ceylon from the earliest period to the present time* (London, 1840); and the other a book on *Forest Life in Ceylon*, 2 vols. (London, 1854).

Knighton and the headmasters of the Central Schools at Galle and Kandy had been trained at the Normal Seminary at Glasgow (begun in 1836), the first institution in Britain for the training of teachers.

[4] There were considerable doubts expressed about the opening of a Central School at Kandy. It was feared that the Kandyans, who were, on the whole, not interested in Government employment, would not appreciate the English education provided in this school. It was also reported that the Kandyans would not pay school fees or buy school books (they were on the whole too poor to afford much money for these). But these gloomy predictions were not fulfilled, and this school proved to be a qualified success.

ment, with the minister becoming the superintendent of his school, appointing and dismissing teachers with the concurrence of the Commission.[1] This aid was originally intended only for schools teaching in the English language, but Gogerly succeeded in getting the Wesleyan schools in the Galle district, and later those at Kollupitiya (a suburb of Colombo) and Trincomalee, on the list of schools qualifying for aid, though these schools taught in the vernacular.[2]

It was in Jaffna, however, where the missionaries laid great emphasis on English education, that the system of aid to mission schools really took root. The first School Commission had started an English school and four vernacular schools there, but these proved to be unsatisfactory and were closed down in 1842. In 1843 other schools were opened under new teachers, but they never really started, as the School Commission found it difficult to superintend these schools effectively. Besides, the mission schools were so well established that the Government saw no need to compete with them. The Government schools were closed and, instead, grants were made to missions – £150 a year each to the C.M.S. and the Wesleyans and £200 a year to the American Mission – with the stipulation that this money was to be spent *in addition* to the amounts already devoted by these missions to the diffusion of English education.[3]

Whatever others may have thought about it, Gogerly looked on this new scheme of aid to missions schools as the first step in a stage that was to lead to radical changes in the existing system of education. He had not ceased to believe in the need for greater emphasis on the vernaculars – particularly in the Government-aided schools – and he looked upon his success in getting some Wesleyan vernacular schools to qualify for aid meant exclusively for English schools, as being no less than the thin edge of the vernacular-education wedge. In 1843 the School Commission made a statement which was, in effect, a cautious step in the direction favoured by Gogerly. It was reported that, although the rules prepared for the guidance of the Commission prevented them from establishing schools,

> exclusively teaching the native languages, they could not remain insensible to their importance; and the necessity of making instruc-

---

[1] Wes.Mss.Cey., I, Gogerly, 24 September 1844.
[2] *Ibid.*   [3] *A/R Sch.Com.* 1843–4.

tion in those languages the preparatory step to English education caused them to pass a resolution [on 1 September 1843] that there be supplied to every elementary school, when necessary, the means of giving instruction in the native languages so as to afford the necessary preparation for English education. It is thought that many natives who would willingly give their children education in their own languages, but who cannot be made to see the advantage of having them taught English, will thus be induced to send their children to Government schools.

This resolution was significant enough when it is remembered that Philip Anstruther, the Chairman of the Commission, was the man responsible for persuading Russell to reject this very policy when it was originally suggested by Mackenzie and Gogerly.

It was one thing to pass this resolution, but quite another to get the Government to accept it as a policy. Gogerly realized that it would take months before the Government could be persuaded to accept it. In September 1844 he revealed his plans to his superiors in London:

> This [education in the vernacular] I have long had in contemplation, and have striven for it at every convenient opportunity. At last I brought it before the Government . . . as a member of the School Commission. It has two [sic] parts: (1) A Normal School . . . (2) A Translating and Printing Department for school books and works of general literature . . . (3) a system of schools to begin in 1846 and to be enlarged each successive year.[1]

It was, in the main, the rejected scheme of 1840. Gogerly was determined that, if this private application failed to move the Government, he would, the following year, 'memorialize the Legislative Council, taking care first to secure if possible a majority'.[2]

By the end of 1844 a touch of urgency had entered his appeals, for he realized that after 1845 it would be increasingly difficult for him to have his way in the Commission. The Government had decided to create a Bishopric of Colombo in 1845; the Archdeacon had been pensioned off, and it was expected that the arrival of the new Bishop would find the Anglican Establishment, its strength recovered, once more a formidable opponent. Gogerly fully expected the Bishop, and the Anglican clergy, to throw difficulties in the way of the Commission. He complained that his plan for

---

[1] Wes.Mss.Cey., I, Gogerly, 24 September 1844.   [2] *Ibid.*

native education was opposed: 'by some influential persons as tending to give too much power to the Wesleyans. Had I been a Minister of the episcopal church instead of a Wesleyan missionary, the plan would have been instantly adopted'.[1] But he was being unduly pessimistic, for Anstruther informed him that the Government proposed a grant of £1,000 for 1845, to aid Gogerly's scheme of native education.[2]

The principle had been accepted and it was now Gogerly's intention to fill in the details. In a letter to Anstruther he laid out a comprehensive plan for native education, the keystone of which was a native normal school for Sinhalese youths (on which £500 was to be spent), with his colleague the Rev. Andrew Kessen as principal and himself as honorary superintendent.[3] The course of education in this school was to be completely in Sinhalese – the subjects taught would be Sinhalese reading and writing, composition and grammar, arithmetic, geometry, mensuration and trigonometry, geography and 'a general view of Ancient and Modern History'. Religious teaching was to be an integral part of this education, and none but Christians would be employed as teachers.

Even more urgent, Gogerly thought, was the need for school textbooks in Sinhalese: a general reading book, an arithmetic book, a geography and one or more histories (with a treatise on geometry, mensuration and trigonometry to follow) being the irreducible minimum. He urged the Government to undertake the printing of this series of school textbooks as well as other works (in Sinhalese) of general interest to a wider public.[4]

He recommended a standing Committee of the School Commission to be appointed to control the Department of Native Education; the members of this standing Committee were to be: Gogerly himself; Rev. J. P. Horsford, Colonial Chaplain; Rev. J. G. McVicar, Presbyterian; and George Lee, the Secretary of the Commission. The Anglican Establishment was in a minority of one in this Committee.[5]

---

[1] Wes.Mss.Cey., I, Gogerly, 22 November 1844.

[2] Wes.Mss.Cey., I, Gogerly, 16 September 1845.

[3] *Ibid.* Gogerly estimated that it would cost £270 to establish the Normal School. Kessen, as Principal, was to have £250 a year since it was a post of very great importance.   [4] *Ibid.*

[5] Wes.Mss.Cey., I, Gogerly, 16 September 1845.

Looking beyond the 1845 budget, he suggested an increased grant for 1846 of £1,250, to be distributed thus: £600 to the schools, £300 to the Normal School, £100 to the Translations Department, and £250 for printing school books. The new schools were to be established in groups of not less than five within a radius of five or six miles. Ministers of all denominations were requested to help in conducting these schools (on the same principles as Chaplains' and Ministers' Schools) and, whenever possible, to serve as superintendents of schools in the vicinity of their stations. In every instance these schools were to teach at least four subjects – reading, writing, arithmetic (including fractions and decimals) and Christianity.[1]

It was, on the whole, a well-thought-out plan, matured by reflection over several years. Its only defect was that it tended to give the Wesleyans a commanding position in the new scheme of education, through Gogerly and – to a lesser extent – Kessen, a position which the Anglicans would not concede to them without a struggle. There was too much at stake, for with the Government supporting education in the vernaculars, it was obvious that the Anglicans themselves would have to adjust their education policy to meet the new situation, if they were not to be completely overshadowed by the Wesleyans who already had the advantage of having pioneered education in the vernaculars in the Sinhalese areas. It is not surprising that when the Government sent Gogerly's scheme to the School Commission, it should have been opposed by the Anglicans, mainly on the grounds that it would throw the whole system of native education into the hands of the Wesleyans.[2]

It was a difficult, even dangerous, position for Gogerly, for his new education proposals were now in danger of provoking an embarrassing sectarian dispute; but he was equal to the occasion. After his scheme had been with the Executive Council for some time, he called on Anstruther, and then on Campbell, and convinced them that the objections of the Anglicans were without foundation. Apparently Campbell was convinced by Gogerly's persuasive arguments, and felt that the apprehensions of the Anglicans – that the Wesleyans would gain a preponderant influence in the new educational structure – were 'unworthy of notice'. A second – and more difficult – problem was the question of finance. Would the Government consent to meet the additional

[1] Wes.Mss.Cey., I, Gogerly, 16 September 1845.   [2] Ibid.

expenses that this new scheme involved? Here again Gogerly's arguments appear to have been persuasive enough, for Campbell was satisfied that the island's revenues could well meet the increased demands on it for native education. And then came the third, and most difficult problem – would Campbell consent to approve this scheme on his own, or would he seek the prior permission of the Colonial Office and thereby jeopardize the whole project? For the Colonial Office was likely to object both to the prominence given to the vernaculars and to the additional expense. Here, Gogerly did not seek to influence Campbell's decision, though he obviously hoped that the scheme would not be sent to the Colonial Office first. Campbell hesitated to carry out the scheme on his own authority, and was inclined to submit it to Lord Stanley; but he changed his mind and approved the project on his own initiative. The money was obtained by a special grant.

Gogerly's lobbying had proved effective. The Commission established the Native Normal School, with Kessen as superintendent on a salary of £250 a year. It is an indication of the extent of Gogerly's influence with the Government that this Native Normal School was established in the rooms on the ground floor of the Wesleyan Mission House in the Pettah in Colombo.[1] No wonder, then, that this institution was always looked upon as a Wesleyan, rather than as a Government, venture.

A sub-committee (in which significantly there was no representative of the Anglican Establishment, or for that matter even one from the C.M.S.) consisting of the Revs. J. G. McVicar and Gogerly, and a layman, G. Lee, was formed for the translation into Sinhalese of books for schools and general purposes. The supervision of this work was left with Gogerly, not however, at his insistence, for he aimed at carrying out his plans with as little personal prominence as possible, in order to avoid antagonizing the Anglicans further. At the same time he urged the Home Society to

> use your influence with Her Majesty's Government to have education in the vernacular languages extended to every part of the Island, not to the exclusion of English, but in aid of it, as I feel confident that Native education will act upon English education by inducing many to study that language from higher motives than those by which the few who attend to it are influenced at present.

[1] Wes.Mss.Cey., I, Gogerly, 16 September 1845.

But there is nothing to indicate that the Home Society moved in the matter.

When the Legislative Council decided in favour of education in the vernacular, Gogerly wrote home in triumph that:

> All opposition to this so far as this Island is concerned is at an end, and its necessity is universally admitted.[1] This is a very great point gained. . . . It is necessary to insert the wedge prudently and resistance will be in vain. . . .

He was already thinking of 1847, by the beginning of which he hoped to get ten or twelve schools established, with the prospect of increasing the number considerably in the course of that year.

But towards the end of 1845, Gogerly's position in the educational system was endangered by the retirement of Philip Anstruther from his post of Colonial Secretary, and what was to be more important, by the creation of the Bishopric of Colombo. The Wesleyans had great fears for their position in the system of education; it was anticipated that the Bishop would not co-operate with the School Commission as it was then constituted, and Gogerly feared that the Commission itself would be superseded and one with a greater representation for the Anglicans substituted. Besides, Anstruther's departure left the post of Chairman of the School Commission vacant. After a great deal of thought, Campbell appointed the Bishop to the post, perhaps because he felt that he could be more dangerous outside the School Commission than inside it.[2] The Bishop and Gogerly offered to co-operate with each other, but the latter was already apprehensive, as he had good reason to be, for the Wesleyans through him, had come to wield an influence out of all proportion to their numbers. Gogerly had charge of two schools at Kollupitiya (paid for by the Government), and had the superintendence of schools at Panadura, Molligoda and Kalutara. At Galle, Bridgnell had his schools paid for by the Government, but they were under his sole control. As Gogerly himself informed his superiors in London, the Wesleyans could not expect more than this.[3]

---

[1] It was generally true that all the missions in Ceylon were at this time convinced of the need for education in the vernaculars.

[2] Wes.Mss.Cey., I, Gogerly, 17 November 1845. It would appear from this letter that Campbell consulted Gogerly before he appointed the Bishop to the post. Gogerly agreed with Campbell that it was safer to have the Bishop on the Commission than out of it.   [3] Wes.Mss.Cey., I, Gogerly, 17 November 1845.

The appointment of the Bishop to the post of chairman of the School Commission marked the end of the period of comparative peace in that body. Anstruther had kept sectarian jealousies in check, and the Commission had worked with smooth efficiency, but the dominance of Gogerly had given the Wesleyans a great deal of influence and prominence, a situation which the Anglicans would not tolerate. The Bishop, who tended to look at most problems from the narrow point of view of the Anglican Establishment, almost at once set about to redress the balance, which in this case meant a reduction in the influence of the Wesleyans. The period immediately following the creation of the Episcopal See of Colombo saw a ruthless campaign against the Wesleyans waged by the Anglicans under the leadership of the Bishop. The Wesleyans could with justice call this phase, 'the most mournful period in the history of the mission. . . .' Schools were erected and services established in the immediate neighbourhood of Wesleyan schools and chapels, 'and the thombo registry and the burial ground were used as instruments of intimidation'.[1]

The only encouragement the Wesleyans had at this time came from the fact that the new Colonial Secretary, Sir James Emerson-Tennent, had been a great friend of the Wesleyans in England and was known to be a strong supporter of missionary enterprise.[2] Gogerly had obtained a letter of introduction to him from the Secretary of the Methodist Mission in England, and he had hopes that it 'may prove sufficient to interest him in our cause in this Island.'[3] A few months after the Bishop's arrival, Gogerly was complaining that Governor Campbell was 'very much in the hands of the Bishop', but at the same time he declared his great faith in Tennent who, it appeared, had promised Gogerly his support.[4] And events proved that he would live up to his promise.

This sudden change in the situation in Ceylon did not deter Gogerly from going ahead with his plans on education. His main aim at the time [July 1846] was to get the vote for Sinhalese education passed by the Legislative Council. He had met both

[1] Spence-Hardy, R., *The Jubilee Memorials of the Wesleyan Mission, South Ceylon, 1814–64*, pp.99, 100.

[2] Mis.Not., X, 515. Tennent had presided at the Annual Missionary Meeting at Exeter Hall in 1841. He had played an important part at the previous annual meeting, too.

[3] Wes.Mss.Cey., I, Gogerly, 17 November 1845.

[4] Wes.Mss.Cey., II, Gogerly, 11 July 1846.

Campbell and Tennent on this matter. He had previously written to them officially as well as privately on it. But, in mid-1846, the Government was pledged only to the Native Normal School, while Gogerly was anxious that the whole scheme of native education should be approved by the Council, and that the grant for native education be included in the estimates for 1846, '. . . or the Normal students will have no work to do'. With the unanimous support of the School Commission, and a promise from Tennent to use his influence, Gogerly had every reason to hope that it would be possible to obtain a grant for thirty native schools, twenty for boys and ten for girls, as a beginning. He wrote home that:

> . . . if this be granted the work will surely increase year by year; the important step being to induce the Government to commence education in the Native Language as they have hitherto supported only English schools. I have every prospect of a grant of £2,600 for education in the Native Languages for 1847.[1]

Eventually he did obtain the grant for thirty schools in 1846, but at the price of alienating the Bishop further. By the middle of 1847 the Bishop and Gogerly were at loggerheads. The Bishop was endeavouring to thwart him in the School Commission and to reduce, in every way possible, the influence of the Wesleyans. He was particularly anxious to crush Kessen's Native Normal School. As a means of achieving this end, he opposed the employment of normal students trained by Kessen, but Gogerly was sufficiently influential at the School Commission to have many of the Bishop's proposals outvoted, particularly those on the Native Normal School. Besides, the Wesleyans had the backing of the Government, particularly of Tennent, who it would appear had introduced Gogerly and Kessen to the new Governor, Viscount Torrington, as the ' . . . two men who were doing more for education than all the others put together'.[2]

Relations between the Wesleyans and the Anglicans deteriorated progressively in the course of 1847. In the Eastern Province, where the rivalry of the two groups was particularly strong, it retarded the progress of the Veddah Mission.[3] In the Western Province the Anglicans entered into fierce competition with the Wesleyans, opening schools and chapels in close proximity to those

[1] Wes.Mss.Cey., II, Gogerly, 11 July 1846.
[2] Wes.Mss.Cey., II, Gogerly, 10 June 1847; Kessen, 10 June 1847.
[3] See below chapter VII.

of the latter. These campaigns which had the active support of the Bishop, culminated in a clash at Negombo in which Torrington was compelled to intervene. He did so with the firm declaration that all missionary groups in Ceylon were of equal standing and that none, not even the Anglicans, were entitled to any special privileges.[1] The Wesleyans were delighted. But the ground was being prepared for the inevitable conflict in the Central School Commission. It came on the issue of the appointment of Kessen, then at the head of the Native Normal Institution, to a vacant post in the Colombo Academy. Kessen applied directly to the Governor for this post, instead of applying through the Central School Commission as he ought to have done. Torrington gave him the appointment, to which the Bishop and the Rev. J. Horsford (Colonial Chaplain) expressed strong objections on the ground that the appointment to that post lay with the Commission. Torrington's defence was that he was unaware of any such regulations; in any event, he disapproved of such a regulation even if it existed.[2] Later he issued a minute declaring that: the administration of funds, the appointment of teachers and all proceedings of the Commission which involved the expenditure of money, should be subject to his approval; and all appointments carrying a salary of over £100 per annum should in the first place be made by him. The Bishop refused to accept this new situation and resigned, along with Horsford. Torrington justified his decision to the Secretary of State on the grounds that large powers were delegated to the Commission without reference

to the responsible Head of the Executive, a circumstance the unusual character of which and the possible inconvenience that might arise therefrom were very much modified by the fact of the Colonial Secretary being appointed to occupy the chair of the Commission. Through his direct intervention as the double organ both of the Commission and of the Government, their respective wishes were reciprocally made known to him, so that practically the Executive had really a direct cognizance of and protanto a participation in all the proceedings of the Commission.[3]

[1] C.O. 54/238, Torrington to Grey, no.99 of 10 September 1847, and no. 105 of 15 September 1847.

Wes.Mss.Cey., II, Gogerly, 14 September 1847; *The Ceylon Examiner*, 8 September 1847; *The Ceylon Times*, 31 August 1847.

[2] C.O. 54/238, Torrington to Grey, no.99 of 10 September 1847.

[3] *Ibid.*

It was implied that, since the Colonial Secretary was no longer Chairman of the School Commission, it was necessary to increase the control of the Government over the Commission. But there was no mistaking the fact that a sharp reduction had been made in the powers of the Commission, for even when Tennent was appointed to the post of Chairman, on the Bishop's resignation, these powers were not restored. Both Earl Grey,[1] the new Secretary of State for the Colonies, and Benjamin Hawes, his Under-Secretary, supported Torrington in his brush with the Bishop, though Hawes[2] feared that the resignation of the Bishop would lead to a revival of sectarian disputes on the Commission, and regretted the loss of the Bishop's services.[3] Torrington, on the other hand, obviously did not regret the resignation of the Bishop.

The sectarian conflicts anticipated by Hawes came without much delay. Having precipitately resigned from the School Commission, the Bishop now demanded its complete remodelling: he wanted a Commission of five lay members and two paid lay officials.[4] The Bishop probably believed that such a Commission would give the Anglicans a stronger voice in educational affairs. Since the great majority of officials and settlers were adherents of the Church of England, the Commission was very likely to have an Anglican majority; and besides, a Commission composed of laymen would perhaps be more amenable to the influence of the Anglican Establishment. Moreover, these laymen were unlikely to devote as much time to their duties as non-conformist clergymen did in the past, and these duties were likely to fall, by default, on the Anglican Establishment.[5]

The case against the Bishop's suggestions for the remodelling of the School Commission was prepared by Tennent,[6] with the

---

[1] C.O. 54/238, Grey's minute of 29 October 1847.

[2] *Ibid.*, Hawes' minute of 28 October 1847.

[3] *The Ceylon Times*, 31 August 1847, attributed the resignation of the Bishop partly at least to the unfriendly attitude of the Governor:

It is said that the Bishop remonstrated with the Governor on the ground, not of the unfitness of the man, but the informality of the proceeding: on which His Excellency told His Lordship that if what was *right* to be done was contrary to *form* the impediment must be removed, and did so incontinently; whereupon the Bishop feeling snubbed resigned. . . .

[4] C.O. 54/243, Torrington to Grey, no.56 of 13 March 1848.

[5] Wes.Mss.Cey., II, Gogerly, 15 February 1848.

[6] Tennent addressed a letter to the Bishop refuting his arguments.

assistance of Gogerly and the Rev. J. D. Palm of the Dutch Reformed Church.[1] They argued that it was impossible to accept the Bishop's views, as the Colony was 'not sufficiently advanced in civilization' for the Central School Commission to be composed entirely of laymen. There were no laymen sufficiently educated, and with sufficient experience of education (and with the leisure to devote their time to education) to take over the work of the School Commission. Tennent did not have to make a stronger defence of the Schools Commission because there was no charge of inefficiency levelled against it by the Bishop; it was merely a lack of confidence in it among the Anglicans. Torrington endorsed Tennent's views and added that the Bishop's animosity towards the Commission could be explained by the fact that, in resigning the post of Chairman, he now naturally felt himself deprived of that additional influence in the work of education and conversion which that post possessed. The Bishop had alleged, as the main cause for his lack of confidence in the Commission, that a struggle for supremacy was taking place in that organization. Torrington brushed this aside with the comment that:

> . . . if there has been any struggle for supremacy in the Commission, which is not a question as yet brought before me, I have a right to conclude that in that struggle [if such there were] the majority of its members who undoubtedly are of the same communion with the Lord Bishop would not be the losers.[2]

But this was less than the truth. Mackenzie had formed the Central School Commission with the clear intention of leaving the Anglicans in a less dominant position than in the previous Commission. The members of the Commission for the greater part of this period were: P. Anstruther as Chairman (till 1846), Rev. J. B. Horsford (Colonial Chaplain), Rev. C. J. McVicar (Presbyterian), Rev. V. C. Antonio (Roman Catholic), Rev. D. J. Gogerly (Wesleyan), Rev. J. Bailey (C.M.S.), J. Armitage (non-official member of the Legislative Council), Sir Anthony Oliphant (Chief Justice) and P. E. Wodehouse (Government Agent, Western Province). It is significant that the Anglicans did not have a majority in the Commission; until the appointment of the Bishop, the Anglican Establishment had only one representative, and

---

[1] C.O. 54/243, Torrington to Grey, no.56 of 13 March 1848.
[2] Ibid.

M

could rely only on P. E. Wodehouse, a staunch High Churchman. The Bishop's relations with the C.M.S. in Ceylon were never very cordial and deteriorated progressively. He may have had greater support from the S.P.G. but that Society was not represented on the Commission. Anstruther was a Presbyterian and Oliphant may have been one himself; at any rate neither of them supported the Anglican Establishment. The government officials on the Committee, apart from Wodehouse, were free from any sectarian bias and supported Anglican and Nonconformist alike. Thus the Anglicans could never hope to gain a majority on a purely sectarian issue, and it has been shown that Gogerly was able to have the Bishop's measures out-voted on more than one occasion.

Faced with Torrington's intransigent attitude, the Bishop had no alternative but to petition Earl Grey on the question of reconstructing the School Commission. Besides, he had a more specific complaint against the School Commission on the appointment of teachers to schools; he felt that the Anglicans were being discriminated against in this matter, and complained also of the disposition on the part of 'one of its clerical members' – he was obviously referring to Gogerly – to exercise an undue influence over some of the young masters of the Normal School in their attendance at places of worship. When Torrington backed the Commission against the Bishop and the Anglicans on this issue, the latter decided to appeal to Earl Grey on this, and the more important issue of reconstructing the School Commission.[1]

Torrington was willing to make certain minor concessions to the Anglicans. They had objected to the appointment of Dr

---

[1] C.O. 54/243, Torrington to Grey, no.56 of 13 March 1848. See enclosed letter of Bishop.

C.O. 54/244, Torrington to Grey, no.76 of 12 April 1848.

Grey MSS., Torrington to Grey, private letter (?) March 1848 (probably 15 March). In this letter Torrington explained to Grey that, apart from the Bishop and a few of his clergy, there was general satisfaction with the Commission. The lay members in that body had confidence in it. He warned Grey that:

> If you agree to the Bishop's Memorial you will cast a vote of censure on the Commission and cause a great *row* in the Colony. I would suggest your replying that you hope things may work well, that the questions raised are *important* and you will take *time* and consider the question; in the meantime direct me to watch and see that all parties have equal justice. . . .

Grey's reply, C.O. 54/244, despatch to Torrington, no.218 of 25 May 1848, faithfully carried out these 'instructions'.

McVicar to the post of Secretary of the Commission. The latter, in order to prevent the aggravation of sectarian jealousies in the School Commission, made a voluntary surrender of this office, and on his resignation Torrington decided to replace him with a layman J. Fraser, the Keeper of the Government Records. And at the same time he decided to appoint another layman, in place of Rev. B. Bailey of the Anglican Establishment (and the Bishop's personal chaplain), to the important post of Inspector of Schools. He believed that these measures would place 'the most important executive officers of the School Commission as far removed as they can hope to be from the suspicion or imputation of sectarian influence'.[1]

The Bishop could have had but little consolation from Earl Grey's reply to his petitions. He regretted the Bishop's decision to resign from the Commission, but refused to accept his proposals for reform, commenting that, while the Bishop declared a want of confidence in the Commission, he had not charged it with inefficiency, and that this was insufficient reason for so fundamental a change as the Bishop suggested. At the same time he urged Torrington to do all that was possible to win back the confidence of the Church of England and to instruct the Commission to see that it did not give any suspicion that it favoured one religious sect against another.

During this period Gogerly wrote home his own version of these events:

> The Bishop and his friends have opposed us much in the School Commission but hitherto without success: he is in consequence displeased with the Government, affirming that it supports sectarianism, and does not give the Church of England its share in the education of the Colony. The correspondence had been lengthy and the last letter which I have seen from the Governor to the Bishop makes 37 pages. The Bishop also wrote to Earl Grey recommending the consti-

---

[1] C.O. 54/244, Torrington to Grey, no.76 of 12 April 1848.

In 1845 the Rev. Brooke Bailey was appointed Inspector of Schools. He was the Head Master of the Colombo Academy. Subsequently he took Holy Orders and was appointed Chaplain to the Bishop of Colombo. In his despatch, no.99 of 10 September 1847 – C.O. 54/238 – Torrington remarked '. . . that representations have been made to me which tend to show that this proceeding coupled with the fact that his tours of inspection are now made in a double capacity have been viewed with some degree of jealousy by those who are not members of the Church of England'.

tution of the Commission be changed, but without success, as the Home Government has supported the Colonial Authorities.[1]

Gogerly had a triumph to report:

> I am happy to say that the Home Government decidedly approved of the plan for education in the vernacular languages, and have kept Mr Kessen's school on the fixed establishment of the Colony. It was, before on the contingent list and required an annual vote of the Legislative Council for the necessary funds: but it is now out of the power of the mere Island influence to discontinue it.[2]

The years 1841–8 were without doubt years of quiet achievement. No other phase in the history of education up to this time, could quite compare with it for constructive achievement. The School Commission which worked well in spite of the bitterness and sectarian disputes that entered with the Bishop, proved to be an efficient instrument in the hands of the right man – a lay head such as Anstruther or Tennent. In this period government expenditure on education rose from £2,999 in 1841 to £11,145 in 1847. More important than this enormous increase in expenditure was the sense of direction and purpose in educational work, and a consciousness of the value of the work that was being done – all of which was notably absent in the work of the first School Commission.

Much of the credit was due to Anstruther, who kept the worst aspects of sectarianism in check, and guided the Commission through its first few formative years; but much more was due to his trusted confidant Gogerly, to whom, above all others, the credit for the achievement of this period must go. He is one of the forgotten men in the educational history of Ceylon, though he left his mark on his age as few others had done. Working with tact and patience, and using all the high qualities of industry, erudition and foresight with which he was endowed, he won Anstruther over to reversing the very policy he had been so largely instrumental in enforcing only a few years earlier. More than that, Gogerly had forced those with whom he was associated into seeing that education in the vernaculars had its place; and his achievement is all the greater when one considers the fact that the keenest intelligences of his day were still insisting on the exclusive virtues of the

---

[1] Wes.Mss.Cey., II, Gogerly, 15 February 1848.
[2] *Ibid.*

English language. Ceylon, thanks to him, was years ahead of India in the appreciation of the value of the vernaculars.

But his success in this sphere was achieved at the sacrifice of his other ideal of a wider expansion of educational facilities. In 1840 he had spoken of one hundred schools teaching in Sinhalese to 6,000 students.[1] In 1846 he was satisfied with thirty schools. Indeed, he could hardly have persuaded the State to accept both vernacular education, and education for the masses. The former was difficult enough; the latter was impossible to achieve because of the enormous expenditure it would have entailed. In any event, persuading the Government to accept vernacular education was achievement enough at that time.

It must not be assumed that, once the Government accepted the principle of education in the vernaculars, it concerned itself mainly with vernacular education and vernacular schools thereafter. English schools and English education remained the main concern of the Government.

Missionary influence on educational policy was particularly strong at this time. But missionary influence as exemplified by Gogerly and as exemplified by the Bishop of Colombo were two different things: the first was missionary influence at his enlightened best, an invigorating and refreshing thing, but the second was missionary influence at its worst, as corrosive of ideals as the shadier aspects of party politics.

After the seven years of achievement which ended with the appointment of Tennent to the post of Chairman, the next eight were years of frustration and disappointment. The economic depression of 1847–8, which marked the end of the coffee boom, compelled the Government to reduce its expenditure drastically. The Government vote on education had reached £11,145 in 1847; it was reduced to a mere £6,000 in 1848. The missionary organizations were in no position to make good the difference. They could not have done so in the best of times, and they were much less likely to do so in 1848, when as a result of the depression at home, the parent societies had curtailed their grants to overseas branches.[2] The Wesleyans, never very strong financially, were among the worst affected. They made a despairing appeal to Government to

[1] Wes.Mss.Cey., I, Gogerly, 15 September 1840.
[2] C.M.S. MSS., C.CE.05, Bishop Chapman's letter of 31 March 1848.

continue the annual grant of £200 to finance the Wesleyan schools,[1] and largely through their influence with Tennent they succeeded, much to their surprise, in having it continued. Gogerly wrote home that, 'I cannot speak in too high terms of the very effectual aid we have at all times received from Sir Emerson Tennent'.[2] Thanks to this continuation of Government aid, the Wesleyan Mission schools survived in better shape than they would have unaided.

In September 1847 the School Commission was informed that the education vote for 1848 would be drastically reduced, and they were requested to institute 'a searching inquiry into the state of the schools with a view to retrenchment'.[3] In a letter of 20 September 1847 Tennent explained the new principles on which Government aid to education was to be based – the principle of 'self-support' as distinguished from the hitherto prevailing system of Government-support to schools '. . . [Henceforth] the interference and contribution of Government ought to be confined to assisting education, and not to providing it exclusively as heretofore. . . .' He added that this new principle was adopted because the Government was 'satisfied that the mass of the population whose children now resort to or are hereafter likely to frequent the public schools, are possessed of sufficient means to contribute something towards the expense of their education.'[4] Events were to prove that this assumption was far from correct. Few parents could afford to pay school fees, and there was a steep drop in attendance at schools when the new system of 'self-support' was introduced.

A committee of the School Commission was appointed to inquire into the state of the schools with a view to retrenchment. The Committee reported that there was a remarkable unanimity of opinion on the 'abstract justice' of the principle of self-support. But the significance of their report lies less in the arguments used to justify the adoption of this new principle[5] (it was after all only a

---

[1] Wes.Mss.Cey., II, Gogerly's letter of 14 April 1848.

[2] Wes.Mss.Cey., II, Gogerly, 11 May 1848.

[3] *A/R Sch.Com.*, 1847–8.   [4] *Ibid.*

[5] The arguments used to justify 'self-support' were disarmingly simple. First, it was contended that while State intervention was necessary, it should not be 'too general or too ostensible'. Secondly, it was argued that school fees were necessary because 'men are not apt to value any blessings that are given to them gratuitously'.

grandiloquent term for economy in education), than in the fact that, for the first time, an effort was made – indeed as a by-product of this attempt to justify self-support – to define the scope and purpose of education, and it was defined in terms that had little connection with religious conversion.

The Committee held that it was in the interest of the State, 'whatever its duty, to educate those whom it governs'. (This was, for its day, a surprisingly radical view. It was nearly a generation later that England awoke to the need to 'educate our masters'.) They added that this was all the more necessary and urgent in the east where 'a knowledge of the rights as well as of the duties of humanity is so deficient and so vague [among the people], and over whom, consequently, the machinery of government must be so much more minute and complex than in countries where half the work of administration is done by the people themselves'.[1] The corollary of this argument was that an educated people would require less government interference in the ordering of their lives, the consummation of which the Committee regarded as a thing of inestimable value.[2]

This conception of the purpose of education was narrow: though it was fundamentally political, it was not, indeed, an education designed to train people for ultimate political freedom, as much as for a less lofty, but more immediately practicable, goal of training them to take over some of the tasks of the administration. The mid-nineteenth century conception of State purpose was narrow and the designs of the Committee naturally pre-supposed this framework. It was very much a preparation for something like local self-government. One suspects, however, that these ideas were the personal views of C. J. MacCarthy, who presided over this Committee, for, generally, few people in Ceylon at this time would have thought of education designed for much more than conversion to Christianity.

The Committee admired the organization of education in Van Diemen's Land, where a system of local rates financed education. They held that the best method of self-support would be such a system of local rates, but since a system of local government did not exist in Ceylon they saw no alternative to an 'indirect assessment' in the shape of increased school fees. There was to be a change 'from an almost nominal payment into a fixed and pro-

[1] *A/R Sch.Com.*, 1847–8.   [2] *A/R Sch.Com.*, 1847–8.

portionate one, according to the nature and extent of the instruction communicated in each class of schools.'

At the same time the Committee graded the schools afresh. Five categories were recognized. There was first, the Colombo Academy, the finest of the Government Schools. It was assumed, and it was probably true, that a majority of the pupils there could afford to pay for their education. The Committee felt that there was no need to continue this school at public expense, and that the fees levied there must cover the costs of running the school. The second category were the Central Schools: the Committee decided that there should be one in each provincial capital, and that each such school was to have a Headmaster and Assistant Master. There were to be no Normal classes. (In the three existing Central Schools there were such classes) A fee of 3s. 6d. a month was to be levied. Thirdly, there were the English elementary schools, forming by far the majority of the Government Schools, which were in future to charge a fee of 1s. 6d. a month. The fourth category were the mixed English and Vernacular Schools charging a fee of 6d. a month; the fifth category consisted of Vernacular Schools charging a fee of 3d. A school which did not fall into any of these categories was the Native Normal Institution. The Committee permitted the continuation of this school only because a contract had been signed between the Government and the students to provide for the maintenance of the latter during their period of study, and to provide them with teaching posts as soon as they finished. The Committee suggested, however, that once the present group of students had completed their education, it would be left to the Government to decide on the fate of that institution.

The guiding factor in this new gradation was undoubtedly economy. This was further emphasized when the Committee laid it down that no future schools were to be established unless buildings and furniture were provided by the people of the locality in which the school was situated.

The region least affected by this new gradation was the Jaffna peninsula, where, since 1843, the Government had left the three missions – the C.M.S., the Wesleyans and the American Mission – in charge of education, and merely provided them with an annual grant of money. This system had proved to be so successful that there was no necessity for purely Government Schools. The Committee decided that there was no change necessary there, and that the annual grants were to continue undiminished.[1]

The Committee had no comment to make on the organization of the School Commission, the subject of so much controversy since the Bishop's resignation, but they did make an attempt to discuss the vital subject of the medium of instruction. There was no unanimity on this question. Some members held that, 'to do any good at all, or communicate any instruction worth acquiring or retaining, we must not only impart quite new knowledge to a native mind, but also impart it through a new medium'.[2] Others maintained that, '. . . an education of this kind, imparted by means of English books, and in the English language, would at best be but a feeble sickly exotic, incapable of taking root in the native soil, much less of bringing forth any fruit'. It was a difficult choice, and the Committee took the line of least resistance by deciding on the middle course. But they made a virtue out of it, as their pompous pronouncement would show.

> Fully agreeing with the advocates of English education as to the paramount importance of a complete renovation of the native mind, of a letting in of new light, they are yet of the opinion that the time is not yet come when that light can be admitted through a new medium. . . . They have therefore made the English language the principal, but not the sole vehicle of instruction. They consider it necessary to keep up the present system of vernacular schools, but in such sub-ordination and distribution as shall make them essentially subordinate to the English schools [3]

The policy of self-support had disastrous consequences. The Colombo Academy, and the three Central Schools, the finest schools of the education system, suffered most. Their staff was retrenched at the very moment when their fees were increased. In 1849 the lower school of the Academy was abolished, fees in the upper school were raised, and three of the European teachers discontinued. The Academy became a school of less than thirty pupils, with two teachers. At Galle and Kandy, the two English Headmasters of the Central Schools were retrenched, school fees were raised, and the schools converted into elementary schools. The Normal classes were abandoned and the training of teachers for the English schools ceased. Only the Colombo Central School,

---

[1] Ibid. [2] Ibid. [3] A/R Sch.Com., 1847–8.

under Kessen, survived, but this had ceased to have Normal classes sometime earlier. With the raising of fees in the Elementary Schools, English, mixed and vernacular there was an immediate fall in attendance leading to the closing of some of them. (When fees were reduced in 1852, however, there was a slight but noticeable increase in attendance.) In the English elementary schools, the main concern of the Commission, the increased fees led to a sharp fall in attendance, and though the fees were reduced in 1852, the attendance did not reach the level of 1848 again in our period. Thus the severity of the depression dictated a policy of strict economy which inevitably led to a fall in attendance and a deterioration of standards.

The situation might not have been so very desperate had the economic depression been the only disturbing factor. The disturbances of 1848 had a more unsettling effect on the administration, whose time, for the next two years, was occupied with the difficult task of preparing a defence of Government policy before the Parliamentary Committee which deliberated on the affairs of Ceylon. Needless to say, neither Torrington nor Tennent had time for much else; in 1849 Tennent went home to defend the administration before the Parliamentary Committee. The senior officials of the administration were deeply divided on these matters and the morale of the public service reached a very low ebb.

Not surprisingly, the record of these years in the sphere of education makes dismal reading. The situation might have improved had Gogerly been in a position to dominate the School Commission as he had previously done, but he was too preoccupied with the task of assuring the survival of the Wesleyan Mission in Ceylon, then under heavy fire from the Anglicans, who were making inroads into the Wesleyan position in the Eastern province in particular.[1]

The disturbances of 1848, however, had one beneficial effect on educational policy, by forcing the Government into a realization of one of the major defects of its educational policy – the neglect of the Kandyan provinces. It is very often stated that the education policy of the Government tended to favour the towns as against the villages,[2] or, on the other hand, the excellence of the education

---

[1] See Wes.Mss.Cey., II, Gogerly's letters of 1849–51 particularly.
[2] Mendis, G. C., *Ceylon Under the British*, p.78.

provided in the Jaffna peninsula by the missionaries is contrasted with the efforts of the Government in the south-west coast.[1] But very rarely has it been pointed out that the real defect was the neglect of the Kandyan provinces. The Government was itself unaware that it had done so little for the Kandyans. In 1847 at a conference called by Torrington to discuss the Buddhist problem, the Kandyan chiefs appealed to the Government to provide more schools, explaining that education had been very much neglected by their own kings, and that the British Government itself had done little in this regard, with the result that the great bulk of the Kandyan people were illiterate. But it was not education in the Sinhalese language that the chiefs wanted for their people; they asserted that the Kandyans wished to learn the English language, and complained that they had neither schools nor teachers.[2] On Torrington's part there were expressions of gratification at this request and vague promises of help, but nothing constructive was done because, just at this time, the effects of the depression were being felt and the decision had already been taken to reduce the education vote substantially for 1848.

If the Government wanted proof of its neglect it had merely to turn to the 8th Report of the Central School Commission. Out of a total expenditure of £10,962 for 1847, £6,481 was spent on the Colombo district and £1,029 on the Galle district. £57 was spent on the Matara district and £252 on the Naval base of Trincomalee. In the Central province £640 was allocated to the Kandy district, while the remoter districts of Badulla and Nuwara Eliya received £48 each. Those districts of the old Kandyan Kingdom now forming part of other provinces did not fare better; Kegalle and Ratnapurna, forming part of the Western province, had to be satisfied with £36 and £47 respectively, while Anuradhapura in the Northern province fared worst. There was no money spent at Anuradhapura.[3]

The number of Government Schools maintained also tended to show the neglect of the Kandyan provinces. Out of a total of 103 Government English Schools (including the Colombo Academy

---

[1] Gratien, L. J., 'The School Commission, 1848–1859', *J.R.A.S.(C.B.)* XXXII, p.40.

[2] C.O. 54/238, Torrington to Grey, no.73 of 12 August 1847.

[3] Jaffna, where the Government subsidised the Missionaries – C.M.S., the Wesleyans and the American Mission, was a special case.

and the Central Schools) there were 36 in the Northern province,[1] 35 in the Western province, 13 in the Eastern province, 12 in the Southern Province and only four in the Central Province. The North-Western Province, half or more of which formed part of the old Kandyan Kingdom, had only three schools. Of the 25 Government vernacular schools established in 1847, 24 were in the Western Province and the other was in the Southern province.

It was C. R. Buller, the Government Agent of the Central province, who first drew attention of the administration to this state of affairs – after the disturbances. In his report on the disturbances, Buller pointed out that there were very few schools in the Kandyan areas,[2] indeed in the years 1815–48 the Government had put up just four schools.[3] He contrasted this with the speed with which the Government's excise policy had dotted the Kandyan areas – not hitherto noted for their consumption of liquor – with arrack taverns. In the same period, the Government had granted permission for the reconstruction of no less than 133 arrack taverns. The Bishop of Colombo in a letter to the S.P.G. referred to the disturbances and commented that:

> In the whole the Central Provinces [sic], the scene of the recent outbreak, we c[d] not remember more than three or four Government schools, and scarcely any missionary efforts out of Kandy itself. The Missions in Kandy both of the Church & the Baptist Missions in Kandy are upheld chiefly by the settlers from the Maritime Provinces, who from Dutch times have been in some way Christianized.[4]

[1] All but three of these schools in Jaffna were run for the Government by the three missions.

American Mission, Annual Grant £200	—	17 schools
Wesleyans	£150	—	10 schools
C.M.S.	£150	—	6 schools

[2] C.O. 54/251, Torrington to Grey, no.165 of 15 September 1848; Buller's report of 13 September 1848, enclosed.

[3] The missionaries too had very few schools in the Kandyan provinces. It must be pointed out that the Wesleyans had no Mission Station in the Central Province (in fact they had only one station in the Kandyan areas at all, and that on the border of the Western Province) and hence no schools. The C.M.S. had a few schools in and around Kandy; the Baptists had more schools, but the number decreased with the passage of time.

[4] S.P.G. MSS., Ceylon, 1840–55. The Bishop of Colombo to the S.P.G. 11 September 1848. On the neglect of the Kandyan provinces by the Government in the matter of educational facilities, see also *The Ceylon Examiner*, 4 November 1848.

The obvious result of this neglect was that the Kandyans were completely outstripped in education by the Tamils of the north and the Sinhalese of the south and the west.

But before the full implications of these facts had had time to register in the minds of the administration, the economies imposed after 1848 reduced the education facilities of the Kandyans even further. The retrenchment left the town of Kandy with one school – the elementary school. The Central School was closed down. In the Nuwara Eliya district there was no school for 15,000 people. There were no schools in Matale. In the Badulla district with a population of 60,000, there was no school house (the building had been burnt down by accident), and there was only one schoolmaster.[1] The only other school in the Central province was the elementary school at Gampola, twelve miles from Kandy; the school was described as being '. . . only nominal, a pack of 20 idle boys in a dirty building, and conducted by one who was never intended for the post he holds'.[2]

It was only after 1850 that there was any increase in the number of schools in the Kandyan areas.[3] The increase, though small, was significant, not least of all because it occurred at a time when Government expenditure on education was generally reduced. It was to these circumstances that Kessen referred when he wrote that 'the gross ignorance of the vast masses of the people – the rebellious proceedings in different [parts] of the Island and other circumstances have awakened the Government more fully than ever to the necessity of educating the people, and of doing so to a great extent in their own language'.[4] He was wrong in attributing this insistence on the vernaculars to a realization of the ignorance of the people, or to the disturbances. But he was right in stating that the disturbances had awakened the Government as never before to the necessity of educating the people – chiefly the Kandyan people.

By the end of 1850 it was clear that Tennent would not return.

[1] *The Ceylon Examiner*, 29 October 1849.   [2] *Ibid.*

[3] *The Government Almanac* for 1856, showed that on 13 December 1855 there were 89 Government Schools in Ceylon, of which 16 were in the Central Province, and 5 in the North-Western. The distribution for the other provinces was as follows: Western Province 52, Southern Province 8, Eastern Province 4 and the Northern Province (where the Government had special arrangements on education) 3.   [4] Wes.Mss.Cey., II, Kessen, 15 August 1848.

Torrington himself was recalled, and this tended to aggravate the instability and confusion in the administration. In the School Commission, too, there were a great many changes, the most important of which was the appointment of C. J. MacCarthy, the Auditor-General, to the position of Chairman by virtue of his appointment to the post of Colonial Secretary. The Wesleyans looked on his appointment with deep despair, for they suspected him of being a Roman Catholic. When MacCarthy went home on leave in 1851, Kessen wrote that 'MacCarthy the newly appointed Colonial Secretary is going home in bad health. His absence will be no loss to us.'[1] MacCarthy was no friend of the Wesleyans, or for that matter, of any other group of Missionaries.[2] The new Governor, Sir George Anderson, was a great believer in balanced budgets, and in no way inclined to spend Government revenues on such things as education, if he could help it. In spite of the slow recovery of the economy, he did not substantially increase expenditure on education. In the years of his administration the deterioration in education, which had commenced in 1848, was only slightly arrested.

What of the influence of the missionaries on the education policy of MacCarthy and Anderson in the meantime? And what particularly of Gogerly? In the early months of Anderson's administration there was some hope that Gogerly might resume his role of confidential adviser.[3] When, in 1852, the Wesleyan Mission in Jaffna was faced with a financial crisis, a Wesleyan missionary wrote to the Home Society that he would be travelling down to Colombo to discuss the situation with 'Mr Gogerly (whose influence is almost paramount in the School Commission) and to wait upon the gov[r] who professes a great regard for our mission'.[4] He had completely over-estimated Gogerly's importance on the Commission in 1852 and the extent of the Governor's support of the Wesleyans.

---

[1] Wes.Mss.Cey., II, Kessen, 13 and 19 March 1851. MacCarthy was not a Roman Catholic but a free-thinking Unitarian.

[2] Wes.Mss.Cey., II, Gogerly, 15 April 1851. In this letter Gogerly referred to the opposition the Wesleyans had from the Bishop and the Anglicans, supported by 'the present Colonial Secretary, a Roman Catholic'.

[3] Miss..Not., XIII (1851) 66–8, Gogerly's letter of 12 December 1850. Here Gogerly refers to Anderson as being well disposed to the Wesleyans; indeed he had promised his support to the Wesleyans in their mission work.

[4] Wes.Mss.Cey., II, Griffith, the Rev. N. D., 5 November 1852.

Curiously, though, everything seemed to favour the Wesleyans. Anderson's main concern at this stage was to settle the Buddhist problem, and in seeking that settlement he had earned the uncompromising opposition of the Anglicans, who were conducting a particularly virulent campaign against his Buddhist policy. What was more natural, then, than for Anderson and the Wesleyans, both faced with the same opponent, to unite forces? But the Bishop of Colombo stood aloof from the Anglican campaign against Anderson, and steadfastly supported the Governor against his own subordinates; Anderson valued this support too much to antagonize the Bishop by backing Gogerly too enthusiastically.

It is very unlikely that Gogerly shared his optimistic comrade's estimate of his position. Gogerly's energies were devoted to saving something of the Wesleyan organization from the assaults of retrenchment and Anglicanism. He probably realized that he could not get Anderson to spend more generously on education. He could hardly succeed when the planters and the Press, with all the resources at their command, had failed to persuade him to spend more on roads and public works.

Gogerly could not have derived much confidence from observing the work of the Government in the sphere of vernacular education. The Government had acknowledged the value of the vernaculars in 1848. The number of vernacular schools run by the Government increased from 24 schools and 855 pupils in 1848 to 45 schools and 1,362 pupils in the course of the next decade.

But it is more instructive, however, to consider the fate of the mixed schools – those in which both English and the vernaculars were used as media of instruction. In these schools the conflict between English and the vernaculars was an unequal one; it was not long before these schools regarded themselves as English schools and neglected the vernaculars (which in some schools was taught only in the lowest classes, whilst in others it was not taught at all, but was only used for purposes of explanation in the lower classes).

Moreover, though in 1848 the Government had acknowledged the value of the vernaculars, that acknowledgement itself had been very lukewarm. The contrast between Tennent's attitude to the vernaculars and MacCarthy's was striking; Tennent had supported vernacular education through conviction; MacCarthy was both lackadaisical and indifferent. His attitude to the Native

Norman School reflected his indifference to the importance of vernacular education. That school, the pivot of the whole system of vernacular education, survived the economies of 1848–9 only because it was not convenient to abolish it immediately. But the threat of abolition hung over it from then onwards. It was clear that, if the principle of vernacular education were ever seriously challenged, there would be few to defend it.

The fact was that after 1848 it was difficult to see anything like a clear policy on matters of education, least of all on such important problems as the medium of instruction. There was always a tendency to abandon vernacular education to the missions.

By 1852, Gogerly and the Wesleyans were confronted with a new and serious obstacle to their plans. In 1848, a Committee of the Executive Council had been appointed to review the fixed establishments of Ceylon (the School Commission was one of them), with a view to a reduction of expenditure. The report was ready by 1849, but it was not until 1850, sent to Earl Grey. In 1851 the report was sent back to Ceylon with instructions that the Legislative and Executive Councils were to report on the economies recommended. In 1852 the report was printed for the House of Commons; and a Committee of the Ceylon Legislative Council was appointed to review it. In 1853 this Committee made its own recommendations: they declared that 'no State support should be given to any but English schools'; recommended '. . . that the Native Normal Institution be dispensed with'; and, more ominous still, they held that the School Commission should be re-organized, excluding the four clerical members and retaining only the five lay members. These recommendations were a complete rejection of all that the Wesleyans had struggled for since the establishment of the new Commission, and an acceptance of the Anglican recommendations that the Bishop had hawked around since his resignation from the Commission.

For the Wesleyans there was another dangerous development, not, however, connected with these reports of the Council. The School Commission had several schools in Moratuwa and its neighbourhood, and since these schools were open to children of all denominations, the Wesleyans had discontinued their own schools in those areas as a measure of economy.[1] At this time the Bishop demanded that these Government Schools should be

[1] Wes.Mss.Cey., II, Gogerly, 26 September 1853.

placed under the superintendence of the Anglican clergy. When the School Commission refused this demand, he applied to Anderson who, realizing that he could not hand these schools over to the Anglicans without making himself a party to the Bishop's opposition to the Wesleyans, decided instead to discontinue all the Government Schools in that neighbourhood. His reasons were that the Government only supplemented the educational labour of others, and that, if other organizations were prepared to undertake education in any district, the School Commission would not keep up schools in opposition to them. Gogerly explained to the Home Committee that 'in consequence of this we must either leave the children of our members to attend the Bishop's schools and have them withdrawn from us to be Puseyites or we must re-establish the schools we formerly discontinued. We are determined to do the latter.'[1] An extract from a letter from another Wesleyan missionary would explain why, at a time when their finances were desperately low, the Wesleyans felt compelled to re-establish their schools rather than accept the alternative of education in Government schools. It expressed the attitude of the average missionary to the whole problem of education:

> But what is this education that the Government would thus afford? Just such an education as certain members of the British Parliament wished to impose on the nation, but which as a Society, we rejected, preferring the expenditure of our own money in order to secure a Christian education. This is just the position here. The people would be taught to read and write though we were to abandon them:— But what is this towards their evangelization?

The problems posed by the Reports of the Councils were more difficult to solve. Although some of his colleagues were extremely pessimistic,[2] and were convinced that these recommendations would be accepted by the Government, Gogerly had more confidence in his ability to preserve at least something of the Wesleyan gains of the last decade. He was confident that the Legislative Council could be persuaded to reject the recommendation that the School Commission be re-organized, and he believed that 'if any change takes place . . . it would be the placing of the Education Department under one responsible officer'. He was equally cer-

[1] Wes.Mss.Cey., II, Gogerly, 26 September 1853.
[2] Kessen was the most pessimistic of them, as his letters of 26 December 1854 and 15 January 1855, in Wes.Mss.Cey., II, show.

N

tain that the Native Normal School would not be abolished, as some of those who had voted against it in the Committee had changed their minds on the subject. At any rate he was determined to use all his influence to prevent the abolition of the Native Normal School, and the projected re-organization of the Commission. But on this occasion the Anglicans were equally determined to have their way. Kessen reported that the 'High Church Party is making strenuous efforts to get the education of the island into its own hands. Most violent expressions have been employed in speaking of the School Commission'.[1] And events were to show that Gogerly had been unduly optimistic.

Gogerly had one last success. When the Principal of the Colombo Academy, the bigoted Anglican clergyman Dr B. Boake, had obtained leave of absence for twelve months, the School Commission requested the Government to appoint Dr Kessen in his place. (Kessen was thus to have control over the Colombo Academy, the Colombo Central School, and the Native Normal Institution, at one and the same time.) Tennent had offered this post to Kessen in 1848, but the appointment had gone to Boake. When the 1848 offer was first made, Kessen had realized that it would place him, '... at the head of Education not only in Sinhalese but also in the English language, such a position as no European has ever occupied. . . .'[2] Now, in 1855, the Government acceded to the Commission's request, partly because Kessen's appointment would be in keeping with the recommendations of the Committee of the Legislative Council, that the Colombo Academy and Colombo Central School should be united under one head.[3]

But Gogerly himself realized that his influence on education policy was almost at an end. He had spent the last seven years saving his policy from the attacks of economy-minded administrators and bigoted Anglicans. Seldom had he been able to influence Anderson's policy as he had those of Mackenzie, Campbell and Torrington. In June 1855 he wrote home in despair that

> the education question will soon come before the Legislative Council . . . it will be decided whether the present Central School Commission is to be continued, or whether some other plan is to be adopted. So much bitter hostility had been manifested by the chaplains of the

[1] Wes.Mss.Cey., II, Kessen, 15 January 1855.
[2] Wes.Mss.Cey., II, Kessen, 15 August 1848.
[3] *Ibid*. Gogerly, 30 March 1855.

Anglican Church to the Wesleyans in reference to this question that I feel inclined to recommend that we depend altogether on our own resources for our Native Schools.[1]

He was not being unduly pessimistic, for in the course of 1855 the School Commission was deprived of its administrative powers,[2] just as in 1847 it had been relieved of a great measure of its financial authority. It became a purely advisory body. All power was vested in the Chairman of the Commission; and since this post was held by the Colonial Secretary, education policy became the direct responsibility of that official. In 1855 the Colonial Secretary was C. J. MacCarthy, no friend of the Wesleyans or of missionary interests in general. Kessen's Native Normal Institution was the next to go. The Government abolished the allowances for pupils at that Institution in 1855.[3] Then, in 1856, Kessen went home and did not return to Ceylon. The school survived until 1858, when the decision was taken to abolish it. Gogerly was still a member of the Commission (he was to be there till 1862) when these decisions were taken. But he did not wield the influence he had before 1848.

[1] *Ibid.* Gogerly, 25 June 1855.
[2] *A/R Sch.Com.*, 1855–6.   [3] *Ibid.*

CHAPTER V

The Problem of Caste[1] – Drifting without a Policy

IN the nineteenth century no policy of social reform could ignore the problems posed by the caste system; for caste was the most formidable obstacle that faced the reformer. Caste consciousness was deeply rooted in the mores of the people, and it would have taken a radical change in the whole climate of opinion before they could be brought to accept any change here.

Neither the administrators nor the missionaries had anything like a clear policy on caste apart from a vague egalitarianism. They were against caste, without knowing very much about it except that it was an obstacle to their programmes of reform.[2] They were convinced that caste was both obnoxious and intolerable, and were opposed to any positive recognition of caste distinctions. Had there been something as morally and socially repugnant as untouchability, it might have been possible to focus attention on it and thereby compel the adoption of a positive programme of action, but untouchability scarcely existed in Ceylon where caste was too nebulous and amorphous to be tackled by a precise and deliberate policy. Besides, the people were so steeped in caste prejudices that there was always the fear that impetuous or precipitate action would lead to unrest. Hence there was always a tendency to 'soft-pedal', to postpone action, to prefer the indirect approach to the direct attack. Thus both administrators and

---

[1] The best recent works on caste in Ceylon are: A. M. Hocart, *Caste a Comparative Study* (1950); B. Ryan, *Caste in Ceylon* (1953); R. Pieris, *Sinhalese Social Organization* (1956); particularly chap. V; and no. 2 of the *Cambridge Papers in Social Anthropology* (1960), entitled *Aspects of Caste in South India, Ceylon and North-West Pakistan*, edited by E. R. Leach.

[2] It is significant that practically every mention of caste in the letters and journals of missionaries working in Ceylon at this time was in relation to its role as an obstacle to conversion. To the missionaries this was the most formidable obstacle to the spread of Christianity, and it was this aspect of the problem that they concentrated on.

missionaries preferred to deal with each specific caste issue as it arose, instead of laying down general principles of universal application.

Caste in Ceylon deviated from the normal Indian pattern. Though there were regional variations in the caste pattern in Ceylon, between the Sinhalese regions on the one hand and the Tamil areas on the other, over the whole island there was a deeply significant absence of the classical Hindu four-fold division of castes; there were no brahmans,[1] no *kshatriyas* and no merchant caste. Instead, in both these regions the dominant caste was the farmer caste, called the *goigama* in the Sinhalese regions and the *vellala* in the Tamil area. This dominant caste, unlike the brahmans of India, was no thin upper crust, but in fact formed the bulk of the population.

If the caste pattern in Ceylon deviated from the Indian norm, the ideology of caste was much the same. As in India, castes were determined by birth, and were endogamous; there were definite restrictions on commensality between members of different castes, and there was the conception of pollution. In certain contexts, especially those concerned with food, sex and ritual, a member of a 'high' caste was liable to be 'polluted' by either direct or indirect contact with a member of a 'low' caste. (There were regional variations in the intensity with which these taboos were observed – taboos on food and water for instance were very much stronger in the Tamil regions, where Hinduism was the dominant religion.) As in India, there was a heirarchical arrangement of castes with various forms of traditional customary behaviour serving to symbolize the differences of rank; the heirarchical arrangement was not quite so rigid in the Sinhalese caste system, the order of precedence was more flexible – there being little agreement on the exact position of some of the lower castes.

Though the Sinhalese themselves possessed the spirit of caste exclusiveness to a great extent, it was scarcely as thorough-going as that which prevailed among the Tamils of the north and the east, who were mainly Hindus. Much the strongest obstacle to missionary enterprise among the Tamils of Ceylon was caste, though caste-consciousness among them was considerably weaker

[1] In the Tamil region of Jaffna and the Eastern Province where Hinduism was the main religion, there were some brahmans, but it is doubtful if they enjoyed the high social position of brahmans in India.

than it was among the Tamils of South India.[1] In a brief history of the American Mission in Ceylon (they worked only in Jaffna) written in 1850, it was observed that caste was still the major obstacle that confronted them.[2] Bishop Chapman of Colombo arriving in Jaffna for the first time in 1846, was quick to observe the caste marks on the foreheads of the people – a practice which did not exist among the Sinhalese – as an indication of the great strength of caste in Jaffna.[3] Mr Justice Stark, Puisne Judge of the Ceylon Supreme Court, in an address to the Ceylon Branch of the Royal Asiatic Society in 1846 on the races of Ceylon, singled out the Tamils as the most caste-conscious of them.[4] And Tennent, writing in 1850, remarked that though

> caste is still strong in the Sinhalese areas . . . [among] Buddhist converts even under the influence of caste, there is no dread of that fearful vengeance of apostacy which exists among the Hindus. . . . The Buddhist does not shudder to think that Christ was the son of a carpenter, associating with fishermen, nor does he recoil to think of temples of Jehovah and sacrifices of oxen and calves, nor does he think it at all objectionable to go to heaven with the pariah or the outcast.[5]

The missionaries were faced with a most awkward problem; any attempt to proceed headlong into an attack on caste would have

[1] *A Brief Sketch of the American Mission in Ceylon*, p.26.
   See also, C.O. 54/204, Campbell to Stanley, no.154 of 18 August 1843.
   The confidential Report of the Bishop of Calcutta, 21 January 1843.
   Tennent, *Christianity in Ceylon*, p.174.
[2] *A Brief Sketch of the American Mission in Ceylon*, pp.10–11.
   In the Archives of the C.M.S. there is an interesting letter on the caste problem in South India written by the Rev. J. Knight, *c.* 1831–2, at the request of a Wesleyan Missionary in Ceylon. This letter referred to the obstacles to the spread of Christianity in South India, but the missionaries working in the Jaffna peninsula believed that Knight's comments were applicable to their region too. And a copy of the letter was filed for reference purposes at the C.M.S. station at Nallur in Jaffna. Knight placed caste first among nine factors which were the most formidable obstacles to the spread of Christianity. In the schedule of obstacles the next four, in order of gravity, all dealt with aspects of the Hindu religion directly or indirectly connected with caste.
   C.M.S. MSS. C/CE/O.20. Letter of the Rev. J. Knight, *c.* 1831–2.
   See also Selkirk, *Recollections of Ceylon*, pp. 292–5.
[3] S.P.G. MSS., The Bishop's Visitation Journal, 1846.
[4] *JRAS(CB)*, I, part 2, 1846–7. Address of Mr Justice Stark on 'The People of Ceylon', p.11.
[5] Tennent, *Christianity in Ceylon*, pp.330 ff.

alienated a good many of their prospective converts, while, on the other hand, to have recognized it as a fact of life, and to have accommodated themselves to it, would have been a betrayal of some of their most fundamental principles.[1] It was their proud boast that theirs was an egalitarian creed; and such a creed could hardly countenance the idea of the inherent inequality of man on which caste was based. Nor could they accept either the heirarchical gradation of the caste system,[2] the inflexibility of caste gradation, or the conception of pollution.

On the whole, they preferred to attack caste but tentatively and cautiously at first. In our period – it was now nearly a quarter of a century since they first began mission work in the north – the missionaries could afford to adopt this attitude for several reasons, not least among them being the fact that the first battles against caste had already been fought in the course of these twenty odd years. Besides, their insistence on equality corresponded with, and indeed supplemented, the egalitarian attitudes of the State acting under the impulse of a blend of Liberalism and Evangelicalism. And in this period, unlike the past, there was an eager demand for education; it was in the schools that the first battles against caste were fought and won.

The missionaries found that the two most effective fields of operation against caste were the schools and the churches. The schools brought children of several castes together under one roof, which was, in itself, a matter amounting almost to a social revolution, so strong were caste prejudices among the Tamils. In all parts of Ceylon the caste of the teacher was a matter of considerable importance, since only a man of the very highest caste could attract a crowd of students, and very often a school-teacher was appointed merely because he had by virtue of his caste-status the influence necessary to gather the children together.[3]

In spite of the increased demand for education, there was some degree of opposition in our period from the students themselves,

[1] It would have been only too easy for the missionaries to have adopted this position; but it is to the credit of the missionaries of our period that they generally refused to do so. Both the Roman Catholics during Portuguese rule in Ceylon, and the Dutch Reformed Church during Dutch rule, tolerated caste distinctions in their churches.

[2] Almost all the missionaries working in Ceylon accepted the class structure of Victorian England.

[3] Tennent, *Ceylon*, II, 157 ff; *Christianity in Ceylon*, pp.330 ff.

when caste distinctions were ignored in the schools, or when traditional taboos on food and water were disregarded. Thus, Hindu students at the Batticotta Seminary of the American Mission were at first unwilling to eat on the mission premises,[1] and the missionaries were sufficiently accommodating as to build a kitchen for them on an adjoining piece of land belonging to a Hindu. When, after a year or so, the kitchen was removed within the mission enclosure, several students left the College – though they were to return later. Some students at this institution also objected to the use of one common well, but they were asked to meet that particular difficulty as best they could.[2] In 1847 when a low-caste Roman Catholic boy was admitted to one of the higher classes of the Wesleyan seminary at Jaffna, the other students refused to let him sit with them, and the native teachers would not interfere. Fifty of the pupils, led by a brahman who was also a pupil, demanded his expulsion and when this was refused, they left the school in a body. They opened one of their own, with the young brahman as their teacher, and, to show their irritation at the Wesleyans, they excluded the Bible and all Christian treatises from the school which they also kept open on the Sabbath. Their venture ultimately failed, and the pupils returned to the Wesleyans.[3]

The American mission would tolerate no caste marks on the foreheads of their students, presumably because caste marks were considered to be an ostentatious display of caste-status.[4] But there was no uniformity in this regard among the various missions working in the Jaffna district. The Wesleyans were prepared to allow these caste marks among their students.[5]

On certain other matters, the missionaries would allow no compromise with principle. Every mission insisted on their converts sitting together as equals in church, however galling this may have been to converts of higher castes, and however much it

---

[1] *A Brief Sketch of the American Mission in Ceylon*, pp.10–11.
Tennent, *Christianity in Ceylon*, pp.145–7.
[2] *A Brief Sketch of the American Mission in Ceylon*, pp.10–11.
[3] Tennent, *Christianity in Ceylon*, p.146.
[4] S.P.G. MSS., The Bishop's Visitation Journal, 1846.
[5] *Ibid*. We have no evidence as regards the attitude of the Anglicans to caste-marks. Could the Bishop's disapproval of the laxity of the Wesleyans on this issue, indicate that the Anglicans in the Jaffna district followed the American practice?

would give offence to the Hindus in their midst. Students were expected to sit together on the same mat in church (or chapel), and all were expected to drink wine from the same cup in the celebration of the communion. These gestures were intended to emphasize the ideal of equality within the Christian community.

Very often there were objections raised against the presence of low-caste Christians in church. In 1842 a perplexed C.M.S. station at Nallur in Jaffna reported that women of the higher castes refused to sit on the same bench with low caste women, '. . . and many not liking that the low cast [*sic*] should be raised to the bench at all.'[1] At Batticaloa, the Wesleyans, under Stott, had much the same problem; he had given great offence to high-caste Hindus by baptizing five lime burners (the lowest caste there) and by permitting them to enter the chapel along with men of higher caste. There were threats to burn down the lime-burners' houses, and to kill them, if they persisted in coming to the chapel. These threats were taken quite seriously as, five years earlier when the weavers 'put on a crown and danced, which as low caste people they were forbidden to do by the custom of caste, [the high caste folk] set one of their houses on fire and put an end to their merriment'.[2] On this occasion, however, threats did not suffice, for the lime-burners found a stalwart champion in Mudaliyar Daniel Somanader, the most eminent convert of the area, and other 'Christian men of caste'[3] who gave them every encouragement.[4]

Equality within the Christian community, and particularly in churches and chapels, was a matter on which the missionaries would make few concessions, even though it gave great offence to those in the higher rungs of the traditional caste heirarchy. Reflecting on this incident at Batticaloa, Stott made the perspicacious comment that 'these heathens don't seem offended at the lime-burners becoming Christians, but their coming to the very chapel where their Christian relations come'.[5] The idea that association with members of a lower caste tended to 'pollute' those of a higher caste, was exceptionally strong among the Hindus of the north and the east; that it was not entirely absent even in the Sinhalese areas,

---

[1] C.M.S. MSS., C.CE.06, A/R C.M.S. Station Nellore [Nallur], 1842.
[2] Wes.Mss.Cey., I, R. Stott, 5 April 1842.
[3] The phrase is Stott's.
[4] Wes.Mss.Cey., I, R. Stott, 5 April 1842.
[5] Wes.Mss.Cey., I, R. Stott, 5 April 1842.

is shown by a caste incident that occurred in 1844 at the Wesleyan mission station at Moratuwa (then a village) on the western coast near Colombo. At Moratuwa the *karawe* or fisher caste was particularly strong, and they were a significant group in the Wesleyan congregation, much to the resentment of the *goigama* people of the area, who threatened the Christian members of their caste group with ostracism if they associated with the *karawe* converts. The Christian converts threatened – in the event of ostracism – to form themselves into a new caste, '[the] Christian caste embracing all who love Christ'.[1]

This example of a religious group meeting together in prayer without considerations of caste served as a great attraction to the lower castes, to whom Christianity was often a refuge and a hope, as an incident at Batticaloa in 1847 illustrates. There was a dispute at Batticaloa between the toddy drawers, a low-caste people, and the Hindu priests, when the latter refused to perform a religious ceremony for them at the time of the threshing of their paddy, as they were accustomed to perform for people of high caste.[2] The toddy drawers consulted together and threatened to embrace Christianity, '. . . as it does not recognize distinctions of caste'.[3] The threat sufficed to wring a grudging submission from the priests (not without some coaxing from a native official), but many of the high caste people were greatly offended. The incident was not without its benefits to the Wesleyan mission there. The missionary in charge remarked that, 'At my last visit to this place, I found the people very attentive to the word, and there are two candidates for baptism.'[4]

Caste, as it exists at the present day [1850] amongst the Buddhists of Ceylon, is purely a social distinction, and entirely disconnected with any sanction or pretensions derivable from their system of religion.[5]

This remark of Tennent's focuses attention on a most significant aspect of the caste problem in the Sinhalese areas of the island,[6]

[1] Wes.Mss.Cey., II, D. J. Gogerly, 22 November 1844.
[2] *Miss.Not.* XII, 40, J. Gillings, 6 November 1847.
[3] *Ibid.*   [4] *Ibid.*   [5] Tennent, *Christianity in Ceylon*, fn., pp.91, 92.
[6] Tennent asserts that among the Sinhalese of the coast the barriers of caste had to a great extent broken down from their longer acquaintance with Europeans, while among the Kandyans the '. . . system flourishes in ranker luxuriance, under the conjoint influence of the Buddhist priest and the headman', *Christianity in Ceylon*, p.91. That caste consciousness was comparatively

where caste consciousness was less marked than among the Tamils of the north and the east.[1] Buddhism, whatever its adherents may have made of it in the course of time, in its purest form had little of the caste exclusiveness of Hinduism. Its teachings were as egalitarian as those of Christianity, and there could be no more trenchant criticism of the caste system than that of the Buddha himself.

The popular Buddhism of the nineteenth century, however, had come to terms with its environment and had accepted, indeed, absorbed caste as it had absorbed so much else that was contrary to the doctrines of Theravada Buddhism.

In the early years of the nineteenth century, however, a reformist spirit appeared among some *bhikkus*, who rejected caste distinctions in the Sangha, formed themselves into a separate group – the Amarapura Nikaya – advocating a return to the purer teachings and practices of the original Buddhism, and preaching against the acceptance of Hindu practices. This movement, which had started in the Maritime provinces, had made great headway in the

---

strong among the Kandyans cannot be denied, but no one with any acquaintance with the letters and diaries of nineteenth-century missionaries can accept his theory that caste barriers among the Sinhalese of the coast had broken down to any great extent, or that any relaxation of caste observances was due to acquaintance with Europeans. Neither the Portuguese nor the Dutch rulers of the Maritime Provinces, had made any significant attempt to break down caste barriers; the Roman Catholic Church as well as the Dutch Reformed Church tolerated caste distinctions. And the Dutch jurists, by giving legal recognition to caste distinctions, particularly in matters relating to land tenure, may have made the system even more rigid than it was.

The working missionaries were quite certain that caste was as much a problem among the Sinhalese of the coast, as it was among the Kandyans, but they were all agreed that caste was not as formidable an obstacle to missionary enterprise among these people as it was among the Tamils. In 1843, the Bishop of Calcutta remarked in the course of a report on the Anglican Establishment that one of the great advantages the missionaries possessed was the relative weakness of caste prejudice among the people. See the confidential report of the Bishop of Calcutta, 21 January 1843, in C.O. 54/204, Campbell to Stanley, no.154 of 18 August 1843. The Bishop's acquaintance was mostly with the Sinhalese of the coast. As for the Kandyan area, the Baptists who had more experience of mission work there than any other mission, seldom mentioned caste as a major obstacle to missionary enterprise.

[1] It is remarkable that missionaries working among the Sinhalese reported caste issues much less frequently than did their contemporaries in the Tamil regions.

Kandyan areas in our period. In 1845 a Christian convert reported that it was rapidly supplanting the 'conservative' Buddhism in the affections of the people in the remote, but important, Sabaragamuwa district, where the new movement was led by a monk belonging to one of the oldest families of the area.[1] It had made rapid gains in the Kandy district, too, where several chiefs supported it, much to the chagrin of the local *bhikkus*. In 1847, at a conference held by Torrington on the question of the State's relations with Buddhism, a sharp division was observed between the chiefs and *bhikkus*, who explained that their suspicion of the chiefs was due in the main to the support given by the latter to the Amarapura Nikaya.[2]

The growth of the Amarapura Nikaya is significant for being the only indigenous movement in any way directed against caste distinctions, and this at a time when even the Government itself was compelled to move with great caution on this issue of caste. Tennent – like many other Christians – attached great importance to the growth in influence of the Amarapura Nikaya; he believed that this schism in the ranks of the *bhikkus* would inevitably facilitate the conversion of the people to Christianity.[3]

But this was another instance when contemporaries overestimated the impact of a new movement, for the new group flattered these hopes for a while and then settled in a groove of its own. And when this one indigenous movement directed against caste petered out, it was left to the missionaries to lead the movement against caste in the Sinhalese areas of the island.

The work of the Baptist missionaries in the Kandyan provinces was the most significant in this respect, both because of the fact that there were very few missionaries of any denomination working in that region, and because of the nature of their response to the peculiar caste problems of Kandyan society. They established a school among the Gahalayas, one of the very lowest in the Kandyan heirarchy of castes, and another among the Rodiyas, a small group of people who formed the only outcasts of the Kandyan society. These people were held in such contempt by the generality of Kandyans that the very fact that a Rodiya or a Gahalaya was

[1] C.O. 54/217, Campbell to Stanley, no.120 of 8 May 1845.
    Memorandum of A. de Silva, schoolmaster of Bentota, 9 January 1845.
[2] C.O. 54/238, Torrington to Grey, no.73 of 12 August 1847.
[3] Tennent, *Christianity in Ceylon*, pp.224 ff.

accepted as a Christian would have sufficed to damn Christianity in their eyes. Mission work among them carried with it a difficulty seldom faced in mission work elsewhere among the Sinhalese – the active opposition of the local people of all castes.

Mackenzie, having seen a Rodiya village while on his way to the Eastern Province at the end of 1839, decided that the Government should assume some responsibility for their welfare. But because it was difficult for the State to undertake a venture of this nature, the co-operation of the missionaries was sought. Mackenzie asked for the assistance of the Baptists, who had a mission station at Matale and were thus best placed for this work, and they agreed to undertake it.[1]

In 1840, at Matale, in spite of the active opposition of some *bhikkus*, Harris, the Baptist missionary at Kandy, baptized twenty-nine persons, five of whom were Rodiyas. Harris was greatly – too greatly, as it later proved to be impressed by his Rodiya converts.[2] He reported that, 'the change appears decisive and genuine. The strongest attachment is manifested towards the Gospel, and death preferred to any cowardice or shame'.[3] His enthusiasm for the Rodiya converts was boundless; he believed that their knowledge and practice of Christianity 'might put many to the blush who have grown up to maturity amid the light and national advantage of England'.[4]

It is a point worth noting that what the Baptists deplored most about the miserable lives of these people was '. . . the necessity to which they are driven of begging for their subsistence'.[5] They believed that Mackenzie himself had been struck most of all 'with the evils of their eleemosynary life'. This was a reflection of the strong conviction among Englishmen of the nineteenth century that hard physical labour was of great importance in the life of an individual, and that idleness and mendicancy were intolerable evils. The Baptists explained that such a life as the Rodiyas led 'must have a tendency to counteract the better principles which a knowledge of Christianity always brings. It cuts the sinews of independent industry, [and] operates as a drawback in leading them forward in the race of civilization.'[6]

---

[1] *A/R Baptist Mission* (1840), printed in *Miss.Her.*, (September, 1840), pp. 22–3.　　[2] *Ibid.*, p.19.　　[3] *Miss.Her.* (1840), p.168.　　[4] *Ibid.*
[5] *A/R Baptist Mission* (1840), printed in the *Miss.Her.*, (1840), p.247.
[6] *Ibid.*

A school was built for the Rodiyas, through Mackenzie's aid. It was supported by the Government, and in recognition of the interest taken in this project by the Governor, it was named the Mackenzie School. The schoolroom also served as a place of public worship, for both children and parents. The Rodiyas were permitted to participate in the activities of the Baptist Chapel at Matale – but with definite restrictions.

> Without hazarding the loss of other hearers, or creating confusion in the assembly, they are likewise permitted now to stand under the verandah of the Matale Chapel; and even this removal of prejudice brings many to the regular Sabbath service.[1]

The mission to the Rodiyas did not last long; after 1842 there is little mention of it in the Baptist journal, the *Missionary Herald*. Harris was far too optimistic about the prospects of this mission; he overestimated the strength of the new faith among the Rodiyas, and completely underestimated the opposition to this project among the Kandyans. Centuries of degradation had left their mark on the Rodiyas; they could hardly understand the meaning of their conversion; and it would have been a brave Rodiya indeed who, on the strength of his conversion to Christianity, claimed equality with high-caste Kandyans. The social pressures against such a step were much too strong. To the Rodiyas, the work of the missionaries was perhaps, like any other charity (the only thing to which they were accustomed), to be accepted with a show of gratitude and to be easily forgotten.

In the course of 1842 Harris left Kandy, after a long quarrel with his fellow Baptist missionary, Dawson. The basis of this quarrel is interesting. Harris was accused of counting as converts to Christianity people who knew nothing of the significance of their conversion, and among other allegations, there was one concerning a Rodiya convert who was found to be living in incest with his daughter.[2] The departure of Harris apparently marked the beginning of the decline of the Rodiya mission.

More significant was the fate of the Baptist chapel at Matale. During the disturbances of 1848 it suffered considerable damage.[3] In 1848 Allen, the Baptist missionary at Kandy, reported that:

---

[1] *A/R Baptist Mission* (1840), printed in the *Miss.Her.* (1840), p.247.

[2] B.M.S. Archives, Ceylon, Box 8.

[3] *Miss.Her.* (1848), Rev. J. Allen's letters of 12 August 1848 and 13 September 1848.

... my greatest grief is that the chapel at Matelle has not escaped, though the building is not much harmed. Everything in it has been wantonly destroyed. Pulpit, chairs, benches, lamps, books – all have gone or broken to pieces. Poor Thomas Garnier the preacher, has lost everything he had, having escaped only with his life. . . . There is no doubt that much of this wanton mischief was done by the very villagers amongst whom we labour, for they hate us with a perfect hatred. . . .[1]

It is possible that this hatred may have been at least partially due to the memory of the Rodiyas at that chapel, for the Kandyan peasants loathed and despised the Rodiyas so much that their presence at the chapel would have been looked upon as an intolerable affront to their customs. (Even today a Rodiya can very seldom enter a Buddhist temple; and a few years ago (1949) the attempt of the Government of Ceylon to admit Rodiya children into a village school at Gampola near Kandy nearly led to a riot.)[2]

The work of the Baptists among the Gahalayas attracted less attention, and lasted longer.[3] A school was established among them at about the same time as the Rodiya school, and, like the latter, with Mackenzie's support. On his departure from Ceylon, the school was at first supported by a private benefactor resident in Kandy, and later it received much more substantial support from the Baptist congregation at Park Street, London.[4]

This regular financial support accounts only partially for the longer life of the Gahalaya school. Proximity to Kandy made it easier for both the missionaries and government officials to supervise its administration, and the school benefited greatly from the keen interest taken in its welfare by the Government Agent of the Central Province, C. R. Buller, and his subordinates. It is possible that this open support given by officials was directed at showing the local population that the missionaries had the support of the State in this venture, and that the State would not countenance caste discrimination directed against the Gahalayas.[5]

---

[1] *Ibid.* Allen, 12 August 1848.

[2] See *Ceylon Daily News*, 18 October 1949, quoted in B. Ryan, *Caste in Ceylon*, pp.236–8.

[3] *The A/R Bapt.Miss.* (1850), states that the Gahalaya school had 'fully answered our expectations'.   [4] *A/R Bapt.Miss.* (1850).

[5] The Gahalaya school earned the hostility of some of the petty headmen of the area, one of them in particular used physical violence against the school teacher, and was imprisoned as a consequence, but on his return from jail, the

These two projects were a positive response to some of the more blatant injustices of the Kandyan caste system; caste discrimination directed against the Gahalayas and the Rodiyas (and more particularly the latter) were the nearest equivalent of untouchability in Ceylon. Because the evils involved in this element of untouchability attracted greater attention, the response they evoked was much more direct and positive than was possible in caste issues in other parts of the island. If missionaries working in the Sinhalese areas of the Maritime provinces could boast of no such ventures as the Gahalaya and Rodiya schools of the Baptists, it is not that caste was less of a problem there, or that the missionaries were less responsive to it, but that the evils of the caste system were more diffused and there was no trace of untouchability to attract measures of amelioration.

In a society such as that of nineteenth-century Ceylon, where the 'prestige' of the Government stood so high, its attitude on issues such as caste was likely to have a greater impact on the minds of the people than the efforts of private organizations and individuals. But this was one of those issues on which the Government was reluctant to commit itself to a positive programme of action. There were occasions, however, when it did commit itself, but in each instance it was a response to an extraordinary situation.

On Mackenzie's initiative, the Government supported the Baptist Rodiya and Gahalaya schools; apart from a trifling grant of money, the Government lent the prestige of its name, and government officials were associated with these projects. These schools, however, were special ventures dealing with problems peculiar to the Kandyan region.

---

school house was burnt down. Buller dismissed him from his post for his complicity in this act of arson, and appointed another in his place.

Apparently, this petty headman had once been a good friend of the school, but he took strong objection to the extra-curricular activities of the schoolteacher who had formed a 'Good Behaviour Society' in the Gahalaya village, the rules of which prohibited the practice of cock-fighting, highway robbery, and the use of intoxicating drinks. The schoolteacher was an enthusiastic temperance worker, and the petty-chieftain, who owned two arrack taverns in the vicinity, stood to lose a great deal of income if the Gahalayas practised what the schoolteacher preached. Perhaps the headman's opposition to the school was based on less sordid considerations than this Baptist version makes it out to be. He may have been expressing the typical Kandyan chieftain's opposition to education for the lower orders of society.

But two decisions of the Government, one taken in 1833 and the other in 1843, focused attention as never before on the State's attitude to caste. In 1833, on the recommendations of the Cole-brooke-Cameron commission, *rajakariya* – the ancient system of forced labour, rigidly conscripted on the basis of caste distinctions – was abolished. Its abolition was the most effective blow against the caste-system in the first half of the nineteenth century. It was erosive of caste in three ways. The social disabilities, to say nothing of the economic disabilities, of a great many people were abolished at once.[1] It helped to facilitate the mobility of labour, as indeed it was meant to do. And the powers of the headmen, the men at the apex of the caste heirarchy, were reduced considerably.

The decision to abolish *rajakariya* left the aristocracy, particularly the Kandyan aristocracy, disgruntled and perturbed, for they were deprived of powers and privileges which had been theirs by long-established tradition. It was one more step in the reduction of the powers of the aristocracy, which the British Government had pursued as a deliberate policy ever since the great rebellion of 1817–18. From 1815 to 1833 the Kandyan provinces had had a separate administrative system reflecting to a certain extent the social structure of a static society based on rank, caste and the ownership of land, but the administrative and legal reforms of 1833 put an end to the Kandyan administrative system. These reforms reduced the powers of the aristocracy even further and each such reduction resulted in some loosening of caste bonds.

This connection between the reduction of the powers of the aristocracy and the loosening of caste bonds was emphasized by the reforms of the jury system of 1843.[2] And on this occasion there was a positive declaration, explicitly directed at caste discrimination. The modern British jury system was introduced to Ceylon by the Charter of Justice of 1810. (This was applicable only to the

---

[1] Caste considerations entered as a factor in the administration of the law whenever the courts were called upon to decide an issue in relation to *rajakariya*, or the obligations of service tenure. When *rajakariya* was abolished the courts no longer had to decide issues of this nature.

[2] Digby, *Forty Years in a Crown Colony*, I, 120 ff.

Perera, E. W., 'Jury System in Ceylon: its origins and incidence', *C.L.R.* 3rd series, III, 1–6.

Report of the Proceedings of the Legislative Council, 1843 Sessions, particularly pp. 121–56.

C.O. 54/216, Campbell to Stanley, no. 4 of 7 January 1845.

o

Maritime provinces. The Kandyan kingdom was still independent.) By a Proclamation of 23 November 1811, clear instructions
were issued on the preparation of jury lists. These lists were to
consist '. . . of all persons resident in their districts, who by their
character and condition may be deemed qualified to sit upon
juries, distinguishing them into their respective classes and
castes.' It was distinctly stated that the word 'classes' referred to
the various communities resident in the Maritime provinces –
'the several classes hereinafter mentioned, that is to say: Burghers,
Native inhabitants, viz: Sinhalese, Malabars and Moors. . . .'

It was left to the *Mudaliyars* of the Supreme Court to draw up
these lists, and in drawing them up they paid little heed to the
spirit of the Proclamation of 23 November 1811. First, they confined the privilege to the more advanced of the Sinhalese castes
and then, in addition to the separate lists for these castes, they
took advantage of the term 'classes' in the Proclamation of 1811
to draw up a 'First Class' Jurors list and a 'Second Class' Jurors
list for each caste. The 'First Class' list consisting of *mudaliyars* and
muhandirams only, and the 'Second Class' list consisting of other
qualified jurors, although in the Proclamation 'classes' referred to
the different communities, and not classes within castes.[1]

This arrangement led to complications which those who drew
up these lists did not anticipate. Soon the list of 'First Class'
jurors of the *goigma* caste contained, in addition to the names
of sons and descendants of the *mudaliyars* and *muhandirams* of
the original list of 1812, the names of persons who were not
de facto chiefs, while the 'Second Class' list contained the names of
several officiating *mudaliyars* and *muhandirams*. By the early 1840s
the anomalies in this system had multiplied; there were as many
mudaliyars and *muhandirams* in the 'Second Class' list as in the 'First
Class' list thought the 'First Class' list was intended to contain
the names of *de facto* chiefs only.[2]

One of the great defects of this system was that 'First Class'
jurors were recruited from a small group of some thirty or forty
families living in and around Colombo, and – so the Government
alleged – any person enjoying their support was practically beyond the reach of the law.[3] Besides, if a member of this group was

[1] Perera, E. W., *op.cit.*
[2] *Ibid.*
[3] C.O. 54/216, Campbell to Stanley, no.4 of 7 January 1845.

accused in a case, he had the right to elect to be tried by his own clique.

These anomalies had somehow escaped Cameron's attention, and survived the radical changes in the judicial system that followed the introduction of the Charter of Justice of 1833.

In 1843 some *mudaliyars* who found themselves in the 'Second Class' list petitioned the Government against the existing system, and the division into classes was withdrawn. But this decision was itself suspended until the whole question was discussed in detail as a result of a counter-petition by the *mudaliyars* of the 'First Class', who asked for the maintenance of the *status quo*. The Government's attempt to introduce legislation to reform this system aroused strong opposition from this latter group, and from the Judges of the Supreme Court.[1] In its origins this was essentially a conflict between two groups of *mudaliyars* of the *goigama* caste, and they would have preferred to have had it remain so; but there were other and more progressive forces at work, who challenged the whole system of caste distinctions in the selection of juries.

Curiously, this new development only strengthened the opposition of the Judiciary to any measure designed to abolish caste distinctions in the selection of juries. They held the view that, however desirable the abolition of caste distinctions may be as a means 'to the general improvement of the native population', yet if no serious practical evil had resulted from the existing arrangement as regards juries, a compulsory measure designed to abolish it would be doing unnecessary violence to the habits and feelings of the people.[2] Apart from reflecting the innate conservatism of the judiciary, and their opposition to the reform of a system to which they had grown accustomed, these views gave expression to a common belief that open attacks on the caste system were imprudent and unlikely to yield much benefit. But the government was not inclined to accept the advice of the judges, and proceeded with the preparation of legislation despite their opposition.

In the meantime, two groups, the *karawe* community and the Moors of Colombo, petitioned the Legislative Council against the existing system as regards the formation of juries. They objected

to the system of classification on the grounds that it has the tendency of retarding the advancement of the natives in civilization, and of

[1] *Ibid.*
[2] C.O. 54/216, Campbell to Stanley, no.4 of 7 January 1845.

creating discord and animosity among peoples of the same caste, and among members of the same family; also that it would impair the efficiency of the system of Trial by Jury, and be the first public recognition and encouragement on the part of the Government of the doctrine [of caste].[1]

The two groups of petitioners were represented by counsel who appeared before the Legislative Council to plead their respective cases; the 'exclusives' were represented by James Stewart, acting Queen's Advocate, and the 'reformers' by Richard (later Sir Richard) Morgan, two young, but easily the ablest, rising lawyers of the day. It is reported in the Proceedings of the Legislative Council that '[the] large number of persons assembled at the Council room evinced the interest excited by the question to be discussed'.[2] It had become a *cause célèbre*.

Stewart's was a difficult task. Had it been merely a question of defending caste distinctions in the jury lists, he could have appealed to the Proclamation of 1811, but it was necessary to argue that the term 'classes' used in that Proclamation referred to classes within castes. This was not the meaning given to that term in the Proclamation, and Morgan had little difficulty in exposing the weakness of the case of the 'exclusives'. As a recent writer put it:

> The position the 'exclusives' were compelled to fall back upon ... was palpably untenable. The accident of having held a 'chief-Headman-ship' in a particular year, i.e. 1812, would not entitle his descendant to have his name inserted in an official list of chiefs nor connote that his progenitor belonged to a privileged class.[3]

In contrast, Morgan's case was much easier. He had the support of the Proclamation of 1811, logic, and, what was more important, the declared intention of the Government to abolish this absurd system. And it was easy for him to expose the hollowness of the pretensions of the 'First Class' jurors.[4]

The Government's attitude was neatly summed up by J. N. Mooyart, Acting Colonial Treasurer:

> Caste, as a social distinction, is incompatible with the progress of civilization. Hereditary privileges not based on personal merits are favourable to a stationary condition of Society, and preclude salutary

---

[1] Proceedings of the Legislative Council (1843), p.121.
[2] *Ibid.*   [3] Perera, E. W., *op. cit.*
[4] Digby, *op. cit.*
Proceedings of the Legislative Council (1843), pp.131–9.

changes and improvements. The principle no longer is recognized; and its opposite is clearly enough admitted on all sides to be a desideration. The measure now introduced to discontinue a recognition which is in reality fictitious is therefore in accordance with the general persuasions, although in a measure at variance with certain predilictions unsupported by the improved understanding and judgement of intelligent natives. . . .[1]

Mooyart expressed the hope that, '[the] example set in that portion of the Maritime Provinces will . . . operate favourably on the Kandyans.'[2] Ordinance No. 9 of 1844

for determining the qualifications and making other provisions in respect of persons liable to serve as jurors and assessors, [enacted] that every free man . . . between the ages of twenty-one and sixty years . . . who shall be of sufficient intelligence and respectability, and shall be able to speak any of the languages following, English, Singalese [sic] or Tamil . . . shall be qualified and shall be liable to serve as a juror and an assessor in the Supreme Court. . . .

There were to be three jury lists:

A list of persons who can speak the English language.
A list of persons who can speak the Singalese [sic] language.
A list of persons who can speak the Tamil language with the right of election of those who can speak more than one language.

Jury lists were no longer prepared on the basis of caste.

Bishop Chapman, commenting on this change in the formation of juries, wrote that 'It seems to be a practical and wise law, and if worked as an experiment in a kindly and fostering spirit at first, which is now the case, it will do much to break down the prejudices of caste'.[3]

Once caste distinction in the formation of juries was abolished, the ideal of equality before the law was taken a stage further. In 1833 the new Charter of Justice had established an uniform judicial system for the whole island, and for all races.[4] And, in the long run, this ideal of equality before the law was in many ways more erosive of caste than the ideal of an equality before God,

---

[1] Proceedings of the Legislative Council (1843), p.154. [2] Ibid.
[3] S.P.G. MSS., The Bishop's Visitation Journal, 1846.
[4] (Ed.) G. C. Mendis, The Colebrooke-Cameron Papers, Vol. I, Introduction pp. xliii ff. In 1833 the separate system of courts for the Kandyan areas was abolished; and distinctions between Europeans and Ceylonese were removed.

since it was more palpable and more dramatic in its impact on the people than the more lofty, but less comprehensible, ideal of an equality before God. Besides, this new concept of equality was associated with a strange God, the God of the strangers who now ruled the country. The fact that, ideally, a Rodiya was the equal of a man of the highest caste in the courts of law, was likely to be more effective in condemning caste than the fact that Rodiyas were members of the Baptist congregation at Matale.

But, by its very nature, the ideal of equality before the law took years before its full effects were felt. It was a matter of decades and generations rather than years. In the meantime, well-publicized decisions such as that on the jury system, in 1843-4, had more immediate effect.[1] In 1853 the Government gave further proof of its discountenance of caste distinctions when Governor Anderson appointed a wealthy Sinhalese capitalist of the *karawe* community (he made his fortune in the coffee industry and in the transport business) to the position of a *mudaliyar* of the Governor's Gate, a position reserved hitherto for the aristocracy alone. There were murmurs of protest against the appointment, but the Governor was not to be dissuaded. And when the *mudaliyar*, in accepting the honour, held a splendid reception, attended by the Governor and the highest officials of the administration, he proved beyond a doubt that caste was no barrier to advancement – if a man had money. To the perceptive mind it would have provided a glimpse of the future, when money would be a fairly effective solvent of the caste system.

But while the administration took this stand against caste distinctions they were too remote from the people for their decisions to have their full force. The law could hold a Rodiya to be the equal of a man of the highest caste, but it was quite another matter to have the latter accept a Rodiya on terms of equality outside the law courts. The missionaries working among the people, and standing, as it were, between them and the administration, could influence at least some of them to change their views on such matters as caste. Working in a mental climate of equality, they were competent auxiliaries in the struggle against caste, supple-

---

[1] A good test of the Government's attitude to caste would have been an analysis – on the basis of caste – of the appointments made to lower rungs of the administration, particularly to such departments as the Police Force. But it is impossible to extract this information from the existing documents.

menting the work of the administration. For the law by itself was not sufficient to destroy caste prejudice. To take just one example, Tennent makes this observation on the impact of British rule on the Rodiyas. Under British rule:

> ... which recognizes no distinction of caste, the status of the Rodiyas has been nominally and even moderately improved. Their disqualification for labour no longer exists: but after centuries of mendicancy and idleness they evince no inclination for work. . . . Socially their hereditary stigma remains unaltered: their contact is still shunned by the Kandyans as pollution and instinctively the Rodiyas crouch to their degradation.[1]

Hence the great significance of the work of the Baptist mission among the Rodiyas; and their proud boast that '... it is the Gospel alone that teaches us that in Christ Jesus we are all one – that there is neither barbarian nor Scythian bond nor free'.[2]

It is perhaps best to conclude this survey of the caste problem in early Victorian Ceylon with a word of caution. Neither the missionaries nor the administrators had made anything like a significant impact on the caste system.[3] Tennent, the most sensitive and perceptive mind among the civil servants of the day, observed with regret that:

> Amongst the pure Sinhalese the ascendancy of caste still exerts a baneful influence over the intellectual as well as the material prosperity of the nation . . . [and] no appreciable progress has yet been made towards its modification or abandonment. . . . But the inference from past experiments of the Government suggests the propriety of abstaining from direct interference and leaving the abatement of the evil to the operation of time and the gradual growth of intelligence.[4]

[1] Tennent, *Ceylon*, II, 189.

[2] *The Miss.Her.* 1840, p.168. Harris, 10 January 1840.

[3] The great strength of caste feeling even among Christian converts was alluded to in the *Annual Report of the Baptist Mission* for 1853, p.37, where it is stated that a Sinhalese Assistant Missionary in a Baptist station near Colombo was dismissed from his post for his violent opposition to the marriage of his daughter to another Sinhalese Baptist pastor of a lower caste than he.

[4] Tennent, *Ceylon*, II, 157, 158.

CHAPTER VI

The Abolition of Slavery

SLAVERY in Ceylon differed fundamentally from plantation slavery as it had existed in the West Indies and Mauritius, and as it then existed in the Americas. Immeasurably milder in form, its abolition was easier because there was no formidable vested interest entrenched in the British Parliament to defend its existence, and besides, the abolition of slavery in the Empire in 1833 (though the Eastern Empire was specifically excluded from the operation of the Act) made it inevitable that slavery in Ceylon could not much longer survive.

By 1832, slavery in the Island was confined to two main regions – the Jaffna peninsula and the Kandyan areas.[1] Though there were far fewer slaves in their region, the main opposition to the abolition of slavery came from the Kandyan aristocracy.

In the Kandyan provinces slaves were the personal property of the owners, liable to perform any service their owners required of them, and disposable in any way the owners thought fit. While the great majority of slaves were domestics, a few were employed on the property of their owners; some even rose to positions of trust on these properties, though this was seldom considered a permanent arrangement.[2] The manner of employing the slave was

---

[1] Accurate figures on the incidence of slavery are difficult to come by. The census returns of 1824 showed 15,350 slaves in the Jaffna district, and it is likely that by 1840 there was a substantial increase in this number, largely because the birth rate exceeded the death rate. In the Sinhalese areas of the Maritime Provinces there were about 1,000 slaves, most of whom belonged to the Dutch inhabitants or their descendants. See (ed.) Mendis, G. C., *The Colebrooke-Cameron Papers*, I, 60. For the Kandyan areas more accurate figures are available. In 1832 there were 2,113 slaves there, of whom 1,067 were males. C.O. 416/20, G20, p.229. The census of 1824 showed 1,787 slaves, and the increase in the number of slaves between 1824 and 1832 was once again because births outnumbered deaths.

[2] The Kandyan treatise on law, the *Niti-Nighanduva*, recognized the following categories of slaves:

Anjato. Born and bred in the family for ages.

Dhanakkito. Purchased from their masters or parents.

entirely at the owner's discretion,[1] and a slave, whatever his caste, was liable to perform such services as his owner might require of him, however low and base these services might be. There were services which only a slave could perform. A free, hired *goigama* dependent could not be compelled to dig a privy, carry water thereto, carry a palanquin or a corpse – all of which a slave, and only a slave, was liable to do for his master.

At the time of the British conquest, a substantial number of Kandyan slaves were very probably insolvent debtors.[2] A person could sell himself into bondage in order to repay a debt, or in order to obtain a loan, and if the debt were not settled during the lifetime of the original debtor it was inherited by his children, who themselves became slaves. On the repayment of the principal the creditor lost the right to the services of the slaves, and no interest was allowed to accumulate, the labour of the slaves being considered an equivalent. There was no recognition of a privileged caste in this matter and it was not unusual for a *goigama* man to become the debtor of persons of lower caste, thus rendering himself liable to become his creditor's slave, in the event of his inability

---

Karamanito. Stolen from a foreign country; captives of war; women who having been expelled from their families for losing caste have become the property of the king.

Saman Dasaviyopagato. Persons who for their livelihood or protection, of their own accord, agree to become slaves for a sum of money; those who steal the property of others, or burn a house or granary belonging to another and are unable to pay compensation to the injured party, become their slaves; persons who borrow money and cannot repay the principal and interest become slaves of their creditors. The sons, and failing the sons, the daughters could be seized as slaves after the death of the parents for debts incurred by the parents. *Niti Nighandhuwa*, 7–12.

See also, Pridham, C., *A Historical, Political and Statistical Account of Ceylon and Its Dependencies.* 2 vols. (London, 1850) II, 223 ff.

Lawrie MSS. It would appear that both Lawrie and Pridham used the same source of information, with the difference that Pridham seldom acknowledged them.

[1] Pridham, *op. cit.* I, 226; C.O. 416/20, G.20, p.229. Extract from the Proceedings of the Board of Commissioners held at Kandy on 25 May 1829.

[2] Pridham, *op. cit.* II, 223 ff.

Davy, J., *An Account of the Interior of Ceylon and of its Inhabitants* (1821), pp. 184 ff.

Lawrie MSS., Vol. 3.

to repay the debt. But when there was the danger of this degradation, a local chief generally paid the debt, and made him his own
slave instead. A creditor of inferior caste or rank to his debtor
could not actually seize him as a slave.[1] Apart from this relief, no
caste was exempted from being made slaves, except the *rodiyas*
whose supposed vileness rendered them useless for this purpose.[2]

Kandyan slave-owners had the right to sell their slaves or to
give them away as dowry, but slaves were very seldom sold. Even
when this happened, families of slaves were not separated except
when they were given as part of a dowry, or on the death of the
owner when, in common with the rest of the deceased's property,
they were distributed among his heirs, but 'in all cases however
every consideration [was] paid to the feelings of the slaves thus
disposed of. . . .'[3] Even in transactions such as these, there were
certain traditional restrictions that limited the slave-owners'
powers: the slave could not be given under any condition to a
person of inferior caste to the slave;[4] nor could a slave be compelled
to receive a spouse of an inferior caste.[5]

Since a great many of the Kandyan slaves were persons who
had sold themselves into slavery in settlement of a debt or in order
to obtain a loan, it is not surprising that their owners had no
absolute rights over them but possessed merely the right to their
services until the debt was repaid. (And, to a great extent, this
explains the Kandyan insistence on compensation for emancipation, an insistence which evoked little sympathy from the Colonial
Office, though the Ceylon Government was inclined to be more
sympathetic to these demands.) Slaves could possess and acquire
landed property and even moveable property independent of their
masters, who could not deprive them of the property so acquired
which descended to the slave's children as if he were a free man,
though if a slave died intestate his owner became his heir at law
and inherited his lands and effects.[6] Slaves were also in every
respect as competent as a free man to give evidence in a court of
law, and quite often, were called upon to witness transactions in
which their owners were concerned.

Though the laws and customs of the country gave the slave
owner the power of punishing his slaves as he wished, short of

[1] Davy, *op. cit.*, Lawrie MSS., III.
[2] *Ibid.*
[3] C.O. 416/20. G.20, p.229.
[4] Davy, *op. cit.*, Lawrie MSS., III.
[5] *Ibid.*
[6] Davy, *op. cit.*

maiming them or putting them to death, such punishments were very rarely inflicted. British officials working in the Kandyan areas reported that '. . . in no part of the world is slavery in a milder form than here [Kandy], cruelty to a slave is scarcely known and in general they are treated more as adopted dependents of the family than as menials.'[1] Indeed there was no reason for ill-using the slaves, for

> The owners [were] the principal landed proprietors of the country who confine their agricultural pursuits merely to the supply of grain for the use of their families and relations – there is therefore no inducement for over-working or otherwise ill-treating their slaves. . . .[2]

Slavery in the Tamil areas of the Jaffna peninsula and the Eastern Province differed from that in other parts of the Island. The bulk of the Tamil slaves were employed as agricultural labourers on the fields of their owners, and were rewarded with a small proportion of the produce.[3] In the Kandyan region slavery was domestic rather than predial, and slaves were employed less as servants than as the retinue or suite of the chiefs. Besides, the Tamil slaves belonged to four particular castes,[4] viz., the *Koviyars*, *Chandars*, *Pallas* and *Nallavars*, among the lowest and most depressed in the Tamil caste heirarchy. (Thus, despite their ultimate emancipation, there was no perceptible improvement in their position; they remained as despised and poverty-stricken as they originally were.) Tamil slave-owners treated their slaves with much less humanity than their Kandyan counterparts.[5]

In Ceylon, the British Government had taken definite measures against slavery in the Maritime provinces, where between 1806 and 1821 a series of regulations on slavery had been enacted, all of

---

[1] C.O. 416/20, G20, p.229; See also C.O. 416/20, G11, p.121 and C.O. 416/20, G12.

[2] C.O. 416/20, G20, p.230.

[3] A competent and thorough survey of slavery among the Tamils of Ceylon is provided in Tambiah, H. W., *The Laws and Customs of the Tamils of Jaffna* (Colombo, 1951), particularly chap. V, and the same author's *The Laws and Customs of the Tamils of Ceylon* (Colombo, 1954).

[4] This is the classification provided in the Tamil legal code, the *Thesawalamai*, but the British regulations on slavery refer only to three castes, viz. the *Koviars*, *Pallas* and *Nallavars*. Thus by the first half of the nineteenth century, the *Chandars* were no longer regarded as slaves.

[5] The British Government, by a proclamation, dated 3 January 1821, abolished the Tamil slave-owners' right to kill or maltreat their slaves.

which sought to compel slave-owners to register their slaves, and imposed the emancipation of such slaves as a penalty for failure to register, or irregular registration.[1] These measures were not introduced into the Kandyan provinces until after 1832, when the Colebrooke–Cameron Commission recommended their introduction to that region.[2]

From 1832 to the final abolition of slavery in 1844, Kandyan conservatism was the great obstacle to emancipation. In January 1832, Governor Sir Robert Wilmot-Horton appealed to the Kandyan chiefs to emancipate their slaves gradually, and suggested the introduction of the system of registration to the Kandyan areas. He pointed out that the advantages of registration were not entirely with the slaves. The system of registration, by declaring who were and who were not slaves, would '. . . remove the obstacles by which free persons of low caste were under present circum-

---

[1] (Ed) Mendis, G. C., *The Colebrooke-Cameron Papers*, I, 59–61, II, 351 ff. Tambiah, H. W., *The Laws and Customs of the Tamils of Jaffna*, pp. 83–7.

A Proclamation dated 15 January 1799, declared that those who were slaves would continue to be slaves. The British Government recognized the customary laws pertaining to slavery. In 1806, however, the first steps for a true register of slaves were taken. Provision was made for the complete emancipation of all those not duly registered within a limited period. The object was probably to ascertain who were *bona fide* slaves and to prevent an increase in their numbers by foreign importation. Slave owners did not register their slaves, but the penalty was not imposed. In 1808 there was another measure with the same object and the same penalty of forfeiture. (These two regulations – no.13 of 1806, and 3 of 1808, required the registration of *Koviar, Nallavar* and *Palla* slaves in Jaffna.) But again there was little registration, and no imposition of the penalty.

In 1816, Sir Alexander Johnston, the Chief Justice, persuaded certain slave-owners of the Maritime Provinces to emancipate children born of slave parents from 12 August 1816, the birthday of the Prince Regent. By Regulation of Government, no.9 of 1818, provision was made to annul all joint-ownership in slaves and to enable slaves to redeem their freedom by purchase. These measures had little effect in Jaffna where slave owners seldom emancipated their slaves voluntarily. Regulation no.8 of 1821 attempted to purchase and free the slave children of the *Koviyar, Nallavar* and *Palla* castes. The regulation enacted that all female children born of a female slave of these castes on, or after, 24 April 1821, shall be free. Their owners were to be compensated; the government paid a sum of two or three rix-dollars according to the caste of the mother.

By 1832, there were less than 1,000 slaves in the Sinhalese areas of the Maritime Provinces, but in the Jaffna district there were over 15,000 slaves.

[2] (Ed.) Mendis, G. C. *op. cit.* I, 61.

stances prevented from the performance of menial services for slave owners under the apprehension of being condemned to slavery'.[1] The Kandyan chiefs refused to accept these suggestions. Their opposition to the abolition of slavery was based less on a desire to maintain slavery as a system, than on the ill-grounded fear that they would be unable to command the attendance of emancipated slaves for the performance of duties which had hitherto pertained solely to those in slavery – such as the preparation of dead bodies for cremation. They entreated the Government to postpone the abolition of slavery for sixty years, and they asked for compensation to the value of the slaves manumitted at the end of this period.[2]

The 'conspiracy' of 1834 following the abolition of *rajakariya*, and its aftermath, the State Trial of 1834, when some of the foremost chieftains of Kandy were tried unsuccessfully for an alleged attempt to revolt, forced Horton to postpone any plans he may have had for the immediate abolition of slavery in the Kandyan areas. The evidence collected at the trial appeared to suggest that one of the main fears of the chiefs was that slavery would be abolished;[3] thereafter Horton came to believe that a frontal assault on slavery would only give a handle to rebellion.[4]

Nevertheless it was impossible to ignore the question of slavery altogether, particularly with Stephen (and Glenelg) at the Colonial Office. The principle of registration was introduced into the Kandyan region, but the penalty for non-registration was not imposed. Then in 1837 a new Ordinance on Slavery Ordinance 3 of 1837 – enacted a triennial review of the slave registers of the Kandyan areas.[5] The operation of the Ordinance was restricted

---

[1] C.O. 54/156, Horton to Glenelg, no.144 of 3 October 1837.

[2] *Ibid.*

[3] See particularly C.O. 54/162, Mackenzie to Glenelg, no.130 of 13 August 1838, in which Mackenzie called attention to the summing up of the Second Puisne Judge at the State Trial, and the evidence of the third Adigar Molligoda, as proof of the great anxiety in the minds of the aristocracy on the question of slavery.

[4] Pridham, *op. cit.* I, 231 ff.

C.O. 54/162, Mackenzie to Glenelg, no.130 of 18 August 1838.

[5] The number of slaves registered in 1838 under the Ordinance of 1837 was 1,044, a reduction of 1,069 since 1832. See C.O. 54/162, Mackenzie to Glenelg, no.130 of 13 August 1838. Since only 66 slaves were emancipated by their owners in this period, it must be assumed that slave owners had neglected to register nearly 1,000 slaves.

to the Kandyan areas, in spite of the fact that there were more slaves in the Tamil regions, largely because the most vehement opposition to the abolition of slavery came from the Kandyan chiefs. The Tamil slave-owners were much less influential.

In 1837, Glenelg used the opportunity provided by the appointment of Mackenzie to succeed Wilmot-Horton, to insist on the speedy abolition of slavery in the Island.[1] Up to this time he had accepted Wilmot-Horton's view that there was a very mild form of slavery in Ceylon, and that it was a good policy to let it die silently.

Mackenzie had a greater awareness of the problems posed by Kandyan conservatism. He believed that with the abolition of *rajakariya* (Mackenzie called it 'Government slavery') the whole system of slavery in Ceylon would be destroyed without disturbance, and warned Glenelg that the political considerations which compelled Wilmot-Horton to postpone the suppression of slavery in the Kandyan areas still existed, and that it was still too soon to make a bold attack on slavery. 'A pre-mature measure will only be the rash fore-runner of certain failure.'[2]

Mackenzie followed Wilmot-Horton in seeking to encourage the chiefs to manumit their slaves without legal compulsion. He did meet with some success, for in 1838 Doloswala Dissave of Sabaragamuva freed his slaves, thirty-nine in all. In recognition of his generosity and as an example and encouragement to others he was awarded a gold medal worth one hundred guineas.[3] Mackenzie was convinced that the 'consummation most to be desired' was 'the free, voluntary, unsolicited emancipation of their slaves, by the slave-owners themselves. . . .'[4]

Glenelg, however, had decided that it was now time to move more boldly in this matter and called on Mackenzie to take measures 'for effecting the entire abolition of slavery at the earliest practicable period'. He insisted on a detailed and complete report on slavery in the island, with an estimate of the amount of compensation to be paid. Mackenzie was instructed not to give the

---

[1] C.O. 55/79, Glenelg to Mackenzie, no. 18 of 2 October 1837.

[2] C.O. 54/162, Mackenzie to Glenelg, no. 130 of 13 August 1838.

[3] Apart from Doloswala Dissave, another chief at Alupota also emancipated his slaves and was awarded a gold medal.

[4] Mackenzie's speech to the Legislative Council on 5 December 1839, in *Governors' Addresses*, I, 63–6.

slave owners the expectation that compensation would be paid unless it was absolutely necessary to do so.[1]

Despite his faith in the policy of persuasion, Mackenzie himself must have realized the efficacy of the system of registration as a means towards the abolition of slavery. In 1838, when registration under Ordinance 3 of 1837 began, only 1,044 slaves were registered, a drop of 1,069 from the figures for 1832. Mackenzie had only to impose the penalty for non-registration and a thousand slaves would have been emancipated, but he was averse to precipitate measures of this nature for fear of upsetting the Kandyan aristocracy. He preferred to wait a while, at least till 1840–1 when the first of the triennial examinations of the slave registers was due, and when the penalty for non-registration would at last be imposed.

This urge to postpone the application of the penalty for non-registration must have been strengthened by difficulties that arose in the Jaffna district, where some excitement prevailed in November 1839 on the question of slavery. Slaves had long been of little value there, and in consequence slave-owners had generally neglected to register their slaves. But an unguarded expression on the part of Justice Jeremie had given rise to the expectation of an Emancipation Act, providing for the payment of compensation to owners, and as a result slave-owners began to register their slaves, and to recall to their service slaves who had generally been left to seek their own subsistence.[2] Had these processes continued, Mackenzie's plans may have been upset, and the abolition of slavery might have become a more complicated process than it was to prove to be. But the Government prudently abstained from any immediate interference with slavery in this region, with the result that the rumours of an Emancipation Act died down, and slave-owners returned to their accustomed laxity as regards registration. The Ceylon government's policy, in Mackenzie's time as in Wilmot-Horton's, was to let the slave-owners neglect the registration of their slaves, and then, when the opportune

---

[1] C.O. 55/79, Glenelg to Mackenzie, no.143 of 21 November 1838.

[2] C.O. 54/203, Campbell to Stanley, no.63 of 17 March 1843. See also Anstruther's memorandum of 23 November 1840 where he states that 'The arrival of Mr Justice Jeremie . . . was for a time productive of some ill-effect. Slave proprietors fancied that his appointment must have something to do with slavery and began to call in their slaves and to look to their titles in the hope that some measure of emancipation and consequent compensation was in progress.'

moment arrived, to emancipate the slaves whose names were not on the register. It was a most sensible policy, and events were to show how very effective it was in the abolition of slavery in Ceylon.

Another outcome of these developments was that Mackenzie did not prepare the report on slavery that the Colonial Office was so anxious to have.

In the years before 1840 it was possible for the Ceylon government to work out its policy on slavery with very little interference from the Colonial Office. Such public opinion as existed in Ceylon did not concern itself with this problem and the missionaries were strangely reluctant to enter the fray. Indeed the silence of the missionaries on an issue of this nature is both surprising and significant.

Their silence may have been due to one, or a combination of several factors. In the Kandyan areas there were very few missionaries (only the C.M.S. and the Baptists had mission stations in and around Kandy) and they were finding it difficult enough to make any headway with their evangelical activities, without having to concern themselves with the social problems of the region in which they worked. But the Baptists in Kandy had embarked on three extraordinarily significant ventures—the Rodiya school, the Gahalaya school and the Mission to the Coffee Plantations – which indicated that they at least were responsive to the challenge of the social problems of the Kandyan provinces. The circumstances in which the first two of these ventures originated may provide a clue to their surprising lack of concern in the question of slavery; in both these instances Baptist activity followed on the initiative of the Government. But as regards slavery, the Government, concerned that publicity and agitation might frustrate their plans, was likely to have been more interested in keeping the initiative in its own hands, and in excluding private individuals and organizations from this sphere of activity.

Besides, since it was the Kandyan aristocracy that benefited chiefly from slavery, the missionaries were hardly likely to lead a sustained public agitation. In Ceylon, as elsewhere, they were always interested in winning the goodwill and gaining the support of the chiefs, and it was only on an issue of great importance (the question of the State's connection with Buddhism was one such issue) that they were willing to agitate against the interests of the aristocracy. Kandyan slavery, so mild in nature that it hardly seemed like slavery at all, was too unimportant an issue on which to antagonize the aristocracy.

The situation was rather different in the Sinhalese areas of the Maritime provinces, where there were very few slaves and where the years 1840–5 saw the reform of the Anglican Church, reforms in education, in the registration of births, marriages and deaths, and new regulations on subsidies for church construction, all issues which caused considerable controversy among the missions and involved them in prolonged agitation. Preoccupied with these issues, the missionaries had little time for less important matters like slavery.

It is more difficult to understand or justify the silence on this question, of the missionaries in the Jaffna peninsula, where there were more slaves than in the rest of Ceylon, and where they – the C.M.S., the Wesleyans and the American Board of Missions – were more powerful than in other parts of the Island. There are two possible explanations for this extraordinary conduct; either the Government was unwilling to allow any agitation on this issue, or the missionaries preferred to devote their time to their evangelical and extremely well-organized educational activities, without any serious concern for the deeper social problems of the society in which they worked, except those – such as caste – which directly affected their evangelical activities. The fact is that missionaries in Ceylon seldom responded to any social problem (other than education) except on the initiative of the State. The evidence would appear to support this second possibility, though not to the exclusion of the first. For even if the Government had discouraged agitation within the Island against slavery, it could not have prevented the missionaries from writing to their home societies on this issue, or showing an interest in it in their journals and diaries. But a search of the Archives of the C.M.S., S.P.G., the Wesleyan and Baptist Mission Societies has failed to reveal any consistent or active missionary interest in the abolition of slavery.

In the years after 1840 the issue of slavery in Ceylon came increasingly to the fore, and it became more and more difficult for the Ceylon Government to continue its policies without interference from home. Anti-slavery societies began to petition on the Colonial Office regularly, calling for an immediate abolition of slavery in Ceylon. They pointed out that, if the regulations of

P

1806–21 had been rigidly enforced, as they should have been, slavery would have been abolished by 1840.[1] They complained that, as a result of neglect on the part of the Ceylon Government, there was actually an increase in the number of slaves between 1806 and 1841. (Superficially this was true, but it was because births outnumbered deaths.) But they found it more difficult to move the Colonial Office to precipitate action in these matters than did those who agitated for a separation of the State from Buddhism, and the reason for this difference would lie rather in the attitude of James Stephen than in the nature of the subject. Stephen, who had done more than most for the abolition of slavery within the British Empire, had a profound knowledge of the subject. He realized that the problem of slavery in Ceylon was only one of marginal importance. Convinced by Horton's arguments that an indirect approach was preferable to a frontal assault (a conviction which was strengthened by Anstruther's comments on the subject), he concluded that the extinction of slavery in Ceylon was a matter of time, and could be effected 'without any intervention of the Government except in the Central Province where it has a firmer root than elsewhere.'[2] Above all else, he understood the vital difference between plantation slavery and slavery as it existed in Ceylon where 'slave property is held as a matter of pomp and state and is not much more than the old feudal relation between a Lord and his vassal.'[3] He therefore refused to take these various anti-slavery societies seriously, declaring that it would be a mere waste of time to debate these problems with them. When they complained of the delay involved in abolishing slavery in Ceylon, he pointed out that the delay was inevitable from the very nature of the problem in Ceylon, and that there was not the same urgency to abolish slavery in Ceylon as there had been elsewhere in the Empire.

The Ceylon Government must have found Stephen's attitude helpful, for they were allowed time in which to test the efficacy of

[1] See the petitions of: the Hibernian Anti-Slavery Society to the Secretary of State for the Colonies, 31 August 1841 in C.O. 54/193; the British and Foreign Anti-Slavery Society, 9 and 10 February 1843, in C.O. 54/208, and a petition, c. November 1845 in C.O. 54/220 from the Committee of the same Society.

[2] Stephen's minute of 28 November 1840 on Anstruther's memorandum, op. cit.

[3] C.O. 54/193, Stephen's minute of 4 September 1841 on the petition of the Hibernian Anti-Slavery Society.

the existing regulations, and these were proving to be quite effective. In 1840 Anstruther explained that nearly all the slaves in the Trincomalee district were declared free by investigating the titles of the owners.

> It was found upon examination that so many penalties and forfeitures had been incurred through total neglect of the registration laws that the owners were glad to emancipate all their slaves to escape from further inquiry. Their loss by doing so was very trifling...[1]

Stephen himself had come to believe in the advantages of this policy as a means to the abolition of slavery in the Island. He wrote that:

> In all countries, and at all times, the multiplication of the species and the consequent cheapness of labour have been the invariable causes of the natural extinction of slavery. On the operation of these causes in Ceylon, we have hitherto relied. But it seems that almost all the slaves have been forfeited from non-registration.[2]

By 1840 he had come to accept the Ceylon Government's policy on slavery in its entirety, for not only did he believe in the efficacy of the policy of registration, but he was also convinced that it was prudent to postpone the imposition of the penalty for non-registration. But his political superiors at the Colonial Office had fewer doubts on the subject. Vernon Smith's comment was brief but decisive. 'I would lean to the forfeiture in my recommendation on this subject.'[3] Lord John Russell took an even more definite stand. In May 1841 he called on Campbell to seize the first favourable opportunity for a total abolition of all vestiges of slavery, and he called for the report that Glenelg had asked for as early as 1838.[4]

Campbell found these peremptory instructions rather disconcerting, particularly because the first examination of the slave registers of the Kandyan areas under the Ordinance of 1837 showed that slavery was almost at an end there.[5] The bulk of the slave-owners had neglected to register their slaves, and this time

---

[1] Anstruther's memorandum, *op. cit.*
[2] Stephen's minute of 28 November 1840 on Anstruther's memorandum, *op. cit.*
[3] Vernon Smith's comment on Stephen's minute above.
[4] C.O. 54/188; Russell to Campbell, no.60 of 31 May 1841.
[5] C.O. 54/196; Campbell to Stanley, no.38 of 10 March 1842.

the penalty for non-registration was imposed. Elated at this success, he sent home a draft ordinance for a renewed registry in the Maritime provinces, as a prelude to any other measures against slavery there.[1] Doubtless Campbell realized that, with the near extinction of slavery in the Kandyan areas hitherto the main obstacle in the path of abolition, it would be easy to bring it to an end in the rest of Ceylon.[2] But his despatch home did not convey this impression, though he did explain that the Regulation (9 of 1818) for the registration of slaves in the Maritime provinces contained no provision for any revision of the registry, and that, in consequence, it was believed that the number of slaves then existing (1841) fell very far short of the numbers shown by the registers. He believed that, apart from being a very useful and necessary measure in any circumstances, it would be very essential to have the registers revised as a preliminary to any report on slavery.[3]

Stephen looked upon this despatch as an unnecessary postponement of the final abolition, now that the Ordinance of 1837 had proved to be so effective in the Kandyan areas.[4] He could not be blamed for coming to this conclusion, as Campbell's despatch was very clumsily drafted. Stephen's annoyance sprang, at least partly, from the fact that, in spite of Russell's reminder, no report on slavery had been sent. He looked forward to this report to provide the necessary information on which the future Colonial Office policy on slavery in Ceylon was to be based. He explained to the new Secretary of State for the Colonies, Lord Stanley, that 'one of the main objects of the required Report was to determine whether it would or would not he right to insist on the forfeiture already incurred by non-registration'. He regretted the lack of information on the subject at the Colonial Office:

> Beyond the simple fact that there are a great many people held in slavery, we have really no official information whatever. . . . It used to be said by Sir W. Horton and others that slavery in Ceylon was a mere name – that the cheapness of human labour disposed everyone to become a slave-owner – that the slaves were kept rather as an

---

[1] Ord. 7 of 1842. 'For making further Provision for Registration of slaves in those parts of the island formerly termed the Maritime Provinces.'

[2] C.O. 54/198, Campbell to Stanley, no.149 of 19 September 1842.

[3] *Ibid.*

[4] Stephen's minute of 29 November 1842 on Campbell to Stanley, no.149 of 19 September 1842 in C.O. 54/198.

affair of pomp and ceremony than with a view to profit – that to register them over again wᵈ be bad policy – that it wᵈ revive dormant rights and create in the minds of the owners vague hopes of compensation which wᵈ lead to the assertion of obsolete Titles – that there were praedial and personal slaves whose condition was essentially different and whose registration it might therefore be unwise to blend together in the same law, supposing any law on the subject expedient. For the last four years demands for information on the whole subject have been made in vain. . . .[1]

With the extinction of slavery in the Kandyan area, the main political obstacle in the way of abolition of slavery in the Island was removed, and the Colonial Office was no longer willing to accept a postponement of its final abolition. Stanley's first despatch to Campbell on the theme of slavery reproached him for his failure to send home the report on slavery that the Colonial Office had repeatedly requested. He also complained that the delay in sending this report resulted in an unnecessary postponement of the final abolition of slavery, since he was reluctant to issue any further instructions without the benefit of the information which only a report of this nature could provide.

It was only at this stage that Campbell explained why this new Act was really necessary.[2] When he received Russell's despatch calling for a report, Campbell had asked the Government Agent of the Northern Province, P. A. Dyke, for a confidential memorandum on the number of slaves there. That official had replied that it was notorious that the provisions of Regulation 9 of 1818 had been very generally neglected, and that therefore any result gathered from the registers must be so misleading as to be practically useless. Moreover, to obtain trustworthy information as to the persons who were legally slaves it would have been necessary to inquire in each case whether the conditions laid down by Regulation 9 of 1818 had been duly complied with, which he had no satisfactory means of doing. Besides, the state of the registers was such that it was easy to re-enter improperly the names of slaves whose registration had been neglected, and in any case of inquiry it would be difficult to prevent this unless under a law providing precautions against fraud. In Dyke's view, and Campbell concurred in it, these precautions could only be provided by such a law as

---

[1] C.O. 54/203, Campbell to Stanley, no.63 of 17 March 1843.
[2] Ibid.

that which had answered so well in the Kandyan provinces. Campbell explained that the revised slave registry would merely permit the renewed registry of slaves who were still subject to slavery under the old law – the District Judges ensuring before registration, that no forfeiture had occured under the former regulation. To prevent the registers being tampered with, these judges were required by instructions to keep the old registers under their own key until the new register should be completed.[1] This explanation satisfied Stanley, who proceeded to ratify the Ordinance. But he refused Campbell's recommendation to allow the payment of compensation to slave-owners.[2]

Campbell had hoped that, just as the first triennial inspection of the Kandyan registers had shown that slavery was almost at an end there, the second triennial inspection (in 1843) would see the complete extinction of slavery in the Kandyan areas. The inspection showed that the number of slaves had been reduced to a mere twentieth of the figures for 1837. But a more spectacular result was obtained in the Jaffna district and in the Sinhalese areas of the Maritime provinces, where the examination of the registers had shown the total extinction of slavery.[3] The number of slaves in Ceylon had been reduced to a mere 55, and Campbell decided that it was not necessary to delay the final abolition of slavery for three years longer, when, at the latest, those remaining on the registers would have been struck off. The policy of the Ceylon Government was thus justified by its complete success, and was achieved without any disturbance. In 1844, slavery was finally declared to be at an end. Ordinance 20 of 1844 'to provide for the total abolition of slavery in Ceylon', the main object of which was to declare that henceforth slavery would be contrary to the law, put an end to all doubt on the subject, and, at the same time, made it unnecessary to keep up the voluminous slave registers then in existence. (So long as even one slave could legally exist in Ceylon it was necessary to preserve this mass of records.)

Thus, the policy of the Ceylon Government had proved to be completely successful sooner than it could have been anticipated. The explanation lies in the fact that in all parts of the island slaves were of such little economic value that their owners did not

[1] *Ibid.*
[2] C.O. 54/203, Stanley to Campbell, no.50 of 5 June 1843.
[3] C.O. 54/204, Campbell to Stanley, no.157 of 28 August 1843.

think it worth their while to go to the trouble, and the trifling expense, of registering them. Indeed, the owners lost little by their emancipation. Another factor – less important than this – was that public opinion itself had begun to change, and chiefs and other slave-owners, anxious to cultivate the friendship of officials and missionaries, were willing to be persuaded to emancipate their slaves as the price of that friendship. The missionaries, as has been pointed out earlier, had little to do with the abolition of slavery, though some of them did hail it as the elimination of yet another obstacle to the progress of Christianity.

CHAPTER VII

A Mission to the Veddahs

It is a sobering thought that in the nineteenth century the continguity of European settlers with uncivilized tribes generally resulted in the gradual demoralization and decay, if not the complete extermination, of the latter. One had but to turn to the Americas and to Australasia for proof of this assertion. The Veddahs, the aborigines of Ceylon living in the forests of Bintenne in the Eastern Province, escaped the fate of the Maoris, the Black-fellows and the American Indians for two reasons. The forests in which they lived were unsuited to the cultivation of the two commercial crops that interested European capitalists in Ceylon at this time, coffee and sugar, and thus had little commercial value. Besides, the climate of that region did not commend itself to European settlement. They were, however, not spared the attentions of administrators and missionaries, but this interference, actuated by sincere humanitarianism, was an attempt at social amelioration conducted from the highest of motives.

The idea of a mission to the Veddahs originated with Glenelg, who instructed Mackenzie, on the latter's appointment to the Governorship of Ceylon in October 1837, to suggest, to the C.M.S. missionaries in Ceylon, the idea of a mission station at Badulla or at Bintenne, or in any other part of the Veddah country. Glenelg was very anxious that an attempt should be made to civilize the Veddahs, and he suggested that the expenses of the mission station should be defrayed from the colonial revenue.[1]

He underestimated the difficulties of the project. He felt that, since there were 'roads' from Kandy and Badulla to Bintenne, communications were not a serious problem. It would have been difficult for him to have visualized the real nature of those jungle tracks into the wilds of Bintenne. In any event his anxiety to civilize the Veddahs was so great that he suggested the construction of a road from Batticaloa on the eastern coast to Badulla, a

[1] C.O. 55/79, Glenelg to Mackenzie, no.18 of 2 October 1837.

most formidable undertaking, to provide reasonable access to the Veddah country.[1]

The Veddahs, by long-established tradition, paid a tribute of bees-wax to the Government of the day. Glenelg suggested that they should be asked to bring this wax to the projected C.M.S. Station in future, not indeed as tribute, but solely in order to exchange it for some of the necessaries and conveniences of civilized life.[2]

It was some time before Mackenzie could get down to the task of financing a mission to the Veddahs. He made a tour of the Eastern Province in 1839, partly, at least, in the hope of seeing these primitive people, and on his return to Colombo he sought to interest the Anglicans in the Veddahs.[3] Getting no response from them, he persuaded the Baptists to consider the idea of a mission to the Veddahs.[4] Two Baptist missionaries toured the Veddah country in the latter half of 1839, but returned convinced that the task was too formidable for them to undertake. Thus is was that the Wesleyans, who had the advantage of a mission station at Batticaloa on the eastern coast, quite close to the Veddah country, were entrusted with this work.[5]

From its inception, the Veddah Mission was a joint venture of the State and the Wesleyans. The Legislative Council made an annual grant of £200, while Mackenzie himself provided £25 a year for the establishment of two schools among the Veddahs, which were appropriately named the 'Mackenzie Schools'.[6] This enthusiasm was not confined to the higher ranges of the administra-

---

[1] Ibid.

[2] C.O. 55/79, Glenelg to Mackenzie, no.18 of 2 October 1837.

[3] S.P.G. MSS. Missionary Returns, IV, The Bishop's (Chapman of Colombo) Visitation Journal, 1846.

Pascoe, C. F., Two Hundred Years of the S.P.G. 1701–1900, p.677.

[4] Miss.Her. (1840), p.168, the Rev. E. Daniel, 20 September 1839.

[5] The Wesleyans at Batticaloa were divided on this issue. Rev. R. Stott, who was an enthusiastic supporter of a mission to the Veddahs, wrote that:

In the estimate of some persons it would not be worth the while for a missionary to make a ten days journey of more than a hundred miles for the sake of preaching to a hundred or a hundred and fifty people, scattered in the jungle, when he might, during the same time, find ten thousand people within a few miles of his own house. . . .

See Stott's letter of 9 September 1840 in Miss.Not., IX, 593.

Stott's enthusiasm won over his more reluctant colleagues.

[6] Miss.Not., X, 56, 57. Ibid., pp.70–2, Stott, 4 January 1842.

tion in Ceylon. Indeed, the experiment[1] could not have succeeded had it not enjoyed the devoted support of men on the spot, particularly Robert Atherton, who held the combined posts of Assistant Government Agent of the Eastern Province and District Judge of Batticaloa, and of the Rev. R. Stott of the Wesleyan mission station at Batticaloa. Mackenzie and the Wesleyans at Colombo could have laid down only the barest outlines of the policy to be followed – the conversion and civilization of the Veddahs;[2] the more important task of effecting that policy was left in the capable hands of Atherton and Stott, working in tandem.[3] The early success of the Veddah Mission was largely due to the fact that these two were able to work so well together. And they worked together mainly because Atherton himself – he had joined the Wesleyan congregation at Batticaloa in early 1841 – was a very enthusiastic Wesleyan lay worker. Together they began the process of turning these timid, primitive hunters into civilized, Christian farmers. Their task was formidable; it was nothing less than that of bringing these Stone Age men into the nineteenth century.

The early reports from Bintenne were encouraging. In 1841 Stott reported that he had converted ninety Veddahs and Sinhalese of Bintenne. He stated that

> forty families have already come down, and are building houses. A considerable number of them are Christians and the rest are anxious to be baptised. Mr Atherton . . . has just returned from Bintenne where he has been to fix their settlements, and gives a very good account of the people. He states that they pray daily, conduct themselves with the greatest propriety, and refrain from all labour on the Sabbath.[4]

[1] Mackenzie's aim, according to Stott, *Miss.Not.*, IX, 593–5 was:
'. . . to give on a lease to each Veddah who is wishing to settle down and cultivate, three acres of land, to assist him in building a house, give him seed grain for the first year, and to provide him with hoes, axes, etc., and, when thirty children can be found to learn, to establish a free school.

[2] *Miss.Not.*, IX, 593. Stott's letter of 9 September 1840 explained that if the Veddahs were settled in one place, they would embrace Christianity. '[They] appear simple and docile, have no false religion, and listen with great attention to spiritual things.'

[3] In August 1840 Stott had undertaken a tour of the Veddah country. Mackenzie had intended to accompany him but his health failed and, at his request, Stott was accompanied by Atherton.

[4] *Miss.Not.*, X, 56, 57.

By the beginning of 1842, 53 families had been settled in the villages with a Mackenzie School in each under Christian schoolmasters. Atherton made the schoolmasters constables in their villages in order 'that they may have the power to protect the Veddahs from ill-disposed Moormen who go to barter with them.'[1] Stott explained that the object of the Moors was 'to keep the Veddahs in their former ignorance, that they may cheat them better in bargaining with them'.[2] But this opposition was of little avail, and Stott reported, triumphantly, that nine out of ten Veddahs wished to embrace Christianity.[3] For Atherton and his wife, Stott had nothing but the highest praise.[4] He was equally well-pleased with the schoolmasters.[5] In November 1842 Atherton wrote to the Wesleyan Mission Society in England that the Veddah mission had made substantial progress. 'Everything is going on there quietly – they are busy cultivating grains, and I have sent them a good supply of coconut palms.'[6] He was making preparations to establish a third Veddah village with its own school, and to settle another forty to sixty families in the course of the next year.

Stott explained to his superiors in London that his attitude to the Veddahs was essentially paternalistic. 'I have received them as children and I think it prudent to keep them as such for a time.'[7] Indeed it is difficult to see what other attitude could have been adopted.

By 1843, the Veddah mission[8] had become a showplace of the Wesleyans in Ceylon. A Wesleyan missionary who visited the Bintenne region in October 1842 reported that what he had seen

[1] *Ibid.*, pp.70–2, Stott, 4 January 1842.
[2] *Ibid.*, pp.56–7.   [3] *Ibid.*, pp.70–2.
[4] Wes.Mss.Cey., I, Stott, 7 January 1842.
[5] *Ibid.*, Stott, 5 April 1842. These two schoolmasters also held services on the Sabbath.
[6] Wes.Mss.Cey., I, Atherton, 4 November 1842. See also *ibid.*, Stott, 19 January 1843. He informed the Society that, in the course of 1842, 18 Veddahs had been converted, 40 more houses were being built, and more than 500 coconut trees were planted. In some of the new villages the Veddahs were planting paddy.
[7] Wes.Mss.Cey., I, Stott, 19 January 1843.
[8] The Wesleyans created a circuit to cover this area – the Bintenne circuit under the Batticaloa Station.

was 'enough to gratify both philanthropist and Christian'.[1] But the very success of the mission had its own peculiar pitfalls, for it attracted so much attention both in Ceylon and in England that there was a danger that other aspects of mission work might be neglected. The Wesleyans in England were warned not 'to lay undue significance or undue relative importance to the work among the Veddahs'.[2] Stott conveyed the same warning in a letter home in April 1843, in which he pointed out that there were not more than 400 Veddahs living in the three villages, the largest of which had no more than 40 houses, while the real field of operations was the coastal region near Batticaloa where several thousand Hindus, Muslims, Buddhists and 'Papists' awaited conversion.[3] Jealous voices were being raised against the mission, and typical of these was a rather insidious comment by a Wesleyan missionary.

> It is to be supposed that the influence of Mr Atherton, considering the station which he holds, has something to do with the conversions that take place; but after a second visit and as much inquiry as circumstances have enabled me to make, I have no hesitation in declaring . . . that in the main this work is of God.[4]

Another Wesleyan missionary, conscious perhaps of the publicity the Mission had attracted, declared in a soft condemnatory tone that:

> . . . were the ingathering in that quarter the effect of instruction apprehended and appreciated by the natives I would rejoice at it; but from what I can learn, the reception of Baptism is the consequence of a general Government-encouraged movement, of a few degraded and most ignorant people from a barbarous though by no means savage to a more civil and social state. It is no doubt an interesting state of things, but how can it be the effect of the preaching of the Gospel? When and by whom was the Gospel preached . . . ?[5]

This latter criticism focuses attention on what, as regards the propagation of Christianity, was the real weakness of the mission. The work of civilization – the construction of houses, the establish-

---

[1] *Miss.Not.*, X, 247, Rev. J. Crowther, 24 October 1842. *C.L.R.* 1st Series, I, 151–2.

[2] *Ibid.* Crowther insisted that the real achievement of Stott was in converting the Hindus and 'Papists' of Batticaloa.

[3] *Miss.Not.*, X, 353, Stott, 20 April 1840.

[4] *Ibid.*, X, 247, Crowther, 24 October 1842.

[5] Wes.Mss.Cey., I, Rev. R. Percival (Jaffna), 5 January 1842.

ment of schools and the introduction of agriculture – seemed successful enough, but the work of conversion was necessarily superficial,[1] a thin veneer over a solid core of paganism. Men were 'converted' to Christianity who hardly had the most elementary notion of what it meant.

But only a discerning – or a jealous – eye could see this defect at this stage. The foundations laid by Atherton and Stott seemed solid enough and the mission continued to expand without much difficulty. The three thriving village settlements served as centres from which civilization gradually spread among the other Veddahs. A fourth village – numbering one hundred and fourteen – applied to the Government for aid,[2] which was readily granted, and another settlement was made. Another village, reluctant to be civilized, was won over, and when it was visited in 1846 the people were found to be cultivating not merely grain for their consumption, but also cotton for their own use in clothing.[3] In June 1845 the Wesleyan missionary at Batticaloa informed the Society that the Veddah mission was flourishing.[4]

The Bishop of Colombo made a visitation to the Eastern Province in 1846; the fame of the Veddah mission was such, that he braved the rigours of the trip to visit the Veddahs. Very impressed by what he saw, he commended the '. . . active zeal and enterprising energy of . . . Mr Atherton'.[5] He was more reluctant and grudging in his praise of the Wesleyans.[6]

The Bishop realized the full significance of the work of the Veddah mission.

The undoubted aborigines of the island, they are now for the first time gathered together, and brought within the reach and blessings of civilization – reclaimed from a wild barbarism, instead of being

[1] C.L.R., 1st Series, I, 151.
[2] S.P.G. MSS., The Bishop's Visitation Journal, 1846, Part II.
[3] Ibid.
[4] Wes.Mss.Cey., I, Rev. R. Pargiter, 30 June 1845.
[5] The Bishop's Visitation Journal, 1846, Part II.
[6] Ibid. Referring to the work of the Wesleyans among the Veddahs, the Bishop remarked:
   . . . if all their work was as well done as it is here, we should have less reason, and far less inclination to blame them. Were all their efforts directed with a single eye to God's Glory than their own numerical increase, the cause of Christianity would gain much, and they would themselves lose nothing.

exterminated or altogether disappearing, from some unknown cause, before the footsteps of civilization.[1]

However, he was no uncritical admirer of the Veddah mission. He observed that the schools were on the verge of being abandoned, partly from the want of teachers, and partly from the indifference of the people themselves. He had carefully examined the Veddahs in their knowledge and understanding of Christianity, and found them ignorant of the very elements of their new faith.[2] He concluded that the Veddah mission was successful, 'as far as their settlement in villages, the formation of homes and families, and consequent social improvement is concerned; but their religious instruction has *all* to be done'. But Stott writing home at much the same time, had no such reservations about his mission. To him, it was an unqualified success.[3]

The Bishop's estimation of the mission proved to be more correct. By 1847 the Veddah mission was on the wane. The schools at Bintenne were given up in 1847, 'as it was found impossible to collect and keep together a sufficient number of scholars to make it worthwhile paying the teachers that amount of salary which they require in consideration of their living in such localities'.[4] Stott, who had worked indefatigably in the cause of the Veddah mission, left Batticaloa, and his successor, the Rev. J. Gillings, even if he had the inclination to work as hard, did not have the resources and the support that favoured Stott.

In 1847 the commercial depression in England and the collapse of the coffee industry in Ceylon saw a drastic reduction in the finances of the Wesleyan mission in Ceylon, and the Veddah mission, showpiece though it was, had become a rather expensive luxury.

But there was more to it than a question of financial assistance. Gillings was not as devoted to the mission as was Stott, who, until

[1] *Ibid.*
[2] The Bishop carefully questioned the Veddahs on their knowledge of Christianity.

> I asked them who made the sun to shine and the rain to fall, and the trees to grow. Answer: God. Where does God dwell? Answer: We don't know. Who was Jesus Christ? Answer: We don't know. I was afraid of proceeding much further, and told them that they should have a school, not for their children only, but for themselves.

[3] Wes.Mss.Cey., II, Stott, 5 March 1846.
[4] A/R North Ceylon Mission (Wesleyan), 1849, p.37.

malaria sapped his constitution, had made at least three visits a
year to the Veddah settlements.[1] The exhorters and catechists
were sent quarterly, but as none of them understood the Veddah
dialect any better than the missionary, they were always obliged
to use an interpreter.[2] The teachers proved a sad disappointment.
Free from the regular supervision to which they were accustomed
under Stott, they neglected their duties, and some of them became
traders. Thus, these teachers, who were formerly appointed and
paid by the Government were discontinued, and the schools
abandoned.[3] The early success of the mission was due to the work
of Atherton and Stott, and of the teachers themselves, not to
mention the regular support of the administration. As long as this
paternalistic interference was maintained, the mission prospered,
but without a resident teacher sincerely devoted to this work it
could not succeed. When, as a consequence of the financial crisis
in Ceylon, Government supplies were withheld or curtailed, only a
careful reappraisal of the needs of the mission could have carried
it through this crisis. But there was no one on the spot capable of
shouldering those responsibilities. By the beginning of 1849 it was
clear that the Wesleyans had virtually abandoned the Veddah
mission; there were fears that others would take over the work
unless they reoccupied it. Gillings lamented that 'it is indeed a
cause of sorrow that such a field should be either allowed to be
uncultivated or given over to another party after having been
begun by ourselves. With our present agency and means we cannot
supply it.'[4] It was at once a confession of failure, and a plea for help;
but the Wesleyan Mission Society at home was in no position to
help.

The Veddahs themselves, deprived of the close supervision they
were accustomed to, returned to their old ways. They were tired
of their new and settled life, and took once again to the jungles.[5]
They forgot their agricultural pursuits; their crops died from want

[1] Wes.Mss.Cey., II, 7, Gillings, J., 8 November 1849. He informed the
mission, in this letter, that he had opened a more fruitful station on the coast
among the Muslims, and that he could therefore devote only a little of his time
to the Veddahs.

[2] Ibid.

[3] A/R North Ceylon Mission (Wesleyan) 1849, p.37.
WesMss.Cey., II, Gillings, J., 8 November 1849

[4] Wes.Mss.Cey., II, Gillings, J., 7 April 1849.

[5] A/R Wesleyan Mission (North Ceylon) 1849, p.38 and 1850, p.46.

of water, and what survived were destroyed by wild elephants. The veneer of Christianity had worn thin; they had reverted to their traditional cults.

> Stating that they had been so long under the power of the devil that he would not allow them to be free, but if they worshipped Christ, would afflict them and their children and cattle with all kinds of disease, they avowed in the strongest manner their determination, whatever might come of so doing, though urgently remonstrated with on the folly and wickedness of such rites, to persist in their heathenish ceremonies . . .[1]

This was Gillings' despairing comment.

Gillings complained that some of the Veddahs were now '. . . wholly intent on worldly things, unwilling to labour at agricultural pursuits, more fond of jungle life, less tractable and submissive to those placed over them, and full of cunning and deceit'. Apparently he had lost heart and had come to the conclusion that it was time for the Wesleyan mission to cut its losses and to abandon the mission to the Veddahs. 'In our present circumstances we can do little or nothing for the Veddahs . . . but pay them occasional visits; and these are but of slender service'.[2] He explained that the Veddahs 'appear to be too migratory to allow of any continuous and systematic effort for their instruction and evangelization'. Besides, the mission station at Batticaloa was so badly understaffed that there was '. . . scarcely sufficient to meet the wants of the places surrounding home'. The mission also found it 'exceedingly difficult to get Singhalese [sic] on whom we can depend'.[3] It is not surprising therefore that he recommended the abandonment of the Veddah mission, in the interests of the work of the Wesleyans elsewhere in the Batticaloa station. Gillings left the fate of the Veddah mission to be decided upon by his superiors at home.

On this occasion Gillings made no mention of a far more serious development, which certainly affected his calculations in these matters, that had put the Wesleyans in the Eastern Province on the defensive. Just at this time, the Anglicans were making a bid to oust the Wesleyans from their position of primacy in mission work in the Eastern Province. The campaign was apparently conducted with the connivance, if not the authority, of the Bishop

---

[1] Wes.Mss.Cey., II, Gillings, J., 8 November 1849.
[2] Ibid.   [3] Ibid.

himself. The extent of its success may be gauged from the fact that by 1850 the Wesleyan community in Batticaloa was badly divided, and had lost some of their most influential members to the Anglicans. The loss of Atherton, who now went over to the Anglicans, was a particularly grievous blow, for much of the success of the Wesleyans in the Eastern Province was due to his exertions on their behalf. With all the fervour of the recently converted, Atherton now worked for the Anglicans, and against the Wesleyans.[1]

He directed his attention to the Veddah mission in particular, and instructed the one remaining Veddah instructor to transfer the Veddahs under his care from the superintendence of the Wesleyans to that of the Bishop of Colombo. The Bishop himself visited Batticaloa. The Veddahs were persuaded, with presents of cloth and axes, to place themselves under the Church of England. The instructor himself had been, until then, a 'Wesleyan by education and profession'.[2] Gillings protested to Torrington against these actions of Atherton and the Veddah instructor (who was paid by the Government), complaining that Atherton had given no reasons for this change, and that the Veddahs were people utterly incapable of deciding for themselves. He had every reason to be bitter about this bit of poaching by the Anglicans because the Veddah mission owed its existence, to a large extent, to the devoted labours of the Wesleyans at Batticaloa. (They had undertaken this project at a time when the Anglicans had failed to respond to Mackenzie's invitation to establish a mission to the Veddahs.) What steps Torrington took in this matter, whether he backed the Wesleyans or the Anglicans, whether he took any interest in the Veddah mission at all, are matters on which there is little evidence in the records. But the rivalry between the Anglicans and Wesleyans continued and the Veddah mission suffered as a consequence.

One result of Atherton's activities was to make Gillings more defiant; in 1849 he had suggested the abandonment of the Veddah mission, but later (1851) he pleaded that this station should not be neglected or abandoned.[3] But neglected and abandoned it was, both by the Wesleyans and the Government. None of Mackenzie's successors as Governor of Ceylon showed the same – or for that

---

[1] A/R North Ceylon Mission (Wesleyan) 1851, p.66. [2] *Ibid.*
[3] Wes.Mss.Cey., II, Gillings, J., 9 August 1851.

matter, any – interest in the Veddah mission. Glenelg had left the Colonial Office before the mission was established, and his successors appear to have been unaware of its existence. Then, when the depression came in 1847, the Government ruthlessly curtailed its expenditure. The grant to the Veddah mission was one of the expendables. The loss of the Government subsidy was a crippling blow; still the mission could have survived if the Wesleyans were financially strong enough to undertake its support entirely on their own. But they were not, and Gillings – until Anglican opposition goaded him to a defiant change of heart – was not inclined to commit scarce resources to an undertaking that seemed on the verge of collapse. The Wesleyan mission itself lost heart and the Anglicans appear to have taken over by default.

The Anglicans ousted the Wesleyans; but the substitution of Anglicans for Wesleyans did the Veddahs little good. It was at best a shallow, selfish triumph in a petty sectarian dispute. The Anglicans proved to be incapable of organizing this work. The Veddah mission was a formidable undertaking at the best of times; it needed unselfish devotion in the face of a rigorous climate, a rugged, inhospitable terrain, and a people who did not understand the work of the missionaries.

The Wesleyans, at least, did not forget the Veddahs. In 1855 a Wesleyan missionary was sent on a tour of the Veddah country, with the intention of reviving the Veddah mission. He reported that 'the poor Veddah Christians are virtually abandoned by the Church Party here. . . .' Instead of the once flourishing Veddah settlements he saw 'dire disease and misery – an alarming amount of both'. He concluded that 'There can be but one opinion as to the speedy fate of this people, viz., extermination by disease.'[1]

Administrative parsimony and sectarian antagonisms together destroyed an enlightened project that might have brought great benefit to the Veddahs and credit to the missionaries.

[1] Wes.Mss.Cey., II, Rev. J. Kilner, 17 September 1855.

Part III

THE expansion of plantation agriculture in Ceylon created an unprecedented demand for a stable and disciplined supply of labour. The bulk of the indigenous population could not be persuaded to work on the plantations, and Ceylon, like the West Indian islands and Mauritius, came to depend almost entirely on immigrant Indian labour. The Indian immigrants who came to Ceylon formed part of a general movement of Indians across the seas to man the plantations of the tropical colonies of the second British Empire. But, while the movement to the sugar islands has been the subject of systematic study, the movement to Ceylon, which was quite as important, has been curiously neglected. In many ways – and largely because of the proximity to India – the movement of immigrants to Ceylon differed considerably from that to the other tropical colonies. And the policies adopted by the Ceylon Government in the years 1840–55 did not follow the West Indian and Mauritian model. For these reasons, if for no others, the problem of Indian immigration to Ceylon is worthy of study.

The first of these two chapters seeks to do two things: to elucidate the nature of problems posed by the immigration of Indian labour; and to analyse the response of Government to these problems. The second deals with the attitude of the missionaries to these problems and their influence, if any, on Government policy. Such a division would normally have presented great difficulties; it would have been both injudicious and inconvenient to make such a separation. But since the missionaries had so little influence on Government policy, it is possible to study the respective reactions of the Government and the missionaries in separation.

If the missionaries had so little influence on Government policy in this sphere, the question naturally arises: why study the reaction of the missionaries to this problem at all? To this the answer is that it is impossible to study a movement that aimed both at conversion and social reform without studying its attitude to one of the gravest social problems of the day. The great social problem created by the immigration of Indians to Ceylon dwarfed most other social problems; and these other problems were in a different category, for they were the problems of the traditional society which both the administrators and missionaries were dedicated to changing. The question of Indian immigrants was a major social problem of the new society that the missionaries, along with the administrators, were helping to create. Hence the need to study the reaction of the missionaries to this problem.

CHAPTER VIII

The Immigration of
Indian Plantation Labour to Ceylon, 1840–55:
the Attitude of the Government

NOTHING was more exasperating or more puzzling to the British planters in Ceylon at this time than the fact that, with the great majority of their plantations established in the old Kandyan kingdom, they were still as dependent on immigrant Indian labour as their contemporaries in the West Indies or Mauritius. Tennent remarked that

> no temptation of wages and no prospect of advantage has hitherto availed to overcome the repugnance of the Sinhalese and the Kandyans to engage in any work on the estates except in the first process of felling of the forests.[1]

A pioneer coffee planter explained that the Kandyans had no incentive to work on the plantations.

> They have as a general rule, their own paddy fields, their own cows, bullocks, their own fruit-gardens; and the tending and managing of these occupy all their attention. Their wants are easily supplied, and unless they wish to present their wives with a new cloth, or to pro-

---

[1] Tennent, *Ceylon*, II, 235 ff.

For the reluctance of the Kandyan peasants to work on the plantations, see also Anon, *Extracts of Letters from Ceylon on Courtship, Marriage etc., with a peep into Jungle Life* (London, 1848).

Boyd, W., 'Autobiography of a peria Durai', *C.L.R.* 1st Series, 11, 376–432, 'Ceylon and Its Pioneers', *ibid.*, 217–84.

Rigg, C. R., 'Coffee Planting in Ceylon', *The Ceylon Examiner*, 16 and 23 June 1852.

C.O. 54/235, Tennent to Grey, no.6 of 21 April 1847.

In this despatch Tennent explained that in the early years of coffee planting, Kandyan peasants did work, but they were discouraged by the brutalities of the superintendents, and frauds concerning their wages.

In the newspapers of these years (1840–55) there is evidence that at times of acute labour shortage, Kandyan peasants and low country Sinhalese turned up for work on the plantations but demanded, and received, substantially higher wages than the Indians.

cure a gun or powder and shot for themselves, they really have no inducement to work on the coffee plantations.[1]

There were other reasons. A more perceptive observer commented:

The [Kandyan] has such a reverence for his patrimonial lands, that were his gain to be quadrupled, he would not abandon their culture. . . . Besides working for hire is repulsive to their national feelings, and is looked upon as almost slavery. The being obliged to obey orders, and to do just what they are commanded is galling to them.[2]

The substantial immigration of Indian labourers to work on the coffee plantations of Ceylon began in the 1830s, and increased to a regular flow in the early 1840s with the expansion of coffee culture in the Central Province.[3] (By 1840 coffee cultivation in Ceylon held the prospect of definite, if not spectacular, success, with over a hundred plantations in the process of formation – in nearly every instance by amateur planters – in every district within thirty miles of Kandy.[4]) In spite of an increase in the number of immigrant labourers, the planters were seldom certain of an adequate supply of labour during the picking season. In the latter half of 1842 the Ceylon planters were faced with the first of those shortages of labour that were to be such a regular feature in the economic history of this period.

In 1842 the Ceylon Agricultural Society was established with the active encouragement and support of the Ceylon Government, with Philip Anstruther – then Colonial Secretary of the Ceylon Government – as its first President. The first problem that faced the Society was this shortage of labour. They appointed a sub-committee to devise a plan to import labour under the auspices of the society, but that sub-committee reported that such a plan would be of little use because no contract entered into with labourers in India would be binding in Ceylon, and besides, even if one were signed when the labourers landed in the north of the

[1] Boyd, W., 'Autobiography', *C.L.R.* 1st Series, 11, pp.249 ff.

[2] Rigg, C. R., *op. cit.*

[3] Between July 1842 and December 1842 there were 13,935 immigrants. In 1843 there were 31,201, while in 1844 and 1845 the numbers had increased to 71,173 and 67,278 respectively.

See *Ceylon Plantation Gazetteer* (1859), pp.169 ff.

[4] See, Lewis, R. E., *Coffee Planting in Ceylon* (Colombo, 1855).

Lewis was a pioneer coffee planter in the Central Province. He became the first editor of *The Ceylon Examiner* in 1846. His small pamphlet still remains one of the most informative studies of the first phase of coffee planting in Ceylon.

Island, it would still be difficult to bring these labourers to the Central Province without 'considerable risks of desertion'. The sub-committee could only suggest that '. . . it would be advantageous to afford them [the immigrant Indians] inducements and facilities to come over on their own responsibility.[1]

Fortunately for the society, the labour situation improved sooner than was anticipated, and they were able to reflect at leisure on the causes of the shortage. The committee observed that though the shortage was serious enough, it was at its worst in January, February and March 1843, after the picking of the crop. They explained that the immigrants normally returned to their homes at this time of the year.[2] There was less agreement among the members of the committee on the causes of labour scarcity during the crop season of 1842. Some attributed it to sickness, the result, it was assumed, of the abnormally heavy rain in the early part of the year, while others referred to a panic that appears to have struck the immigrant Indians, inducing them to leave the country earlier than they anticipated. They did not indicate what caused this panic.[3]

Faced with this labour shortage, the Society demanded government assistance in promoting the immigration of Indian labourers. They suggested that the State should provide rudimentary welfare facilities for the immigrants – chiefly 'rest-houses' and wells – on the road from the arid north-west coast (the immigrants came by boat from the south-west coast of India to Talaimannar or Arippu) to the plantations in Kandyan areas.[4] These facilities were a prime necessity because this road, a mere path through the jungle, lay through some of the most difficult country in Ceylon, in respect of climate – the flat, malarious, densely forested lands of the present North Central Province. At the end of the journey there stood the hills of the Central Province, with their heavy rains and cool climate, where the coffee estates were. Further on, beyond Kandy, it was wetter still, colder, and the terrain more rugged and mountainous.[5] A contemporary coffee planter observed that:

[1] *Proc/C.A.S.*, 1st Report 1842, pp.1–18.

[2] *Ibid.*, 3rd Report 1843, pp.1–4.

[3] There may have been an epidemic of cholera at this time. During such outbreaks, Indian immigrants deserted the estates and rushed home.

[4] *Proc/C.A.S.*, 1st Report 1842, pp.30–31; 3rd Report 1843, pp.2–4.

[5] C.O. 54/235, Tennent to Grey, no.6 of 21 April 1847, Knighton, W., *Forest Life in Ceylon*, I, 171 ff. Millie, P. D., *Memoirs of a Coffee Planter*.

Few gangs of coolies arrived on the estates without some deaths occuring on the road, but more took place after arrival on the estates, being worn with the journey and change of climate . . . it is generally some time before the cooly gets hardened.[1]

The newspapers of the day, reflecting planter opinion, were as interested in the labour problem as the Ceylon Agricultural Society, but the solutions they suggested were more radical. They held out to the Ceylon Government the example of the Governments of the West Indies and Mauritius, which sponsored and even financed the immigration of Indian plantation labourers. *The Colombo Observer* argued that the '. . . condition of the planters in the interior . . . is rapidly approaching to that of the West Indies . . .' and insisted that the Ceylon Government was 'as much bound to undertake this duty [of importing labour] as the Governments of the several West Indian islands, or even more here as the expense would be so trifling here as compared to what it is there.'[2] This was to be a very familiar demand of the planters in the years ahead, but the Government ignored it in 1843 – and it was to ignore it in the future, too.

The Ceylon Government maintained that there was a significant difference between the immigration of Indian labour to Ceylon, and that to the West Indies and Mauritius; the former, they insisted was more akin to the seasonal immigration of Irish agricultural labourers to England.[3] The facts certainly support this argument, since coffee plantations (unlike the tea plantations of the future) did not require a large permanent labour force. The demand for labour reached its peak during the picking season, generally mid-August to early November. This happened to coincide with the slack season on the rice fields of South India, thus enabling

---

[1] Millie, *op. cit.*, chap. XIV. (The pages of this book are not numbered.)

[2] *The Colombo Observer*, 13 July 1843.

[3] See C.O. 54/235, Tennent to Grey, no.6 of 21 April 1847; and particularly Tennent's correspondence with the Indian Government.

The Colonial Office had reached this same conclusion on their own as early as 1840–1. See C.O. 54/185, Anstruther's memorandum of 28 November 1840. In this memorandum, Anstruther referred, among other things, to the dependence of the planters in Ceylon on immigrant labour from India; he recommended State sponsored immigration. In the margin, against this comment, an official of the Colonial Office had written (in pencil) the remark that Indian immigration to Ceylon 'was more analogous of the Irish to England' than the 'Hill Coolies' (from India) to the West Indies.

peasants from there to make an annual trip to Ceylon during the coffee-picking season, and to return home in time for the next harvest.

One of the distinguishing features of British colonial activity in this period was the remarkable interest taken by the Imperial Government, as well as the governments of the several West Indian islands (and British Guiana) and Mauritius, in the immigration of Indians. This active State intervention was the result of exceptional circumstances, the abolition of slavery in the West Indies and Mauritius, and the fear that unless a regular supply of free labour was available there would be a complete breakdown in the economy of these territories. At every stage, this immigration from India was rigidly controlled and carefully supervised by the Imperial Government, the East India Company in India, and the receiving territories. To a large extent this close supervision was the result of Evangelical agitation in England and India, an agitation inspired by a determination to prevent any possibility of the old slave-owners converting indentured labour into a new form of slavery. Besides, the Evangelicals had a vested interest in the success of the experiment of free labour in the West Indies and Mauritius. Only the gravity of these problems compelled these governments, imperial and local, to intervene in a sphere of activity specifically barred to the State by contemporary social and economic theories.[1] In Ceylon, where there was no problem of plantation slavery, the Government's policy was to leave the importation of labour to the planters themselves, who in their turn left this business in the capable but unscrupulous hands of the more enterprising of the labourers.

In the early years of coffee planting, plantation owners sent their own agents to India to recruit labour, but later on the Indians come on their own, forming themselves into gangs of from twenty-five to one hundred. They selected one of themselves as *kangany*, or headman, and this individual guided them on their journey, negotiated their engagements, and ultimately superintended their labour, receiving for these services a fraction of the wages of each labourer. The kangany supervised the work of his gang of twenty-five or thirty or, if it were smaller, he would him-

---

[1] The most satisfactory study of these problems is found in Miss I. M. Cumpston's recent work, *Indians Overseas in British Territories, 1834-54* (Oxford, 1953). See also Mellor, G., *British Imperial Trusteeship, 1783-1850* (London, 1951).

self work as a labourer. All labour gangs on the estates would be under a head-kangany who acted as an intermediary between the estate-superintendents and the labour force regarding the payment of wages. Apart from his fixed monthly wages for supervising the work of the labour force, he was also paid a trifling commission, called 'head money', by the estate, for each labourer who turned out for work. It was thus in the interests of the kangany to provide as many labourers as he could. The kangany was the medium of all advances made to the labourers, and he was often the sole debtor to the estate.[1]

It must, however, be noted that the term kangany had several meanings. In the first phase of coffee planting in Ceylon, he was generally a 'democratically' elected leader, but there were others who were merely agents of the planters. The Ceylon Agricultural Society suggested that some of them should be induced to establish themselves as agents for recruiting labour, providing advances from their own funds to men who did not have the means to come across to Ceylon.[2] They came to assume this role of planter's agent increasingly after 1850. There was a third category of kangany, who earned a living by 'crimping' labourers from one plantation to another, and were particularly active during periods of labour scarcity.

To leave the importation of labour to the planters and the kanganies was to invite abuse, exploitation and neglect. The records indicate that the most widespread abuse was the neglect and harsh treatment of sick labourers. In 1843, the Ceylon Agricultural Society reported that it viewed 'with feelings of great pain the destitution of the sick labouring poor, which has arrived at such a pitch as to call forth the most serious attention of everyone interested in agriculture.' They warned the planters that, 'unless some internal arrangement be made upon estates, higher authorities will most assuredly intervene to compel the adoption of some system which shall exonerate the agricultural interest of seeing the roads choked up with the sick, the dying and the dead.'[3] The hospital of the Kandy Friend-in-Need Society, founded in 1838 for the benefit of the poor and the sick in the town of Kandy, had

[1] An excellent description of the kangany system is provided in Millie, *op. cit.*, chap. III.
[2] *Proc/C.A.S.*, 3rd Report, pp.50 ff.
[3] *Ibid.* 2nd Report, pp.4 ff.

by 1840 become almost exclusively a hospital for sick immigrant labourers, who generally entered it in '. . . a miserable state from disease and starvation'.[1] It was not one of the original aims of this hospital to attend to sick immigrant labourers, but for obvious humanitarian reasons the Kandy Friend-in-Need Society could not very well ignore them. The pressure on the hospital from these immigrant labourers became so great, and it was increasing annually, that an appeal was made to the Government for assistance. Though this appeal was made as early as 1840, the first contribution from the Government came only in 1843, and even then it was a trifling sum of £40, which was increased in 1844 to £50. At its fifth anniversary meeting, the Kandy Friend-in-Need Society appealed to the planters for assistance, rightly arguing that 'those who induce the immigration of coolies are in duty bound to contribute to their necessities when afflicted with sickness'.[2] This appeal was backed by the Ceylon Agricultural Society, which suggested that every estate should make an annual contribution of £3. The appeal of the Ceylon Agricultural Society concluded thus:

> It requires but a glance at the road-side in the neighbourhood of Kandy to be convinced of the frightful amount of disease and misery which prevails and the Committee in performing this act which they consider to be their sacred duty, cannot but be persuaded that their call will be unanimously successful.[3]

Only six estates made any contribution at all in 1843. In 1844 the number of estates making this annual contribution had increased to sixteen, but still the bulk of the funds came from public subscriptions.

The Government was as negligent of its duties to immigrant labour as were the planters. After much cajoling, it made a trifling annual contribution to the hospital of the Kandy Friend-in-Need Society. During Stewart Mackenzie's administration it had constructed four sheds (called 'rest-houses') on the road from Puttalam to Kurunegala. The Government passed a Labour Ordinance designed, above all else, to regulate the duration of labour contracts.[4]

[1] The 3rd A/R Kandy F.I.N.S., p.5.
[2] The 6th A/R Kandy F.I.N.S., pp.6–8.
[3] *Proc/C.A.S.* 2nd Report, pp.4–5.
[4] The duration of the labour contract was to be one calendar year.

This ordinance had originally been prepared by Wilmot-Horton at a time when there was no significant movement of Indian emigrants to Ceylon. It was meant to be no more than the introduction to Ceylon of the main principles of English master and servant legislation, but the Colonial Office disallowed it because it discriminated too much in favour of the employer.[1] Glenelg recommended that the Ordinance should be submitted again in an amended form, with the alteration or deletion of those clauses which the Colonial Office had found objectionable.[2] Stewart Mackenzie, Wilmot-Horton's successor, resubmitted the Ordinance without the amendments suggested by Glenelg, but with the addition of a few new clauses which, by favouring the employer even more emphatically, made it all the more objectionable.[3] There was the significant difference that Mackenzie's Ordinance was drafted largely to deal with immigrant labour, and in its drafting he, and his Executive Council – the bulk of whom were planters – had the planters' interest in mind.

The Colonial Office decided that the Ordinance would not be confirmed 'unless an amendment included the whole of the accommodation conveyed by Lord Glenelg . . . or unless some satisfactory reason shall be given why they should not be adopted'.[4] It was left to Mackenzie's successor, Sir Colin Campbell, to submit the Ordinance with the amendments suggested by the Colonial Office, among which the most important was the clause that sub-

[1] The Colonial Office made three important criticisms of this Ordinance: that it embraced engagements made beyond the island; that it empowered the District Courts to inflict severe punishments; and that there was no reciprocal scale of punishments for the offences of masters against their servants.

[2] C.O. 54/182, Mackenzie to Russell, no.187 of 9 December 1840.

[3] Of particular significance in this regard was Mackenzie's recommendation that breaches of labour contracts should not be settled in the civil courts, but – in the interests of speedy settlements – should be tried by the criminal courts. It followed that breaches of labour contracts would become criminal offences liable to severe punishments. Since there was no reciprocal scale of punishments for employers, this ordinance was liable to be very oppressive to the immigrant labourer.

Mackenzie explained that the provisions of this ordinance were not to be compulsory, but binding only on those who were willing to enter into these engagements. And he argued that, in the long run, the ordinance would benefit the workers because employers would be forced to pay attention to the workers' welfare if their services were to be retained for any appreciable length of time.

[4] C.O. 54/182, Russell to Mackenzie, no.27 of 3 March 1841.

jected an employer who failed to honour an engagement to a fine of £10 or, in default, imprisonment for a period of three months. James Stephen found that it met the requirement laid down by Glenelg and, on his recommendation, Russell confirmed it.[1]

Thus the Government's response to the problem created by the immigration of plantation labourers was neither positive nor enlightened. First, there was the very novelty of the problem; it would take many years before the administration accustomed itself to it, and by a process of trial and error evolved some satisfactory approach. Secondly, the idea of Government intervention was obnoxious to administrators of this period, brought up to accept the infallibility of the theories of *laissez-faire*. State intervention in the immigration of labour to the West Indies and Mauritius was the result of the working of uniquely important factors; it was not, in the opinion of these officials, a precedent to be followed in Ceylon. Thirdly, since the labour shortage of 1842–3 there had been a steady improvement in the labour situation, and – until 1846 – no complaints of a serious labour scarcity.

In 1846 there was an acute shortage of labour in Ceylon. With new land coming into production a bumper crop was anticipated, but in that year the number of Indian immigrants was very nearly halved.[2] Planter agitation for State-sponsored and State-subsidized immigration increased in volume and intensity. The Ceylon Government was jolted out of its lethargy, and Campbell, near the end of his administration in Ceylon, made the first attempt to examine critically the whole basis of Indian immigration in Ceylon.[3]

While Campbell was searching for these remedies, the planters' agitation assumed a defiant tone. At a meeting held at Kandy on 9 June 1846, they prepared a memorial to the Secretary of State,

---

[1] C.O. 54/190, Campbell to Russell, no.88 of 1 October 1841 and Stanley's reply, no.75 of 23 March 1842.

[2] Between 1845 and 1847 the acreage under coffee nearly doubled. In 1845 there was 26,429¾ acres; in 1847 there were 52,722½ acres.

See Grey MSS., Torrington to Grey, 9 June 1848.

Yet in 1845 there had been 67,278 immigrant labourers, but in 1846 this had dropped to 34,971.

See *Ceylon Plantation Gazeteer* for 1859, p.169.

[3] C.O. 54/224, Campbell to Stanley, no.45 of 14 February 1846 and C.O. 54/227, Campbell to Grey, no.72 of 11 November 1846.

laying all the blame for the labour shortage on the Ceylon Government: the neglect by the Government of the medical care of the immigrants; the absence of hospital facilities; and the difficulties of the march on the northern road.[1] During the legislative sessions of 1846, the non-official numbers of the Legislative Council sought to initiate some discussion of this subject, and they even prepared a draft Ordinance designed to promote State-sponsored and State-subsidized immigration, but the Government refused to accept this principle or the Ordinance. (Constitutionally, the non-officials had no right to introduce legislation in the Council.)

This turn of events had the effect of hardening Campbell's attitude to the planters. In any event, once the blame for this acute shortage of labour had been openly and boldly laid on the administration itself, he had to defend its record. In the last few months of his administration, he devoted a great deal of time to this task. He left this in the hands of his new, and able Colonial Secretary, Sir James Emerson-Tennent.

In the meantime there was one unexpected development; the great publicity given in the local Press to these controversies on Indian immigration, and, particularly to the Ordinance prepared by the non-officials in the Legislative Council, attracted the attention of the Madras Government. Though the immigration of labourers for plantation labour in Ceylon was officially frowned upon, the Madras Government had turned a blind eye on a movement of such obvious benefit to its citizens. As the law stood it was illegal to abet the emigration of labourers from India except to Mauritius, British Guiana, Jamaica and Trinidad. But once it had become a matter of controversy, it was impossible to ignore it any longer. The Governor-General of India in Council expressed readiness to discuss the problem of Indian immigrant labour with the Ceylon Government. The negotiations on behalf of the Ceylon Government were conducted with great skill by Tennent, who throughout these discussions insisted that the treatment accorded to these immigrants was both benevolent and enlightened and that there was little need for stringent legislation like that which controlled the traffic to Mauritius and the West Indies. This was less than the truth, but the Indian Government, only too willing to please, did not raise awkward questions. They agreed to include Ceylon in the schedule of territories to which Indian immigration

[1] C.O. 54/227, Campbell to Grey, no.72 of 11 November 1846.

was officially approved, on condition that she would not become an *entrepôt* for immigration to other colonies in evasion of the law. This latter guarantee was easily given (since Ceylon never was an *entrepôt* for the emigration of Indians) and, with it, a promise that effective measures would be taken to protect the labourers on the estates. Thereupon, the Indian Government removed the legal restrictions on emigration to Ceylon.[1]

Campbell left Ceylon in 1847. Between his departure and the arrival of his successor, Viscount Torrington, there was an interval of a little over a month, during which Tennent was appointed Lieut.-Governor of Ceylon. In this short space of time he sent home two despatches on the coffee industry of Ceylon, one of which dealt at length with the problem of immigrant labour. This latter despatch[2] was the product of months of quiet preparation. The lucidity of its argument and the brilliance of its language combine to make it one of the best half-dozen despatches ever written by a Ceylon civil servant. Indeed it is more a Blue Book than a despatch reminding one of the great Blue Books of Victorian England. And like the latter, it strikes the imagination as much by the touch of moral indignation that pervades it as by its impressive array of facts and figures. Tennent's arguments were so forcefully put and his logic so irresistible that one is apt to be overwhelmed by it all and to forget that this despatch was written at a time of acute controversy (at a time when the planters had boldly accused the Government of being directly responsible for the labour crisis of 1846) and was, basically, a defence of the Government's record. That was its fundamental defect. The carefully-selected evidence and the skilfully-marshalled arguments led to one conclusion: the labour crisis of 1846 was the result of the planters' negligence and ill-treatment of the immigrants. For Tennent, and the administration he defended so well, this was a most comfortable conclusion. But Tennent's despatch had concealed as many facts as it had revealed.

Tennent attributed the great shortage of labour in 1846 to three causes: the better than average harvest in South India; the bad weather, the heavy rain and high winds which prevented the boats from coming over; but most of all, and this he emphasized over

---

[1] Cumpston, I. M., *Indians Overseas in British Territories*, fn., p.116.
  C.O. 54/235, Tennent to Grey, no.6 of 21 April 1847.
[2] C.O. 54/235, Tennent to Grey, no.6 of 21 April 1847.

and over again, the callous neglect and the cruelties of the planters. But one factor which Tennent did not consider, or perhaps deliberately concealed since it would weaken his case, was the terrible epidemic of cholera that ravaged Ceylon in the years 1845 and 1846. Cholera, like smallpox, was a regular scourge in Ceylon, but the outbreak of 1845 was unprecedented in its severity, carrying off whole villages in the planting districts and a great many labourers on the estates.[1] The epidemic claimed 3,500 victims in the Kandyan areas in three months.[2] A pioneer coffee planter wrote that:

> . . . fully one-fifth of the population of Kandy was carried off during the few short weeks that the pestilence lasted. . . . It spread to the Dumbara and Peradeniya estates and in one or two cases almost cleared off the whole of the coolies, whilst the remainder fled in the vain hope of eluding its grasp.[3]

The significance of an epidemic of cholera for the immigrant labourers in Ceylon was that they generally panicked during such an outbreak, fled to their homes and did not return until they were certain the epidemic was over. The newspapers of the day were full of reports of this epidemic. Bishop Chapman's Visitation Journal for 1846 contains a description of a visit to Kandy to hold a thanksgiving service after the epidemic was over, and to comfort as many of the soldiers of the 95th Regiment as had survived.[4] One-third of this regiment died of cholera in a fortnight.[5] It is also significant that the Government grant to the Kandy Friend-in-Need Society Hospital, normally £40 to £50 per annum, reached the unprecedented figure of £317 in 1846.[6]

Tennent ignored this epidemic, for his aim was to focus all

---

[1] Boyd, W., 'Ceylon and its Pioneers', *C.L.R.* 1st Series, II, 281.
   See also, *A Historical Sketch of the Baptist Mission in Ceylon* (1850), p.34.
   This pamphlet refers to a 'dreadful attack of cholera' in Kandy in 1845, an attack 'which prevailed to an extent never known before'. Two despatches, Campbell to Stanley, no.18 of 13 January 1846 and no.49 of 16 February 1846 in C.O. 54/223, refer to the effects of this epidemic in the north of the island. In the Jaffna district there had been 3,219 deaths in November and December 1845 and 3,655 deaths from the beginning of 1846 to 16 February 1846.

[2] Boyd, *op. cit.*   [3] *Ibid.*

[4] S.P.G. MSS., Ceylon 1840–55. The Bishop's Visitation Journal for 1846. Anon, *Memorials of Bishop Chapman*, pp.42 ff.

[5] Boyd, *op. cit.*

[6] 9th and 10th A/R Kandy F.I.N.S.

attention on the harsh treatment of the labourers. And it was necessary to do so, for the Colonial Office had no idea that conditions on the coffee plantations in Ceylon were so deplorably bad, or that the death rate among the Indian immigrants to Ceylon was so high. In their despatches, Campbell and Anstruther had concentrated attention on just one aspect of Indian immigration; they insisted that the wages paid to these immigrants were higher than they ought to have been.[1] Besides, it was Tennent's aim to effect a radical change in the State's attitude to the problem of immigrant labour; there was to be no State-sponsored or State-subsidized immigration, but the State was to intervene to protect the immigrants from the planters. By concentrating on the short-comings of the planters, and by concealing the equally serious shortcomings of the Government, Tennent hoped to get the Colonial Office to approve this change of policy.

In describing conditions on the estates Tennent, did not have to resort to hyperbole, for the plain truth was sufficiently distressing. He commented that the labourers lived in grossly over-crowded and insanitary huts on the estates. Wages were not punctually paid, and were frequently months in arrears, or even withheld alto-gether. When the labourers complained against this, they '... were silenced by blows and personal restraint'. Little or no notice was taken of the sick; they were sometimes driven off to die on the roadside. Those who died were buried without inquest or inquiry. Those who died on the roadside were buried by the police. Tennent's comments on the neglect of the sick labourers would indicate that there had been no improvement in this regard since the early 1840s, when the Ceylon Agricultural Society and the Kandy Friend-in-Need Society had drawn the attention of the planters – and the Government – to this problem. The appeals and exhortations of these societies had been of little avail.

---

[1] See, C.O. 54/189, Campbell to Russell, no.53 of 9 August 1841. *The Report of the Sub-Committee of the Legislative Council on the Grain Duty* (1841), par-ticularly pp.5 ff., and the evidence of E. J. Darley, R. Christian and H. Ritchie, all merchants and planters, and G. Turnour then Acting Colonial Secretary (and himself a coffee planter). James Stephen was not impressed by all this talk of high wages. In his minute of 16 Oct 1841 (on Campbell's despatch to Russell, no.53 of 9 August 1841 in C.O. 54/189) he commented, 'So the rich invariably argue in all parts of the world. Whatever gives them a great com-mand of the labour of the Poor on lower terms, they who hire such labour, will always regard as a public benefit. . . .'

R

Tennent complained that the planters did not convey sick labourers 'to the hospitals of the Government'. However, the truth was that there was no Government hospital in Kandy.[1] Apart from the garrison hospital in Kandy, which did not admit civilians, the only other hospital was that run by the Friend-in-Need Society, towards the maintenance of which the Government contributed a paltry sum of money, normally between £40 and £50 annually. There was, apart from 'hospitals' at Gampola and Matale, little else in the way of medical facilities provided by the Government in the whole of the Central Province. By the skilful and unscrupulous use of statistics, Tennent sought to impress upon the Colonial Office that the Government, unlike the planters, had not neglected these workers. According to Tennent the total Government contribution 'to institutions exclusively used by the immigrants' was as follows:

$$
\begin{array}{lrrr}
1843 & \pounds & 186 & 10 \ 11 \\
1844 & \pounds & 207 & 5 \ \ 0\frac{1}{4} \\
1845 & \pounds & 811 & 1 \ \ 8\frac{1}{2} \\
1846 & \pounds 1{,}590 & 0 & \ \ 3\frac{3}{4} \\
\end{array}
$$

The sum spent on medical and charitable institutions described as those to which the immigrants were admitted equally with the natives of Ceylon was:

$$
\begin{array}{lrrr}
1843 & \pounds 1{,}242 & 5 & 2\frac{3}{4} \\
1844 & \pounds 1{,}185 & 11 & 9\frac{1}{2} \\
1845 & \pounds 2{,}597 & 0 & 1 \\
1846 & \pounds 4{,}010 & 17 & 6\frac{1}{4} \\
\end{array}
$$

These figures were misleading, and it would not be too much to say, deliberately so, because Tennent did not indicate how he had arrived at them. Row upon row of statistics were set out in impressive array, all designed to conceal the government's neglect of the immigrant labourers. The Colonial Office was hardly likely to know that the Ceylon officials themselves had very little confidence in the statistics provided by government departments; the collection of statistics in the colony was at best haphazard and unscientific, at worst a matter of deliberate invention. There is nothing to suggest that the statistics used by Tennent were in any

[1] *Rep.Fxd.Est.*, p.210. Even the term 'hospital' used in this context is dangerously misleading. The 'hospitals' in the planting districts were generally unsanitary shacks which the sick entered at their peril.

way more reliable or accurate than those usually provided by Ceylon officials. These statistics are far less reliable than those provided in the minutes of evidence given before the committee of the Executive Council examining the fixed establishments of Ceylon in 1848–9. The total Government expenditure on medical institutions in Ceylon, 1848–9, was as follows:[1]

Western Province: Colombo district £8,176 16s. od.; Kegalle £90; Ratnapura £90.

North-Western Province: Puttalam district £45; Kurunegala £45.

Southern Province: Galle district £144; Matara £54; Hambantota £72.

Northern Province: Jaffna district £255; Mannar £40; Anuradhapura £36; Mullaitivu £18.

Eastern Province: Trincomalee district £139 10s.; Batticaloa £45.

Central Province: Kandy district £177; Badulla £24; Eliya – Nil.

These figures reveal that the bulk of this expenditure was on the Colombo district, where there were very few coffee plantations. Very few Indian labourers used the port of Colombo. The coffee estates were concentrated in the districts of Kandy and Kurunegala, while the Badulla, Kegalla and Nuwara Eliya districts were in the process of development. The four districts of the Northern Province, and the two districts of the North-Western Province are important in our calculations, since almost all the Indian immigrants landed on the north-west coast and made their way to the coffee estates through these districts. An analysis of the expenditure on these districts would show how very little was spent there and, when it is considered that these sums of money included expenditure on both immigrant labour and the natives of Ceylon, it would seem that very little indeed could have been spent on the immigrants.

From a careful reading of Tennent's despatch it would be clear that the death-rate among the Indian immigrants to Ceylon was very high. *The Colombo Observer* (in 1849) showed that, in the period from 1841 to 1849, about 70,000, or 25 per cent of the immigrants

[1] *Rep.Fxd.Est.*, pp.113–15

had died in Ceylon of various causes![1] But Tennent was curiously reluctant to dwell at length on this theme, and when he did so, he adroitly made it appear mainly as the result of the planters' neglect. The high death rate was the result of several causes. The first of these was undoubtedly the neglect of the planters. Next, there was the utter inadequacy of the medical facilities provided by the Government in the planting districts and on the route from the north-west coast to the estates. The long walk from the coast to the estates was the third, and perhaps the major, contributory factor to this high death rate. Both the Government and the planters drew attention to the heavy mortality on this march to the estates, but each laid the blame exclusively on the other. The planters pointed out that there were few rest-houses or hospitals on the road through malaria-infested jungles and sparsely populated districts. For long stretches there was no drinking water. It was suggested that those who survived this march were unfit for hard work and, their constitutions sapped by this ordeal, often succumbed to disease after a brief stay on the estates.

This was at least partly true, but this does not exonerate the planters from the charge of gross neglect of their workers. Tennent laid all the blame on the planters. He introduced the novel argument that the immigrants arrived in the planting districts in fair or good health, but returned home so worn out and emaciated by disease that large numbers died on the journey home; in fact that the death rate on the march was higher on their way home than on their entry into Ceylon. It was a difficult argument to maintain, and all the evidence he provided in support lay in three reports by Ceylon officials.[2] Superficially at least, these reports – since they were all prepared during this investigation – would provide conclusive proof, but Ceylon officials were not above providing just the evidence necessary to support an official argument, particularly an argument as weak as Tennent's. It is significant that the opinions of a Government official not involved in this investigation – Dr Willisford, later the Chief Government Medical Officer[3] – and the Bishop of Colombo, Bishop Chapman, would indicate that

---

[1] *The Colombo Observer*, 1, 10 and 13 October 1849.
    See also, *The Ceylon Plantation Gazeteer* for 1859, pp.167–9.
[2] The three officials were: the Assistant Government Kurunegala; the Superintendent of Police, Kandy; and the Police Magistrate, Kandy.
[3] *Rep.Fxd.Est.*, pp.212 ff.

Tennent and the other officials had overstated their case;[1] and that the planters were to a great extent correct in their assertion that the poverty of the immigrants *on their arrival* in Ceylon, and the difficulties of the northern road were, together, greatly responsible for the high death-rate on the march.

Apart from this, there was the fact that cholera and smallpox were regular scourges in Ceylon and that epidemics of cholera took heavy tolls of life. Finally, that these immigrant labourers were so vulnerable to disease was as much their own fault as it was that of the planters or the Government. Even when hospital facilities were available, they were reluctant to enter hospital, and those who did so seldom went there voluntarily, and when admitted were *in extremis* and no treatment was possible. The immigrant's aim was to collect as much money as he possibly could while in Ceylon, and so he worked when he was not really fit. The hours of work were long and the wages – the opinions of planters and administrators notwithstanding – were low. So he very often stinted on his food to save part of his earnings, living on herbs, roots and even carrion flesh, all of which made him very susceptible to disease.

Conditions might have been better if Campbell's Labour Ordinance had not been of such little use to the labourer. The general opinion of officials was that the law was availed of mainly by the planters, and that the labourers were either ignorant of its existence or incapable of making much use of it. J S Colepepper, the Superintendent of Police at Kandy, remarked that the law operated 'fully to the satisfaction of the employer, but the labourer seldom avails himself of it even when it was pointed out to him, and is advised to do so'.[2] The Police Magistrates of Kandy and Gampola agreed with this opinion, the former commenting that 'The Coolies are nearly all ignorant that any law exists for regulating agreements,' and the latter explained that the 'law is in itself a good one, but the [Indian immigrant] is ignorant of the protection it provides . . . thus he becomes an easy prey to his knowing and unrelenting master'.[3]

Many of the abuses on the estates stemmed from the very nature of planting organizations in Ceylon, and the type of men involved.

[1] S.P.G. MSS., Ceylon 1840–55, Bishop Chapman, 21 November 1847.
[2] C.O. 54/235, Tennent to Grey, no.6 of 21 April 1847.
[3] *Ibid.*

On the one hand there were the large agency houses like Ackland, Boyd and Company, with their headquarters in Colombo, or Hudson, Chandler and Company at Kandy, employing scores of Europeans as overseers and superintendents. These organizations were too remote to have anything like a first-hand knowledge of conditions on the estates. They depended to a great extent on the superintendents and these men were, as Tennent pointed out, very often non-commissioned officers of regiments stationed in Ceylon, men without any experience at all of coffee planting.[1] Contemporary observers were even more uncomplimentary in their remarks. A pioneer coffee planter referred to these superintendents in these terms: 'In the course of time all the riff-raff of the round world came here. . . . And we came to have a floating scum of coffee planters.'[2] William Boyd, another pioneer coffee planter, commented that, '. . . these men used their coolies with disgraceful injustice and cruelty'.[3]

Apart from the agency houses, there were the small individual property owners, many of whom were merely market-gardeners and men of small means, operating on borrowed money or on their own meagre savings, hoping in the course of a few years to increase their capital and to return home when they had done so. At this time the experts seldom gave the coffee plantations more than a dozen years of life.[4] Quick profits were all that mattered, and the easiest way to quick profits was to stint on wages, housing and medical facilities. Thus, whether it was at the hands of the superintendents or the small capitalists, immigrants received harsh and shabby treatment.

One Government official described conditions on the coffee estates as being as bad as plantation slavery in the West Indies; another official compared it to 'Egyptian bondage'. Tennent, in more sober language, asserted that

the conditions of the coolies on the estates and their treatment by their employers was not in every instance or in every particular such as humanity or even policy would have required in order to encourage and secure a continuation of their resort to Ceylon.[5]

[1] C.O. 54/235, Tennent to Grey, no.6 of 21 April 1847.
[2] Anon., *Days of Old* (c. 1870). Two pioneer coffee planters describe conditions on the coffee estates in the 1840s.
[3] Boyd, W., 'Ceylon and its Pioneers', *C.L.R.*., 1st Series, II, 296.
[4] Sabodiniere, W., *The Coffee Planter of Ceylon*, p.46.
[5] C.O. 54/235, Tennent to Grey, no.6 of 21 April 1847.

Tennent's despatch was more than a mere condemnation of the planters. It is a deeply significant document, which provided the Colonial Office, for the first time, with a detailed study of the problems of Indian immigration to Ceylon. Biased, lopsided and tendentious though it was, few could fail to be impressed by the deep humanity that pervaded it, and its urgent concern for the welfare of the immigrants. More important, this despatch contained the first clear enunciation of Government policy on this subject. Where there had previously been apathy, neglect and ignorance, here was a firm declaration of principles. In Tennent's own words the obligation of the Government to the Indian immigrants was

> to expedite their journeys by safe and healthy roads, to protect them from violence, or ill-treatment by the way, to provide them with shelter when necessary and with medical [facilities] . . . when overtaken by illness; to afford them the protection of the law when defrauded or abused, to insist on their humane and becoming treatment when employed on the estates, and to ensure them security in their country with the earnings of their labour.[1]

This was a very positive conception of the duties of the Government.

To give effect to this policy of protection and welfare, Tennent recommended the appointment of a new category of officials to be called Protectors of Coolies, who were to be given wide powers to examine living conditions on the estates, and to inspect books and check-rolls of estate agents and superintendents. In other respects their powers were very restricted – in the event of any infringment of regulations, they could merely inform the labourers of the nature of their redress and the means of obtaining it from the nearest magistrate. Also, there were to be more magistrates in the planting districts. He did not suggest any radical changes in Campbell's Labour Ordinance, but merely recommended that Ordinance 14 of 1845, which sanctioned contracts for three years in the case of labour employed by Government departments, should be amended to allow the planters too to benefit from these longer contracts.

These measures, particularly the appointment of Protectors of Coolies and more magistrates, would have entailed additional expenditure, but Tennent felt that this could be met by a stamp

---

[1] C.O. 54/235, Tennent to Grey, no.6 of 21 April 1847.

duty on labour contracts, and by an annual levy on the planters for each immigrant employed on the estates.

But much the most significant of Tennent's recommendations was that Indian labourers should be settled in Ceylon. This policy of settlement had two aspects; on a lower level there were to be allotments of land for market gardening and the rearing of live-stock and poultry. These allotments were to be in the planting districts, and they were designed to diminish '. . . the difficulties which are now experienced in providing suitable supplies [of food] in districts remote from villages and bazaars'. At a different and more important level, there were to be settlements of Indians in the Northern Province (now the North Central Province). Tennent saw the urgent need for a stable supply of labour in Ceylon, independent of the vagaries of the rice and palmyra crop in South India, and he connected this with the equally important problem of making Ceylon self-sufficient in rice.

Immensely impressed by the vast network of canals and irriga-tion tanks in the Northern Province, dilapidated but capable of repair, it was his hope to convert this flat malarial region into what it had once been, the granary of Ceylon, by settling Indians there. Apparently he had little faith in the local peasantry. The demand for labour on coffee estates was seasonal and was heaviest at crop time, which generally coincided with the slack season in the paddy fields of the Northern Province. These settlers could both develop the Northern Province and supply the plantations with their labour in the picking season.

Welfare and settlement were the two bases of Tennent's policy, with settlement the more important of the two. The Colonial Office had a much narrower view in this matter, and when the planters' demands for State-sponsored immigration were received, the Colonial Office took its stand on *laissez-faire* principles, reply-ing that it was not the business of the State to take any active part in inviting or promoting the transit of immigrant labourers be-tween India and Ceylon. The official view was that if a section of the population, particularly a powerful section such as the planters, were confronted with a problem, it was up to them to find a solu-tion. This was not the Colonial Office policy on immigration to the West Indies and to Mauritius, but in those colonies there was the vital difference that it was the abolition of slavery that had necessitated the introduction of free immigrant labour. It was for this reason that the Colonial Office had accepted the principle of State-sponsored immigration there. Not only was immigration sponsored and subsidized by those colonies, but the Colonial Office, largely at the insistence of the Evangelicals, had introduced legislation to control this immigration with a view to checking and preventing abuses and ensuring that the system of indentured labour did not degenerate into another form of slavery. Thus State interference in the immigration of Indians to the West Indies and Mauritius was the result of unique and important factors operating there. In Ceylon, where these factors were absent, the Colonial Office was unwilling to let the administration play any active role in this immigration. When Tennent's despatch was sent to the Colonial Land and Emigration Commissioners, it came back with the comment that State intervention would be of little use and that the greatest security for any improvement lay in the planters becoming 'alive to their interests in protecting the labourers'.[1] Even Earl Grey concurred on this view, commenting that the best solution seemed to be 'the arousing [of] the coffee planters to the necessity of greater vigilance in the prevention of abuses by which they must in the end be themselves the greatest sufferers'.[2] At the same time, he realized that the situation in Ceylon called for a more positive approach and he indicated that he was willing to support Tennent's policy of State intervention. But, as regards Ceylon, Grey and the Colonial Office never really conquered their *laissez-faire* inhibitions.

Just at this time the Colonial Office was making a comprehensive review of the financial structure and revenue system of Ceylon. Towards the end of 1846 the Ceylon Government, on Grey's instructions, examined its financial and commercial policies with a view to making them conform to Grey's *laissez-faire* and free-trade ideals.[3] By far the most substantial contribution towards this end was another and equally brilliant report by Tennent – his *Report on the Finance and Commerce of Ceylon* – in which he advocated sweeping changes of Government policy: steep reductions if not total abolition of export and import duties; the equalization of duties on British and foreign imports; and a radical transformation of the tax structure, with the emphasis shifting decisively from

[1] C.O. 54/241, the Colonial Land and Emigration Commissioners to James Stephen, letter of 27 July 1847.
[2] C.O. 54/241, Grey's minute of 30 July 1847.   [3] *Rep.Fin.Com.*

export and import duties to direct taxes. The foundation of the new system was to be a general land tax. Grey had appointed a committee of the Colonial Office to report on Tennent's recommendations.[1] Grey had apparently sent Campbell's last few depatches on Indian immigration to this committee.

The report of Grey's committee referred, among other matters, to the question of Indian immigration to Ceylon. Its recommendations in this regard are significant, both because Grey adopted them as the basis of his own policy, and because of their acceptance of a more positive role by the State. There was a remarkable similarity between their recommendations and those of Tennent, particularly on the welfare aspect of State intervention. The committee suggested: that a steam vessel should ply between India and Ceylon for the use of the immigrants; that rest-houses, wells and bazaars should be established on the line of march; and that officers should be appointed to assist and advise the immigrants and to direct them to the areas where labour would be in the greatest demand. These were recommendations which the Ceylon Agricultural Society had been making for several years. They did not believe that the financing of these projects would be any great problem.

Grey's committee and Grey himself[2] were attracted by the idea of settlement, but its views on the subject were rather confused. While Tennent suggested Indian settlement primarily as a means of solving the problem of labour for the plantations, Grey and his committee were more attracted by the prospect of using Indian settlers to develop the agricultural potential of the Northern Province;[3] as for the immigrant plantation labourers, Grey's committee recom-

---

[1] The members of this committee were B. Hawes, Under-Secretary of State at the Colonial Office; H. Tufnell; J. G. Shaw-Lefevre and R. Bird. Their report was dated 13 April 1847, and was sent to Ceylon in Grey's despatch to Torrington, no.40 of 18 June 1847.

[2] See C.O. 54/241, Grey's minute of 30 July 1847.

[3] C.O. 55/89, Grey to Torrington, no.67 of 7 August 1847, Grey's Committee recommended that these settlers should be granted small plots of land on an almost nominal rent for the first year or two, but increasing thereafter and attaining its maximum about the sixth or seventh year. They suggested that whole village communities should be induced to settle down in Ceylon, with their headmen and priests, their own modes and customs and their own forms of village 'self-government'.

At this time Grey had recommended some such scheme for Mauritius. See Cumpston, *op. cit.* pp.112, 113. Mellor, G., *op. cit.* pp.217 ff.

mended that lands allotted them 'should not be sufficiently large to induce them to devote the greater part of their time to cultivation on their own account'. It believed that experience in other colonies showed that ease in obtaining land was the main cause of difficulty in commanding the services of hired labour. Grey adopted these recommendations in their entirety and made them the basis of his reply to Tennent's suggestion that settlement of Indians should be an integral part of a new policy on the immigration of Indian plantation labour in Ceylon.

It was left to Viscount Torrington, the new Governor of Ceylon, to work out the new policy on Indian immigration. Grey's committee had recommended that the new Governor be furnished with ' . . . copies of the papers which had been presented to Parliament on the subject of coolie labourers in Mauritius and the West Indies'.[1] Before he left England, Torrington was briefed on the subject by Grey; it would appear that Grey had impressed upon him that he should pay particular attention to the settlement of Indians.[2] And Torrington was urged to investigate the possibility of a settlement of Chinese in Ceylon to develop the Northern Province and to provide some of the skilled labour on the plantations.[3] This emphasis on settlement[4] was a natural development in the age of Edward Gibbon Wakefield; an age which saw the settlement of the British territories of Australia and New Zealand.

From the moment of his arrival in Ceylon, Torrington was concerned with the problem of Indian immigration. In his first letter to Grey, he wrote that 'the treatment of the unfortunate Coolies on the coffee estates (in some at least) has been shameful'.[5] He

---

[1] *Rep.Fin.Com.*, p.29.

[2] Grey MSS., Torrington to Grey, 14 March 1847. It is very likely that at this stage Grey was thinking more of agricultural development than of labour for the plantations.

[3] C.O. 54/240, Torrington to Grey, no.155 of 12 November 1847, and Grey to Torrington, no.158 of 11 January 1848. After careful consideration of the costs of the project Torrington reported that Chinese settlement would be far more expensive than that of Indians.

[4] Even Campbell had been attracted by the possibilities of settlement, but he was thinking more of the settlement of English artisans for skilled labour on the plantations and in government departments concerned with public works. See C.O. 54/224, Campbell to Stanley, no.45 of 14 February 1846; and C.O. 54/227. Campbell to Grey, no.72 of 11 November 1846.

[5] Grey MSS., Torrington to Grey, 6 June 1847.

informed Grey that Major Thomas Skinner, the Commissioner of Roads, was preparing a report on the best means of bringing these immigrant labourers to Ceylon.

Torrington began the preparation of a 'Coolie Ordinance'. He had decided that it would be imprudent to consult the Executive Council on this matter because, 'Everybody here has estates, and are liable consequently to interested motives'.[1] He drafted the Ordinance himself, with the assistance of his private secretary. The new Ordinance, in effect, accepted the welfare aspects of Tennent's proposals (and of Grey's committee); the finances were to be provided by a tax on the planters.[2]

But this Ordinance was never put into effect, for Torrington had arrived in Ceylon at a most inopportune moment. A depression of unparalleled severity reduced the prosperous coffee industry to bankruptcy, and it became impossible to tax the planters to finance welfare measures for immigrant labour. Nor, since its own revenues were as seriously affected by the depression, could the Government afford to finance these measures out of its own resources. The Ordinance was thus shelved.

Torrington found that by 1847 the labour shortage of 1846 was only a bitter memory. In 1847 there was not only a great surplus of labour,[3] but the immigrant labourers had arrived earlier in the year than usual and found themselves stranded in Ceylon without employment and faced with starvation. The plantations were without the resources to employ them before crop time and the pitiful condition of these men, many of them sick and half-starved, made it necessary for the Government to step in. It was impossible to let them go back to India for that would have led to another scarcity of labour at crop time. Torrington employed them in draining the pestilential Bogambara lake in Kandy until it was time for the

---

[1] Grey MSS., Torrington to Grey, 16 September 1847, and 14 October 1847.

It was typical of Torrington's general incompetence as an administrator that he should have been ignorant of the fact that Tennent had no financial interests at all in Ceylon, while Skinner was a coffee planter.

[2] *Ibid.*

[3] *The Colombo Observer*, 28 June 1847, reports a meeting of the Ceylon Agricultural Society on 18 June 1847, to consider the problems arising out of this excess of labour.

The Ceylon Examiner, 7 July 1847, reported that there was a 'great superabundance of labour' in the planting districts. Also see the issues of this newspaper for 17, 21 and 24 July 1847.

picking of the crop.[1] But he earned a stiff rebuke from Grey for providing the immigrants with this temporary employment. Apparently, it should have been left to the planters themselves to support these immigrants while they waited for the picking season.[2]

Much more disastrous in their consequences were the disturbances that occurred in July 1848 in the Central Province, the heart of the coffee area. Breaking out just before the picking season, the disturbances threatened the finances of the estates and the resources of the Government alike.[3] Moreover, the Government was acutely conscious of the fact that these disturbances could seriously affect the labour supply to the estates, by frightening those who intended to come to Ceylon, and causing panic among those already on the estates. It was easier to deal with this first possibility than with the second, and the means adopted was that of keeping prospective immigrants informed of the facts of the situation in Ceylon, particularly the fact of the early and easy suppression of the disturbances.[4]

At the same time, largely as a result of the depression, non-payment of wages was more widespread in the years 1847–8 than it had ever been before. In the period of ten months ending in March 1848, there had been 2,584 complaints by immigrant labourers (about non-payment of wages) at the District Court of Kandy alone.[5] Torrington commented that, if there were a shortage of labour in the picking season of 1848, it would not be the result of the disturbances but of the 'disheartening effect upon the coolies of having been kept months in arrear of wages due to them in the course of the past season, and indeed at the present time'.[6] There was little the Government could do directly to compel employers to fulfil their obligations. It could, however, make it easier for immigrant labourers to appeal to the courts. Thus, at the suggestion of S. Hanna, the Police Magistrate of Kandy,

---

[1] C.O. 54/238, Torrington to Grey, no.68 of 5 August 1847; C.O. 54/244, Torrington to Grey, no.3 of 5 January 1848.

The Ceylon Examiner, 21 July 1847, reported that the Government was employing these starving immigrants to fill up the lower lake at Kandy at 3d. a day.

[2] C.O. 55/89, Grey to Torrington, no.134 of 24 November 1847.
[3] Grey MSS., Torrington to Grey, 11 August 1848.
[4] C.O. 54/250, Torrington to Grey, no.145 of 15 August 1848.
[5] C.O. 54/258, Torrington to Grey, no.52 of 13 April 1849.
[6] C.O. 54/250, Torrington to Grey, no.145 of 15 August 1848.

labourers suing for their wages were permitted to file plaint at the various Courts of Requests without the payment of the usual stamp fees. Again, when the owner of an estate was absent from Ceylon, the Courts had no authority to seize his property to pay his labourers' wages. At Hanna's suggestion, Torrington amended the law to enable the courts to do so. It was also enacted, again at Hanna's suggestion, that the labourers' claims for wages should have priority over every other charge on the estates.[1]

During the disturbances there were fears that the Indian labourers on the estates would panic and that potential immigrants would be discouraged by this political instability from coming into the heart of the coffee country. But it was soon proved that these fears were without foundation. Both Hanna and the Superintendent of Police at Kandy, L. B. Dunuvilla, testified that the Indians had not fled the country during the disturbances; far from deserting the estates for fear of the Kandyans, they had, on the few estates that had been attacked by the 'rebels', put up a courageous defence. Nor had there been a shortage of labour, except on those estates which had not paid their labourers regularly. And the labourers who came to the Island were not unduly worried about the disturbances.[2]

The depression and the disturbances postponed the imposition of any welfare legislation; all that the Government could do was to meet each problem as it arose with some practical but temporary solution. But, if welfare legislation had been unfortunately shelved, the disturbances made the policy of settlement for the first time seem a practical solution.

It would appear that Torrington had arrived with specific instructions from Grey that a scheme of settlement should be attempted,[3] but after a few months in the Colony he veered round to Tennent's, rather than Grey's, conception of settlement.[4] Tennent's project was much the more realistic of the two. He always

[1] C.O. 54/258, Torrington to Grey, no.52 of 13 April 1849.
[2] *Ibid.*
[3] *The Third Report on Ceylon* (1850), p.253, Tennent's evidence.
[4] Grey MSS., Torrington to Grey, 13 October 1847. In this letter, Torrington explained that, while he had great faith in the policy of settling Indians in the Northern Province on the lines suggested by Grey, he nevertheless felt that such a settlement must benefit the planters, too. '[It] will encourage the coolies to come here with more confidence, and in the end it will ensure a sufficient supply of labour and *at a reduced rate.*'

looked upon the settlement of Indians in Ceylon as a means of providing the planters with a regular supply of labour, free from the uncertainties of the existing system of immigration. On the other hand, Grey's ideas on settlement were confused and unrealistic. His scheme of settlement was not designed to benefit the plantations, and it is not certain that it would have helped develop the Northern Province either.

The disturbances provided an unexpected opportunity to give Tennent's scheme of settlement a trial. But he gave his scheme a new and diabolical twist when he suggested that the Kandyan peasantry should be expelled from the disturbed districts (which happened to be the richest planting districts) and Indian labourers be settled on their lands.[1] On 14 August 1848 he wrote to Torrington that '. . . the opportunity that now presents itself of locating a race of Malabars in these important positions on the lands to be forfeited by the rebels, is one which I earnestly trust your Lordship will not allow to pass unimproved'.[2]

Torrington had himself been thinking on these lines; in a letter to Grey he remarked that a settlement of Malabars on lands to be confiscated from the rebels 'would have an excellent effect'. 'A population would soon spring up that would act as a check on the Kandyans and gradually be the means of giving us a supply of labour without sending to the coast.'[3]

In his examination before the Parliamentary Committee on Ceylon in 1849–50, Tennent sought to explain that all he had in mind was his old scheme of a settlement of Indians in the Northern province. This was obviously incorrect, because 'the lands forfeited by the rebels' were in Kurunegala, Matale and Kandy far from the Northern province. When he found that the Committee seemed unimpressed by this explanation, he changed his story slightly and suggested that he meant merely the establishment of Indian settlements to the north of Kandy in the disturbed districts of Kurunegala and Matale, but out of contact with the Kandyans. As late as 1850 he was still prepared to insist that attempts were being made to settle Indians in the Northern Province, but this statement was at variance with the facts, for the scheme of Indian settlement in Kandy or in the Northern Province was never

---

[1] *The Third Report on Ceylon* (1850), Tennent's evidence, p.253.
[2] *Ibid.*, p.274.
[3] Grey MSS., Torrington to Grey, 11 August 1848.

attempted. He explained that his scheme of 1848 was not put into effect only because the confiscations of land fell far short of what had been anticipated. These schemes, however, were abandoned not for the reason that Tennent gave but because the disturbances had opened the eyes of the administration to the fact that the Kandyans objected to the presence of the Indians and they would have actively opposed these schemes of settlement. This fact is implicit in Tennent's evidence before the Parliamentary Committee. And it is significant that after 1850 these plans were quietly but permanently abandoned.

After 1850 it was impossible to think of a policy of settlement as a practicable solution of the problem of immigrant labour, since the policital risks were much too great. It could only be a policy of welfare, and Governor Sir George Anderson, Torrington's successor, seemed ideally suited to implement it because of his acquaintance with similar problems in the colony of Mauritius, where Indian immigration was sponsored and subsidized, and the immigrants themselves protected, by the State. Besides, there was the legislation prepared by Tennent and Torrington, the implementation of which had only been postponed by the severity of the depression. But Anderson, by instinct and training a doctrinaire of the *laissez-faire* school, did not see the need for such legislation in Ceylon, and, after Grey's departure from the Colonial Office in 1852, there was no one there to remind him of his obligations in these matters.

Ceylon's coffee industry had emerged from the depression healthier and stronger than it had been before, with scientific cultivation and trained superintendents the rule rather than the exception, and, despite the loss after 1851 of the last vestiges of protection in the home market, the industry made a steady advance. There was also an increase in the immigration of Indians – from 1850 to 1855 it averaged nearly 50,000 a year – but, despite this increase, the planters lived in fear of labour shortages and on occasions there were actual shortages. Thus 1851 was, on the whole, a year of labour scarcity, when very few estates could get all the labour they required during the picking season.[1] In 1852 there was so great a surplus of labour that, after almost all the planters had had their supply, many thousands of Indians were

---

[1] *The Colombo Observer*, 12 June and 16 October 1851.
The Ceylon Times, 13 June and 16 September 1851.

unable to obtain work.[1] For one thing they had come too early; but in any event there were too many of them. So much so that *The Ceylon Times* suggested that owners of estates should raise the money to hire boats to send this surplus labour back to India free of charge. That newspaper recommended to Anderson the example of Torrington, who in similar circumstances had employed starving immigrant labourers on Government works in 1847. But there was no response from Anderson to this appeal and the Government stood aloof, leaving the planters to deal with the problem as best they could.[2] As a consequence of this superabundance of labour in 1852, and the inability of the immigrants to get work as readily as they formerly could, there was a reluctance to leave their homes in 1853 and this caused a shortage of labour sufficiently serious to warrant the despatch by the planters of much more than the normal number of *kanganis* to South India.[3]

Moreover, there was another epidemic of cholera in Ceylon; the appearance of this disease at Mannar and along the route to the interior, particularly in some of the coffee estates around Matale, caused much anxiety because the Indians generally panicked during these epidemics and fled from the infected areas in an attempt to make their way home. Many immigrants actually turned back when they heard of the epidemic, and some of the Indians working on the plantations fled in panic.[4] A hundred of them were drowned when the overcrowded boat in which they sailed was wrecked in a storm.[5] But the labour situation eased during the picking season and labour, though not abundant, was sufficient to save the crop.[6] 1854 saw an immigration of Indians on the scale of 1852;[7] once again they had arrived earlier than was necessary, but the planters having learnt from their experience of 1852 employed extra labourers, in return for their food, in order to retain them for the picking of the crop which was expected to be both earlier and heavier than usual.[8] Further, in 1854 the

[1] *The Colombo Observer*, 11 August and 16 September 1852.
The Ceylon Times, 27 July 1852.
[2] *The Ceylon Times*, 27 July 1852.
[3] *The Colombo Observer*, 11 July and 11 August 1853.
[4] *The Colombo Observer*, 12 September 1853.
[5] *The Colombo Observer*, 28 March 1853.
[6] *The Colombo Observer*, 12 and 26 September, 13 and 27 October 1853.
[7] *The Ceylon Times*, 13 and 24 January and 14 February 1854.
[8] *The Ceylon Times*, 23 June and 29 August 1854.
S

planters were beginning to have fears for the future; for the Madras Government had announced a large irrigation and public works programme and the Ceylon planters feared that this would deprive them of their workers.[1] Still, the enlightened (if largely from self-interest) attitude of the planters in providing for this surplus labour from their own resources without waiting for Government intervention stands in sharp contrast to the attitude of their predecessors in the days of the 'coffee mania'.

It must not be assumed that the abuses of the past in the treatment of the labourers had completely vanished. The planters indeed had improved – they were a better class of men, by training and education, than the old planters of the 'coffee mania', but there were newer and equally vicious evils in the treatment of the immigrant labourers involving, not the planters so much as their kanganies – and the 'coast advance' system. In this phase of planting activity there was a great change in the nature of the kangany; he was much less the 'democratically' elected leader of a gang of labourers, and much more an employers' agent. There was also another type of kangany, contemptuously referred to as 'crimps', who intercepted labourers on the road for a livelihood and took them to plantations which paid the 'crimps'. Some of these were accustomed to waylay labourers from the line of march, and then to take them from one estate to another, drawing an income from every new employer but giving none a regular supply of labour. 'Crimping' was very common at times of labour scarcity.[2]

Under the 'coast advance' system the kangany undertook to supply planters with labourers on the payment of an agreed sum of money. He then took an advance from his employers (to buy rice and other necessities for the labourers he was to bring along) went over to India,[3] made arrangements with a gang of labourers and brought them over to the estates. The expenses incurred in recruiting labour were entered in the estate 'Debt Account' as a charge against the kangany and his recruits; this amount, divided

[1] *The Ceylon Times*, 26 September 1854. This newspaper, in its issue of 23 June 1854 explained that this large and early influx of labourers was the result of the dry weather and bad harvest in South India. The labour supply was larger in 1854 than in previous years because, with the failure of the rice crop, the peasants needed to find money to pay their land-tax.

[2] *The Colombo Observer*, 23 September 1853.

[3] At times the Kangany instead of going to centres of recruitment would get the necessary labour recruited through his relatives in India.

among them, became the debt with which every labourer started work on the estates, and at the end of his stay he was paid his wages in a lump sum – minus his share of the 'Debt Account'. On some estates it was the practice to pay the kangany a bonus for the labourers he recruited, but only after these labourers had worked on the estates for six months to one year.

This system of recruitment became deplorably corrupt. The kanganies spent only a fraction of the 'coast advance' on the immigrant labourers, keeping the bulk of it for themselves. It was estimated that only about a third of the money charged to the labourer was actually received by him. It could be said, without much exaggeration, that the cruelties inflicted upon the labourers by the kanganies under this system were as vicious as any the immigrants had to face on the estates before 1850. Hundreds of men died on the way to the estates and those who survived arrived on the estates in a semi-starved and fatigued condition. The kanganies made little allowance for those who, through exhaustion or ill-health, could not keep pace with the rest. The longer the gang was on the road, the more the cost of their food, and the kanganies pressed on with all possible speed to extract as large a profit as they could out of these transactions. Since only a fraction of the 'coast advance' was spent by the kangany, he could afford to bring more than the required number of labourers, and thus make up for the 'wastage' on the journey. If a much larger number than the estates required survived the journey, he could always find employment for the surplus on the neighbouring estates; but he was safe even if he failed to find such employment, because there was no law whereby arrangements made with the labourer in India could be enforced in Ceylon. Formerly the kangany was chosen by the labourers themselves and had an incentive to get as many of them as possible to the estates alive and well, since after their employment he received from each individual a small monthly payment.

It is a measure of Anderson's lack of interest in the problem of Indian immigration that in the whole period of his administration he wrote less than six despatches on this theme. Two of these dealt with the correspondence with the Madras Government on the question of accommodation on coolie ships. And no mention was made in these despatches of the coast advance system, its abuses and its terrible toll of life. To reconstruct the history of

Indian immigration to Ceylon in Anderson's time we have to rely on Ward's despatches and the newspapers.[1]

The abuses of the 'coast advance system' were of such a nature that only enlightened government intervention could have checked them. The Government could have imposed the legislation prepared by Tennent and Torrington, but at no stage was Anderson interested in introducing this legislation. He could have amended Campbell's Labour Ordinance to make it more effective, by enabling the immigrant labourers to make as much use of it as the planters did. In 1854 *The Colombo Observer* drew attention to the inadequacies of the existing labour legislation and called for its reform:

> The law between master and man is short, plain and excellent; a Coolie by refusal to obey a simple order renders himself liable to a month's imprisonment; and such punishment has been inflicted, but the law . . . should also enforce due care on the part of the manager.[2]

Anderson made no attempt to remedy these defects.

Legislation apart, the most urgent need was for the provision of adequate shelter for the immigrants on the road from the coast to the plantations. It would appear that it was this road that took the greatest toll of life. From the limits of the Northern Province to Matale, a distance of 40 miles, there was no shelter at all.[3] In 1848 a large shed had been erected at Dambulla but this had been allowed to go to ruin.[4] A few Matale planters bore the cost of a shed at Matale, substantially built and within easy reach of water.[5] The Chamber of Commerce subscribed the money for a shed and a well at Colombo[6] (but only a very small percentage of the immigrants took boat to Colombo). There was no shelter at Kandy and the immigrant labourers were compelled to sleep on the bund of the Kandy lake.[7] The great need was for more rest-

---

[1] Ward's account of numerous deaths on the road from the coast has been questioned as untrue or exaggerated. It is suggested that he was merely seeking to strengthen the case for State intervention, at a time when the whole question of Indian immigration was being thoroughly examined. But the newspapers of that day provide ample confirmation on the question of a heavy death rate on the march.

[2] *The Colombo Observer*, 24 July 1854.
[3] *The Colombo Observer*, 12 September 1853.   [4] *Ibid.*
[5] *The Colombo Observer*, 21 April 1854.
[6] *The Colombo Observer*, 28 August 1853.
[7] *The Colombo Observer*, 24 July 1854.

houses, more hospitals, more officials on the road; but in the five years of Anderson's administration not one new official was appointed by the Government and not one new rest-house or hospital was built. Agitation for more rest-houses and hospitals on this road increased considerably in and after 1854, when the news reached Ceylon of the projected irrigation and public works programme of the Madras Government; and the agitation returned to the old theme of Government-sponsored immigration. At a meeting of the planters held at Kandy on 7 October 1854, a resolution was passed calling on the Government to aid the immigration of Indian labourers to Ceylon. While the mover of the resolution concentrated on this issue, the seconder (a non-official member of the Legislative Council and a prominent planter, J. Swan) called attention to the lack of rest-houses and wells on the roads to the planting districts, remarking that gangs of immigrants turned back frightened by the heavy mortality on these roads.[1] These demands were taken up with greater enthusiasm by the newly founded Ceylon Planters' Association (the Ceylon Agricultural Society did not survive the depression) which suggested that Ceylon should adopt the Mauritian policy of importing plantation labour at the cost of the Government.[2] These appeals had little effect on Anderson, who was not to be converted to a policy of State intervention even by reminders that he himself had followed this policy in Mauritius.

He was compelled to pay attention, however, when the Madras Government, who had previously raised this matter in 1847, expressed concern at the overcrowding of the native passenger vessels that brought labourers from India to the ports of the Northern Province or to Colombo.[3] In 1847 regulations had been im-

---

[1] *The Colombo Observer*, 7 and 18 October 1854.

[2] *The Colombo Observer*, 4 December 1854. Report of the meeting of the Ceylon Planters' Association held on 11 November 1854.

The Ceylon Planters' Association laid great emphasis on the need for rest-houses on the road from the coast to the plantations. They also suggested that two steamers – to be bought by the Ceylon Government – should ply between India and Ceylon for the purpose of transporting immigrant labourers who were to be brought in free of charge. (The immigrants, however, were to pay a reasonable fare for the return passage home.)

[3] It must be emphasized that the overcrowding of passenger vessels from India was not something that affected the great mass of the Indian immigrants, who could not afford the means for this brief sea voyage of four days. They

posed by the Madras Government limiting the number of persons who might embark on these vessels, but these regulations were in need of overhaul by 1853. The great defect of these regulations was that while they restricted the number of passengers to Ceylon, there were no restrictions on the number of passengers from Ceylon to India. In 1853 the schooner *Colombo* (29 tons) entered Tutucorin harbour with a load of 204 passengers, while another boat of 80 tons carried 400 passengers.[1] Anderson could no longer ignore the problem, especially because the vessel *Colombo* was caught in a storm shortly after leaving Colombo with a great number of Indian labourers aboard. The ship was wrecked, and of the 150 on board at least 100 were drowned.[2] *The Colombo Observer* remarked that

> this catastrophe will probably lead to the enforcement of the Passengers' Act here. These native vessels are nearly always over-crowded but on the present occasion there was an additional motive ... in the prevailing fear of cholera which has broken out at Colombo.[3]

The Government was compelled to act. The Queen's Advocate, H. C. Selby, was of the opinion that the Passengers' Act of 1853 (15 & 16 Vic., Cap. 44) was applicable to all voyages from Ceylon to any part of India, and he suggested that it should be brought into operation by issuing a proclamation. But the Executive Council feared that this Act was not suited to voyages from Ceylon to the coast of India (it was too short a distance), and that its introduction would injure the planters by raising costs. On the recommendations of the Executive Council, Anderson submitted, for the approval of the Secretary of State, a Local Ordinance regulating the number of passengers proceeding from Ceylon to India. The Ordinance was approved by the Home Government;[4] it constituted the total of Anderson's efforts to solve the problems created by the immigration of Indian plantation labour to Ceylon.

---

usually walked down to the southern tip of the Indian peninsula and made their way by dhony or catamaran to Talaimannar on the north-west coast of Ceylon, a brief distance of about twenty miles.

[1] C.O. 54/299, Anderson to Newcastle, no.106 of 20 August 1853.

[2] *The Colombo Observer*, 28 March 1853.

[3] *Ibid.*

[4] C.O. 54/299, Anderson to Newcastle, no.106 of 20 August 1853.

C.O. 386/110, Land and Emigration Commissioners to Herman Merivale, 11 February 1854.

Indeed Anderson's administration marks the end of a distinct phase in Government policy with regard to the immigration of Indian labourers. It was a phase in which *laissez-faire* attitudes proved to be stronger than humanitarian considerations. In this sense the practice in Ceylon proved to be radically different from that in the West Indies and Mauritius, where humanitarianism and the principles of Imperial trusteeship triumphed over the prevailing *laissez-faire* theories.

CHAPTER IX

Missionary Organizations and the Problems of Indian Immigration to Ceylon

THE problems created by the immigration of Indian plantation labour to Ceylon dwarfed the other social problems of the day, and while these latter were associated with the traditional society, which both administrators and missionaries were dedicated to changing, the question of Indian immigration was the major social problem of the new capitalist society, that the missionaries, along with the administrators, were helping the planters to create. But nothing reveals the narrowness of the missionaries' vision in matters of social policy so much as their indifference to and neglect of this the gravest social problem of the day. Not that they failed altogether to respond to it, but their response was not equal to the gravity of the issues that faced them.

The Baptists stationed at Kandy were the first to plan a mission to the immigrant Indian labourers. The Rev. C. Dawson, and his associate at Kandy, had preached to them on several occasions and, in 1841, had concluded that these immigrants offered a new opportunity for work and conversion. At the same time, he was keenly aware of the peculiar difficulties that faced the Baptists, among the more formidable of which was the fact that while a few of the coffee planters were favourable to the preaching of the Gospel to their labourers, many planters particularly those who had come to Ceylon from Jamaica, showed 'no disposition to encourage the labours of the Baptist Missionaries.'[1]

The Baptists went ahead with the project of a 'Coffee Plantation Estates Mission'. Neither the 'Jamaican' planters nor the Anglicans were in a position to prevent its establishment, for, as Dawson noted, unlike Jamaica, Ceylon was '. . . a land of freedom and obstacles which once existed in Jamaica were not to be met with here'.[2] But the Baptists themselves realized the limits of their

---

[1] *Miss.Her.* (November, 1841), pp.168 ff., Rev. C. C. Dawson, 14 August 1841.   [2] *Ibid.*

freedom. They could establish a mission, but it was up to the planters to allow them to visit their estates, and though there were over 100 plantations in the Kandyan areas only a dozen or so welcomed the mission.[1] Dependent as the Baptists were on the goodwill of the planters, they could hardly (even if they were so inclined) take an interest in the living conditions of the labourers, the discipline on the estates, and such other matters. But it does appear that the Baptists were not inclined to interest themselves in these matters and they merely concerned themselves with the conversion of these labourers to Christianity. As Dawson explained, the Mission '. . . originated in an anxious concern for the salvation of this class of our fellow-creatures'.[2] He commented on 'the laudable anxiety of several proprietors of estates to have Christian instruction imparted to their degraded and idolatrous labourers'.[3]

In May 1842 Dawson and his colleagues, 'encouraged by assurances of sanction and co-operation from several proprietors of estates', commenced a series of exploratory visits. The plan, proposed and agreed to by the planters who consented to allow the Baptists to visit their estates, was to set aside an hour ('in addition to the hours allowed for food and rest') once a week, or a fortnight, when their labourers could receive 'Christian instruction'. A school was established for the education of the children of the immigrant labourers, but Dawson explained that much greater emphasis was laid on instruction by 'Exhortation, reading the word of God, distributing religious tracts, private conversations and prayer'. The expense of this mission – including the school – was £6 10s. a month. There was also regular preaching at the 'Coolie Bungalow' erected by some planters connected with the Ceylon Agricultural Society. Dawson was agreeably surprised at the warmth of the reception he got from the labourers. He wrote that most of them

> had been brought up under the influence of the darkest systems of idolatry, and taught to worship images of wood and stone. . . . Few and indistinct were the ideas they were capable at first of receiving. . . . They nevertheless listened with deep attention, and many of them manifested a degree of seriousness hardly to be expected from persons so sunk in ignorance and sin.

[1] *Miss.Her.* (October 1842), Rev. C. Daniel, 20 June 1842.
[2] *Missions in Ceylon, 1842–55, Report of the Plantation Mission Kandy* (1842), pp. 1 ff.   [3] *Ibid.*

It was not only the labourers who were receptive, for the number of estates that welcomed Dawson had increased to eighteen by the end of 1842.[1]

The diary of the first month's work of the Plantations Mission has this entry for 14 May 1842.[2] Dawson reported a warm welcome at the estate of George Bird at Kundasale, where he addressed a gathering of about one hundred immigrant labourers. Bird, one of the pioneer coffee planters, and also one of the more enlightened (he was among the first to respond to the appeal of the Kandy Friend-in-Need Society for a contribution to the maintenance of their hospital) was anxious to establish a school for the education of the children of the labourers. He gave Dawson the utmost encouragement and drew the latter's attention to the fact that there were over a thousand labourers on the neighbouring estates wholly 'destitute of religious instruction'.

But Dawson did not have to be reminded that Bird's attitude to his mission was in no way representative of the majority of planters. On the same day that he had been so warmly received by Bird at Kundasale, Dawson returned home to find a note from Hudson, the owner of a sugar plantation at Peradeniya, refusing to allow the preaching of the Gospel to his labourers.

Apart from this embarrassing dependence on the whims and prejudices of individual planters, Dawson had two other difficulties. One of these concerned the wandering life of these immigrants; he could never be certain that the same group of men would turn up at the same estate the next year.[3] But he took some consolation in the fact that at least some of these men were likely to carry the message of Christianity to their homes in India. On a different level, there was the lack of a 'good pious interpreter who understands the Singhalese [sic] and Tamil languages'.[4] This problem was soon solved by the employment of a native assistant – T. Garnier, a person of Dutch extraction who had a command of the Tamil and Sinhalese languages.

By the end of 1842, it was reported that this mission bade 'fair to produce extensive good'. In October alone, thirty-six visits

---

[1] *Ibid.*

[2] *Miss.Her.* (October 1842), pp.356 ff.

[3] *Missions in Ceylon, 1842–55, Report of the Plantation Mission Kandy* (1842), pp.6 ff.

[4] *Miss.Her.* (October 1842), p.357.

had been made to the estates. But it was only in 1844 that the first converts were made. At Pallekelle estate in Kundasale, Dawson baptized three men 'who [promised] to be the first fruit of an abundant harvest'.[1] But his increasing responsibilities in the Baptist Mission in Ceylon, left him little time for the Plantations Mission, and Garnier took over that work. Garnier appears to have won the confidence of the planters quite soon, for when over-exertion incapacitated him for a brief spell in September 1844, the planters to show their personal regard for him, raised nearly £20 to buy him a strong horse, so that he would 'be able to visit more estates at the expenditure of less bodily strength'.[2] In the course of 1845 Garnier was established at Kundasale, four miles from Kandy, an excellent location from which to conduct the affairs of this mission.[3]

But two factors seem to have upset the progress of the Plantations Mission. One was the transfer of Garnier to Matale (15 miles from Kandy) where he had to devote his time to the mission station. The other was the effect of the disturbances of 1848 on the Baptists in the Central Province. The mission station at Matale was wrecked by the rebels: Garnier barely escaped with his life, only to be arrested by the Government on the ludicrous charge of conspiring with them.[4] Though he was released later on, the animosity of Torrington towards Dr Christopher Elliott, the editor of *The Columbo Observer* and a leading Baptist layman, led the Government to suspect all Baptists as potential trouble-makers.[5] After 1848 the mission to the plantations recovered, but it was never the force it might have been.[6]

The Anglicans, too, were interested in a mission to the immigrant labourers, but in their case the initiative came from the

[1] *Ibid.* (August 1844), p.330, Rev. C. Daniel, 18 May 1844.

Ibid. (September 1844), p.342, Dawson, 4 June 1844.

[2] *Ibid.* (December 1844), p.392, Dawson, 25 September 1844.

[3] *Ibid.* (August 1846), p.244, Dawson, 15 and 21 January 1846.

[4] *Miss.Her.* (1848), the Rev. J. Allen's letters of 12 August 1848 and 13 September 1848.

[5] Grey MSS., Torrington to Grey, 8 August 1848.

[6] *A/R Baptist Mission* (1853), p.39, mentions that the Rev. J. Allen and Garnier made several visits to coffee estates 'within a circle of about 50 miles in diameter'. At a conference of Baptist missionaries in Ceylon, 1855, attention was drawn to the importance of this work among the Indian immigrants.

Bishop of Madras, who, in 1842, several months after the Baptist mission to the plantations was established, urged the Colonial Chaplain at Kandy, the Rev. William Oakley, to investigate the possibilities of such a mission. The latter's response did not lack a measure of enthusiasm; he agreed that such a mission was a necessity for the number of immigrants was increasing, while 'their present condition called loudly the sympathy and assistance of Christians', a comment which suggests that Oakley was aware of the privations and affliction of the immigrant labourers in the vicinity of Kandy. Besides, from a narrow sectarian point of view there was the danger that if the Anglicans did not undertake this work, missionary activity among the immigrant Indians would become a monopoly of the Baptists.[1]

Oakley called for a separate mission to the immigrant Indians, and, since neither he nor the C.M.S. missionary at Kandy had the time to undertake such work, he recommended that a missionary, preferably a European, should be sent out to organize it with the assistance of four or five Tamil-speaking native assistants who would act as interpreters. The European missionary's chief duty would be to visit the plantations with a view to converting 'the Superintendents, conductors and others'; he was to have a central residence, but on his tours he would stay a few days on each estate lodging with the superintendents and the conductors. It was assumed that a few of the planters would support the mission, and though Oakley did not mention it, he probably realized that, as Anglicans, they would be more welcome to the planters than the Baptists who were always suspect at this time as subversives and trouble-makers.

These inquiries and plans brought no tangible results. But once more – this time after the arrival of Bishop Chapman of Colombo in 1845 – the Anglicans made an attempt to establish a mission to the Indian labourers, and once again the initiative came from Madras rather than Ceylon.[2] Two C.M.S. missionaries visited Ceylon on a special mission of enquiry into the spiritual condition of the Indian immigrants. The inquiry was undertaken with the sanction of the Bishop of Madras, and the Bishop of Colombo, in

[1] S.P.G.Mss.Cey., 1840–55, The Rev. W. Oakley to the Bishop of Madras, 29 August 1842.

[2] C.M.S. MSS., C.CE.O.5, Bishop Chapman's letters of 24 November 1845 and 8 April 1846.

explaining why it was being held, commented that '. . . the charge is a grave and distressing one against us: it is said that many [immigrant labourers] who have been converted to X'tianity in India, from neglect during their temporary residence in Ceylon return relapsed heathens home'.[1]

The result of the inquiry was a recommendation that one or two missionaries should be appointed to lead a mission to the immigrant Indians; they were to be assisted by trained Tamil catechists, who were to visit the estates and to have direct and continuous contact with the labourers. The migrants, it was suggested, should bring letters of recommendation from the missionaries in their villages. The Bishop of Colombo recommended that it would be better still to station a missionary on the north-west coast at the point at which the immigrants usually land, 'especially as their migratory habits when dispersed to seek for employment offers the principal difficulty to our plan'.[2] This scheme, like the previous one, did not see the light of day.

It was only in 1854 that the Anglicans launched their mission to the estates – the Tamil Coolie Mission. The man primarily responsible for its commencement was a layman, J. Murdoch, one-time Headmaster of the Central School, Kandy, and later Secretary of the Christian Literature Society. He was accustomed to ride out from Kandy on Saturdays to visit the isolated coffee plantations in that district to hold services for the planters, and on one of these visits he discovered little groups of Christians – immigrant labourers from Tinnevelly.[3] In 1854, when the Rev. W. Knight, one of the Secretaries of the C.M.S., was on a tour of inspection of the C.M.S. stations in Ceylon, Murdoch suggested that Tamil catechists from Tinnevelly should be invited to Ceylon to minister to these small Christian groups and to evangelize the non-Christians.[4]

Murdoch found Knight an eager supporter of this plan. After a visit to the Matale district, Knight returned convinced that the immigrants were likely to be more easily converted than the Kandyans, because they appeared to be less reserved and more

[1] Bishop Chapman's letter of 8 April 1846, *op. cit.*

[2] *Ibid.*

[3] Whitehouse, *Padre Rowlands of Ceylon*, pp.42 ff; (ed.) Beven, F. L., *A History of the Diocese of Colombo*, pp.178 ff.

[4] *Ibid.*

demonstrative and affectionate. The fact that, while the Kandyans clung to their homes, the Indian Tamils were enterprising enough to emigrate to all parts of the Empire, made the latter all the more attractive to Knight. Besides, he was convinced that these immigrants would ultimately prevail over the Kandyans, and that 'a body of Christianized Tamils in the centre of Ceylon would make their influence felt from one shore to the other. They would work like leaven in the inert mass.'[1]

In practice, however, the Tamil Coolie Mission emphasized the limited nature of its aims from its very inception. Its purpose was 'not so much to reach the non-Christian as to shepherd Christians'.[2] The first report of the Mission was even clearer on this matter. It declared that 'the object of the Mission is purely spiritual. Its efforts are directed at the evangelization of the Tamil Coolies and the supply of the means of grace to such of them as are already Christians.'[3]

This mission was supported almost entirely by funds provided by a group of planters who formed themselves into an association which undertook to provide small churches and schools for worship and instruction.[4] A mission such as this, with its aims so narrowly defined and so dependent on the financial support of a group of planters, could hardly concern itself with the formidable social problems connected with the immigration of Indian labour to Ceylon.

From the plans of the Anglicans, and the practice of the Baptists, it is clear that they had little interest in anything other than the conversion of these immigrants to Christianity. It cannot be said that the missionaries were unaware of conditions on the estates and the high death rate among the immigrants, because the Baptists had a mission station at Kandy and another at Matale both centres of coffee production, while the C.M.S. were among the leading figures in the Kandy Friend-in-Need Society and its hospital. The Bishop's correspondence would indicate that he was aware of the high death-rate among the immigrants.[5] But no

[1] Quoted in *The Colombo Observer*, 14 December 1854.
[2] Whitehouse, *op. cit.*, p. 43.
[3] Quoted in (ed.) Bevan, F. L., *op. cit.* p.178.
[4] *Ibid.*, p.179.
[5] See particularly S.P.G. MSS., Ceylon 1840–55, Bishop Chapman, 12 November 1847.

missionary voices were raised against the planters, much less the Government, on this issue.

In 1847 there was an incident which revealed the nature of the missionary response to this problem. An Indian journal, *The Madras Atheneum*, reported the speech of an S.P.G. missionary, the Rev. T. Brotherton, at a meeting of the South Indian Temperance Union where he made the charges that only a third of the emigrants to Ceylon returned to their villages in South India (the death rate was so high); that half the emigrants became habitual drunkards while in Ceylon; and that those who returned to their villages became a corrupting influence there. When this speech was reported in the Ceylon newspapers, both *The Ceylon Examiner* and *The Colombo Observer*, concentrating on the weaker of Brotherton's allegations, the question of drunkenness, condemned him outright for 'misleading' the public. Brotherton played into their hands by emphasizing this question of drunkenness when there was very little proof to support his allegation.[1]

His charges may not have attracted so much attention had they not followed the great publicity given to the problem of immigrant Indian labour after the labour shortage of 1846. Besides, other Indian newspapers, particularly those controlled or influenced by missionary organizations, sought to draw the attention of the East India Company to the distressing position of immigrant Indian labour in Ceylon. The most influential of these journals, *The Bengal Harkaru*, which had played a leading role in securing Government interference in the emigration of labourers to the West Indies and Mauritius, took up the cause of the immigrants in Ceylon and strove to raise opposition to emigration to Ceylon until conditions there had improved.[2] That newspaper drew attention to the high death rate on the march to the estates, asserting that the 'high road from Midnapore to Juggernauth [*sic*] is not (in a sickly season in July) more clearly defined by the dying, the dead and the bones of those who have been left to perish by the

---

[1] *The Madras Atheneum's* account of Brotherton's speech was published in *The Ceylon Examiner* of 28 August 1847, and *The Colombo Observer* of 26 August 1847. *The Colombo Observer* called upon the planters to defend themselves against these allegations. There may have been some element of truth in Brotherton's allegation because *The Colombo Observer* remarked that the two C.M.S. missionaries from Madras who had visited Ceylon in 1845–6 had come, partly at least, to investigate charges similar to those made by Brotherton.

[2] *The Bengal Harkaru*, 13 August 1847.

way, than is the whole line from Trincomalee to the Hills.'[1] *The Colombo Observer* took issue with *The Bengal Harkaru* on this statement, and declared, with more confidence than was warranted by the facts, that in the previous five years no more than 1,000 coolies had died on the march.[2] Two years later the *Observer* itself changed its opinion radically, and proved beyond reasonable doubt that the death-rate among the Indian emigrants was at least 25 per cent, if not more.[3]

The Colombo Observer, in the meantime, wrote to several missionaries asking whether Brotherton's allegation of drunkenness among the immigrant Indians was correct; at the same time, it urged the planters to defend themselves against this allegation.[4] Letters poured in from planters attacking Brotherton, and one after another the missionaries wrote in, either confessing total ignorance of conditions among the immigrant labourers, or claiming that sickness or death among them was due to very much the same causes that the planters had emphasized: the lack of shelter on the road from the coast to the estates; their exposure to the elements on this journey; and to their folly in stinting on food to save money to take back with them. All the missionaries agreed that the Indians were not habitual drunkards, but were on the contrary a sober race of people.[5]

Brotherton earned the disapproval of the Bishop of Colombo, who wrote to the S.P.G. in London and to the Bishop of Madras in defence of the planters. He referred to Brotherton's assertion that 'of every 500 Coolies who came from India to Ceylon, one half or two thirds *die of* drunkenness & the rest return only to corrupt their fellows',[6] and complained that this was a gross exaggeration, and one which had resulted in a very prejudicial

---

[1] *Ibid.* The vast majority of the Indian labourers landed on the north-west coast, and not at Trincomalee, which was on the eastern coast.

[2] *The Colombo Observer*, 29 August 1847.

[3] *Ibid.*, 1 October 1849; 4 October 1849 and 13 October 1849. See Appendix VII.

[4] *Ibid.*, 26 August 1847.

[5] *Ibid.*, 24 January 1848. See letters of: the Rev. J. Smith, Scotch Colonial Chaplain, 9 November 1847; the Rev. A. Reinard, Roman Catholic, 9 November 1847; the Rev. H. H. Von Dadelzen, Colonial Chaplain, 22 November 1847; the Rev. J. Allen, Baptist Missionary, 1 December 1847.

[6] S.P.G. MSS., Ceylon 1840–55, Bishop Chapman to S.P.G., 12 November 1847.

effect on public opinion in Ceylon against the Society and its missionaries. 'How can you expect us, the Merchants & Planters say, to support a society, which so wantonly wrongs & slanders us?' The Bishop was eager to mollify the merchants and planters whose support was so essential to the Anglicans. He explained 'that the Indian labourers who periodically migrate to this island for the higher wages to be earned on the coffee estates than in their own country are far more a hoarding than a drinking race of people. They live scantily and scrape together all they can to carry back with them'.[1] Then, turning to Brotherton's charge, the Bishop insisted that there were no deaths from drunkenness, though '[Very] many died from fatigue & exhaustion in the pitiable condition in wh[ich] they come, from sickness, jungle-fever & dysentery in their long & weary travel through uncleared & most unhealthy country'.[2] The Bishop appears to have been more interested in proving Brotherton wrong on the charge of drunkenness, than in expressing any concern for the deplorable condition of the labourers, or in condemning a system that resulted in such an inordinately heavy sacrifice of human lives. The missionaries all emerge from this incident with little credit, for they showed themselves to be more concerned with the superficial issue of drunkenness, than the immeasurably more serious problem of a high death rate.

The Bishop's protest had its desired effect. Brotherton apologized, but his apology is more illuminating than his original contention.[3] He explained that, in the course of his mission work in the Tanjore district, he found that Indian labourers of the lower castes – 'the Palla and Pariah castes' – were in the habit of spending a great deal of money on liquor, and investigations revealed that they had acquired a taste for it while in Ceylon, where liquor was comparatively cheap. There had been temptation to use it there under the mistaken notion that it was a preventive against cholera and malaria. He found that the higher caste emigrants were not so fond of liquor. Brotherton declared that his investigation had also revealed that a good many of the immigrants died in Ceylon: he had mistakenly attributed these deaths to liquor, but he was now certain that liquor had little to do with it. He stated

---

[1] *Ibid.*   [2] *Ibid.*
[3] This apology was printed in *The Colombo Observer*, 17 February 1848, and *The Ceylon Times*, 18 February 1848.

T

that his remarks should be modified to read that many Coolies died in Ceylon; some, perhaps of liquor, but that liquor was not the main cause of death. Implicit in this statement was a criticism of the planters and the administration in Ceylon, for ignoring this problem of a high death rate. His letter was no mere apology; it was a rebuke to his critics in Ceylon and a challenge to them to concentrate on the main issue – the high death rate among the Indian Coolies – instead of on the minor one of drunkenness. But this challenge was not accepted by the administration, the Press, the planters or the missionaries. They were satisfied with accepting the statement as an apology, pure and simple.

The response of the missionaries to the problem of Indian immigration, the most formidable social problem of the day, could hardly be described as energetic or enlightened. They displayed no deep concern for the physical suffering that this system of immigration involved, but concentrated exclusively on the spiritual welfare of the immigrants. This emphasis on spiritual salvation was, perhaps, a natural and wholly understandable one where nineteenth-century missionaries are concerned, but it reveals a certain rigidity of approach, a narrowness of outlook and a deplorable lack of sympathy and understanding. It was not merely that they did not see, but many of them did not care to see. They were interested in the immigrants as potential converts, or as converted men to be kept within the fold. But they made no attempt to speak out against the treatment of the Indians in Ceylon, though they could hardly have been unaware of conditions on the estates. It is not surprising that the missionaries had so little influence on Government policy on Indian immigration, for they did not seek to influence it. There is no evidence to suggest that they protested either privately, or – much less likely – publicly, against the abuses in the system of immigration. In 1846–7 the question of Indian immigration was in the limelight in Ceylon, with discussions in the Legislative Council and in the Press, but not once – except during the Brotherton controversy – did the missionaries intervene in these discussions. The fact that no missionary voices were raised against the planters in such circumstances, contrasts rather unfavourably with the attitude of their colleagues in Bengal who were in the forefront of the movement against abuses on the indigo plantations.

It is curious too that apart from the missionaries in Ceylon, the Evangelicals in England, who were actively interested in the immigration of Indians to the West Indies and Mauritius, should have shown so little interest in the immigration of Indians to Ceylon, in spite of the fact that the death rate among the Indian immigrants to Ceylon was considerably higher, and abuses in the system more widespread. The explanation would seem to be that they were interested in immigration to the West Indies because it followed on the abolition of slavery. Evangelical interest in – and antipathy to – Indian immigration stemmed from their anxiety to see that the transition of the slave to the status of a free labourer should not be thwarted by unfair competition from immigrant labour. Because of the absence of this situation in Ceylon, the immigration problem never attracted the same public attention in England. It is claimed, probably with justice, that the rigid control of Indian immigration by the Colonial Office and the Colonial Governments of the West Indies and Mauritius, which the Evangelicals secured and supported

. . . saved the great mortality and hardship which would have sprung from continuation of the system of private speculation.[1]

In Ceylon, where this 'system of private speculation' flourished, there was both 'great mortality and hardship', little administrative interference and no public outcry.

[1] Cumpston, *op. cit.*, p.176.

CHAPTER X

Epilogue

THE first two decades of Queen Victoria's reign saw British missionary organizations make their first sustained bid to 'conquer' the East for Christianity. In the process of evangelization they made their own distinct contribution to the evolution of the Second British Empire, though their endeavours in this regard have attracted less attention than those of the soldiers and administrators.

These missionaries displayed a confidence that sprang from a strong conviction that theirs was a creed that surpassed all others, and from a belief that their efforts at proselytism must certainly culminate in the triumph of Christianity at the expense of all other religions. This confidence occasionally bred complacency, but more often it served to heighten an already acute sense of the urgency and immensity of their task. A Baptist journal published in Ceylon summed up these missionary aspirations thus:

> The whole of mankind must be converted or endure the bitter pangs of eternal death. There is no alternative; we must have true religion or ruin.[1]

Their appeals for support and assistance struck a responsive chord in the hearts of those who governed the Empire. Glenelg and Stephen were Evangelicals both, while Russell, Stanley, Gladstone and Grey shared this outlook even if they were not Evangelicals themselves.

In Ceylon the impact of this Evangelical drive in Imperial policy became more pronounced with the appointment of Stewart Mackenzie as Governor, and the arrival of Glenelg's despatch of 2 October 1837.[2] This long and rambling document is a landmark in the history of the colony, marking as it did the beginning of a policy of active, if limited, support by the Government for proselytism. Every paragraph in it bore the impress of the Evangelical faith of Glenelg and Stephen.

[1] *The Investigator* (February 1842), p.87.
[2] C.O. 55/79, Glenelg to Mackenzie, no.18 of 2 October 1837.

In the peculiar circumstances of Ceylon, however, the immediate consequences of the new policy was to aggravate the sectarian animosity that already existed in such large measure in the field of missionary enterprise in the Island. The Anglican Establishment there, a stronghold of High Church principles and Tory ideas, more devoted to the preservation of its many privileges than to the business of propagating Christianity, was in need of radical reform. Thus a clash between reformist Evangelicalism and High Church Anglicanism was almost inevitable. The process of reform was painful, long drawn out, and marked by bitter sectarian rivalries. When it was a matter of reform within the Anglican Establishment, the noncomformist missions stood discreetly aloof, but when more important issues were involved, such as the establishment of the principle of equality between the various Christian groups in Ceylon, or when it came to depriving the Anglicans of some of their more important and vexatious privileges, they brought great pressure to bear on the Government.

Education was always the core of the Evangelical programme of action. Controversies on education served to aggravate sectarian animosities, these conflicts being the extension to Ceylon of that general struggle between Anglicans and Dissenters for the control of education in England.

But in no aspect of policy did the impact of Evangelicalism loom larger than on the question of the severance of the connection of the State with Buddhism. The missionary groups were united on this as on no other issue, largely through a conviction that this association with Buddhism was a connection with idolatry. There was, besides, a strong belief that the withdrawal of State support, more than any other measure, would accelerate the decline of Buddhism. To a large extent these factors explain the unity displayed by the missionaries on this issue, the vehemence of their arguments, and the sense of urgency that impelled them to oppose all concessions to the Buddhists.

Apart from Mackenzie (and he too, only in the last year of his administration), none of the other Governors of Ceylon displayed any anxiety to go back on the promises made at the Kandyan Convention; they were aware of the legal and moral difficulties involved, and the potential political dangers of a precipitate severance of the connection of the State with Buddhism. The administration in Ceylon stood aloof from these campaigns, refusing to be coerced into indiscreet action by this missionary agitation. In this instance, however, the missionary campaign succeeded only because of the influence they were able to wield at the Colonial Office. The missionaries won a most significant victory; they brought to an end the age-long connection of Buddhism with the rulers of Ceylon; and their triumph was all the more significant for having been won in spite of the resolute opposition of the Ceylon Government. No other achievement of theirs was so completely their own.

A study of the Buddhist problem reveals a constant factor in the working of Colonial policy – where a fundamental principle was at issue, it was the Colonial Office that laid down the policy to be followed. At this time, the initiative in most aspects of policy lay with the Ceylon Government.[1] It is not that the Colonial Office placidly let the Ceylon Government take the more active role, but there was a tacit recognition of the practical difficulties inherent in a situation where a despatch to Ceylon – the usual means of communication – took eight weeks or more to reach its destination.[2] The Colonial Office, therefore, preferred to concentrate on matters of importance.

There appears to have been a general recognition of what these matters of importance were and they seem to have been dependent on three factors. First, there were the personal interests of individual Secretaries of State. Secondly, there was the question of public opinion at home. If any pressure groups – the missionaries are a good example – had the support of public opinion, they could influence the policies of the Colonial Office and the Ceylon Government. And thirdly, as long as James Stephen was at the Colonial Office he had as great an influence on policy-making as his

---

[1] Education policy is a case in point. In 1840–41 Russell and Stephen refused to accept Mackenzie's proposals on vernacular education. In spite of this, when, in the course of the next few years, 1843–7, the Ceylon government gradually gave vernacular education a prominent place in the system of education, the Colonial Office hardly realized that this fundamental change had taken place. There was no protest against this change of policy.

[2] There may have been other factors as well. Reading through the despatches, minutes and memoranda of the Colonial Office one is struck by the fact that even the senior permanent officials were much less informed on the affairs of Ceylon than their successors of the 1860s were to be. It is not surprising, then, that the Ceylon officials played a more positive role in the initiation of policy.

political superiors. Where any two of these factors coincided in support of a policy, such as in Stephen's opposition (based largely on an almost dogmatic belief in the orthodox theory on the medium of instruction in the Eastern Empire) to the emphasis laid on the vernacular languages in Mackenzie's education proposals of 1840–1, the Ceylon Government was compelled to conform to the recommendations of the Colonial Office. And where all three factors operated as they did in the case of the Buddhist problem, the Colonial Office laid down the policy, and compelled a reluctant Ceylon administration to implement it even though the latter knew it to be both intemperate and dangerous.

On the question of Buddhism, the missionaries displayed an acute understanding of the mechanics of colonial policy. They were quick to realize that on this issue their great strength lay in the support of public opinion at home; it was a matter of bringing pressure to bear on the Colonial Office. Their task was simplified by the fact that Stephen felt as strongly on this matter as they did, and was more than willing to fight their battles for them.

Indeed, if the study of Buddhist policy reveals anything as regards the actual administration of colonial affairs, it is the importance of Stephen in the making of policy. On this issue, his was the guiding hand and he was more a policy maker than a civil servant. Here he was at his best and worst; determined and thorough, consistent and persuasive but at the same time pigheaded and bigoted.

Religious issues figure prominently in the study of social policy in Ceylon at this time for two reasons – the strength of the missionary movement (to say nothing of the extent of State support it received) and the fact that the State's relations with Buddhism proved to be a matter of acute and prolonged controversy. But there was more to social policy than a mere concern with religious issues alone.

In Ceylon, unlike India, there were no glaring social evils associated with the indigenous religions – no *sati, thugi* or *meriah* sacrifices and no ritual ceremonies of the sort associated with the Temple of Jaganath. There were, however, other less formidable problems, those of the traditional Sinhalese society – mass illiteracy, slavery, caste and the problem of the aboriginal Veddahs. The traditional society had no solutions for these problems and no remedies for these evils; indeed, there was hardly a realization that these were evils or problems at all. In Ceylon there was no equivalent of the Brahmo Samaj, no Ram Mohan Roy, and the initiative in all these measures of social reform had to come from above to a much greater extent than in India.

Inspired by Evangelicalism, the British Government interested itself in all these problems; it directed that the mild form of slavery then existing in Ceylon should be gradually abolished, and that the State should take a paternal interest in the Veddahs, protecting them, civilizing them and, if possible, converting them to Christianity. Caste was too amorphous and nebulous a problem to be tackled by a deliberate and precise policy, and apart from a vague egalitarianism there was no clear policy on caste. The missionaries had little influence on the actual formulation of these policies; their role in these projects was that of auxiliaries and assistants with a great deal of influence on the day to day running of these schemes. Their assistance was indispensable because the State could not have conducted these projects by itself, since it did not have the men and the administrative structure for it. Besides there was a great deal of agreement between the administrators and the missionaries on the basic aims of these schemes – 'civilization' and conversion. The missionaries were interested in these projects because of the rich dividends they expected in converts; they were, after all, eroding the traditional society at its weakest links; they were converting to Christianity men who they believed had a grievance against the old society.

The abolition of slavery in Ceylon does not fit into this pattern, for in this instance it was the Ceylon Government alone that set the pace. Even the Colonial Office, strangely enough (for this was a matter that could easily have roused influential pressure groups at home, and in which the Secretaries of State, and above all James Stephen had a deep personal concern), allowed the Ceylon Government to assume the initiative with little interference from home. The missionary groups in Ceylon showed little interest in the abolition of slavery, and were content to let the State handle the problem on its own. They were not encouraged to take an active part, but their conduct on this issue would seem to suggest as much a lack of interest as the lack of an invitation to participate.

This issue provides further proof of the importance of James Stephen in the formulation of Colonial Office policy. Evangelical concern for the abolition of slavery in the empire might have had its impact on colonial policy on slavery in Ceylon; the Colonial Office might have issued peremptory instructions and laid down a rigid policy to be followed. That this did not happen was largely the result of Stephen's advice. The contrast with Buddhist policy is obvious. There Stephen's approach was emotional; he had little knowledge of the subject; but in his opinion a vital principle was involved, for among the Crown Colonies only in Ceylon was there this close connection of the State with a religion other than Anglican Christianity. On the question of slavery, the issue had already been settled in 1833, and though the various anti-slavery societies still agitated against its survival in Ceylon (and India) it was clear that the problem was only one of marginal importance. Such differences as existed between the Colonial Office and the Ceylon Government were merely on the question of means; there was complete agreement in the end, the abolition of slavery.

The greatest social problem of the day, however, was not one associated with the traditional society but with the new capitalist society that was growing up in Ceylon – the problem of the migrant Indian labourers on the coffee plantations, nearly 25 per cent of whom died in Ceylon. It was a grim tale of neglect by the Government and harsh treatment by the planters. The narrowness of the missionaries' vision in matters of social policy is shown in their indifference to and neglect of this problem.

The abuses in this system of immigration were so widespread that after 1847 the Ceylon Government changed its *laissez faire* policy and sought to adopt some of the protective measures then in use in the West Indies and Mauritius. This State intervention, reluctant and late though it was, owed little to the interest of the missionaries in these immigrants. And it must be remembered that in the nineteenth century State intervention in these problems was contrary to the generally-accepted social and economic theories of the day; the State intervened only because the abuses in the system were so great that humanitarian interests triumphed over abstract theories.

The attitude of the missionaries to this problem was different. The Baptists and the Anglicans had missions to the migrant Indians, but they were interested in the immigrants only as potential converts, or as Christians to be kept within the fold. They kept silent, although they could hardly have been ignorant of the abuses of the immigration system; no missionary voice was raised against the planters or in urging upon the Government the adoption of protective or welfare measures.

It was, unhappily, characteristic of the missionary movement in Ceylon at this time, that they seldom interested themselves in a social problem if it was not likely to bring rich dividends in converts. Missionary societies in Ceylon, unlike their contemporaries in India, concentrated their energies on the process of conversion alone, and were rarely interested in social reform for its own sake.

Despite these shortcomings, however, they brought a new vigour and vitality to the solution of some of the social problems of their day. And if their energies were often directed at undermining the ancient religions and the traditional culture of Ceylon, they were put to more enlightened uses as well.

APPENDIX I

GOVERNORS OF CEYLON

1837–41	The Hon. J. A. S. Mackenzie
1841–47	Sir Colin Campbell
1847–50	Viscount Torrington
1850–55	Sir George Anderson

COLONIAL SECRETARIES OF THE CEYLON GOVERNMENT

1830–45	Philip Anstruther
1845–50	Sir James Emerson-Tennent
1850–60	Charles (later Sir Charles) MacCarthy

THE KANDYAN CONVENTION
[Proclamation of 2 March 1815]

AT a Convention held on the second day of March in the year of Christ 1815, and the Cingalese year 1736, at the Palace in the City of Kandy, between His Excellency Lieutenant-General ROBERT BROWNRIGG, Governor and Commander in Chief in and over the British Settlements and Territories in the Island of Ceylon, acting in the name and on behalf of His Majesty George the Third King, and His Royal Highness George Prince of Wales Regent, of the United Kingdom of Great Britain and Ireland, on the one part, and the Adigars, Dessaves and other principal Chiefs of the Kandyan Provinces on behalf of the Inhabitants, and in presence of the Mohattales, Corals, Vidahns and other subordinate Headmen from the several Provinces and of the people then and there assembled on the other part, it is agreed and established as follows.

1. That the cruelties and oppressions of the Malabar Ruler in the arbitrary and unjust infliction of bodily tortures and the pains of Death without Trial and sometimes without an accusation or the possibility of a crime, and in the general contempt and contravention of all Civil Rights have become flagrant, enormous and intolerable, the acts and maxims of His Government being equally and entirely devoid of that Justice which should secure the safety of his subjects, and of that good faith which might obtain a beneficial intercourse with the neighbouring Settlements.

2. That the Rajah Sri Wickreme Rajah Sinha by the habitual violation of the chief and most sacred duties of a Sovereign, has forfeited all claims to that title of the powers annexed to the same, and is declared fallen and deposed from the Office of King – His family and relatives whether in the ascending, descending or collateral line, and whether by affinity or blood, are also for ever excluded from the Throne – and all claim and title of the Malabar race to the dominion of the Kandyan Provinces is abolished and extinguished.

3. That all male persons being or pretending to be relations of the late Rajah Sri Wickreme Rajah Sinha either by affinity or blood and whether in the ascending, descending or collateral line, are hereby declared enemies to the Government of the Kandyan Provinces and excluded and prohibited from entering those Provinces on any pretence whatever, without a written permission for that purpose by the authority

of the British Government, under the pains and penalties of Martial Law, which is hereby declared to be in force for that purpose – and all male persons of the Malabar cast now expelled from the said Provinces are under the same penalties prohibited from returning except with the permission before mentioned.

4. The Dominion of the Kandyan Provinces is vested in the Sovereign of the British Empire, and to be exercised through the Governors or Lieut.-Governors of Ceylon for the time being and their accredited Agents, saving to the Adigars, Dessaves, Mohattales, Corals, Vidhaans and all other chief and subordinate Native Headmen, lawfully appointed by authority of the British Government, the Rights, Privileges and Powers of their respective Offices, and to all classes of the people the safety of their persons and property, with their Civil Rights and immunities, according to the laws, institutions and customs established and in force amongst them.

5. The Religion of Boodhoo professed by the Chiefs and inhabitants of these Provinces is declared inviolable, and its Rites, Ministers and Places of Worship are to be maintained and protected.

6. Every species of bodily torture, and all mutilation of limb, member or organ, are prohibited and abolished.

7. No sentence of Death can be carried into execution against any inhabitant except by the written Warrant of the British Governor or Lieut.-Governor for the time being, founded on a Report of the case made to him through the accredited Agent or Agents of the Government resident in the Interior, in whose presence all trials for Capital offences are to take place.

8. Subject to these Conditions, the administration of Civil and Criminal Justice and Police over the Kandyan inhabitants of the said Provinces is to be exercised according to established Forms and by the ordinary authorities, saving always the inherent Right of Government to redress grievances and reform abuses in all instances whatever, whether particular or general, where such interposition shall become necessary.

9. Over all other persons Civil or Military residing in or resorting to these Provinces not being Kandyans, Civil and Criminal Justice together with Policy, shall until the pleasure of His Majesty's Government in England may be otherwise declared, be administered in manner following.

1st. All persons not being Commissioned or Non-Commissioned Military Officers, Soldiers or Followers of the Army usually held liable to Military Discipline, shall be subject to the Magistracy of the accredited Agent or Agents of the British Government in all cases except charges of Murder, which shall be tried by special Commissions to be issued from time to time by the Governor for that purpose. Provided always as to such Charges of Murder wherein any British subject may be defendant, who might be tried for the same by the Laws of the United Kingdom of Great Britain and Ireland in force for the Trial of offences committed by British Subjects in Foreign Parts, no such British Subject shall be tried on any charge of Murder alleged to have been perpetrated in the Kandyan Provinces, otherwise than by virtue of such Laws of the United Kingdom.

2nd. Commissioned or Non-Commissioned Military Officers, Soldiers or followers of the Army usually held amenable to Military Discipline, shall in all Civil and Criminal Cases wherein they may be Defendants be liable to the Laws, Regulations and Customs of war, reserving to the Governor and Commander-in-Chief in all cases falling under this ninth Article, an unlimited right of review over every proceeding, Civil or Military, had by virtue thereof, and reserving also full power to make such particular provisions comformably to the general spirit of the said Article as may be found necessary to carry its principle into full effect.

10. Provided always that the operation of the several preceding clauses shall not be contravened by the provisions of any temporary or partial proclamation published during the advance of the Army; which provisions, in so far as incompatible with the said preceding articles, are hereby repealed.

11. The Royal Dues and Revenues of the Kandyan Provinces are to be managed and collected for His Majesty's use and the support of the Provincial Establishment according to lawful Custom and under the direction and superintendence of the accredited Agent or Agents of the British Government.

12. His Excellency the Governor will adopt provisionally and recommend to the confirmation of His Royal Highness the Prince Regent in the name and on behalf of His Majesty such Dispositions in favour of the trade of these Provinces, as may facilitate the Exports of their products, and improve the Returns, whether in Money, or in Salt, Cloths, or other Commodities, useful and desirable to the Inhabitants of the Kandyan Country.

GOD SAVE THE KING

(Signed) ROBERT BROWNRIGG,
> *Governor*

> (Signed) EYHELEPOLA MOLLIGODDA
> *1st. Adikar & Dissave of the 7 Korles*

(Signed) PELIME TALAWE
            2nd. Adikar & Dissave of Saffregam

„   PELIME TALAWE
            Dissave of the 4 Korles

„   MONARAWILA
            Dissave of Ouwa

„   RATWATTE
            Dissave of Matele

„   MOLLIGODDA
            Dissave of the 3 Korles

„   DULLEYWE
            Dissave of Walapane

„   MILLAWA
            Dissave of Welasse and Bintenne

„   GALAGAMA
            Dissave of Tamankada

„   GALAGODA
            Dissave of Nuwara Kalawiya

In the presence of J. D'OYLY
    Chief Translator to Govt.

            JAMES SUTHERLAND
    Dep. Sec. to Govt.

THE PROCLAMATION OF 21 NOVEMBER 1818
ISSUED AFTER THE REBELLION OF 1818
[Amending Proclamation of 1815]

Buddhism

16. As well Priests as all the Ceremonies and Processions of the Budhoo Religion shall receive the Respect which in former times was shewn them; at the same time it is no wise to be understood that the protection of Government is to be denied to the Peaceable exercise by all other Persons of the Religion which they respectively profess or to the erection under due License from His Excellency of Places of Worship in proper Situations.

A LIST OF THE BHIKKUS AND BASNAYAKE NILAMES
APPOINTED BY THE GOVERNMENT

Bhikkus

The Malwatta Establishment: The Maha Nayaka [The Head of the
Order], The Anu Nayaka, the 2nd. Anu Nayaka, the Chief Priests
of the temples of Gangarama, Walgampaya, Deldeniya, Hingula,
Welegoda, Dewanagala, Anuradhapura, Adam's Peak, Alutnuwara
and Dippitiya.

The Asgiriya Establishment: The Maha Nayaka, the Anu Nayaka and
the Chief Priest of the temple of Dambulla.
The Government also appointed the following Basnayaka Nilames
whose Devales came under the jurisdiction of Asgiriya.

The Basnayaka Nilames of Bamba [ragala], Mutiyangana,
Mahiyangana and Huduhumpola.

The Government Almanac for 1839 gives the following list of Basnayaka Nilames appointed by the Government.

Central Province. Kandy District.

The Diyawadana Nilame of the Temple of the Tooth.

The Basnayaka Nilames of the Maha Vishnu, Natha, Kataragama
and Pattini Devales in Kandy.

The Basnayaka Nilames of Maha Devale (Hanguranketa), Walla-
hagoda (Udapalata), Gangoda (Udapalata), Lankatilleke (Udunuwara), Embekke (Udunuwara), Wegiriya (Udunuwara), Dodan-
wala (Udunuwara), Pasgama (Udunuwara).

Badulla. The Basnayaka Nilames of Mahakataragama Devale, Hora-
guna and Saman Devales.

Matale. The Basnayake Nilame of Embekke.

Madawalatenne. The Basnayaka Nilame of Alawatugoda.

Western Province.

The Basnayaka Nilames of Wilbave, Jangura (*sic*), Kandawala,
Kirindagala, Gonawa, all in the Seven Korales.

Southern Province.

The Basnayaka Nilames of Maha Saman Devale (Ratnapura),
Alutnuwara (Ratnapura) and Kataragama (Alupota).

APPENDIX V

GOVERNMENT EXPENDITURE ON KANDYAN RELIGIOUS CEREMONIES

The Bill for 1839 was as follows:

For the Esala Perahera, the main religious ceremony connected with the Temple of the Tooth Kandy and its ancillary devales.

The cost of sundry articles for the use of the temple of the Tooth, and the 4 devales [the Nata, Kataragama, Pattini and the Maha Vishnu] since the Perahera	£ 3	10	6
For the traditional dances	£ 3	13	2½
For outstanding devales	£ 4	5	1
To carry the canopy over the karanduwa (the receptacle for the Sacred Tooth relic)	£ 0	16	0
For oil and rags	£ 3	15	0
	£15	19	9½

The Government also paid for certain other festivals, among which were

The Avurudda Festival [The New Year ceremony]	£ 5	10	5
The Nanamura Festival	£ 6	19	2¾
The 5 Wahala Pinkamas	£25	4	0¾
The Katina Pinkama	£43	13	8¼
The Kartiya Festival	£ 5	11	8¼
The Alut Sal Festival	£11	7	5¼
The Waliya kun ceremony	£ 4	1	1

APPENDIX VI

LIST OF CIVIL SERVANTS WHO HAD INVESTED IN THE PLANTING INDUSTRY IN CEYLON

(a) Ackland's List. In his evidence before the Parliamentary Committee on Ceylon, *2nd. Report on Ceylon* (1850) p.303, the Ceylon planter George Ackland showed that on a single day in 1840, the following Civil Servants had bought 13,275 acres of land in the Ambagamuwa District (Central Province).

The Rt. Hon. J. S. Mackenzie, Governor	1,120 acres
The Hon, W. O. Carr (Puisne Justice) and Capt. T. Skinner (Commissioner of Roads)	862 ,,
F. B. Norris (Surveyor-General) and others	762 ,,
G. Turnour (Government Agent, Central Province, and at that time Acting Colonial Secretary)	2,217 ,,
H. Wright (District Judge, Kandy) and G. Bird	1,751 ,,
Sir R. Arbuthnot (Commander of the Forces) and Capt. Winslow (A.D.C.)	855 ,,
T. Oswin Esq. (District Judge)	545 ,,
C. R. Buller (later, Government Agent, Central Province)	764 ,,
Capt. Layard and others	2,264 ,,
P. E. Wodehouse (Government Agent, and Assistant Colonial Secretary)	2,135 ,,
	13,275

(b) Tennent's List. Tennent in his evidence before the Parliamentary Committee on Ceylon, 3rd. Report pp.352–3, stated that the following officials held lands in Ceylon before the Colonial office restricted the planting activities of Civil Servants in Ceylon in 1845.

	Acres	
The Rt. Hon. J. S. Mackenzie	11,200	(This figure is probably a misprint for 1,120)
W. O. Carr and T. Skinner	1,100	
P. E. Wodehouse	900	
G. Turnour	2,217	
C. R. Buller	1,929	
F. B. Norris	1,633	

	acres
T. Oswin	545
Philip Anstruther	3,793
T. Skinner (by himself)	56
T. Robertson	516
G. Bird (Ceylon Rifles) and	
H. Wright (Auditor General)	780

Other landowners included 'The Second Puisne Judge; the District Judge of Jaffna; the District Judge Trincomallee; the Assistant Colonial Secretary; the Government Agent of the North-Western Province; the Assistant Government Agent, Batticaloa; the Assistant Government Agent, Kegalla; the District Judge, Chilaw; the Assistant Government Agent Kurunegala, the Assistant Government Agent, Kandy; the Assistant Government Agent, Colombo; the District Judge, Kandy; the Post Master General; the Collector of Customs; the District Judge Colombo; the Fiscal Colombo; the Assistant Civil Engineer; the Assistant Surveyor; the Commissioner of Requests; the Master Attendant of Colombo; the Police Magistrate, Kandy; the Deputy Queen's Advocate and some judicial functionaries.'

Tennent, evidence in *3rd. Report on Ceylon*, pp.352–3.

Tennent's list contains two significant omissions. The Chief Justice, Sir Anthony Oliphant owned a coffee plantation (at Nuwara Eliya), as did the Archdeacon of Colombo, the Rev. J. M. S. Glennie, who owned 1,976 acres of land at Pussellawa.

THE DEATH RATE AMONG THE INDIAN IMMIGRANTS TO CEYLON, 1841–8

THE question of the death rate among the Indian immigrants to Ceylon became a subject of controversy in 1849. There had been an incidental reference to the subject in 1847 (during the Brotherton controversy) but apart from that there had been no serious discussion of the problem previously. In its issue of 1 October 1849, *The Colombo Observer* estimated that in the years from 1841 to 1848, about 70,000 or 25 per cent of the Indian immigrants to Ceylon had died in the island of various causes: the arrivals in Ceylon had been 265,467 men, 5,155 women and 2,250 children, while departures had been only 129,360 men, 2,639 women and 1,519 children, leaving about half the immigrants unaccounted for. *The Colombo Observer* calculated that assuming the number of these immigrants remaining in Ceylon at around 50,000, there would still have been between 70,000 and 90,000 deaths. They were inclined to accept the lower figure in order to allow as wide a margin of error as possible.

These calculations were based on figures published in the annual Year Books of the Ceylon Government, and it is significant that the Government did not challenge their accuracy. Only *The Ceylon Times* made a feeble attempt to challenge them; indeed, there was no attempt to deny that the death rate was very high, they merely asked if it was as high as 25 per cent.

In its issue of 4 October 1849, *The Colombo Observer* sought to defend its charge by contrasting the position of the Indian immigrants in Mauritius with that of their counterparts in Ceylon, and emphasized the advantages enjoyed by the former.[1] It was pointed out that despite all these advantages there had been – between 1 January 1843 and 30 July 1849 – 6,884 deaths in Mauritius out of a total of 63,407 immigrants, a death rate of a little over 10 per cent. *The Colombo Observer* suggested that in these circumstances the figure of 25 per cent for Ceylon was not an exaggeration. In the issue of this newspaper of 13 October 1849, a correspondent estimated that in the period 1841–8, the death rate on the plantations alone (presumably without the death rate

---

[1] Apparently the climate there was decidedly healthier; there was nothing to compare with the horrors of the 'march' to the hills on an unhealthy road, as in Ceylon; and stringent legislation protected the interests of the immigrant labourer. Among other things, the immigrants in Mauritius were secured by law in the enjoyment of certain articles of food.

on the march) was at least 12 per cent of the immigrants. The same correspondent pointed out that death rate varied with the elevation of the estate; that it was lower in the hills than in the Dumbara region and the estates under 1,700 feet in elevation. In Dumbara in 1840, for a good many months the death rate was as high as 5 per cent of the immigrant labourers on the estates *per month*.

These same calculations were published ten years later by A. M. Ferguson in *The Ceylon Plantation Gazetteer* for 1859 (pp.167–9). He maintained that the figure of 25 per cent for the years 1841–8 was accurate. He had, after all, allowed for a figure of 50,000 Indians remaining in Ceylon though it was very unlikely that anything like this number did stay behind. And he had also accepted the lower figure of 70,000 deaths in preference to the higher one of 90,000. The Secretary of the Ceylon Agricultural Society suggested that, while the figures for arrivals in Ceylon were accurate enough, those for departure did not take cognizance of the Indian labourers who left Ceylon in *dhonies* at other than authorized stations. He calculated that as many as 25 per cent of the immigrants left Ceylon by this means. But Ferguson replied that even accepting this calculation – and he saw no reason to believe that it was accurate – it still left about 25 per cent of the Coolies unaccounted for and therefore presumably dead.

There is on the whole good reason for accepting this figure of a death rate of 25 per cent as being fairly accurate. It was based on official statistics, and the Government did not challenge its accuracy in 1849 or even in 1859; the planters and the other newspapers did not effectively challenge it either. Besides, it was not based on the mere difference between arrivals and departures, but allowed for a wide margin of error. Neither Ferguson nor *The Colombo Observer* was hostile to the planters, and in raising this issue they appear to have been actuated solely by disinterested humanitarianism.

For the period 1849 to 1855 the statistics still showed a difference between arrivals and departures, but it was not as wide as it was for the earlier period. Presumably the death rate was not so high as 25 per cent in this period. But as late as 1858 Governor Sir Henry Ward could comment that:

> . . . it is no exaggeration to say that many hundreds of these poor creatures perish annually, from want, and disease. . . . Hundreds die of actual starvation upon the road. . . .[1] The immigration of Indians was still accompanied by . . . a large sacrifice of life. . . .[2]

[1] C.O. 54/347, Ward to Bulwer–Lytton, no.131 of 15 November 1858.
[2] *Ibid.*

Bibliography

I. Manuscript Sources – Official

At the Public Record Office, Chancery Lane, London
The most important of the official manuscript sources is the series of Colonial Office documents, C.O. 54/ which contains the despatches of the Governors of Ceylon, along with their enclosures, Colonial office minutes and memoranda, and drafts of despatches from the Secretary of State. The volumes in the C.O. 54/ series catalogued under the category 'Public Offices' (one or two each year) contain the Colonial Office correspondence with other Government Departments, while the 'Miscellaneous' Volumes contain letters from officials and private individuals, and occasionally, memoranda from private persons, or officials in their personal capacity.

The C.O. 55/ series contains the despatches of the Secretary of State to the Governor of Ceylon. This series must be read along with the corresponding volume in the C.O. 54/ series, but generally, C.O. 54/ contains all the despatches to and from the Secretary of State, and only very occasionally does it happen that a despatch to Ceylon is filed only in the C.O. 55/ series.

C.O. 56/   The Legislative Enactments of the Government of Ceylon.

C.O. 57/   Reads as Sessional Papers, but this title is misleading as the volumes for this period in this series do not contain any Sessional Papers. They contain instead the minutes of the proceedings of the Legislative and Executive Councils of Ceylon.

C.O. 58/   *The Ceylon Government Gazette.*

C.O. 59/   A miscellaneous series, which contains bound volumes of local newspapers for this period, and the Annual Blue Books of the Ceylon Government.

C.O. 381/   Vols. 26, 27 and 28 contain commissions and instructions to the Governors and Lieut.-Governors of Ceylon from 1837–72.

There are occasional references to Ceylon in the series, C.O. 110/, C.O. 323/, and C.O. 386/.

C.O. 326/   Correspondence, Register of in-letters. This series is the General Register for the Colonies. Separate registers for the different colonies appear to have been kept from 1849 and are catalogued in the C.O. 357/ series.

C.O. 416/   This series contains the 32 volumes of evidence collected by the Commissioners of Eastern Inquiry (1828–31) – The Colebrooke-Cameron Commission.

II. Manuscript Sources – Private

The Grey MSS.   The papers of the Third Earl Grey, Secretary of State for War and the Colonies, 1846–52.
At the Prior's Kitchen, University of Durham, Durham City.

Grey encouraged colonial governors and senior officials to write to him privately. These letters frequently explained and amplified what was stated in the official despatches.

These papers are of exceptional importance in the study of the history of this period. Of the material on Ceylon the most important are, Grey's correspondence with Sir George Anderson, C.J. (later Sir Charles) MacCarthy and the 7th Viscount Torrington. Grey's relations with Tennent were decidedly cold and unfriendly and, as a consequence, they rarely corresponded with each other.

The Mackenzie MSS.   At the Government Archives, Gangodavila, Ceylon.

A much less valuable source of information than the Grey MSS., these papers consist of draft despatches, reports, private letters and diaries of Mackenzie's tours in various parts of Ceylon. There are 33 files of papers in all. It must be mentioned that six of these files contain material relating to the years 1815 to 1836.

The Lawrie MSS.   At the Library of the Commonwealth Relations Office, London.

These MSS. consist of five volumes of papers relating to Kandyan Law and History collected by A. C. Lawrie who had a distinguished career in the Judiciary in Ceylon. He was appointed District Judge of Kandy in 1873, and a Puisne Justice of the Ceylon Supreme Court in 1892, retiring in 1901 as Senior Puisne Justice and Acting Chief Justice. He had a thorough knowledge of Sinhalese and he made a deep study of the Kandyan records of the early British administration. And these MSS. provide a useful source of information on the social and economic structure of the Kandyan Provinces.

Mention might also be made of a manuscript of much slighter importance – the *Griffith MSS*. At the Library of the University of Ceylon, Peradeniya, Ceylon.

This was a manuscript diary kept by Lucinda Darby Griffith, the wife of an army officer, Major G. D. Griffith, stationed in Ceylon in the years 1841–2. The numerous illustrations in the diary were the work of Major Griffith.

III. Manuscript Sources – Missionary

Baptist Missionary Society:

The archives of the Society were damaged by enemy action in the last war. Of the papers on Ceylon that have survived, only those in Box 8 (1841–2) and Packets 11 and 15 refer to this period. No letters have survived for this period; but extracts from letters of the period are published, along with other material in *The Missionary Herald*.

Mention must be made of a manuscript in the Library entitled 'Letters from Various Fields collected by Dr E. B. Underhill, 1842–55'. It contains 10 letters, nine of which refer mainly to the Mission station of Kottigahawatte, and the other is a petition to the Government requesting equal treatment for the Baptists on the registration of marriages.

The C.M.S. Archives:

Contain an enormous amount of information on missionary activity in Ceylon. It is easily the most extensive source of such information. The material on Ceylon is arranged under C.CE.CEYLON MISSION, as follows: C.CE.E1 Early correspondence 1815–20; C.CE.1, 1–2 individual letter books, outgoing 1854–78, 2 quarto vols; C.CE.L, 1–5 Letter Books (outgoing) 1820–50, 5 vols; C.CE.M, 1–18 Mission Books, incoming 1819–61, 12 large folio vols. C.CE.O1– C.CE.20, 19 Boxes containing original letters, Journals of Missionaries and other papers.

The S.P.G. Archives:

There are two volumes of MSS. dealing with this period. In the category 'E' MSS, there is the volume of letters, reports, etc., entitled 'Missionary Returns. Ceylon 1840–55'. Volume A. In the same category of 'E' MSS. there is a box of letters, reports, etc., entitled 'Missionary Reports India and Ceylon 1852–55'. Volume F.

The Wesleyan Missionary Society:

Both from the extent of their activity in Ceylon, and their influence
with the Government, the Wesleyan MSS. are an extremely valuable
source of information. Only the letters (incoming) of the Missionaries
have survived. (Unfortunately, the Journals of the Missionaries have
not survived.) For this period the letters in Files 1 and 11 are all that
are available. Their importance can hardly be overestimated.

File 1, 1837–45; File 11, 1846–57.

IV. Published Documents

*Addresses Delivered in the Legislative Council of Ceylon by Governors of the
Colony, Together with Replies of Council.* 4 vols. Government Press,
Colombo Ceylon, 1876, 1877, 1900 and 1915.

Aitchison, C. U. *A Collection of Treaties, engagements and sanads relating to
India and neighbouring countries.* 5th ed. (Calcutta, 1931.)

Bell, K. N. and Morrell, W. P. *Select Documents on British Colonial Policy.
1830–60.* (O.U.P., 1928.)

Mendis, G. C. *The Colebrooke-Cameron Papers.* 2 vols. (Oxford, 1957.)

Missionary Sources.

Annual Reports, of the Baptist Mission Society, Church Missionary
Society, The Society For the Propagation of the Gospel, and the
Wesleyan Missionary Society, for the years 1840–55. I have also con-
sulted the following Missionary Journals.

The Missionary Herald (Baptist).
The Church Missionary Recorder.
The Journal of the S.P.G. (MSS.)
Missionary Notices (Wesleyan)

PARLIAMENT
Hansard

In the period, 1840–55, Ceylon very rarely figured in the debates in
Parliament. There were very few questions raised in the House of
Commons on affairs in Ceylon. In the years before 1847, Questions in
the House of Commons were mainly on the Civil Service; there was
only one Question on an important issue like Buddhism.

The disturbances of 1848 and their aftermath – the appointment of the
Parliamentary Committee – naturally aroused greater interest in

Ceylon, and during the years 1848–51 there was a spate of Questions, and Motions on the affairs of Ceylon.

In the years 1852–3 the problem of Buddhism figured more prominently, but there was less interest in this question than there had been on the disturbances.

Sessional Papers, House of Commons

		Vol.
Correspondence on the abolition of slavery.	1843	(568) LVIII, 1
Minutes and correspondence on the Civil Service.	1845	(640) XXXI, 49
Accounts – Revenue and Expenditure.	1845	(530) VIII, 178
Imports of Sugar and Coffee. 1831–46.	1847	(647) LIX
Existing Tariffs, Revenue, Imports and Exports.	1847	(93) XLI
Dismissal of Langslow.	1047	(495) XLI
Correspondence regarding Railways	1847	(716) LXIII, 323
Reports and Correspondence on the Finance and Revenue of Ceylon.	1847–8	(933) XLII, (Command)
Abstracts of Import and Export Duties	1847–8	(41) XLII, 99
Despatch on Commercial Difficulties	1847–8	(369) XLII, 103
Correspondence on the Constitution	1847–8	(1005) XLVI (Command)

Ceylon – Reports of Select Committees of the House of Commons (1849–50)

1st Report from the Select Committee on Ceylon and British Guiana.	1849	(297) XI,	1
2nd Report	1849	(573) XI,	467
3rd Report	1849	(591) XI,	471
1st Report from the Select Committee on Ceylon,	1850	(66) XII,	1
2nd Report	1850	(106) XII,	35

3rd Report. 1850 (605) XII; (655) XII; 1851 (36) VII, Parts I and II.

Sessional Papers, House of Commons

Papers Relative to the Affairs of Ceylon	1849	(1018) XXXVI,

Report of the Commission sent
  to Ceylon   1851   (99) XXIII, 51
Evidence taken by the Commis-
  sion sent to Ceylon.   1851   (534) XXII, 65

This report and the evidence collected was the work of two Civil
Servants of the East India Company, sent to Ceylon on the instructions
of Parliament to investigate questions arising from the issue of certain
proclamations during the disturbances of 1848 by Capt. Albert Watson.

Papers Relative to the Affairs of
  Ceylon.   1851   (1301) XXXV, (Command)
The Court Martial of Capt.
  Watson   1851   (1413) XXXV, (Command)
Report of the Committee of the
  Executive Council on the
  Fixed Establishments of Cey-
  lon.   1852   (568) XXVI
Idolatry of the Natives   1852–3   (410) LXV
                                  1852–3   (927) LXV
                                  1852–3   (985) LXV

State of the Colony. Letter by Viscount Torrington on the state of the
Colony. 1857. (45 Session 2.) XXVIII.

V. Newspapers and Journals

I have consulted *The Colombo Observer*, *The Ceylon Times*, *The Ceylon
Herald* (ceased publication in 1845) and *The Ceylon Examiner* (commenced
publication in 1846). These were the only newspapers published in
Ceylon at this time. Of the journals and newspapers published in
England, I have made use of *The Times*, *The Spectator*, and *The Economist*. But these have, on the whole, been less useful than the missionary
journals listed under the heading 'Published Sources – (Missionary)'.

VI. Other Works

(A) BRITISH COLONIAL POLICY AND RELATED SUBJECTS

Adderley, C. B. (Lord Norton), *Review of The Colonial Policy of Lord John Russell's Administration, by Earl Grey, 1853, and of Subsequent Colonial History* (London, 1869).

Ballhatchet, K. A., *Social Policy and Social Change in Western India, 1817–30* (London, 1957).

Bearce, G. D., *British Attitudes towards India 1784–1858* (Oxford, 1961).

Bertram Sir Anton, *The Colonial Service* (London, 1930).

Bodelsen, C. A., *Studies in Mid-Victorian Imperialism* (Copenhagen, 1924).

The Cambridge History of the British Empire, Vol. II, *The Growth of the New Empire, 1783–1870* (Cambridge, 1940). Vol. III, *The Empire Commonwealth 1870–1919* (Cambridge, 1953).

Carrington, C. E., *The British Overseas* (Cambridge, 1950).

Cumpston, I. M., *Indians Overseas in British Territories, 1834–54* (Oxford, 1953).

Dicey, A. V., *Lectures on the Relations between Law and Public Opinion in England during the Nineteenth Century*, 2nd ed. (London 1914).

Egerton, H. E., *A Short History of British Colonial Policy*, 9th ed. (London, 1932).

Grey, The Third Earl, *The Colonial Policy of Lord John Russell's Administration*, 2 vols., 2nd ed. (1853).

Hall, H. L., *The Colonial Office: A History* (London, 1937).

Ingham, K., *Reformers in India, 1793–1833* (Cambridge, 1956).

Knaplund, P., *The British Empire, 1815–1939* (New York, 1941).

Knaplund, P., *Sir James Stephen and the British Colonial System, 1813–47* (University of Wisconsin Press, 1953).

Knorr, K. E., *British Colonial Theories, 1570–1850* (The University of Toronto Press, 1941).

Kondapi, C., *Indians Overseas, 1838–1949* (Oxford, 1950).

McCulloch, S. C. (ed.), *British Humanitarianism, Essays honouring Frank J. Klinberg* (Philadelphia, 1950).

Mellor, G., *British Imperial Trusteeship, 1783–1850* (London, 1951).

Merivale, H., *Lectures on Colonization and Colonies*; delivered before the University of Oxford in 1839, 1840 and 1841, 2nd ed. (London 1861).

Morrell, W. P., *British Colonial Policy in the Age of Peel and Russell* (Oxford, 1930).

Newton, A. P., *One Hundred Years of the British Empire* (New York, 1940).

Schuyler, R. L., *The Fall of the Old Colonial System* (Oxford, 1951).

Stokes, E. T., *The English Utilitarians and India* (Oxford, 1959).

Walker, E. A., *The British Empire: Its Structure and Spirit* (Oxford, 1943).

Williamson, J. A., *A Short History of British Expansion*, 2 vols. (London, 1930).

Young, D. M., *The Colonial Office in the Early Nineteenth Century* (London, 1961).

VII. Other Works

(B) MISSIONARY SOCIETIES, AND MISSIONARY ACTIVITY

Chatterton, E., *A History of the Church of England in India, since the Early Days of the East India Company* (London, 1924).

Findlay, G. G., and Holdsworth, W. W., *A History of the Wesleyan Methodist Missionary Society*, 5 vols. (London, 1924).

Latourette, K. S., *A History of the Expansion of Christianity, Vol. 6, The Great Century in North Africa and Asia, A.D. 1800 to A.D. 1914* (London and New York, 1945).

Pascoe, C. F., *Two Hundred Years of the S.P.G., 1701–1901* (London, 1901).

Sherring, M. A., *A History of Protestant Missions in India, 1706–1882* (London, 1884).

Stock, E., *The History of the C.M.S.*, 5 vols. (London, 1899–1900).

Thompson, H. P., *The History of the Society for the Propagation of the Gospel in Foreign Parts, 1701–1950* (London, 1951).

Townshend, W. J., Workman, H. B., and Eayrs, G., *A new History of Methodism*, 2 vols. (London, 1909).

VIII. Other Works

(c) CEYLON

Bailey, S. D., *Ceylon* (London, 1952).

Barrow, Sir George, *Ceylon, Past and Present* (London, 1857).

Bennett, J. W., *Ceylon and Its Capabilities* (London, 1845).

Bertolacci, A., *A View of the Commercial, Agricultural and Financial Interests of Ceylon* (London, 1817).

ed. Beven, F. L., *A History of the Diocese of Colombo*, Centenary Volume (Colombo, 1946).

Casie-Chetty, S., *A Gazetteer of Ceylon* (Colombo, 1834).

Codrington, H. W., *Ancient Land Tenure and Revenue in Ceylon* (Colombo, 1939).
A Short History of Ceylon, 2nd. ed. (London, 1935).

'Colonist', *A Few Remarks upon Colonel Forbes' Pamphlet on Recent Disturbances in Ceylon* (Colombo, 1850).
Is Ceylon to be sacrificed at the shrine of the party? (Colombo, 1850).

Davy, J., *An Account of the Interior of Ceylon and Its Inhabitants* (London, 1821).

de Silva, C. R., *Ceylon under the British Occupation, 1796–1832*, 2 vols. (Colombo, 1942).

Digby, W., *Forty Years of official and unofficial life in an Oriental Crown Colony, The Life of Sir Richard F. Morgan*, 2 vols. (London and Madras, 1879).

D'Oyly, Sir John, *A Sketch of the Kandyan Constitution*, ed. L. J. B. Turner, (Colombo, 1929).

Extracts of Letters from Ceylon on Courtship, Marriage etc., with a peep into Jungle Life, (London, 1848).

Ferguson, A. M., *Ceylon, Summary of useful Information and Plantation Gazetteer* (Colombo, 1859).
The Ceylon Commonplace Book; Directory; Read Book, and Compendium of Useful Information for 1861 (Colombo, 1861).

ed. Ferguson, J., *Pioneers of the Planting Enterprise of Ceylon from 1830 onwards*, 3 vols. (Colombo, 1894, 1898, 1900).

Forbes, J., *Eleven Years in Ceylon: Comprising sketches of the Field Sports and Natural History of that Colony; an Account of Its History and Antiquities*, 2 vols. (London, 1840).
Recent Disturbances and Military Executions in Ceylon (London, 1850).

Gratiaen, L. J., *The Story of Our Schools. The First School Commission, 1832–1841* (Colombo, 1927).

Hocart, A. M., *Caste: A Comparative Study* (London, 1950).

Hayley, F. A., *A Treatise on the Laws and Customs of the Sinhalese* (Colombo, 1923).

Henderson, R., *A History of the Rebellion in Ceylon, during Lord Torrington's Government* (London, 1868).

Knighton, W., *A History of Ceylon from the earliest period to the Present time* (London, 1840).
Forest Life in Ceylon, 2 vols. (London, 1854).

Lawrie, A. C., *A Gazetteer of the Central Province of Ceylon*, 2 vols. (1896).

Lewis, F., *A Few Pioneer Estates and Early Pioneers in Ceylon* (Colombo, 1924).

Lewis, J. P., *List of Inscriptions on Tombstones and Monuments in Ceylon, of Historical or Local Interest with an obituary of persons Uncommemorated* (Colombo, 1913).

Lewis, R. E., *Coffee Planting in Ceylon, Past and Present* (Colombo, 1855).

Mendis, G. C., *Ceylon under the British*, 3rd revised ed. (Colombo, 1952).

Millie, P. D., *Thirty Years Ago, or Reminiscences of the Early Days of Coffee Planting in Ceylon* (Colombo, 1878).

Mills, L. A., *Ceylon under British Rule* (Oxford, 1933).

Payne, C. W., *Ceylon, Its Products, Capabilities and Climate* (London, 1854).

Phear, Sir John B., *The Aryan Village in India and Ceylon* (London, 1880).

'Philalethes', *Letters on Colonial Policy, Particularly as applicable to Ceylon* (London, 1833).

Pieris, P. E., *Tri Sinhale – The Last Phase, 1796–1815*, 3rd ed. (Colombo, 1945).
Sinhale and the Patriots, 1815–1818 (Colombo, 1953).
The Sir Paul Pieris Felicitation Volume (Colombo, 1956).

Pieris, R., *Sinhalese Social Organisation*, (Colombo, 1956).

Pridham, C., *An Historical, Political and Statistical Account of Ceylon and its Dependencies*, 2 vols. (London, 1849).

Sabonadiere, W., *The Coffee Planter of Ceylon* (Colombo, c. 1866.).

Sarkar, N. K., *The Demography of Ceylon* (Colombo, 1957).

Sirr, H. C., *Ceylon and the Cingalese*, 2 vols. (London, 1850).

Skinner, T., *Fifty Years in Ceylon* (London, 1891).

Spence-Hardy, R., *Eastern Monachism* (London, 1850).
A Manual of Buddhism and Its Modern Development (London, 1853).

Steuart, J., *Notes on Ceylon, and Its Affairs, During a Period of 38 years ending in 1855* (London, 1862).
Notes on the Monetary System and Cinnamon Revenue of Ceylon to which are appended some observations on the change of policy in 1833 (Colombo, 1850).
Observations on Col. Forbes' Pamphlet on the recent Rebellion in Ceylon in a letter addressed to a friend (Colombo, 1850).

Tambiah, H. W., *The Laws and Customs of the Tamils of Ceylon* (Colombo, 1954).
The Laws and Customs of the Tamils of Jaffna (Colombo, 1951).

Tennent, Sir James-Emerson, *Ceylon. An Account of the Island, Physical, Historical and Topographical*, 2 vols. 4th ed. (London, 1860).
Christianity in Ceylon (London, 1850).

Toussaint, J. R., *Annals of the Ceylon Civil Service* (Colombo, 1935).

Villiers, Sir Thomas, *Mercantile Lore* (Colombo, 1940).

Wydham, II. A., *Native Education* (Oxford, 1933).

IX. Other Works

(D) PAMPHLETS AND BOOKS ON MISSIONARY ACTIVITY IN CEYLON

Boake, B., *A Brief Account of the origin and nature of the Connexion between the British Government and the idolatrous systems of religion prevalent in the island of Ceylon and of the extent to which that connection still exists*, (Colombo n.d., probably 1855).

Casie Chetty, S., *A Sketch of the Rise and Progress of the Catholic Church in Ceylon* (Colombo, 1848).

Chater, H. J., *Ceylon Advancing* (London, 1955).

Daniel, E., *Reminiscences of Two Years of Missionary labours in the jungles of Ceylon, containing a narrative of exertions made to benefit its neglected population; and an introduction to excite Christians to afford their assistance in advancing the Missionary Enterprise* (Kandy, Ceylon, 1843).

Lankalankaraya (Sinhalese), *The Story of the Baptist Mission Society in Ceylon, 1812–1912* (Colombo, 1914).

Minutes of a Conference of Missionaries and native pastors, held at Colombo, June 26th–30th (1855).
x

Moscrop, T., and Restarick, A. E., *Ceylon and Its Methodism* (London. n.d.).

Peggs, J., *The British Connection with Idolatry in the island of Ceylon* (London, 1843).
The Present State of the British Connection with Idolatry in Ceylon (London, 1843).

Spence-Hardy, R., *The British Government and the Idolatry of Ceylon* (Colombo, 1839).
The Jubilee Memorials of the Wesleyan Mission, South Ceylon, 1814–64, (Colombo, 1864).

X. Pamphlets and Books on Missionary Activity in Ceylon

ANONYMOUS, AND OTHERS WRITTEN UNDER PSEUDONYMS

A Brief Sketch of the American Ceylon Mission (Jaffna, Ceylon, 1849).

A Historical Sketch of the Baptist Mission in Ceylon, from its commencement to the present time with introductory remarks (Kandy, Ceylon, 1850).

Civis, *A Letter to the Editor of the Ceylon Herald, occasioned by the question of the Rt. Hon. J. A. S. Mackenzie as to the 'National Church' of the United Kingdom and Ceylon.* (Colombo, 17 March 1840).

Civis the Second, *The Non-Existence of a National Church and the Injustice of Established Religion* (Colombo, 1840).

Six Letters of Vetus [Bailey, (Benjamin) Archbishop of Colombo] *to the Editor of the Ceylon Times, on the Connection of the British Government with the Buddhist Idolatry of Ceylon* (Colombo, 1852).

Three Letters on the Necessity of a Church Establishment in Ceylon (Colombo, c. 1846).

What we want in Ceylon, and how we may get it. An address to European Christians (Colombo, 1840).

XI. Articles

Banks, M., 'Caste in Jaffna', *Cambridge Papers in Social Anthropology*, Vol. 2, 61–77.

Beaglehole, J. C., 'The Colonial Office 1782–1854', *H.S.A.N.Z.*, I, 170–89.

Boyd, W., 'The Autobiography of a Peria Durai', *C.L.R.* 1st series II, 376–432.
'Ceylon and Its Pioneers', *ibid*, 217–84.

Casie Chetty, S., 'Some Account of the Rodiyas, with a specimen of their language', *J.R.A.S.(C.B.)* II, No. 8, 171–80.

Gallagher, J., and Robinson R., 'The Imperialism of Free Trade', *Econ.Hist.Rev.*, 2nd series, VI, (1953), No. 1, 1 ff.

Hardy, S. M., 'Wilmot-Horton's Government of Ceylon, 1831–1837', *University of Birmingham Historical Journal*, VII, No. 2, 180–99.

Ingham, K., 'The English Evangelicals and the Pilgrim Tax in India, 1800–1862', *The Journal of Ecclesiastical History*, Vol. 3, (1952).

Knaplund, P., 'Mr. Over Secretary Stephen', *J.M.H.* I, 40–66.

Ferguson, A. M., 'Ceylon, 1837–46'
'Ceylon, 1847–60', *C.L.R.* 1st series, II and III.

Fernando, C. N. V., 'Christianity in the British Period', *U.C.R.* VII, 135–41.
'Christian Missionary Enterprise in the Early British Period I', *ibid*, 198–207.
II, *ibid*, 269–81.
III, *ibid*, *U.C.R.* VIII, 110–15.
IV, *ibid*, 203–6.
'Some Aspects of Christian Missionary Enterprise in the Early British Period: (1796 1830) vi', *ibid*, 269–71.
'Christian Missions IX: Some Aspects of Baptist and Wesleyan Work from 1827–64', *U.C.R.* IX, 106–112.
'Christian Missions X: Some Aspects of the work of the American Missionaries in the Jaffna District from 1827–66', *ibid*, 191–201.

Gillings, J., 'On the Veddahs of Bintenne'. *J.R.A.S. (C.B.)* II, No. 7, 83–99.

Gratiaen, L. J., 'The Central School Commission 1841–8', *ibid*. Vol. 31, 488–568.
'The School Commission – 1848–1859', *ibid*, Vol. 32, 37–54.

Manning, H. T., 'The Colonial Policy of the Whig Ministers 1830–1837', *Canadian Historical Review*, Vol. 33, 203–37, 341–68.

Pares, R., 'Economic Factors in the History of the Empire', *Econ.Hist. Rev.* VII, No. 2, 119 ff.

Pieris, R., 'Society and Ideology in Ceylon during a "Time of Troubles" 1796–1850 Part I', *U.C.R.* IX, 171–85.

Part II, *ibid*, 266–79.

Part III, *ibid*, *U.C.R.* X, 79–102.

Raghavan, Iyer, 'Utilitarianism and All That – The Political Theory of British Imperialism in India', *St. Anthony's Papers, VII, South Asian Affairs*, No. 1, 9–71.

Tinker, H., 'People and Government in Southern Asia', *Transactions of the Royal Historical Society*, 5th series, IX, 141–68.

Van Den Driesen, I. H., 'Coffee Cultivation in Ceylon', I, *C.H.J.*, III, 31–61.

II, *ibid.*, 156–72.

'Plantation Agriculture, and Land Sales Policy in Ceylon – The First Phase, 1836–1886, *U.C.R.* XIV.

'Land Sales Policy and Some Aspects of the Problems of Tenure, Part II 1836–1886', *ibid.* XV.

Ward, J. M., '*The Colonial Policy of Lord John Russell's Administration*', *H.S.A.N.Z.* IX, 244–62.

'The Retirement of a Titan: James Stephen, 1847–50', *J.M.H.* XXXI, 189–205.

Williams, T., 'The Colonial Office in the Thirties', *H.S.A.N.Z.* II, 141–60.

Yalman, N., 'The Flexibility of Caste Principles in a Kandyan Community', *Cambridge Papers in Social Anthropology*, Vol. 2, 78–112.

Index